Sport and Political Ideology

D1572274

Sport and Political Ideology

BY JOHN M. HOBERMAN

 University of Texas Press, Austin

Requests for permission to reproduce material from this work
should be sent to Permissions, University of Texas Press, Box 7819,
Austin, Texas 78712.

LIBRARY OF CONGRESS CATALOGING IN PUBLICATION DATA

Hoberman, John M. (John Milton), 1944–
    Sport and political ideology.
    Bibliography: p.
    Includes index.
    1. Sports and state. 2. Sports—Philosophy. 3. Right
and left (Political science). I. Title.
GV706.8.H62   1984   796'.01   83-27415
ISBN 0-292-77587-3
ISBN 0-292-77588-1 (pbk.)

For **Louisa,** who believed *quia absurdum.*

Contents

Acknowledgments

I would like to thank the many friends and colleagues who, over many years, have provided both information and encouragement during the preparation of this book. In particular, I wish to thank Horst Huber for providing long, and scrupulously annotated, translations from the Chinese and Tom Koch for research assistance above and beyond the call of duty. And I am grateful to the University Research Institute of the University of Texas at Austin for supporting this work.

1. Sport in the Age of Ideology

Sport and Ideology

The idea that sport is somehow an intrinsically political phenomenon has never been explained. In fact, sport is less known for its political character than for its legendary effects. One example among many is the tumultuous homecoming (Munich, 1954) of the West German World Cup soccer champions, upon which occasion the president of the German Football Association invoked the ancient Teutonic thunder god Wotan to express his nationalistic euphoria. To some observers, this massive demonstration—and the singing of "Deutschland, Deutschland über alles" during the game—represented the sudden postwar recrudescence of a German nationalism which had hitherto been repressed.[1] Such episodes are unquestionably of political significance. The problem is that awe at the seemingly hypnotic powers of sport has a way of deferring indefinitely more specific inquiries into sport's relationship to political life.

The relationship of sport to political ideology is constantly in evidence but rarely subjected to convincing proof. This is due to the fact that while sport may serve as an advertisement for a given ideology—indeed, for virtually any ideology—this is not the deeper sort of relationship which conjoins sport and the political sphere. For if any political ideology can advertise itself through sport, this in itself shows that on this level there is nothing at all distinctive about the relationship which obtains between sport and any given ideology. On this level, sport functions as an undifferentiated vehicle of self-assertion by the state. The specific form it takes as a culture is inconsequential; that it should serve the greater glory of the state—any state—is the sole criterion for its appropriation and use.

An approximation to a genuinely ideological approach to sport can be seen in an official declaration issued in November 1977, when Cuba withdrew from an international amateur baseball tournament which was to be held that month in Nicaragua. The official Cuban press agency called the selection of Nicaragua (then ruled by the dictator Somoza) as the tournament site "the most brutal negation of the very principles that sport should uphold" and claimed that Nicaragua did not meet "minimum conditions of moral order that every sports event should have."[2] It should be noted that in this case, even though a Communist government had declared sport to be incompatible with the excesses of a right-wing dictatorship, the judgment pronounced was not in terms of the familiar ideological spectrum running from Right to Left; here sport was declared to be compatible only with a humanitarian ideology prescribing "minimum conditions of moral order" which presumably could be met by non-Socialist societies other than Nicaragua. Cuba had, after all, sent its athletes to the Montreal Olympiad of 1976. So the relevant ideological division in this case is one which separates the humanitarian from the nonhumanitarian. What this proclamation omits is a principled definition of what these conditions actually are, a definition equivalent to an ideological signature.

This book interprets the major sport ideologies of the twentieth century as distinct expressions of political doctrine. It assumes that the great ideological division of Left from Right, dating back (like the term "ideology" itself) to the French Revolution, is both real and historically significant. It further assumes that fascist, liberal-democratic, and Communist societies have distinct political anthropologies or idealized models of the exemplary citizen which constitute complex answers to the fundamental question of philosophical anthropology: "What is a human being?" "Ideological differentiation" is the term I have applied to genuine ideological differences which originate in different conceptions of what human beings are, what their capacities are, and what sort of social order best serves their needs. In this sense, "political anthropology" is the *fons et origo* of political conflict in the modern world.

Political ideologies are also prescriptive. "If I know what your understanding of life is," the Swiss theologian Emil Brunner writes, "I can tell you what sort of state, sciences, art and economic and social order you will create."[3] Such an assertion may be faulted for its tautological character, presuming as it does a virtually omniscient observer. Nevertheless, it contains an important element of truth which becomes more visible the more totalitarian the society to which it is applied. Any attempt to correlate the values embodied in American sport with ideological positions will be difficult, simply because American sport, its "ideological" content notwithstanding, has no official status.[4] The sport culture of post-1949 China, on the other hand, registers ideological change with the sensitivity of a barometer (chapter 10). In this sense, Brunner might well have added sport to his list of social phenomena which derive from a society's *Weltanschauung*. It is, after all, the declared ambition of each totalitarianism to infuse its own ideological content into every sphere of life. To choose only one example, "the hierarchy of the arts established by Marxist esthetics on the basis of their intelligibility can lead only to the subordination of art and the artist to the imperatives of a philosophical, or often a purely political, doctrine."[5] As we shall see in chapter 9, official East German ideology calls for the subordination of art to sport, precisely because the sport culture of the GDR is considered a faithful expression of state ideology.

"Ideology" is defined by *Webster's Dictionary* as "a systematic scheme or coordinated body of ideas or concepts, especially about human life or culture." Such a category easily encompasses ideas about sport, its cultural benefits, and its baneful effects on society.

"Ideology" can be further defined as containing both explicit content and implicit assumptions. "Any systematic set of attitudes and beliefs, whether about the nature of the universe, political policy, family structure and patterns or family planning, can be 'explained' with reference to a wider ideological context which may in its turn be related to a deeper ideological structure that uses for its terms an appeal to economic factors, reason or emotion, or an appeal to a personality-based process of which the subject may be unaware."[6] The "ideological content" of official political doctrine must be derived from "a deeper ideological structure" in which both rational and irrational impulses have roles to play. Classic texts on ideology like Marx and Engels' *The German Ideology* (1846) or Karl Mannheim's *Ideology and Utopia* (1929) stress the idea that ideologies cannot and should not be taken at face value, that there are always two levels at work: on the one hand, what is said; on the other, what it might mean, given either the intentions of the ideologist or the larger implications of which he or she or the audience may be unaware. This book attempts to connect these two levels by relating doctrines of sport to the subjective world of values, attitudes, passions, and temperaments, and to the objective world of historical conditions.

In the context of history, an ideology is a philosophy with ambitions. Marxism, for example, has been called "a dynamic *Weltanschauung*."[7] Or as Jean-Paul Sartre puts it, "a philosophy, when it is at the height of its power, is never presented as something inert, as the passive, already terminated unity of knowledge. Born from the movement of society, it is itself a movement and acts upon the future."[8] "Every great ideology," Henri Lefebvre writes, "strives to achieve universality."[9] Ideological ambition can, in turn, be interpreted in a positive or negative light. Clifford Geertz has pointed out that ideology, whatever its pathological possibilities, is of undoubted value to society: "The function of ideology is to make an autonomous politics possible by providing the authoritative concepts that render it meaningful, the suasive images by means of which it can be sensibly grasped." The critique of ideological ambition, on the other hand, emphasizes that ideology, as Geertz says, "may indeed lose touch with reality in an orgy of autistic fantasy,"[10] that ideology incorporates illusion.

This is the viewpoint which has its origins in Marx's denunciation of "the chimeras, the ideas, dogmas, imaginary beings, under the yoke of which men are pining away,"[11] a critique which is continued—though not from the Marxian position—by Freud. In "The Question of a Weltanschauung" (1933), Freud defines this term as "an intellectual construction which solves all the problems of our existence uniformly on the basis of one over-riding hypothesis, which accordingly leaves no question unanswered and in which everything that interests us finds its fixed place. It will easily be understood that the possession of a Weltanschauung of this kind is among the ideal wishes of human beings." But it is to precisely this temptation, says Freud, that Marxism itself has succumbed: "although practical Marxism has mercilessly cleared away all idealistic systems and illusions, it has itself developed illusions which are no less questionable and unprovable than the earlier ones." Seeing ideology as a fatal trap, Freud can offer nothing more than the hope that "intellect—the scientific spirit, reason—may in process of time establish a dictatorship in the mental life of man."[12]

Freud's definition of Weltanschauung is inadequate if only because it calls, in effect, for that "end of ideology" which, having been proclaimed,[13] has never actually occurred. Freud's seigneurial (and ahistorical) attitude overlooks ideology's functional role. The Yugoslav writer Mihajlo Mihajlov points out that, despite the "irrefutable fact that at present all the dominant ideologies are disintegrating," it is only superficiality or obscurantism which claims that ideology is unnecessary. Ideology, he says,

> is a definite all-embracing system of ideas in one's social consciousness (it used to be called more precisely Weltanschauung—"world view"). Thus, we can talk about Marxist ideology and the ideology of classical liberalism, which permits ideological pluralism, solidarism, existentialism, struc-

turalism, national-socialism, Zionism, socialism. We can also talk about the ideology of Catholicism, and even Freud's psychoanalysis, because of their attempt to give a total explanation of human life.

However, the more profound meaning of the concept of ideology is not in a system of definite ideas but in the very existence of man's consciousness about life, the cosmos and himself—the consciousness that he tries to express by the system of ideas: *Weltanschauung*. And without this consciousness about himself and the world, man cannot live on earth.[14]

The concept of ideology is important to this book for three major reasons. First, I have assumed that every ideology of historical significance presupposes an official anthropology, or what Mihajlov calls an ideological self-consciousness, which is held to be authoritative. I have further assumed that the interpretation of the body and its potential for athleticism by a political ideology is rooted in basic assumptions about the essence of human beings: what constitute their permanent and ephemeral traits, how they can be changed, the origins and consequences of their relations with others, the sources of their deepest satisfactions.

Second, the historical argument of this essay takes as its point of departure the great ideological struggle between "revolutionary" and "counterrevolutionary" ideas (and armies) which dates from 1789. I am aware, of course, that the terms "Left" and "Right" are approximations and, as Mannheim might put it, "pseudo-unities" to some extent. Nevertheless, and despite the transformations which these idea-complexes have undergone over the past two centuries, I persist in viewing them as both historically intact and mutually antagonistic. (It is Mannheim who finds in the modern struggle of ideologies "the tearing off of disguises" and even "the will to psychic annihilation."[15]) I agree with Ernst Nolte that fascism is *inter alia* "a form of anti-Marxism."[16] I take seriously the historical significance, if not the perfect sincerity, of Mussolini's claim that fascism is "the precise negation of that doctrine which formed the basis of the so-called Scientific or Marxian Socialism," that fascism "attacks the whole complex of democratic ideologies and rejects them both in their theoretical premises and in their applications of practical manifestations."[17] "At a very early stage," Nolte points out, "Mussolini instructed the thinkers and journalists of the regime to regard fascism as the categorical and wholesale denial of the French revolution, and it was precisely this denial that formed the daily bread of the National Socialist polemic."[18] The power of ideology at a given point in history resides not in the sincerity with which it is embraced, but in the authority which it has accumulated and continues to exercise.[19]

The "will to psychic annihilation" has been at least as evident in Communist polemics, the aggressive and categorical nature of which is well known. To a greater degree than their fascist contemporaries, Communist politicians have treated ideology as a force. "From Lenin on down, Soviet leaders have regarded ideas as realities, believing that ideas are just as real in terms of their possible effect on the lives of people as is anything material that can be seen or heard or felt."[20] This book interprets the political cultures of sport as proxy warriors in a larger ideological conflict which has pitted Marxist dogma, in its variety, against its two historical adversaries: first, fascism, and then the postwar non-Communist bloc, which runs the gamut from quasi-fascist (anti-Marxist) dictatorships to the (anti-Marxist) liberal democracies.

Third, I have assumed that the infusion of ideological content into sport during the twentieth century illustrates a more general phenomenon—the penetration of political ideology into almost all forms of culture, the depth and breadth of this penetration depending on the ideological ambitions of the regime being discussed. In the totalitarian political cultures we may speak of the virtual ubiquity of ideological demands. "It was only toward the middle of the twentieth century," Czeslaw Milosz writes, "that the inhabitants of many European countries came, in general unpleasantly, to the realization that their fate could be influenced directly by intricate and abstruse books of philosophy. Their bread, their work, their private lives began to depend on this or that decision in disputes on principles to which, until then, they had never paid any attention."[21] Let us choose an example from the world of sport. It is difficult for a citizen of a Western society to imagine that a text on physical education would take it upon itself to denounce "subjective idealism," or that artists might be admonished to imitate athletes for ideological reasons.[22] Yet the fact is that "intricate and abstruse" philosophy has penetrated that far into East German life.

The intrusions of ideology into our own everyday lives are much less evident. As the historian Jonathan Spence has remarked,

> It is difficult for us to ascribe "ideological" values to [popular] diversions. We shy away from such ascription as an unwholesome pastime, as something smacking of cant or dogmatism, even though we are aware how much time we spend

simply looking at these mass entertainments, and how great an influence they seem to have on our children and on our acquaintances (though rarely of course on ourselves). We praise what seem to be flashes of insight as long as there are not too many of them; we applaud social realism but not "social realism." And though we acknowledge that we live in a bourgeois-capitalist society, we are not generally interested in discussing bourgeois-capitalist art, nor in giving much weight to the fact that such art may mislead and distort.[23]

In Europe, where the competing political ideologies are more sharply defined and have long played a greater role in public life, the situation is very different. As the French "New Philosopher" Bernard-Henry Lévy writes, "We have a Marxist urbanism, a Marxist psychoanalysis, a Marxist aesthetic, a Marxist numismatics. There is no longer any realm of knowledge that Marxism fails to have a look at, no area off limits, no taboo territory. There are no cultural fronts to which it fails to send cohorts of researchers with the mission to 'intervene,' as the jargon would have it."[24] To an increasing extent in France, such efforts on the Left are being matched by an aggressive critique of modernity formulated by the extreme Right.[25] This is not the case in the United States, and it is for this reason that this book explores a specifically European world.

The Symbolic Power of Sport

It is the purpose of this book to demonstrate how interpretations of sport and the athletic body vary according to the ideological position from which they are viewed. At the same time, sport in our era exercises a deep hold on the human imagination which is virtually universal and which does not seem to vary from society to society at this level of emotion. The nature of this appeal, and in particular its transideological dimension, must be addressed in a study of sport's ideological variability. To this end we may interpret sport as a type of dramatic performance, analogous to extreme theatrical moments envisioned by certain avant-garde thinkers discussed below.

Sport provides the human body with dramatic possibilities rarely realized on the stage. Speed, force, dexterity—these are expressive modes which, given the proper magnitude or intensity, possess an inherent "drama." But sport and the theatre represent two distinct kinds of drama which seldom coincide. The separate sources of meaning upon which these "performances" draw, their distinct frameworks of artifice, the different types of effort required, and the dissimilar modes of empathy they evoke all confirm that the theatre and the stadium do not generally constitute a single dramatic forum.

Such differences do not, however, preclude the fusion of sport and theatre. The relationship between these two forms of drama is best understood by examining two aesthetic (and explicitly political) doctrines which have played important roles in the avant-garde theatre of this century: futurism and expressionism. The manifestos of both movements, which together span a period from about 1910 to 1925, claim affinities to movement, speed, the dynamic body, and the concept of sport which unites them.

It is in this sense that sport can be considered a form of expressionism.[26] By this I mean that sport can take the form of a drama for which an ideology of dynamism in the service of human self-expression becomes the ultimate value. The idea that sport is an expressionism in a more technical sense, as well, is suggested by the frequency with which athletic imagery appears in the writings of German expressionists during the period 1910 to 1925. "There are no more bellies, no more drooping breasts. The torso of the artwork grows out of taut thighs into noble hips and ascends from there into the trunk which radiates training and proportion" (Kasimir Edschmid, 1918).[27] Kurt Pinthus (1925) writes of "our nerves trained and hardened like the musculature of a boxer."[28]

In a 1929 manifesto the expressionist playwright Georg Kaiser declares: "The purpose of being is the attainment of record achievements. Record achievements in all areas. The man of record achievements is the dominant type of this age, which will begin tomorrow and never end. The Hindu inactive-panactive man is being outdated in our zones: the panactive man vibrates here at a speed that makes motion invisible."[29] For Kaiser, the record performance becomes an example of that rhetoric of excess so dear to certain members of the expressionist movement. The same submission to dynamism *per se* is evident in Ortega y Gasset's paean to the record performance: "It is a constant and well-known fact that in physical effort connected with sport, performances are 'put up' to-day which excel to an extraordinary degree those known in the past. It is not enough to wonder at each one in particular and to note that it beats the record, we must note the impression that their frequency leaves on the mind, convincing us that the human organism possesses in our days capacities superior to any it has previously had."[30] Here the dynamism of modern sport derives from its tangible index of intensifying human powers.[31] For the Italian futurist (and fascist) Filippo Marinetti, record setting added one more element of pandemonium to his revolutionary theatre: "The Variety Theater is a school of heroism in the difficulty of setting records and conquering resistances, and it creates on the stage the strong, sane atmosphere of danger (e.g. death-diving 'looping the loop' on bicycles, in cars, and on horseback)" (1931). Or: "To your immense system of leveled and intercommunicating stomachs, to your tedious national refectory, we oppose our marvellous anarchic paradise of absolute freedom, art, talent, progress, heroism, fantasy, enthusiasm, gaiety, variety, novel, speed, record-setting. . . ." (1920). And it is Marinetti, prophet of "The New Religion-Morality of Speed" and the development of "pugnacious, muscular, and violently dynamic" male babies, who best captures the essence of sportive expressionism in his definition of *heroism, or the synthetic need to transcend human powers, the ascensional force of the race.*[32]

Sportive expressionism, as noted above, is inherently theatrical in a certain sense. Revolutionary dramatists like Bertolt Brecht and Antonin Artaud saw sport, in fact, as an analogue to avant-garde theatre. Brecht, an expressionist playwright before he became a Marxist one, actually considered the sporting audience superior to that of the legitimate theatre. "There seems to be nothing to stop the theatre from having its own form of 'sport.' If only someone could take those buildings designed for theatrical purposes . . . and treat them as more or less empty spaces for the successful pursuit of 'sport,' then they would be used in a way that might mean something to a contemporary public that earns real contemporary money and eats real contemporary beef." "We pin our hopes," he says, "on the sporting public."[33] For Brecht, John Willett has written, "sport was a form of entertainment whose principles ought to be taken over by the theatre, with the stage as a brightly lit ring devoid of all mystique, demanding a critical irreverent attitude on the part of the audience."[34] "The actor," says the quasi-mystical Artaud, "is an athlete of the heart."

> What the athlete depends upon in running is what the actor depends upon in shouting a passionate curse, but the actor's course is altogether interior.
> All the tricks of wrestling, boxing, the hundred yard dash, high-jumping, etc., find analogous organic bases in the movement of the passions; they have the same physical points of support.[35]

Another, and far more systematic, athleticism can be seen in the early "propagandist theatre" of the Bolsheviks. The revolt of the famous director Vsevolod Meyerhold against the method of Stanislavski "emphasizes the fact that the psychologically exaggerated method of his former teacher suffers from lack of equilibrium; the proportion between soul and body in Stanislavski's actors is weighted against the body . . . The over-developed soul is generally found in Stanislavski's company in alliance with a degenerate physique, unfit for any gymnastic exercises, which, by its unregulated mechanism and clumsy movements, is a constant hindrance to the players," whereas Meyerhold "demanded the most intensive practice of physical culture," and suggested that practitioners of his "biomechanics" study the suppleness of cats.[36] "It may be remarked," says this observer, "that these ideas have a good deal in common with the prevailing political tendencies, which are also directed exclusively to *physical action* and *dynamic momentum* [emphasis added]." Meyerhold's political aim is to train the actor to be "an instrument for social manifestos."[37]

Sportive expressionism employs the body as its aesthetic vehicle. Nor is the aesthetic use of the body ideologically specific. For Meyerhold's "biomechanical" actor, the "instrument" of an ultra-Left ideology, "the cultivation of his body is his first social duty. The whole world of feeling is, as it were, to be extensified in this way, and the body and the limbs are to be the sole instruments of the actor."[38] For the Nazi sport theorist Alfred Baeumler, "The body in motion is completely transformed into expression."[39] Prior to the ideological differentiation of this "expression" into different political messages, the body achieves the status of sheer spectacle. L. Moholy-Nagy, stage designer for the Berlin State Opera, describes his Mechanized Eccentric, "a concentration of stage action in its purest form," in these terms: "The effect of this body mechanism (*Körpermechanik*) (in circus performance and athletic events, for example) arises essentially from the spectator's astonishment or shock at the potentialities of his *own* organism as demonstrated to him by others. This is a subjective effect. Here the human body is the sole medium of configuration (*Gestaltung*)."[40] It remains for the political culture which employs the dramatized body to decide whether its ultimate purpose is the liberation or the subjugation of the astonished spectator.

Every age, says Kasimir Edschmid, has had its own expressionism.[41] The "sportive expressionism" of our century is a modernism, inextricably bound up with the cult of the machine, nationalism, the modern metropolis, and the public style of totalitarian politics.

It is Marinetti's fanatical (and eloquent) devotion to the "great new idea that runs through modern life: the idea of mechanical beauty," coupled with his affinity for the dynamic element in sport, which makes him the great sportive expressionist of his era. (Among our own contemporaries his equivalent is the deceased Japanese novelist Yukio Mishima.) An important development of the period 1910 to 1930 is that the automobile and the airplane became essentially sportive symbols of modernity. "Speed," says Marinetti, "having as its essence the intuitive synthesis of every force in movement, is naturally *pure.*"[42]

The use of sport festivals for nationalistic purposes, as George Mosse has shown, derives from the gymnastics movement of nineteenth-century Germany, which was in turn only one form of a developing "national liturgy." "From the start of the nineteenth century, the classical tended to be confused with the monumental. They mixed the Roman tradition of the Colosseum with the Greek ideal of beauty. This urge toward the monumental, what Winckelmann would have called the exaggeration of form, was a logical consequence of the heightened national impetus: national grandeur had to be symbolized."[43] The fusion of rhythmic bodies into a symbolic whole has become a standard element of totalitarian liturgy and the most familiar image of sportive expressionism.[44]

Modern sport is a part of the urban milieu, a thematic conjunction which dates from the Weimar Republic and the cultural style known as the New Sobriety (1917–1933).[45] "Jazz, movies and sports," notes Wolfgang Rothe, "constitute the trio that determined popular culture until 1933. A disjunction between play and sports arose: play was the old, sports the new."[46] Sport's new associations with crowds, the mass media, machines, and dynamism *per se* made it a stylistic expression of the city. Sport is also associated with the regimen of the metropolis, its focus on rapid processes and the cult of efficiency: "Americanism, businesslike energy stripped of superfluous sensitivity, the principle of rationalization in everything—on the job, in the organization of everyday living, even in the sphere of personal relationships—practicality, an active interest in technology and in sports: these were the characteristic features of the style."[47]

Sportive expressionism, in the form of the sport festival, has become an element of totalitarian style. "The rendering of movement in grandiose and rigid patterns," Susan Sontag has pointed out, is common to both Fascist and Communist regimes, "for such choreography rehearses the very unity of the polity. Hence mass athletic demonstrations, a choreography and display of bodies, are a valued activity in all totalitarian countries."[48] Philip Rieff notes in this type of ceremony a displacement of mind by muscle: "Rhythm bulwarks mass discipline by further linking expectation to acquiescence. Coordinated movement—marching, saluting, chanting in unison—expresses the muscular imagination of the garrison state's ceremonial forms. A rhythm is a promise and, as such, a full alternative to political rhetoric."[49]

Sportive expressionism can employ the heroic-athletic individual in an agonistic state (the distorted face crossing the finish line) or the rhythmic choreography of the mass (thousands of gymnasts on the stadium field). These styles differ in that, while the rhythmic mass presents a flawless image, "by more naive Nazi aesthetic standards, genuine effort—as in the straining veined bodies and popping eyes of the athletes in [Leni Riefenstahl's] Olympiad"[50]—constitutes an aesthetic imperfection. It is worth noting here that Ernst Kris interprets the victor's grimace, "the risus artificialis of the athlete," as an expressive failure to integrate emotional impulses.[51] This "artificial smile," analogous to the symbolic shriek of the expressionists, is therefore profoundly ambiguous. From the standpoint of sportive or expressionist aesthetics, it is an emblem of victory; from the standpoint of psychoanalysis, it is the mask of inner defeat.

Sport and Ideological Differentiation

Sportive expressionism appeals to all ideological temperaments. In other words, it is a universal aesthetic before it is differentiated into divergent ideological messages. Hegel refers to this undifferentiated state in reflecting on the games of ancient Greece: "Sport [Wettkämpfe] presents the higher seriousness; for in it Nature is wrought into Spirit, and although in these contests the subject has not advanced to the highest grade of serious thought, yet in this exercise of the physical powers, man shows his Freedom, viz. that he has transformed his body to an organ of Spirit."[52] Writing long before the modern age of sport, Hegel does not assign himself the task of speculating about sport as a culturally pluralistic phenomenon. Jean-Jacques Rousseau and Friedrich Schiller, however, had already done just that. Prior to the ideological differentiation of sport, which is primarily a twentieth-century development, both had observed cultural differentiation. Rousseau recommends the preservation of national sporting traditions: "Look at Spain, where the bullfights have done much to keep a certain vigor alive in the people. For the same purpose, Poland should take care to revive the circuses in which its young men used to take their exercise, and make of them arenas of honor and competition."[53] Schiller employs sportive diversion as a cultural diagnostic: "To confine ourselves to the modern world, if we compare the horse races in London, the bull fights in Madrid, the spectacles of former days in Paris, the gondola races in Venice, the animal baiting in Vienna and the gay, attractive life of the Corso at Rome, it cannot be difficult to differentiate subtly between the tastes of these several peoples."[54] It is the advent of Marxism which is primarily responsible for transforming an issue of national taste into one of ideological taste.

"In itself," Georges Magnane states, "sport can be neither 'progressive' nor 'regressive.' Like every social fact, it is a perpetual creation of the men who practice and organize it, and who are, in turn, transformed by their very creation."[55] It is the symmetry of this thesis, reflecting the transideological appeal of sportive expressionism, which makes it a persuasive one. But is it true? As we shall see, the assumption that sport *ab ovo* is ideologically inert may not be justified. If, as I argue below, the body is in fact an "ideological variable," this in itself suggests that certain ideological differences may correspond to divergent attitudes toward the body and its sportive self-expression. It is "a special property of muscles," Yukio Mishima writes, "that they [feed] the imagination of others while remaining totally devoid of imagination themselves . . ."[56] But it remains to be seen whether they feed all imaginations in the same way.

The fundamental treatments of "ideological differentiation" appear in chapters 2, 3, and 4. It may be useful to rehearse these arguments briefly. Chapter 2, The Labor-Leisure Dialectic and the Origins of Ideology, describes how a political ideology's interpretation of sport is determined in part by the relative importance it assigns to labor and to play as modes of human experience; conservative and Marxist ideologists have argued over which of these modes appeared first in human prehistory. The significance of such theoretical issues is illustrated, for example, by Henri Lefebvre's insistence that defining man as *homo ludens* "never justifies separating man from his material foundations . . ."[57] As a Marxist, Lefebvre cannot accommodate the idea of an autonomous play-impulse which can compete with labor for primacy as an existential category. Chapter 3, The Body as an Ideological Variable: Sportive Imagery of Leadership and the State, argues that the political anthropologies of Left and Right can be distinguished by studying their resistance to, or affinity for, sportive imagery of leadership and the state. Fascist leaders, not Communist or Socialist ones,[58] are portrayed as "political athletes," primarily because this role offers narcissistic opportunities of which Socialist and Communist doctrine disapprove. Similarly, sportive metaphors are rarely used to characterize a Communist state. Typically, it is the conservative Ortega y Gasset who sees Europe's "muscles flabby for want of exercise";[59] but even when East German officials, in a rare deviation into such imagery, depict their society as a *leistungsfähigen* (fit, productive) *Staat*,[60] the sportive connotation must compete with the industrial one; and once again the category of labor predominates. Chapter 4, The Political Psychologies of the Sportive and Antisportive Temperaments, argues that there is a fascist temperament which shows an affinity to athleticism and the sphere of the body itself which the Left has not shared. This estrangement from the body raises larger questions about how Marxist political cultures deal with other nonrational types of human experience, such as art, religion, and sexuality.

Chapters 5 through 11 pursue the historical consequences of ideological differentiation through a series of official and unofficial doctrines which attribute political or cultural significance to sport and the body. Chapter 5 surveys the conservative critiques (and appreciations) of sport which appeared in response to the rise of mass sport and the pursuit of the record performance after the First World War. Chapter 6 examines the racialistic sport doctrine of Nazi Germany. Chapter 7 describes the early Marxist sport ideologies of the Bolsheviks and the German workers' sport movement (1893–1933). Chapters 8 and 9 deal with the most highly developed Socialist sport cultures, those of the Soviet Union and East Germany, which represent the later (and revisionist) phase of Marxist sport culture. Chapter 10 examines the Maoist (1949–1976) and post-Maoist sport ideologies of the People's Republic of China. And Chapter 11 analyzes the neo-Marxist critique of sport which emerged in France and West Germany in the wake of the political and intellectual upheavals of 1968.

Can a type of physical culture express a specific ideology? Generally speaking, the Left's answer to this question has been no. In 1931 the workers' sport theorist Helmut Wagner maintains that it "is not the specific type of sport which is 'socialist,' but rather the new element inherent in the transformation of physical culture, in the transformation of its content and context. The idea that certain types of sport belong to the future and others to the past is, for the most part, too mechanical and therefore false." The point is that sport's healthy "biological-psychological core" is distinct from its "social-historical form,"[61] which may be wholesome (Socialist) or unwholesome (bourgeois). The quality of any sport, in other words, is a function of the political culture in which it occurs; as the sport historian Horst Ueberhorst has noted, "It was incumbent upon the leaders of workers' sport to demonstrate that, on the sports field, genuine, humanitarian forces were released in the socialist camp, while this was only apparently the case among the bourgeois."[62] Soviet ideologists assume that any kind of "bourgeois" sport is inherently decadent.[63]

Non-Marxist answers to this question are less categorical. Ernst von Salomon, right-wing extremist, novelist, and one of the murderers of Walter Rathenau, writes that "gymnastics are something quite different from sport. Sport is passionate, while gymnastics are an attitude toward the world, the racial metaphysics of the body."[64] Pierre de Coubertin, founder of the modern Olympic movement, claims that sport, too, "can even induce in the mind an inclination toward certain philosophical doctrines," such as Stoicism or fatalism.[65] Hitler extolled boxing above other sports.[66] None of these ideas is ideologically acceptable from a Marxist standpoint.

Is there a political ideology which is estranged from the ethical content of sport ("fair play")? Certain anti-Communists claim this is the case: "indeed, the very conception of fair play is completely foreign to its nature," Jules Monnerot writes in his *Sociology of Communism*.[67] And in *Darkness at Noon*, Arthur Koestler has the old Bolshevik Rubashov make the same point. "We were the first to replace the nineteenth century's liberal ethics of 'fair play' by the revolutionary ethics of the twentieth century. In that also we were right: a revolution conducted according to the rules of cricket is an absurdity."[68] What is more, this attitude toward sportsmanship has its ideological counterpoint. Fascism's documented contempt for "fair play" notwithstanding, it is the fascists or their sympathizers who interpret war as sport and sentimentalize about the cult of the noble adversary. It is the sport-minded British fascist Oswald Mosley who repeatedly invokes "the mysterious fraternity of arms."[69] It is the French fascist Maurice Bardèche who exults in the inane dream of a reconciliation between the fascist and the *résistant* of the Second World War—"heroes" both.[70] And it is the Nazi fellow-traveler Montgomery Belgion who protests the Nuremberg Trials as constituting unsportsmanlike behavior.[71]

Can a sportive style have ideological content? East German soccer teams have claimed that their style of play is "collectivistic" and discourages the cult of the star performer.[72] The West German weekly *Der Spiegel* once concluded that a "system-immanent dogmatism" had actually retarded the development of East German soccer by criticizing dribbling, running, and heretical individualism.[73] And during the age of Maoist sport in China, newspapers reported that a visiting Albanian team had "given in their play, attractive evidence of the spiritual world picture created by Comrade Enver Hoxha."[74]

Such ambitious claims are, however, infrequent. It seems to be generally acknowledged that "Although framed in ideology, the playing field itself is not a canvas for socialist realism . . ."[75]

Blood Sport as an Ideological Variable

"If only there were still danger connected with hunting," writes Hermann Göring, "as in the days when men used spears for killing game. But today, when anybody with a fat belly can safely shoot the animal down from a distance. . . . Hunting and horse racing are the last remnants of a dead feudal world." On at least one occasion Göring's passion for hunting led to intramural squabbling around Hitler's conference table. When his fellow hunter Ribbentrop returned in September 1939 from his second Moscow conference with a German-Soviet treaty and proudly pointed out an enormous hunting preserve Stalin had presented him as a gift, Göring flew into a jealous rage.[76]

It would be a mistake to assume that a predilection for hunting, despite its sadistic overtones, was especially compatible with Nazi ideology. For one thing, as Göring himself puts it: "I joined the party because I was a revolutionary, not because of any ideological nonsense."[77] For another, it is a matter of record that Soviet and Eastern bloc leaders—Lenin,[78] Stalin, Khrushchev, Tito, Ceausescu—have hunted, presumably without doctrinal qualms. Indeed, it may also be the case here that ideological considerations are simply moot. "Stalin's attitude toward hunting," Khrushchev writes in his memoirs, "usually depended on what sort of mood he was in. If he were in an especially good mood, he might even think about going on a hunt himself. But there were other times when he sat at home and complained bitterly about hunters. His occasional opposition to hunting wasn't based on his conviction that all life was sacred—far from it!—but simply on his feeling that hunting was a waste of time."[79] A second example may be adduced to show how immune hunting can be from political orthodoxy. Although he is hardly a Kremlin ideologist, the poet Yevgeny Yevtushenko writes in some ways from a "Soviet point of view." "Hunting," he writes in 1966, "is precious to me precisely because of this feeling we lose in the canyon-like streets of modern cities. Sad as it is to admit, hunting is being enraptured with nature and at the same time murdering it. Still, I am unable to renounce hunting—the voice of my ancestors is stronger than all my vegetarian, sentimental gnawings of conscience."[80] This passage could have been taken almost verbatim from Ortega y Gasset's *Medi-*

tations on Hunting (1943), the personal testament of a profoundly anti-Socialist mind.

The profound latent ideological issue in hunting is the deliberate taking of life by civilized people, an apparent conflict which has made hunting a minor ideological issue for the British Left. When in June 1978 the Labour party's home policy committee recommended that the party should agree to ban blood sports (the original version having included fishing), a Conservative MP remarked: "It is the first time that blood sports have been made a party political issue."[81] This is not quite accurate. "Since the end of the Second World War," a Labour MP writes two weeks later, "a number of Labour MPs have introduced Private Members Bills in Parliament to abolish live hare coursing, and to a lesser extent other blood sports. In 1976 the Labour Government took over the Abolition of Live Hare Coursing Bill, which was only lost when it was shunted off to a House of Lords select committee." This commentator refers to "a strong feeling in Labour's ranks that blood sports are morally wrong, outdated and cruel" and to the "strong aristocratic flavour" of debate on the subject in the House of Lords and finally appeals to the moral authority of Sir Thomas More's *Utopia* (1516), which does indeed state that "a hunter kills and mutilates poor little creatures purely for his own amusement."[82] However, the controversy provoked by the proposed ban defeated it even within the ranks of Labour. The *Times* of London weighed in with a scathing editorial, warning of "the vexatious imposition of a largely agnostic conscience."[83] Two weeks after first being publicized, the proposal was shelved by the party's National Executive Committee as politically unacceptable.[84]

The British debate illuminates the profound moral roots of hunting's ideological variability. "Those who live in the countryside," the *Times* editorial states, "already deeply resent the arrogance of the town and believe their own culture to be more deeply rooted and more healthy. The more traditional of them feel that a progressive conscience which enthusiastically approves the abortion of infants by the million while being concerned to prohibit the killing of a few hundred foxes is dangerously sentimental and dangerously unbalanced." The Socialist "conscience" as it pertains to hunting originates, at least in part, in a feeling of horror at the spectacle of oppression. E. Tangye Lean points out that Kingsley Martin, the English Socialist and editor of the *New Statesman* (1931–1961), "was on the side of the hunted fox and the hare. He remembered in childhood 'cattle being driven through the streets by men mercilessly hitting their bony backs with heavy sticks, driving them to the market and slaughter.'"[85] In 1902, J. A. Hobson identified hunting as a "vital ingredient" of the sportive urge behind imperialistic predation.[86] Both men respond to the spectacle of sadism and domination; but there is a crucial difference in that in Hobson's example the sadistic urge to hunt has been transformed into political economy in the form of imperialism itself. The theme of domination as it applies to hunting can also be transformed—and, in the process, denatured—by interpreting reform not as the abolition of hunting, but as its democratization. In East Germany, the recovery of hunting tradition has been rendered ideologically acceptable by endowing it with a "moral-pedagogical" function and by putting it back "in the hands of the people"; hunting is reclaimed from the old aristocratic monopoly, and a blow is struck against an ancient class privilege.[87]

Boxing demonstrates a somewhat greater degree of ideological differentiation. The Socialist bloc, in accordance with the "hygienist" norms of early Bolshevism, proscribes professional boxing in favor of its "amateur" variant, presumably sparing the athlete both moral and physical injury. For example, the Sandinista revolutionaries who overthrew the Nicaraguan dictatorship of Anastasio Somoza in 1979 abolished professional boxing two years later.[88] "Often," a junta member stated, "they don't let a boxer's wounds heal, and we cannot tolerate poor and marginal boys of our country continuing to submit to the ring just for a little money."[89] An East German polemic against the professional sport of the West claimed in 1975 that medical guidelines enforced by Socialist countries virtually exclude the possibility of serious injury.[90] It is notable, however, that the author, aside from this passing reference to hygienist concerns, devotes an entire chapter on boxing to detailing the seamy business practices of cynical managers who have left their fighters destitute in a hard, capitalist world.

This critique of boxing, addressing not the sport but its societal context, is profoundly evasive. For the real issue here, as in the case of hunting, is human aggression and its encouragement or proscription by political ideology. It is not a representative of East German mobilization (military, industrial, sportive) but a representative of the deeply humane workers' sport movement of Weimar Germany who decries the bloodlust of the boxing spectacle.[91] As we shall see in chapter 7, this is only one of many ways in which the workers' sport movement differentiated itself ideologically from the East German sport culture which would later claim to be its faithful executor. But this schism on the Left should not obscure an important example of ideological differentiation: a difference between Fascist and leftist interpretations of boxing which is suggested by Hitler's ring-ing endorsement. The real ideological variable here is that human capacity for violence and aggression which fascism celebrates and Marxist-Leninist doctrine attempts to subordinate to the rational faculties.[92] It was Mussolini who called punching "an exquisitely fascist means of self-expression."[93] Chapters 3 and 4 should make it clear why such an idea has never been acceptable on the Left.

There is, in addition, a historical example of a profound polarization of views on boxing which does not conform to the fundamental ideological division of Left versus Right which this book attempts to illuminate. For as Henning Eichberg has pointed out, both the Left and the Right in Germany during the interwar period experienced internal divisions with regard to boxing. Hitler's enthusiasm was opposed by a tenacious *völkisch* conservatism which saw boxing as "foreign and unaesthetic," while the disapproval of the Socialist sportsmen was, in turn, contradicted by the enthusiasm of Bertolt Brecht. The real dichotomy here, as Eichberg notes, is between modernity—represented by the odd couple of Brecht and Hitler—and its nostalgic opponents in both camps.[94]

Old Socialist scruples about blood sport surfaced in Portugal in the wake of the Leftist revolution of April 1974. By 1975 the Communist-controlled television and radio networks refused to broadcast live bullfights and claimed that a good Communist should not attend bullfights;[95] according to a law of 1928, it is illegal to kill a bull in public in Portugal. By 1977 the Socialist government, like the nation, was deeply divided on this issue. The prime minister, Mario Soares, stated, "The Spanish bullfight is a cruel spectacle, but we Portuguese are a nonviolent people and so we developed our own sport, which is more horsemanship than anything else." It is worth noting that this statement seeks its authority not in Socialist ideology, but in national identity. And as if to demonstrate the volatile nature of this issue, the president of the bullfighters' union sought revocation of the 1928 law by appealing to the fact of the revolution itself: "If Portugal is going through a revolution in every area, why not in bullfighting?"[96] This statement shows, of course, a comic insouciance toward the ideological content of the revolution. But this controversy, like the British example, demonstrates how difficult it is to impose ideological orthodoxy in this sphere of human activity.

A Postscript on Ideology and American Sport

At some point during the Great Depression, a young black writer in Chicago named Richard Wright sought an appointment with a rather arrogant black Communist named Buddy Nealson, a man who "had spoken before Stalin himself." " 'You can write,' he snorted. 'I read that article you wrote for the *New Masses* about Joe Louis. First political treatment of sports we've yet had.' "[97] However insignificant this episode may be for the history of the American Left, it does suggest that, after forty years of Socialist sport in Europe, it may never have occurred to the most politically dogmatic members of American society that sport might be a matter of ideological interest. Nor has this idea found much favor among the less dogmatic. Ideological conflict, after all, has played a less significant role in American political life than in most of Europe over the past century, one reason being the absence of a politically significant Marxist tradition in the United States and the ideological tensions which would have resulted from its influence.

Sport is a latently political issue in any society, since the cultural themes which inhere in a sport culture are potentially ideological in a political sense. This latent political content becomes more evident when one considers some major polarities which bear on sport and the political world: amateurism versus professionalism, individualism versus collectivism, male supremacy versus feminism, nationalism versus internationalism, sensationalism versus (moral-political) hygienism (e.g., boxing). All of these thematic conflicts belong to the world of sport, and all are of ideological significance in a larger sense.

These issues are as relevant to American sport as they are to sport in Europe or elsewhere. American sport carries a very substantial ideological load of ideas about masculinity, femininity, celebrity, patriotism, heroism, narcissism, race, violence, and more. Nevertheless, this book is devoted to European, not American, intellectual history.

As I have suggested above, this is due to the very modest role well-defined ideologies play in American political life. In this country the very word "ideology" has taken on a connotation of fanaticism, with the result that political ideology in America has a diffuse and shifting character. One need only think of how often Democratic and Republican positions are virtually indistinguishable, or how easy it is to convene "bipartisan" commissions for the express purpose of depoliticizing controversial issues before their potential to mobilize ideological passions becomes too evident. American sport is, indeed, heavily laden with "ideological" content, but it is rarely recognized as such. In Europe, on the other hand, the ideologizing—and hence the intellectualizing—of political discourse is much more pronounced.

Over the last twenty-five years, three American sport ideologies have been evident: a centrist neo-Hellenism, similar to the Olympic ideology, which incorporates standard nationalist and international-ist themes; a conservatism which includes both critical and vitalis-tic elements; and a leftist critique which includes liberal antiauthori-tarian and neo-Marxist positions.

Centrist neo-Hellenism is evident in a sport manifesto pub-lished in *Sports Illustrated* (a semiofficial journal of presidential and vice-presidential sport philosophy) in December 1960 by President-Elect John F. Kennedy. Invoking the familiar idealized picture of clas-sical Greek athleticism, the author states that "the same civilization which produced some of our highest achievements of philosophy and drama, government and art, also gave us a belief in the im-portance of physical soundness which has become a part of Western tradition; from the *mens sana in corpore sano* of the Romans to the British belief that the playing field of Eton brought victory on the battlefields of Europe. This knowledge, the knowledge that the physical well-being of the citizen is an important foundation for the vigor and vitality of all the activities of the nation, is as old as West-ern civilization. But it is knowledge which today, in America, we are in danger of forgetting."[98] The frequency with which these stereo-types appear in official statements is due to their ideological neu-trality; just below the surface, however, cultural reverence for the ancients thinly veils a hortatory nationalism. The openly aggressive variant of this position, as enunciated by Robert F. Kennedy in 1964, stresses that it is "in our national interest that we regain our Olym-pic superiority—that we once again give the world visible proof of our inner strength and vitality."[99] The internationalist variant, as presented by the director of the Peace Corps in 1963, adopts a practi-cal idealism which sees sport as a "universal language": "Unlike many academic subjects, sports lack ideological and propaganda content. They are least vulnerable to charges of 'neo-colonialism' and 'cultural imperialism.'"[100]

The most detailed conservative sport doctrine offered by an American politician was published in 1971 by the most ideologically self-conscious of recent vice-presidents, Spiro T. Agnew. Here one finds an open resentment of "those who intellectualize against ath-letic competition," which is valued as a ritual producing "personal cohesiveness" and a guarantee against the development of a society populated by "identical lemmings." There is an element of social de-spair in the idea that sport "is one of the few bits of glue that hold our society together," and a denunciation of Maoist sport and its pe-culiar etiquette—"all that nonsense of the 'exquisite Chinese taste' in not putting their best players against us."[101] A second, more tradition-minded conservative position deemphasizes competition and the theme of vitality by praising the "genuine athleticism" of British university students.[102] Finally, there is sheer conservative scorn for the naive indignation of the neo-Marxist who cannot fathom sport's power to captivate the working class.[103]

The Left position offers an eclectic critique of authoritarian and racist behavior in the world of sport, which is interpreted as a symptom of a more general social malignancy.[104] It may or may not incorporate elements of Marxist doctrine.[105] It should be noted that the Marxist critique of sport has yet to find its first sophisticated American exponent.

2. The Labor-Leisure Dialectic and the Origins of Ideology

The Problem of Origins

At the origin of the great ideological division between Left and Right which has given shape to the modern political era, there stands a riddle of apparently scholastic obscurity: Which came first in human prehistory—labor or play? The ideological struggle over this territory has been waged on the assumption that precedence is authority, since the question of origins involves an extraordinary authority indeed: a godlike prerogative, the absolute power of creation itself. The more prominent ideological contestants in this struggle have been Marx, Engels, and Georgi Plekhanov, representing the anthropological primacy of labor, and cultural conservatives like Max Scheler, José Ortega y Gasset, Johan Huizinga, and Josef Pieper, responding on behalf of a philosophy of culture which, while not disdaining labor, assigns to it neither the significance nor the dignity with which it has been invested by the Marxist tradition. Even Jean-Paul Sartre puts in an appearance, and to rather surprising effect. This debate features two questions, one historical and the other anthropological: 1. Was the first human society the creation of sportive or labor-oriented impulses? 2. Is labor or play the "absolutely primary category of life" (Huizinga)? In which sphere do the most meaningful human experiences have their origin? Is utilitarianism or nonutilitarianism the correct philosophy of culture?

It is the categorical nature of this somewhat abstruse argument which makes it an ideological one in the deepest sense. The fascist "conception of life," Mussolini writes in 1932, "makes Fascism *the precise negation* of that doctrine which formed the basis of the so-called Scientific or Marxian Socialism: the doctrine of historical Materialism [emphasis added]."[1] As we shall see, this principle of categorical differences also applies to the problem of the origin of the state and to the anthropological debate over a hypothetical original human essence.

The Marxists and Prehistory

How has the Marxist tradition coped with the problem of prehistory? As Lewis Feuer has pointed out, Marx recognized that the anthropological science of the nineteenth century threatened the basis of historical materialism: "The new science was bringing consciously to the fore the significance of mythology and the irrational side of man. Marx and Engels, at a loss as to how to accommodate these new findings to their standpoint, in effect decided to exempt primitive societies from the workings of historical materialism." Engels expressed a certain exasperation: "While still maintaining that 'economic necessity was the main driving force of the progressive knowledge of nature,' he felt it 'would surely be pedantic to try and find economic causes for all this primitive nonsense.' Thus the primitive world, with its myths and magic, was consigned to an irrational realm, beyond historical materialism."[2] Only recently has Marxist thought overcome this original inhibition regarding the domain of the nonrational as a whole; for this reason, among others, its interpretation of play as a psychological and social phenomenon has lagged behind that of non-Marxist theory.[3]

We may also observe that Marx's early interest in literature and aesthetics was subjected to self-censorship,[4] on the grounds that it, too, represented a kind of "primitive nonsense": "Apparently . . . poetic creation represented formlessness, chaos, and danger to Marx. Writing to his father in 1837, Marx refers to the 'broad and shapeless expressions of unnatural feeling' which permeate his early poetry. 'Everything real grew vague,' he wrote, 'and all that is vague lacks boundaries.'" Marx and Engels, Maynard Solomon continues, effected (at a later date) an "early subordination of their aesthetic proclivities to the requirements of a revolutionary movement."[5] Both the myth and magic of prehistory and the unpredictable, eruptive, "unnatural" character of poetry belong to the irrational domain which includes the play impulse. What is crucial is that the nonrational as a whole is put under a Marxist proscription. As we shall see in the next chapter, Marxist attitudes toward the irrational have had a profound impact on Marxist theories of sport.

Marx's antipathy toward the primitive excesses of prehistorical humans did not, however, preclude the use of prehistory for theoretical purposes. "Marx writes that 'the socialist tendency' takes 'the primitive age of each nation' as its pattern (Marx to Engels, March 25, 1868), and the Marxist model of the future is the primitive matriarchal communism of prehistory purged of its terror." This, of course, is the premise which eventually found its way into

Engels' *The Origin of the Family, Private Property, and the State*
(1883). But Marx—like his contemporaries—does not address the
question of what prehistorical experience was really like. Discussing
the origins of the labor process in *Capital*, he distinguishes between
"primitive" and "human" stages in the evolution of labor: "We are
not now dealing with those primitive instinctive forms of labour
that remind us of the mere animal. An immeasurable interval of
time separates the state of things in which a man brings his labour-
power to market for sale as a commodity, from that state in which
human labour was still in its first instinctive stage. We presuppose
labour in a form that stamps it as exclusively human. . . . At the end
of every labour process, we get a result that already existed in the
imagination of the labourer at its commencement."[6] Marx presumably did not foresee that the prehistorical territory in which "those
primitive instinctive forms of labour" occurred would become an
ideological battleground on which the proxies of Labor and Play
would tilt at each other in a contest of indefinite duration.

But if Marx did not ascribe a future significance to this quarrel,
he did recognize its contemporary function in his polemic against
the neo-Hegelians in *The German Ideology* (1846). Here Marx and
Engels note sarcastically that what they refer to as "the great historical wisdom of the Germans" will "invent the 'prehistoric era'";
"they seize upon this 'prehistory' with special eagerness because
they imagine themselves safe there from interference on the part of
'crude facts,' and, at the same time, because there they can give full
rein to their speculative impulse and set up and knock down hy-
potheses by the thousand."[7] This is a fair criticism (and long in advance) of that unbridled anthropological imagination of which Ortega is one representative, for example, in "The Sportive Origin of
the State" (1924). What it overlooks is the fact that some forty years
later Engels would be offering, in *The Origin of the Family*, the fruits
of his own "speculative impulse" regarding prehistory, a theory
heavily influenced by Marx's notes on Lewis H. Morgan, the American anthropologist and author of *Tribal Society* (1877).[8] Neither
could foresee that their ideological inheritors would, in an essentially imaginative way, interpret prehistory in order to derive sport
from the labor process.

One of Engels' roles as a theorist was to address the prehistorical issue directly. "Life," Marx and Engels observe in *The German
Ideology*, "involves before everything else eating and drinking, a
habitation, clothing and many other things. *The first historical act*
is thus the production of the means to satisfy these needs, the production of material life itself [emphasis added]."[9] In the final chapter

of his *Dialectics of Nature*, titled "The Part Played by Labour in the Transition from Ape to Man," Engels calls labor "the primary basic condition for all human existence" and proposes his own chronology: "First comes labour, after it, and then side by side with it, articulate speech—these were the two most essential stimuli under the influence of which the brain of the ape gradually changed into that of a man . . ." Engels does not doubt that labor was the original mode of human self-expression; at the same time, however, he is at pains to explain why this was not more widely understood. It is the religious phenomenon, he claims, which has obscured "the origin of man":

> Law and politics arose, and with them the fantastic reflection of human things in the human mind: religion. . . . All merit for the swift advance of civilisation was ascribed to the mind, to the development and activity of the brain. Men became accustomed to explain their actions from their thoughts, instead of from their needs . . . and so there arose in the course of time that idealistic outlook on the world which, especially since the decline of the ancient world, has dominated men's minds. It still rules them to such a degree that even the most materialistic natural scientists of the Darwinian school are still unable to form any clear idea of the origin of man, because under this ideological influence they do not recognise the part that has been played by labour.[10]

The primacy of labor, says Engels, is an issue of ideological consequence. The first Marxist thinker to interpret the apparent antithesis of labor and play as a matter of ideological moment is Georgi Plekhanov, the most important Russian Marxist before Lenin and a founder of the first Russian Social Democratic party. (It is worth noting that Plekhanov could not have read this passage by Engels, since *The Dialectics of Nature* remained unpublished at Engels' death in 1895 and was first issued in 1927.) Plekhanov's approach to the subject of prehistorical human origins combines intellectual humility and a dogmatic logic. In "The Materialist Conception of History" (1897), he openly concedes that the prehistoric human remains an enigma: "But our ideas of 'primitive man' are merely conjectures."[11] But in "Labor, Play, and Art," the third of his *Letters without Address* (1900), Plekhanov recognizes that Marxist theory must control the territory of prehistory lest it forfeit a crucial authority.

The point of Plekhanov's essay is to refute an idea proposed by the German anthropologist Karl Bücher: "*Labour,* as known among the primitive peoples, is in itself a somewhat vague phenomenon. The closer we approach the point where its development commences the nearer it approaches, both in form and content, to play." Plekhanov then alerts his reader to the gravity of this issue and quotes Bücher again:

> The development of manufacture apparently always begins with the painting of the body, the tattooing, piercing or distortion of various parts of the body, after which, little by little the preparation of ornaments, masks, drawings on bark, hieroglyphs and similar occupations develop. . . . Thus, technical skills are elaborated in play and only gradually acquire useful application. And therefore the previously accepted sequence of stages in development must be replaced by their direct opposite: play is older than labour, and art is older than the production of useful objects.

"Now you can understand," Plekhanov continues,

> why I asked you to pay particular attention to Bücher's words: they have the closest relationship to the historical theory which I am defending. If play indeed is older than labour and if art is indeed older than the production of useful objects, then the materialist explanation of history, at any rate as expounded by the author of *Capital, will not stand up to the criticism of facts* and all my reasoning must be turned upside down: I shall have to argue about the dependence of economics on art and not about the dependence of art on economics. But is Bücher right?

The answer, of course, is that he is not, and to demonstrate why, Plekhanov invokes Herbert Spencer's *Principles of Psychology* (1872): "According to Spencer, beasts of prey clearly show us that their play consists of sham hunting and sham fighting. . . . What does this mean? It means that in animals the content of play is determined by such activity as assists in the support of their existence. Which comes first then—play before utilitarian activity, or utilitarian activity before play? It is clear that utilitarian activity *precedes play, that the former is 'older' than the latter.*" Plekhanov accepts the animal analogy without a qualm: "In other words *activity among human beings in pursuit of utilitarian ends*, that is, activity essential to support the existence of individuals and the whole of society, *also precedes play and is the factor which determines its content.* Such is the conclusion that follows logically from what Spencer says about play."[12]

The Marxists on Labor and Play

Although Plekhanov pursued this argument in defense of Marx, his defense is philosophically incompetent from the standpoint of more recent, and ostensibly more sophisticated, Marxist theorists, not all of whom seem to be aware of Plekhanov's role in this ideological dispute. Plekhanov's error was to have succumbed to the temptation to argue the merits of categories (*labor* and *play*) which, from a later Marxist perspective, are not simple, antithetical essences. Maynard Solomon has pointed out that Marx distinguished between two (qualitatively different) types of labor: "Plekhanov fails to make Marx's crucial distinction between 'primitive instinctive forms of labour' and labour in its 'exclusively human' form." In addition, the relationship between labor and play is to be construed not as antithetical, but as dialectical: "Play is a dialectical coordinate of labor. The *creative* element of labor is the imagination, the free 'play' of a man's 'bodily and mental powers.' To participate in creative, human labor, man withdraws from the instinctive, repetitive labor process and turns it into play, into mimetic representation, into illusion, into art, so that when he returns to labor it may be transformed into a conscious, supra-instinctive, freedom-creating activity. Work and play are a unity of opposites peculiar to the human species. In this sense, play is the philosophy, the art of work. To argue priority is ultimately non-dialectical." It should, however, be noted that Solomon has managed to inject a play element into Marxian thought by seizing on a specific quotation—"At the end of every labour-process, we get a result that already existed in the imagination of the labourer at its commencement"—which does not suggest the *ludique* as it is usually understood.[13] What is more, his alleged "unity of opposites" is a pure hypothesis, and at least as arbitrary as its (historically documented) ideological adversary: the absolute separation of labor and play as existential categories. The Marxian quotation to which he appeals implies nothing, no matter how imaginative the extrapolation, comparable to the primal ludic impulse described by Schiller, Ortega, and Huizinga. It is clear, for example, that for the latter two the *ludique* can include a latent demonic element which Marx, surely, would never have incorporated into his notion of creative activity. Such a difference in the interpretation of play is a measure of the conceptual apartheid which separates Left and Right on the issue of the labor-leisure dialectic.

The alleged artificiality of the labor/play dichotomy is alluded to by the French Marxist Henri Lefebvre: "Anthropology has a domain of its own, and man can be defined as *sapiens, faber, ludens,* etc. Such definition never justifies separating man from his material foundation, or dissociating culture from nature, or what is acquired from what is spontaneously given."[14] Lefebvre seems to suggest here that any of these categories is by itself basically arbitrary and an abstraction from a larger whole; *homo ludens,* for example, must be reconciled with his "material foundation," implying a merger with *homo faber,* the (productive) manipulator of matter. But Lefebvre does not pursue the "unity of opposites" strategy here or in *Everyday Life in the Modern World,* where "the death of the ludic spirit" is mourned,[15] even as the *ludique* itself, presented as a self-evident Romantic virtue, is left unintegrated with a labor process it might have transformed.

Lefebvre, as Richard Gombin has noted, "indicates a degree of optimism when he affirms that it is by and through leisure that modern man will express his revolt against the break-up of his everyday life and the way it is being made increasingly banal."[16] "*Society of leisure* perhaps?" Lefebvre asks in *Everyday Life.* "Indeed, the most remarkable aspect of the transition we are living through is not so much the passage from want to affluence as the passage from labour to leisure. We are undergoing the uneasy mutation of our major 'values,' the mutation of an epoch. Who can deny that leisure is acquiring an ever increasing importance in France and in all so-called industrial societies? The stress of 'modern life' makes amusements, distractions and relaxation a necessity, as the theoreticians of leisure with their following of journalists and popularizers never tire of repeating. A new universal social phenomenon, the holiday, has displaced anxiety and is becoming its focal point." Lefebvre's response to this "new universal social phenomenon" has relinquished the traditional Marxist optimism in favor of a more cautious prognosis: "Leisure contains the future, it is the new horizon, but the transition promises to be long and dangerous." For Lefebvre, "modern life" is characterized by alienated forms of both labor and leisure: "Today leisure is first of all and for (nearly) all a temporary break with everyday life. We are undergoing a painful and premature revision of all our old 'values'; leisure is no longer a festival, the reward of labour, and it is not yet a freely chosen activity pursued for itself, it is a generalized display: television, cinema, tourism. Alienated leisure dwells within 'hygienic ghettos' and such as 'the ghetto of creativity and hobbies.'"[17]

Lefebvre's assertion that "amusements, distractions and relaxation" have become "a necessity" represents a major concession by a serious Marxist theorist. A century after Marx, labor has exhausted its allegedly utopian possibilities, and its ancient antithesis assumes a (hypothetical) salvational role. In one sense, Lefebvre's portrait of the existential bankruptcy of labor marks a return to the early Marx and his portrait of labor under primitive capitalist conditions. Marx's view of the labor-leisure dialectic as it applies to mid-nineteenth century proletarian life is given in the context of his denunciation of political economy in the "Economic and Philosophical Manuscripts of 1844," where he calls political economy

> the science of denial, of starvation, of *saving* [which] actually goes so far as to *save* man the *need* for fresh *air* or physical *exercise*. This science of the marvels of industry is at the same time the science of *asceticism*, and its true ideal is the *ascetic* but *rapacious* skinflint and the ascetic but *productive* slave. Self-denial, the denial of life and of all human needs, is its principal doctrine. The less you eat, drink, buy books, go to the theatre, go dancing, go drinking, think, love, theorize, sing, paint, fence, etc., the more you *save* and the greater will become that treasure which neither moths nor maggots can consume—your *capital*. The less you *are*, the less you give expression to your life, the more you *have*, the greater is your *alienated* life and the more you store up of your estranged life. Everything which the political economist takes from you in terms of life and humanity, he restores to you in the form of *money* and *wealth*, and everything which you are unable to do, your money can do for you: it can eat, drink, go dancing, go to the theatre, it can appropriate art, learning, historical curiosities, political power, it can travel, it is *capable* of doing all those things for you; it can buy everything; it is genuine *wealth*, genuine *ability*. But for all that, it only *likes* to create itself, to buy itself, for after all everything else is its servant. . . . So all passions and all activity are lost in greed.[18]

Clearly, Marx has a notion of recuperative labor; and out of sympathy for the exhausted worker—unlike the fastidious cultural conservative or the neo-Marxist critic of "alienated" leisure—Marx does not scorn it. Here it is not an "evil luxury," to quote Max Scheler's sarcastic paraphrasing of the utilitarian critique of leisure, but a humane respite from an inhuman labor regimen as well as a basic human need to which capitalism blinds the worker. What is more, Marx has glimpsed "alienated leisure" as a form of denatured experi-

ence, suggesting a potential fulfillment which "the science of denial" has robbed of its real substance. Marx does not provide a vision
of leisure activity as an end in itself, though this issue has its problematic aspect. In his commentary on James Mill's *Elements of Political Economy*, Marx does write, "My labor would be a *free manifestation of life* and an *enjoyment of life*."[19] But the interpolation of
the ludic element into this kind of labor misses the point, which is
Marx's belief in the degree to which labor can represent human potential as a whole. This retrospective interpolation appeals to
post-Marxian generations who have encountered the labor-leisure dialectic in its post-Marxian phase of development, which has incorporated a respect for the play element (see Lefebvre) of which Marx
simply had no idea. James Riordan offers the following interpretation: "Whether games playing contained its own justification within
itself or whether its value was to be sought in ulterior ends was not a
question specifically raised by Marx. The Marxist vision of the
future, however, does seem to imply that work and physical recreation will merge, or that work will be elevated to the plane of recreation by the removal of the yokes of specialisation and compulsion.
But Marx evidently did not envisage recreation under communism
as simply games—rather as a fusion of worklike activities within
play." The utopian ludic element which some, like Riordan, discern
in Marx has not done very well in societies which claim to be Marxist. As Riordan himself points out, "sport in the Soviet Union is by
no means a matter of fun and games; it is not the 'garden' of human
activities. Physical culture is on a par with mental culture and has
important functions to discharge."[20]

It is difficult to overlook the fact that Marx, who did not live to
see the age of mass sport, was a theorist of labor rather than of leisure; it remained for Eastern bloc ideologues and Western Frankfurt
Marxists to attack, in their respective styles, the corruption of "bourgeois" leisure and "bourgeois" sport. As the French leisure sociologist Joffre Dumazedier has pointed out, "All the great social doctrinaires of the 19th century had a presentiment of the coming of
leisure. But none foresaw the ambiguity of this phenomenon. For
Marx, leisure is 'the space for human development' [in the *Grun-
drisse*], for Proudhon it is the time of 'free compositions'; for Au-
guste Comte, it is the possibility of promoting 'popular astronomy,'
etc. . . . . This identification of leisure with popular instruction is still
a familiar one in Soviet sociology. And in France, too, a certain
tendency in this direction of 'continuing education' reflects this
concept of leisure."[21]

What does Dumazedier mean by the "ambiguity" of mass leisure which Marx and his contemporaries had missed? Presumably, the fact that leisure could become an opiate as well as a recuperation from labor. It is the twentieth-century Herbert Marcuse, not the nineteenth-century Marx, who warns of "the growing passivity of leisure-time activities" and of "society's direct management of the nascent ego through the mass media, school and sports teams, gangs, etc."[22] In short, a genuine Marxist, or neo-Marxist, critique of sport had to wait until leisure had revealed its own alienating and soporific possibilities. Had Marx lived another twenty or thirty years, he would have seen new dimensions of the labor-leisure dialectic appearing all around him, both in the social process and, eventually, in the work of social theorists.

Neo-Marxist theory today has two ways to construe the labor-leisure dialectic. The first accords play the status of an autonomous and important mode of human activity which is endowed with nothing less than the power to transform the human condition. This position, to which Henri Lefebvre subscribes, has been presented more systematically by Francis Hearn. Hearn is a revisionist who does not even address the issue of "alienated" leisure; his purpose is to establish the significance of play which Marxist theory has overlooked: "The centrality of the category of labor to the Marxian dialectic has fostered in large measure the neglect of play and the denunciation of any serious effort to appreciate the potentially liberating qualities of the noninstrumental."[23] This is, however, a somewhat misleading formulation, since Hearn actually finds play to be anything but "noninstrumental."

Departing from Jürgen Habermas' theory of the emancipating potential within language,[24] Hearn describes three "developmental connections between play and language": "first, play shares many of the liberating properties which characterize language. Second, play complements and, at times, initiates the self-formative process associated with language. And, third, the distortion of play may be more easily overcome than the distortion of language, and, accordingly, it may be wiser to concentrate immediate efforts on the unblocking of play." Play is nothing less than "indispensable to the self-formative process of the species and of the individual"; it is "a genetically adaptive process" which "contributes to evolutionary growth." Like the cultural conservative, Hearn treats play as an essence which can be suppressed but which never changes; in effect, he joins Huizinga in mourning the devitalization of the play-impulse during the industrial regimentation of the nineteenth century. But unlike Huizinga, Hearn associates the play-impulse with political revolt; it contains a "critique of the present order" while it aids and abets "the persistence of the rebellious disposition."[25] This kind of revisionism assumes, in other words, that the substance of Huizinga's classic paean to the *ludique* can be stolen out from under his nose and put to work under very different auspices. A weakness of Hearn's treatise is that he never confronts this inconvenient debt to an ideological adversary.

Play, Hearn claims, "does not conceal or deny reality, rather it reorders and represents it by making it more manageable and meaningful."[26] The second neo-Marxist interpretation, as exemplified by Lawrence M. Hinman, is not so uncritical of the play element. Unlike Hearn, Hinman does not exalt play as a wholesome, and even revolutionary, vitalism but prefers to emphasize what Hearn in effect evades: the problem of alienation. Hinman claims that "in the 1844 manuscripts and the notes on Mill's *Elements of Political Economy*, Marx provides the basis for both a theory of the alienated character of play and leisure in capitalist society and an indication of the characteristics of unalienated play and leisure." "It will be shown," he continues, "that Marx's position involves *an overcoming of the dichotomy between work and play found* in capitalist society and *a rethinking of the traditional categories* in terms of which work and play as forms of human activity are understood. This discussion leads to the question of *whether there is any meaningful distinction between work and play* in their unalienated forms [emphasis added]."[27]

Hinman ascribes to play both positive and negative effects, though he emphasizes the latter:

Play is negated insofar as it is not productive of human life, its freedom is restricted to the realm of appearance, its enjoyability is not rooted in our life and species-existence, its mediations between people and their comrades and between the individual and one's species-being take place only on the level of appearance, it is not rooted in and transformative of human needs, it does not mediate between us and nature, it remains isolated in the imagination, and its many-sidedness is not integrated into the primary life-world. *Play is affirmed* insofar as it is creative of human life, is free, conscious activity, opens up new relations among people and transforms humanity's nature, transforms human needs and nature through imaginative, world-transformative activity, provides a continuing affirmation of the many-sidedness of human activity. In this sense, unalienated *praxis* retains many of the characteristics traditionally associated with play, but fundamentally transforms them by destroying their isolation from humanity's primary species-activity [emphasis added].[28]

In one sense, the primary difference between these two neo-Marxisms is that the first confronts the Marxist intellectual tradition with evidence of its myopic approach to the *ludique*, while the second attempts to defend Marxism from that very charge by finding in the early Marx "the foundation of a theory of play and leisure." Hinman concedes, however, that his notion of "unalienated *praxis*" remains "problematic"; in fact, an ironic aspect of his position is that this very notion forces Hinman to give lessons in Marxism to Marx. In the early writings, "Marx developed a dialectical concept of needs . . . which surpassed previous theories of human needs and opened the way for an understanding of how the dichotomy between necessity and freedom could be overcome. This dichotomy, reflected in that between work and leisure, was one which existed only at specific stages in our development, stages characterized by scarcity."[29] Let us set aside the question of whether the (hypothetical) removal of scarcity would "overcome" the labor-leisure dichotomy. Hinman's more immediate problem is that Marx had committed the indiscretion of contradicting his own thoughts of 1844. In *Capital* Marx had written: "In fact, the realm of freedom actually begins only where working which is determined by necessity and external purposefulness ceases; thus in the very nature of things it lies beyond the sphere of actual material production. . . . Beyond [the realm of necessity] begins that development of human energy which is an end in itself, the true realm of freedom, which, however, can blossom forth only with this realm of necessity as its basis. The shortening of the working-day is its basic prerequisite."[30] In a word, Marx divorces "the realm of freedom" from "the sphere of actual material production." Marx's error, says Hinman, is that he failed "to overcome the categories of the society that he was criticizing and thereby falls into traps that he himself had earlier elucidated." The shortening of the working day represents, for the more ambitious Hinman, a pathetic attempt to bring about an essentially dishonorable compromise, a quantitative solution where only a qualitative one—the fusing of freedom and labor—will do. As he points out, "The distinction between the realm of freedom and that of necessity negates the notion of unalienated *praxis* as the overcoming of the dichotomy between work and play."[31] How could Marx have resigned himself to "the doctrine of the two realms"?

Modern Communist ideology does not resign itself to this doctrine. On the contrary, Eastern bloc theory proclaims the advent of a human condition which will not require leisure (in the "bourgeois" sense of the term) at all. "Certain western sociologists," two Soviet leisure experts write in 1959, "try to view leisure as a complete distancing of man from work, as something opposed to work. We cannot agree with such ideas. Leisure in a communist society is not a fleeing from work but one of the transitional forms to a truly communist form of work, at which point the latter becomes enjoyment and the primary vital need."[32] A corollary to this idea appeared several years ago in an East German broadcast: "Our freedom on the sports field is based upon the fundamental freedom from exploitation, the labor of each for all, etc."[33] In other words, social existence is a seamless whole which cannot be subdivided into spheres of different existential value in the manner of a cultural conservative like Huizinga. Social life is free *in toto*, or it is unfree in the same manner. There is no privileged or transcendent area. As the Soviet sociologists put it, "Leisure in Soviet society is not the affirmation of the individual in an imaginary world but his affirmation in a real one . . ."[34] Once again there is an East German corollary. In an article which appeared in 1972 in the official journal of the Central Committee of the Socialist Unity party, it is maintained that "*Kulturarbeit* [work in the field of culture] in accordance with the motto 'Leisure—Art and Enjoyment' is no 'hobby movement.' In capitalist countries a 'hobby movement' is often the expression of an escape from a conflict-ridden social world and into peripheral regions." Thanks to the humanistic character of East German society, the author concludes, there is simply no need for "mental narrowness or vacuity" to exist.[35] A few issues later the same journal published another article dealing with the leisure category, to which sport belongs as a creative social activity. "Corresponding to its historical mission, its characteristics, and ideals," the author writes, "the revolutionary working class establishes an entirely new relationship to entertainment. Under capitalist conditions the struggle of the working class against exploitation and oppression was linked with the demand that the influence of the late bourgeois amusement industry, with its narcotizing, diverting, and pacifying effects, be driven back." He goes on to point out that it is the abolition of the contradiction between labor and leisure, among other things, which "makes possible a rich variety of amusements and relaxations which are based upon educational, moral, and aesthetic values," all of this "in the service of forming the socialist personality."[36] Small wonder that East German sport sociology is considered an instrument for the creation of an "optimistic" way of life.[37]

Nor have the East German ideologists who resolve the labor-leisure dialectic in this fashion overlooked the prehistorical theme with which we began. Plekhanov's insistence on the primacy of labor over play has survived as a basic principle of sport sociology in the GDR. In one of his works on sport in antiquity, including the prehistorical period, the sport historian Gerhard Lukas, while terming "sportive activity" a primordial human phenomenon, nevertheless makes a point of situating its origin in the "labor process." What is more, Lukas posits an analogy between sport and religion, arguing that religion (like pure play) must be denied the status of an "original" human experience; he implies that there is a similar analogy between sport and art by denying that "aesthetic joy" is the source of art.[38]

The East German kinesthesiologist Kurt Meinel has put forth a Marxist anthropology of human movement of considerably greater theoretical ambition than that of Lukas. Meinel makes three fundamental points. First, he maintains that "the genesis of movement" in human beings developed as a direct result of individuals' interactions with their environment, that is, the social structure in which they found themselves. This premise—which Lukas, interestingly enough, has seen fit to challenge in a heretical passage of his own—aims at refuting the notion of an innate play-impulse, which might well resist integration into a "rational" social praxis. Meinel's second claim is standard Marxist fare: human movement (*die menschliche Motorik*) is a product of labor and its project of securing the conditions for human survival; once again the idea of an innate, spontaneous urge is rejected. Third, and most interestingly, Meinel claims that movement plays a fundamental (*grundlegende*) role in the "psychic, spiritual, moral, and aesthetic-cultural development of mankind."[39] This is an important, and perhaps unsettling, idea in that it appears to assimilate mental functioning to physical functioning, which is qualitatively less complex. This is another idea which goes back to Plekhanov, whom Meinel does not cite:

> Bücher has formed the conclusion that "at the primitive stage of their development, work, music and poetry were a fused whole, work being the chief element in this trinity, and music and poetry of secondary importance." In his opinion, "the origin of poetry is to be sought in work," and he goes on to remark that no language arranges words making up a sentence in ordinary speech in a rhythmical pattern. It is therefore improbable that men arrived at measured, poetical speech through the use of their everyday language—the inner logic of that language operates against that. How, then, is one to ex-

plain the origin of measured, poetical speech? Bücher is of the opinion that *the measured and rhythmical movements of the body transmitted the laws of their coordination* to figurative, poetical speech. This is all the more probable if one recalls that at the lower stages of development rhythmical movements of the body are usually accompanied by singing. But what is the explanation of the coordination of bodily movements? It lies in the nature of the processes of production. Thus, "the origin of poetry is to be sought in productive activities" [emphasis added].[40]

But are the "rhythmical movements of the body" and "the laws of their coordination" compatible with an autonomous mental life? Indeed, the spectre of the robot is evoked when Meinel states that movement's contribution to personality development will be determined by the current state of technology.[41] Such an attitude, not to speak of the East German athlete's transformation into an instrument of "production," testifies to the historical importance of the labor-leisure dialectic and to the ideological importance of Plekhanov's dogmas concerning labor and the body.

The Conservatives and Prehistory

We have seen that an anthropological dogma of precedence is actually a dogma about anthropological values. Ernst Cassirer has pointed out that the same principle applies to the question of the origin of the state. "Only a few thinkers," he writes, "were so naive as to assume that the 'origin' of the state, as explained in the theories of the social contract, gave us an insight into its beginnings. Obviously we cannot assign a definite moment of human history at which the state made its first appearance. . . . What they are seeking for is not the beginning, but the 'principle' of the state—its *raison d'etre*. . . . What we are looking for is an origin in reason, not in time."[42] Or, in the case of Ortega y Gasset, an origin in unreason, as we shall see. In either case, origins prefigure values.

It should be noted that antiutilitarianism does not invariably require a doctrine of precedence which finds play at the origin of culture. Friedrich Schiller's famous concept of the play-impulse (*Spieltrieb*) is not a historical antecedent to the doctrine of the primordiality of play. Schiller does adopt (in 1795) the cultural conservative's position on labor and the utilitarian ideology: "But today Necessity is master, and bends a degraded humanity beneath its tyrannous yoke. *Utility* is the great idol of the age, to which all powers must do service and all talents swear allegiance. In these clumsy scales the spiritual service of Art has no weight; deprived of all encouragement, she flees from the noisy mart of our century." It is "precisely play, and play alone, that makes man complete and displays at once his twofold nature." But for Schiller the play-impulse is not historically primordial; on the contrary, it is antithetical to the primeval condition of humanity: "And what sort of phenomenon is it that proclaims the approach of the savage to humanity? So far as we consult history, it is the same in all races who have escaped from the slavery of the animal state: a delight in *appearance*, a disposition towards *ornament* and *play*."[43] For Schiller, play is the result of culture, not its origin.

Let us now return to the problem of the primordial and existentially primary human activity, but from the standpoint of twentieth-century cultural conservatism. Max Scheler, the German philosopher and social thinker of the 1920s and 1930s, recognizes that "the problem of the origin of *civilization* and *culture*" is raised by the ideal of utility, which he harshly criticizes. "Here again, considerations of utility are supposed to have brought about the formation of tools, science, the origin of language, and the development of art and religion."[44] This is intolerable to Scheler, whose attack on utilitarianism and the labor theory of value is based on his critique of the "bourgeois mentality" and the psychology of *ressentiment*,[45] a notion he had borrowed from Nietzsche's *On the Genealogy of Morals* (1887). Nietzsche himself, as Judith Shklar points out, was only one of many nineteenth-century romantics whose "hatred of utility" was due to "the fact that utilitarianism was the spirit of the age, that it was the philosophy of a mediocre, undramatic society."[46]

Scheler begins his essay "Cognition and Work" with the observation that the pathos which modern people associate with the word "work" has been intensifying since antiquity, and he finds the sharpest expression of this pathos in the *Communist Manifesto*, in the Marxian thesis that work is "the sole creator of all *Bildung und Kultur*."[47] Paraphrasing the Marxian position on labor, an analyst of East German society comments: "The central motif of the Marxian philosophy of man is 'self-realization': Man creates himself and realizes himself only through labor. Basically, labor is the only means by which man can live in society and understand his own history. Furthermore, only through the process of working can man transcend his alienated state. . . . Marx therefore evaluates all society from the perspective of the sphere of labor."[48]

It is precisely the categorical aspect of the Marxian interpretation of labor—the utter hegemony with which it rules over all of human existence—which has driven certain non-Marxist thinkers into revolt against the idea of a culture in which labor rules as an absolute value. Scheler joins Marx in condemning the existential status of work under capitalism; the crucial difference between these two classic, and irreconcilable, positions is that Scheler 1. assigns a subordinate status to the work function, which he denigrates as possessing no real creativity—in short, he simply negates the Marxian position; and 2. holds up as an ideal a vitalistic principle representing "the pure expression of life" in which "bodily training in all its forms" plays an important role, even if capitalist civilization has debased this activity down to the level of mere "sport," a theme heard frequently from conservative cultural critics of the interwar period. The point here is that for the twentieth-century cultural conservative like Scheler, the body and sport constitute either a salvational vessel containing a vital force which is more important than work— which is beyond redemption—or, in their debased form, they represent a form of leisure which is ultimately utilitarian rather than ludic in character because it offers a recuperation from work, or just the boredom pervading society, and nothing more. It is worthwhile here to quote at length from Scheler's *Ressentiment* (1915) in order to understand the categorical position he opposes to Marx. It cannot, however, be quite as categorical as the Marxian position if only because it must, realistically, provide a role for Marx's hegemonic category, that of labor, even as it glorifies as "superior" an opposed principle on which human life is to be based:

Now life itself—the sheer *existence* of an individual, a race, a nation—must be justified by its *usefulness* for a *wider* community. It is not enough if this life in itself contains higher values than usefulness can represent—its existence must be "earned." The right to live and exist, which the older morality included among the "natural rights," is denied both in theory and practice. On the contrary: if a man cannot adapt himself to the mechanism of the utilitarian civilization and the human activity it happens to require at the moment, he "*should*" be destroyed, no matter how great his vital values may be. According to the earlier notion, life in its aimless *activity*, its mere "respiration" and its characteristic inner processes, represents an intrinsic fulness of value; all useful actions are destined to *serve* it, and all mechanisms are only means to aid its *freer* development. Life is, as it were, the *innate lord and master of the inanimate world*, it does *not* owe its value to the benefits derived from its adaptation to the inanimate world and to its capacity for being useful. But this original view is replaced by the feeling that the pure expression of life is only ballast and evil luxury—a kind of "atavistic survival" of forms of behavior and action that were useful long ago. . . . In accordance with this basic idea, the ability to treat life as an intrinsic value disappears in theory and practice. Therefore we lose all understanding for a *technique of life*—be it a technique of propagation, be it a social and individual technique for the intensification of vital forces. Most older civilizations had such techniques: the castes for the selection of the best and for the advancement of physical, intellectual, and moral hereditary values; the fixed, almost automatic systems for the distribution of cultural goods; the many forms of asceticism, exercise, contest, knightly tournament; India's caste system and asceticism; the estate system, races, games, and the Gymnasium of ancient Greece; the estate system, asceticism, knightly games and tournaments of the Middle Ages; the training of a Japanese Samurai; the ancient Chinese rank order and system of education—all these embody the same idea: that a dead mechanical technique stands below a vital technique, that life and the abundance of its forces deserves to be developed for its own sake—without reference to professional usefulness! Modern civilization is alone in lacking such a vital technique—and not only in practice: it has lost its pure idea! Even the last remnants of a social hierarchy—as a meaningful selection of the best and an image of the aristocracy that pervades all living nature—are cast overboard, and society is atomized in order to free the forces required for doing better business. The "estate"—a concept in which noble blood and tradition determine the unity of the group—is replaced by the mere "class," a group unified by property, certain external customs ruled by fashion, and "culture." Bodily training in all its forms is nothing but "recreation" from work or the gathering of strength for renewed useful labor—it is never valuable *in itself* as a pure play of vital forces. There is no longer the slightest understanding for the exercise of vital functions for the sake of life (nor indeed for the exercise of thought for the sake of thought, as in the dialectics of the ancients)—everything is done for the sake of work. . . . Mechanical chance governs everything. "True seriousness" pertains to business and work alone, and all the rest is only "fun." Even modern "sports" are nothing but recreation from work, and by no means a manifestation of free vitality at whose service work itself should be.[49]

"As history, Scheler's construction is fantastic and pure mythology."[50] But the fundamental ideological division could not be clearer: will "work" be in the service of "free vitality" or will it swallow it? Scheler shares with Marx the nostalgia for a preindustrial world; but unlike Marx, he goes beyond the celebration of its "organic unity" to posit as its principle the *ludique* itself: the play principle which would be accorded a primary historical role at the origin of society by the Spanish philosopher of culture José Ortega y Gasset, who was influenced by Scheler and wrote a laudatory obituary upon his death.[51]

In "The Sportive Origin of the State" (1924), Ortega presents the labor-leisure dichotomy in the context of a version of prehistory which, like Scheler's, is quite fantastic. Ortega first divides "organic phenomena—animal and human—into two great classes of activity, one original, creative, vital par excellence—that is, spontaneous and disinterested; the other of utilitarian character, in which the first is put to use and mechanized." His strategy is to dichotomize and then draw his own invidious comparison: "all utilitarian actions aiming at adaptation, all mere reaction to pressing needs, must be considered as secondary vital functions, while the first and original activity of life is always spontaneous, effusive, overflowing, a liberal expansion of pre-existing energies." The dichotomy between the utilitarian and the original, the adaptive, and the spontaneous, is then given concrete form: "If the classic instance of the obligatory effort which strictly satisfies a need is to be found in what man calls work, the other, the effort *ex abundantia cordis*, becomes most manifest in sport. We thus feel induced to invert the inveterate hierarchy. Sportive activity seems to us the foremost and creative, the most exalted, serious, and important part of life, while labor ranks second as its derivative and precipitate."[52]

At the origin of this dichotomy Ortega sets his prehistorical fantasy. The "first social organization," he says, was a confederation of predatory adolescent gangs: "They all felt, without knowing why, a strange and mysterious disgust for the familiar women of their own blood with whom they live in the horde and an appetite sharpened by imagination for the others, those alien women, unknown, unseen, or only fleetingly espied. And now one of the most prodigious events of human history takes place, an event from which gigantic consequences have sprung. They decide to rape girls of distant hordes. . . . and war is born for the service of love." At the same time, these adventurous youths are proto-sportsmen: "the primeval political association is the secret society; and while it serves the pleasures of feasting and drinking, it is at the same time the place where the first religious and athletic asceticism is practiced. We must not forget that the literal translation of the word 'asceticism' is 'training exercise.' The monks took it over from the sport vocabulary of the Greek athletes. *Ascesis* was the regime of the life of an athlete, and it was crammed with exercises and privations." The moral of this violent story is that "the first human society is precisely the opposite of a reaction to imposed necessities," that "in the beginning there is vigor and not utility." "Wherever we find the truly original genesis of a political organism, whenever we catch a glimpse of the birth of a state, we infallibly come upon the youth clubs which dance and fight." Ortega's thesis, in a phrase, is that of "the irrational historical origin of the state." But, as we have already seen, the question of primordial origins actually involves an invidious comparison between two basic modes of experience. It is for this reason that Ortega confesses, "I have sought to use the origin of the state as an instance of the creative power inherent in the activity of sport."[53]

What does all of this mean? Ortega's argument amounts to a polemical anthropology which—in its flagrant theatricality, its denigration of labor, and its rejection of "socialistic dogma"—is obviously directed against a utilitarian, or Marxist, mentality whose worst failing seems to be a crucial lack of imagination, a failure of ambition on behalf of the human spirit. "We cannot breathe," Ortega writes, "confined to a realm of secondary and intermediate themes." There is no evidence that Ortega was aware of the theories of prehistory advanced by Engels or Plekhanov. In fact, he did not have to be, since his larger target was the nineteenth century as a whole, "utilitarian throughout."[54] This indictment of an entire century as drab and prosaic would eventually be taken up by Ortega's ideological comrade-in-arms, the Dutch historian and cultural critic Johan Huizinga.

Johan Huizinga and Josef Pieper versus the Marxists

Huizinga's famous *Homo Ludens: A Study of the Play-Element in Culture* (1938) is the most important and influential non-Marxist contribution to the labor-leisure debate of the past century. It should be noted at the outset that it is not Huizinga's purpose to define man as *homo ludens* in a one-dimensional sense. "A brief introduction to the *Homo Ludens*," Karl Weintraub has noted, "makes clear that Huizinga thought of man as *homo sapiens* plus *homo faber* plus *homo ludens*; yet the book may leave the impression that man can be completely circumscribed as *homo ludens*. Economic realities were vital to his conception of culture; yet he rarely discusses them. Rationality is the bolt which locks out chaos; yet the weight of his sentences plays down the importance of rationality. . . . Thus Huizinga achieved unity and structure of argument often by elaborating only one aspect of this complete opinion."[55]

Such selectivity, which in practice amounts to a stylizing of culture and history, has a rhetorical and sometimes a polemical purpose. Huizinga's exaggerated stress on the *ludique* is intended as a polemical compensation for the utilitarian bias of industrial civilization. At the same time, Huizinga placed a limit on the degree to which he was willing to construe the labor-leisure dialectic in a polemical fashion. John Ruskin, he notes, "sees mankind divided from the very beginning into 'two races, one of workers, and the other of players: one tilling the ground, manufacturing, building, and otherwise providing for the necessities of life; the other part proudly idle, and continually therefore needing recreation, in which they use the productive and laborious orders partly as their cattle, and partly as their puppets or pieces in the game of death.'" For Huizinga, this is a species of vulgar Nietzscheanism: "There is," he states, "a taint of the Superman in this declaration of Ruskin's, and a touch of cheap illusionism . . ." Huizinga's loyalty to "the sphere of ethics," not to mention the horror he felt for the "demented" age of Hitler, precluded any endorsement of such a hierarchical reading of the labor-leisure dichotomy.[56] His polemical intent is to be found elsewhere.

Like "The Sportive Origin of the State" (to which it makes only cursory reference in a footnote), *Homo Ludens* amounts to a kind of perfect anti-Marxian argument. For Huizinga, Marxian economic determinism is a "shameful misconception," an accusation the author offers in sorrow rather than in anger, as he does not share Marx's taste for ideological combat. Huizinga's arguments are, consequently, usually implicitly rather than explicitly anti-Marxist: his task is to demonstrate the utterly indefinable, irreducible character of play so that he may demonstrate in turn a source of human action which lies outside of the historical process. "What makes Huizinga interesting from a theoretical point of view is his insistence that the cultural historian should not use a diachronic approach to history, but should study the past as if no element of time were involved in history at all; the absence of progress in history implied for him that there was no progression or direction to this historical process."[57]

This is Huizinga's way of answering the Marxian emphasis on "making history"—he simply makes history irrelevant to this "absolutely primary category of life," claiming that "genuine, pure play is one of the main bases of civilization," that "civilization arises and unfolds as play."[58]

In these claims we encounter the familiar anthropological argument over precedence, which is invoked here to promote the claims of "the primaeval soil of play." "Play is older than culture, for culture, however inadequately defined, always presupposes human society, and animals have not waited for man to teach them their playing"; "play is older and more original than civilization." Just as Plekhanov cited Herbert Spencer and Wilhelm Wundt ("Play is the child of labour"), Huizinga summons the testimony of the anthropologist Leo Frobenius: "In the remote past, so Frobenius thinks, man first assimilated the phenomena of vegetation and animal life and then conceived an idea of time and space, of months and seasons, of the course of the sun and moon. And now he plays this great processional order of existence in a sacred play, in and through which he actualizes anew, or 'recreates,' the events represented and thus helps to maintain the cosmic order. Frobenius draws even more far-reaching conclusions from this 'playing at nature.' He deems it the starting-point of all social order and social institutions. Through this ritual play, savage society acquires its rude forms of government."[59] This is Huizinga's version of "the sportive origin of the state."

As an accomplished historian—and unlike Ortega—Huizinga could not attest to the literal truth of Frobenius' vision: "We can leave aside," he says, "the question of how far this explanation of ritual regicide and the whole underlying conception can be taken as 'proved.'"[60] To such caution about prehistorical speculations Ortega had a blunt, and consummately romantic, reply: "How can we live turning a deaf ear to the last dramatic questions?"[61] Still, the fact is that Huizinga was finally unable to "turn a deaf ear" to primordial speculations, toward which he showed a deep ambivalence. "I can no longer remember," he writes in 1943, "when precisely I hit upon the idea that historical understanding is like a vision . . ."[62] In *Homo Ludens*, historiographical scruples virtually dissolve in the elegant impressionism that made Huizinga famous. The ambivalence alluded to above is curiously evident in his definition of "Romanticism" as "a tendency to retrovert all emotional and aesthetic life to an idealized past where everything is blurred, structureless, charged with mystery and terror. The delineation of such an ideal space for thought is itself a play-process."[63] Can Huizinga have been unaware of how closely this image fits the imaginative project of his *Homo Ludens*? Like Plekhanov, who confesses that "our ideas of 'primitive man' are merely conjectures," Huizinga both recognizes the fantasy element which plays a role in excavating "the primaeval soil of play," and then proceeds to endorse that vision of prehistory to which he is temperamentally, and therefore ideologically, drawn.[64]

Huizinga's hostility to Marxism is subtle in that it manages to be both temperate and visceral. His insistence that play possesses "a non-materialistic quality," that "it is not matter,"[65] derives from an unshakable determination to segregate the play-element from a materialistic philosophy whose most virulent form is a Marxist one. But Huizinga also shares Ortega's aristocratic condescension toward the great totalitarianisms of the age. The proper style for such spirits is to find communism and fascism less alarming than disappointing, horrific experiments which have pointedly failed.

The play-element must be maintained in its immaculate condition of indefinability: "play is a function of the living, but is not susceptible of exact definition either logically, biologically, or aesthetically. The play-concept must always remain distinct from all the other forms of thought in which we express the structure of mental and social life."[66] Robert Anchor ascribes this rather tortuous project to Huizinga's need for a unifying conception which could be derived from the multifarious details of cultural history.[67] But this explanation is only part of the truth; what it lacks is a sense of the play-concept's ideological function, which will in turn prepare the way for Huizinga's use of sport as an index of cultural degeneration (see chapter 5). The unstated purpose of Huizinga's essay on play is to devalue the political sphere as a whole and to portray the Marxist vision of humanity as irrelevant to human concerns.

Josef Pieper's *Leisure: The Basis of Culture* (1947) is another work by a conservative thinker whose single-minded pursuit of the labor-leisure dichotomy aims at elevating the antiutilitarian impulse to virtually sacred status and then propounding a critique of modernity based upon what he perceives to be the decline of a sacred value. Pieper's concept of "leisure" is, of course, analogous to Huizinga's notion of "play"; and he is far less reticent than Huizinga about acknowledging the ideological significance of his favored category: "There is no doubt of one thing: the world of the 'worker' is taking shape with dynamic force—with such a velocity that, rightly or wrongly, one is tempted to speak of daemonic force in history." Pieper's target is "that inhuman state characteristic of labour under totalitarianism: the ultimate typing of the worker to production," which in turn produces "the look of the 'worker': the fixed, mask-like readiness to suffer *in vacuo*, without relation to anything. It is the absence of any connection with reality or real values that is distinctive . . ."[68]

It is curious that Pieper does not cite Huizinga, whose basic doctrine he shares. Both, for example, found civilization upon religious values. Huizinga frequently uses words like "sacred" and "holy": "in the form and function of play, itself an independent entity which is senseless and irrational, man's consciousness that he is embedded in a sacred order of things finds its first, highest, and holiest expression."[69] (It is significant that Huizinga here ascribes consciousness of the sacred to "man" rather than to himself, choosing to speak more as an anthropologist than as a believer.) Pieper is a Catholic philosopher who does not share Huizinga's cross-cultural comparativism, his principled religious eclecticism. Both thinkers, however, employ the idea of the sacred in an antiutilitarian fashion. For Huizinga, the "sacred order of things" precedes, both as an event and as a value, the world of labor. Pieper is more direct: "Cut off from the worship of the divine, leisure becomes laziness and work inhuman." In addition, his fidelity to the words of Aquinas makes possible a critique of labor far more ambitious than anything offered by Huizinga. "The essence of virtue consists in the good rather than the difficult," Saint Thomas writes in the *Summa Theologica*, and Pieper shows just how subversive a notion this is in "the world of planned diligence and 'total labor.'"[70]

Whereas Huizinga is too genteel to fire open broadsides at the Marxists—as opposed to their "shameful misconceptions"—Pieper is openly anti-Communist: "The 'total work' state needs the spiritually impoverished, one-track mind of the 'functionary'; and he, in his turn, is naturally inclined to find complete satisfaction in his 'service' . . ." Pieper even claims that it is the Church rather than the Communist state which will rescue the proletariat: "whereas the 'total work' State declares all un-useful work 'undesirable,' and even expropriates free time in the service of work, there is one Institution in the world which forbids useful activity, and servile work, on particular days, and in this way prepares, as it were, a sphere for a non-proletarian existence."[71] Compared with Huizinga, then, Pieper's polemic represents an intensification of both religious and political consciousness on behalf of the antiutilitarian ideology we have been examining.

Pieper was among the many Catholic conservatives to attack Jean-Paul Sartre and his "atheistic existentialism" during the late 1940s. Replying, in effect, to *What Is Literature?* (1947) and its doctrine of *littérature engagée*, Pieper takes Sartre to task for perversely changing the relationship between the writer's work and what he or she earns by producing it. Pieper's argument rests on an important distinction between the concept of "honorarium," which "implies that an incommensurability exists between performance and recompense," and the concept of "wage," which is "intended as payment for the specific work": "Jean-Paul Sartre announces that the writer, who has in the past so seldom 'established a relation between his work and its material recompense,' must learn to regard himself as 'a worker who receives the reward of his effort.' There, the incommensurability between the achievement and the reward, as it is implied and expressed in an 'honorarium,' is declared non-existent even in the field of philosophy and poetry which are, on the contrary, simply 'intellectual work.'"[72] This act of leveling, Pieper suggests, is tantamount to a disastrous merging of mind and matter, quality and quantity—in a word, the consummate *trahison des clercs*. Gabriel Marcel, too, attacks "the crudely materialistic foundation of the doctrine" of *Being and Nothingness* (1943).[73] Both speak in the attenuated accents of Huizinga's anti-Marxist idiom, banishing Sartre first to "the world of planned diligence and 'total labour'" and then to the ranks of its "materialistic" apologists.

Sartre does not, however, present so unambiguous an ideological target. If we penetrate far enough into *Being and Nothingness* to find Sartre's comments on the labor-leisure dialectic, we discover an interesting identification, not with the Left, with which Sartre is customarily associated, but with the right-wing position: ". . . the power to know leisure," Pieper writes, "is the power to overstep the boundaries of the workaday world and reach out to superhuman life-giving existential forces that refresh and renew us before we turn back to our daily work. Only in genuine leisure does a 'gate to freedom' open."[74] Sartre, too, is interested in conjoining play and freedom: "Play, like Kierkegaard's irony, releases subjectivity. What is play indeed if not an activity of which man is the first origin, for which man himself sets the rules and which has no consequences except according to the rules posited. As soon as a man apprehends himself as free and wishes to use his freedom . . . then his activity is play. . . . His goal, which he aims at through sports or pantomime or games, is to attain himself as a certain being, precisely the being which is in question in his being." The "function of the [play] act is to make manifest and to present to *itself* the absolute freedom which is the very being of the person." Sartre adds to these passages a long and striking appreciation of *sport*:

Ultimately a desire can be only the desire *to be* or the desire *to have*. On the other hand, it is seldom that play is pure of all appropriative tendency. I am passing over the desire of achieving a good performance or of beating a record which can act as a stimulant for the sportsman; I am not even speaking of the desire 'to have' a handsome body and harmonious muscles. . . . These desires do not always enter in and besides they are not fundamental. But there is always in sport an appropriative component. In reality sport is a free transformation of the worldly environment into the supporting element of the action. This fact makes it creative like art. The environment may be a field of snow, an Alpine slope. To see it is already to possess it.

These are not the only passages in *Being and Nothingness* which seek to confer nothing less than an existential dignity on sport; only once does Sartre use an example taken from the world of sport in a pejorative sense.[75] But the really astonishing passage on play in this book opposes its spirit of freedom to "materialism," "revolutionaries," and the "serious" Marx himself. The characterology which Sartre sets up on the basis of this dichotomy portrays the ideological conflict over the labor-leisure dialectic in a manner that cultural conservatives would find entirely satisfactory. Small wonder that the later Sartre made a point of disavowing this interpretation of play.[76]

It might seem like an exaggeration to suggest that a typology of ideological temperaments can be built upon different responses to as apparently obscure an index of political character as the labor-leisure dialectic. Yet this is exactly what Sartre does and what I have been proposing all along, since what is at stake is nothing else than competing interpretations of the human project and its ultimate, existentially primary experience. "Even if it has long since been forgotten," Eugen Fink writes, "human play is the symbolic act of representing the meaning of the world and life."[77] As we have seen, this is an inherently ideological claim, since it simultaneously excludes a contrary interpretation with which it has competed historically. The French philosopher Gaston Bachelard has expressed the "conservative" position in its most basic terms: "it is in *joy* and not in sorrow that man discovered his intellect. The conquest of *the superfluous* gives us greater spiritual excitement than the conquest of *the necessary*. Man is a creation of *desire*, not a creation of *need* [emphasis added]."[78] Bachelard's formulation captures the essence of the "sportive" style rather than the challenge of survival itself, greater rather than lesser "spiritual excitement." Bachelard presents us, in effect, with opposed visions of abundance and scarcity. The temperament which interprets human existence as a realm of abundance will be characterized by a profound exuberance which experiences life as an "incitement," as Ortega puts it: "Thus we imagine the magnificent stallion whom Caligula called *Incitatus* and made a member of the Roman Senate." The mentality of scarcity cannot fathom, and will oppose, the "exuberant" pursuit of style, an enmity which Ortega describes in biological terms reminiscent of Nietzsche's contempt for the psychology of resentment: "Abundance of possibilities is a symptom of thriving life, as utilitarianism, the attitude of confining oneself to the strictly necessary, like the sick man who begrudges every expenditure of energy, discloses weakness and waning of life."[79]

The Metaphysical Roots of the Quarrel

The two primary interpretations of the labor-leisure dialectic are irreconcilable; this has been openly recognized by the ideologists who have conducted this somewhat intermittent, but coherent, public dispute since the days of Engels and Plekhanov. Just as Pieper, Huizinga, and Ortega recognize the Marxist adversary, so has the Marxist adversary recognized them. The author of a Stalinist tract on sport published in East Berlin in 1961, for example, claims that Western sport lacks any valid ideological foundation: "All attempts to justify Western sport on an ideological basis, whether through the philosophy of an Ortega y Gasset or a Huizinga, or by means of neo-thomistic and neo-vitalistic world-views, are doomed to failure, because no ideologue of the imperialistic bourgeoisie is capable of producing thoughts which will save the cause of progress."[80] The "neo-thomistic" type is very probably Josef Pieper; the enmity is mutual.

The power to create is the power to determine the meaning of the creation and the laws which govern it—this is the significance of the anthropological issue which Right and Left have contested during the past century. Were people created, ultimately, to work or to play? In the utilitarianism and labor fetishism of the Left, the Right sees slavery, boredom, and confinement within the mundane; in the irrationality and leisure fetishism of the Right, the Left sees perversity and a squandering of human energies. What is more, the idea of a synthesis of labor and play into a utopian third mode of existence remains a fantasy.[81] As we have seen, the attempt by certain neo-Marxist theorists to infuse a play-element into Marx's early concept of labor founders on Marx's unwillingness to dissolve the labor-leisure dichotomy to the satisfaction of his inheritors. Nor is there anything ludic about this futuristic passage from *Capital*: "from the factory system budded, as Robert Owen has shown us in detail, the germ of the education of the future, an education that will, in the case of every child over a given age, combine productive labour with instruction and gymnastics, not only as one of the methods of adding to the efficiency of production, but as the only method of producing fully developed human beings."[82]

There is, however, at least one dichotomy (knowledge versus desire) which the Marxian vision does abolish; but, as Perry Anderson demonstrates, this synthesis does not lead in the direction of the *ludique*:

> For Marx . . . "knowledge" was itself a fundamental and illimitable human "desire." Science, far from being sequestered in a few excentric rural retreats, would pervade all economic life, providing the normal framework of everyday production. Manual and mental labour would exchange and coalesce at progressively higher levels of integration, in rhythm with moving forces of production. Creative work would not necessarily be carefree pleasure. Marx had another, less sensuous paradigm than handicrafts in mind when he thought of unalienated labour. Rebuking Fourier for the notion that such work would be like "play," which he scorned as the dream of "a naive shop-girl," he wrote: "Really free work, such as composing, is at the same time the most grimly serious, the most intense exertion." The image of the artist here is closer to that of Beethoven or Flaubert than—say—Blake or Chaucer . . .[83]

The essence of the Marxian vision retains its asceticism, even within the province of art. Eventually, Lenin would take such asceticism once step further by refusing to listen to Beethoven at all.[84]

The myth of the primordial character of play is usually associated with a notion of divinity. "With a word whose depth surpasses all logical understanding," Huizinga writes in 1936, "Plato once called men the playthings of the gods. To-day one might say that man everywhere uses the world as his plaything."[85] The impious humankind which manipulates the world with such wanton insouciance has, of course, been infected by Marx and his "materialistic" century. Huizinga speaks with a modest, even evasive, piety which adjures open polemics, but the outlines of this profound (metaphysical) quarrel with the Marxian vision are clear. ". . . never before in the history of the West," says Pieper, "has the world of work advanced such bold claims, insisted so strongly on its own 'totality.'"[86]

Huizinga and Pieper confront here the same enemy: the unlimited hubris of industrial man, the godless Prometheanism of Marx, whose version of the labor-leisure dialectic grows out of his view of humans and creation.

"The basis of irreligious criticism is: *Man makes religion*, religion does not make man," Marx writes in 1844.[87] Such a principle is, of course, diametrically opposed to the Christian anthropology of Pieper and Huizinga, who situate the primordiality of the play-impulse in "divine" or "sacred" origins. But Marx takes this dispute back to the moment of creation itself: "One of the key ideas in Marx's picture of man," David McLellan notes, "is that man is his own creator; any being that lived by the favour of another was a dependent being. Accordingly, Marx rejects the idea that the world was created . . ."[88] In the "Paris Manuscripts," Marx writes, "Since for socialist man, however, the entire so-called world history is only the creation of man through human labour and the development of nature for man, he has evident and incontrovertible proof of his self-creation, his own formation process."[89] Huizinga, in turn, attacks not only Marx's anticreationism ("the world as [man's] plaything"), but its consequences: "This grotesque over-estimation of the economic factor was conditioned by our worship of technological progress, which was itself the fruit of rationalism and utilitarianism after they killed the mysteries and acquitted man of guilt and sin." Sin can burden only a created being, not a self-created one. But are the "mysteries" of pagan or Christian origin? Huizinga is too anthropologically inclined not to combine them; the anthropologist in him is fascinated by "the very core of comparative religion: the nature and essence of ritual and mystery."[90] By demystifying the creation itself, Marx—without even realizing it—denies the play-element its primordial authority and ushers in the hegemony of labor.

A related aspect of this ideological dispute concerns the origin of the state. "The rise of the state among the Athenians," according to Engels in *The Origin of the Family*, "is a particularly typical example of the formation of a state; first, the process takes place in a pure form, without any interference through use of violent force, either from without or from within . . ."[91] This is the perfect antithesis of Ortega's vision: "Whenever we find the truly original genesis of a political organism, whenever we catch a glimpse of the birth of a state, we infallibly come upon the youth clubs which dance and fight."[92] As late as 1980, we find the British Marxist Perry Anderson complaining about a volume which propounds "the view that the origin of the State in primitive societies lies in the masochistic 'desire' to be dominated of the oppressed classes themselves. . . . Neither Marxism or socialism have anything to gain from traffic with [the notion of 'desire'], unless it is given what in this irrationalism it is so expressly constructed to refuse—a clear and observable meaning."[93] Anderson upholds Marxist tradition by refusing to countenance what Ortega termed "the irrational historical origin of the state." As Anderson later notes, Marx fuses desire with knowledge to create a form of "free work" which is actually "the most intense exertion." Marx, in short, deanarchizes desire so as to harness it to the engines of production. To the cultural conservatives, this represents an obscene truncation of the play-element. It is interesting to note that Anderson sees himself doing battle with "a fashionable philosophy of Parisian irrationalism." As we have seen, however, the struggle over "the origin of the State" is older than he seems to realize.

3. The Body as an Ideological Variable: Sportive Imagery of Leadership and the State

Theoretical Introduction

"Forme is Power," Hobbes remarks in *Leviathan*, "because being a promise of Good, it recommendeth men to the favour of women and strangers."[1] The idea that "Forme is Power," that an inherent charisma resides within the shapely and well-muscled torso, is as old as the warrior-kings of ancient times. Even in late medieval Europe, a king was sometimes referred to as *rex athleta Christi*—"an athlete of Christ."[2] It is a sign of the psychological force of this image that, even as physical strength has become irrelevant to political stature, statesmen have been promoted, and have promoted themselves, as physically statuesque. "His justice," Curzio Malaparte writes of Mussolini, "is of the body, not of the mind."[3] Such images are, of course, as insubstantial as they are impressive. "The predominant trait of this seemingly muscular power," an observer writes of Kwame Nkrumah in 1969, "is its fragility"—and this despite Nkrumah's "handsome build" and his title of *Kokodurni* (brave warrior).[4]

The principle that "Forme is Power" can also be applied to the state itself. A "body politic" may be interpreted as virile or decrepit, athletic or debased. This chapter presents a history of this "sportive" imagery of leadership and the state, particularly as it has flourished during the twentieth century, an age when, as Heidegger lamented, "a boxer is regarded as a nation's great man."[5]

The central thesis to be argued here is that Marxist and non-Marxist political cultures can be distinguished by employing the image of the body, and in particular the image of the athletic male body, as an ideological variable. Different attitudes toward the body point to significant disagreements which divide the respective political anthropologies of Left and Right: conceptions of leadership which differ on the propriety of charismatic appeals and narcissistic self-display, diametrically opposite views on the use of racialistic ideas, different views on the propriety of appealing to the irrational affinities of the populace, and divergent conceptions of the state as a community. These fundamental disagreements eventually take the form of opposed, and irreconcilable, ideologies of sport.

As suggested above, the image of the athletic body has led a double life: first, as a metaphor of the political leader and, second, as a metaphor of the body politic. The thesis of this chapter is that, while the Western political tradition offers numerous examples of such imagery, its twentieth-century development has bifurcated sharply along the lines of the two "extreme" political ideologies of our epoch. While fascist ideologists and a variety of fellow-travelers have shown a marked affinity for these images, Marxist writers and official ideologists have consistently refused to employ athletic imagery in the service of leadership and the Communist state. In one sense this refusal represents a remarkable political asceticism, since these metaphors have an obvious appeal to the imagination of any public. This abstinence can be explained as an act of ideological discipline. Ideological appeals more powerful than the temptation to accommodate sport-minded populations must have enforced such restraint. At the other ideological extreme, the appeal of such images to the mentalities of the extreme Right, including fascists of the pre- and postwar eras, must be accounted for. In the end this inquiry should justify itself as political research of the widest application: "For ideological dispositions to sport, we realize, are grounded in political psychology, which in turn finds its own sources in questions of philosophy. In this sense, sport can function as a powerful instrument in the search for the origins of ideology itself."[6]

Narcissistic Types of Body Display

The archetypal status of the body metaphors described above stretches back to antiquity. We may assume that the prototype of the ruler-athlete image was the warrior. According to Gaetano Mosca, "In primitive societies that are still in the early stages of organization, military valor is the quality that most readily opens access to the ruling, or political, class. In societies of advanced civilization, war is the exceptional condition. It may be regarded as virtually normal in societies that are in the initial stages of their development; and the individuals who show the greatest ability in war easily gain supremacy over their fellows—the bravest become chiefs."[7] Although the modern political world has given the idea of leadership a more cerebral accent, until recently the primitive notion of physically powerful leadership was both alive and exercising

a public fascination far out of proportion to its geopolitical significance. The case of the deposed Field Marshal Idi Amin Dada of
Uganda is notable for its unique combination of "primitive" and
"modern" elements. A huge and athletic man who had in fact been
the heavyweight boxing champion of Uganda, Amin adopted a public style which emphasized his warriorlike virtues: "There were attempts on his life, which later did influence him to add more protec-
tion than he had previously granted himself. But considering his
vulnerability to the revenge of a wide spectrum of political foes, perhaps Amin has remained relatively daring and even foolhardy in his
attitude to personal security. Once again this particular form of
courage has been a kind of public exhibitionism." This, along with
an athletic exhibitionism described below, is the "primitive" side of
Amin—the persona and its charismatic elements. The "modern" aspect is the fact that Idi Amin the political figure is the creation of a
sport-minded colonial regime which virtually selected him for his
virility: "he was the type of material the British officers liked in the
ranks—physically large at six feet four inches and uneducated. The
theory was that material of this type responded better to orders and
were braver in battle. He endeared himself to his commanders by becoming the Ugandan heavy-weight boxing champion . . . and by taking up rugby, where even if his skills were limited, his weight as a
second-row forward was a valuable contribution."[8] In his study of
charismatic leadership in the Third World, Jean Lacouture includes
among his "showmen of behavior" a type which easily accommodates the Amin style:

> Thus, the leader is at once a destroyer of colonialist alien-
> ation and a defender against neocolonial penetration. But occa-
> sionally he serves as a glorious shield for hidden operations or
> as an alibi for citizens' collective refusal to shoulder their own
> responsibilities. In that case, the leader will have helped only
> to camouflage the reality of neocolonialism or of collective res-
> ignation, and the personification [of the nation by the leader]
> will seem nothing more than *a childish disease of power*
> [emphasis added].[9]

Exhibitionism is a primary characteristic of this "childish disease," and athletic posturing is perhaps its most dramatic form. A
government brochure on the ruler of Togo includes the following description: "With his athletic build, supple bearing, sparkling style,
General Gnassingbe Eyadema is a force of nature . . ."[10] Such a claim
makes explicit what is implicit in a series of challenges Amin has

issued to various parties to dramatize the athletic dimension of his authority. In November 1978 he challenged the president of Tanzania, Julius Nyerere, to a boxing match in order to settle a war over border territory, offering in addition "to fight Nyerere with one arm tied and weights on his legs so the Tanzanian 'would have a sporting chance.'"[11] In December 1978 it was announced that Amin would fight a popular Japanese wrestler.

The amused and vaguely scandalized reception accorded the athletic buffoonery which counterpointed this dictator's savagery is a measure of the deracination of leadership (from its primitive origins) in a modern political world. But the athletic exhibitionism of African dictators is unique only in its naiveté, in the unabashed quality of its narcissism. The "primitive" narcissism of Amin and Eyadema finds its "modern" equivalent in the public style of an Oswald Mosley, once a promising and then a failed politician, who achieved much notoriety during the 1930s and the wartime period as the leader of the British Union of Fascists. The relatively favorable public responses to his autobiography (1968) and Skidelsky's apologetic biography (1975) demonstrate that a "cultured" narcissism— even one which incorporates an almost obsessive pride in physical prowess—can find a respectful audience denied more "primitive" expressions of self-love. Mosley's style combined an insouciant intellectual narcissism quite unaware of its stilted mediocrity with an athletic vanity derived from the aristocratic sporting ethos with which he identified. "He is the only man in the House of Commons," an observer writes, "who has made an Art of himself."[12] Mosley's cousin James Lees-Milne offers a similar impression: "He was madly in love with his own words. . . . The posturing, the grimacing, the switching on and off of those gleaming teeth, and the overall swashbuckling, so purposeful and calculated, were more likely to appeal to Mayfair flappers than to sway indigent workers in the Potteries. I did not then, and do not now, think that the art of coquetry ought to be introduced into politics."[13] Mosley's physical narcissism assumed forms more subtle than his constant references to previous sporting conquests. John Strachey recalls "the period when Mosley saw himself as Byron rather than Mussolini; and to me it was infinitely preferable. He was certainly a powerful swimmer and used to disappear at intervals into the lagoon to commune with himself."[14] There is also a sheer biological narcissism: "My most competent professional advisors support me with the information that my way of living and my family constitution should with ordinary luck give me many more years at the height of my powers"—an innocent comment until one grasps the pathological egocentricity which pervades his narrative. It should be understood that Mosley was a man who had to assure himself and others that his experiences were richer and more satisfying than those of other men and that he had known the finest comradeship war and sport could offer. There is probably no modern political figure for whom sport was more important, and its significance extended to his conception of leadership. "A man in office," he writes, "should surely live like an athlete in light training . . ."[15] Mosley's biographer has offered a persuasive interpretation of Mosley's conjoining of the statesman and the athlete: Mosley, he suggests, "sought to transcend the dichotomy between the puritan and the libertine, the thinker and the doer, by the concept of the athlete. . . . The statesman, according to Mosley, should be like the athlete who has trained himself to 'peak' at the right moment."[16] In so doing, Mosley immediately links the idea of leadership with the possibility of physical self-display.

The contrast we have observed sets a "primitive" and "naive" athletic-narcissistic style against a "modern" one which makes certain claims to refinement. Both, however, are redolent of infantile egocentricity and self-display. Mosley has always considered himself to be a man of culture, but his yearning for the "Hellenic" is painful to behold. In neither of its basic forms does athletic narcissism escape the stigma of pathology.

If the two styles just examined exemplify a narcissism of physical prowess, it may be noted that a political figure can also offer his public a narcissism of physical degeneration. In the case of King Farouk, deposed by Gamal Abdel Nasser in 1952, we encounter a type of narcissism which virtually scorns the customary male pride in musculature: "The face and the profile were gradually engulfed in a sea of flesh. His obesity became grotesque and provocative; his playboy fancies and utter unreliability were a public disgrace. When the summer of 1952 arrived, the Egyptian people were left with an extraordinary spectacle of public affairs to gaze upon, the joint collapse of an image and a form of government." A political figure, in short, is responsible for being physically presentable. But if Farouk found disgrace in obesity, Prince Sihanouk of Cambodia, a consummate showman and talented egoist of great style, found in it a pathos he had the genius to dramatize. Jean Lacouture has given us the following portrait of Sihanouk's sporting persona:

> When Norodom Sihanouk, son of the Kings of Angkor, played football in the palace stadium and, with his government team, won a 1−0 victory over Parliament's team (as in November 1963), was it to affirm the supremacy of the executive over the

legislative arm? Or to demonstrate the nobility of physical activity? Or to set an example for Khmer youth?

He did it for all these reasons—and to lose weight. His size appalled him. His tendency to put on weight was a torment. For years he spent three months out of every twelve taking a cure in Grasse. Then he discovered that the sports he had enjoyed all his life were a solution to the problem. After that, his ministers, high officials, deputies, and officers (and, of course, the masses) were regularly invited to football or volleyball games. With the nation's cooperation, the Prince would whittle down.

Can you push incarnation beyond the literal disembodiment of the leader? Let him reduce to the point where he swims inside his uniforms, and the nation, too, will be in the swim. Let him perspire, and we shall all be the more agile for it. But the collective limb-shaking will produce the individual slenderness, and the people will feel greater pride in itself because the leader cuts a handsome figure. Leadership becomes identification at this stage of complicity. I/we am/are the nation.[17]

In its Chaplinesque inversion of the heroic pose, Sihanouk's physical exhibitionism constitutes an ironic commentary on narcissism itself. Even more important, it makes mock of the cult of virility which underlies every form of athletic exhibitionism save his own. It is the comic, and therefore humane, style which puts Sihanouk's self-display at the furthest possible remove from the rigid and obscene posturings of the fascist male.

Sportive Imagery and the Leader: The Fascist Political Athlete

"The Fascist leader," Eugen Weber has written, "conquers a crowd and subdues it as he would a woman or a horse."[18] The fascist leader is, in short, an athlete, whether sexual or equestrian. In either case, he takes pride in the act of mastery itself. It is worth noting that history has produced a distinctly nonfascist variant of the political-leader-as-heroic-athlete. In his "Angostura Address" of February 15, 1819, Simón Bolívar offers the following portrait:

A republican magistrate is an individual set apart from society, charged with checking the impulse of the people toward license and the propensity of judges and administrators toward abuse of the laws. He is directly subject to the legislative body, the senate, and the people: he is the one man who resists the combined pressure of the opinions, interests, and passions of the social state and who, as Carnot states, does little more than struggle constantly with the urge to dominate and the desire to escape domination. He is, in brief, an athlete pitted against a multitude of athletes.[19]

Like any heroic figure, Bolívar's magistrate has heroic traits: he is a being apart, he summons forth a Herculean muscularity of will. But he is a republican magistrate. Unlike Weber's fascist leader, he does not glory in the urge to dominate; he grapples with it as one of several forces with which he must contend. He is therefore a suffering hero rather than a triumphant one. He is denied both triumph and the fascist's exultation over those he masters. Most important, the republican athlete is constrained by the very political structure within which he acts. He does not enjoy the (fascist) luxury of rule by charisma, and from the fascist standpoint he is an athlete in chains. He is an athlete whose discontent grows out of the fact of civilization itself.

The difference between republican and fascist "political athletes" may be illustrated by applying a distinction suggested by Eric Bentley. Bentley's collective term for Carlyle, Nietzsche, Wagner, and Shaw is "Heroic Vitalists," who "cling to the aesthetic attitude to the hero—which is one of sheer wonder unmitigated by sociological considerations." Bentley amplifies this point by noting that Carlyle had "admired grandeur more than utility and defiance more than defence. This admiration is a symptom of the Heroic Vitalist's attempt to infuse aesthetic standards into history and politics."[20] The choice, Bentley suggests, is between awe on the one hand and real politics ("sociological considerations") on the other. The republican athlete is heroic in his willingness to endure the sociological factor, the fascist in his contempt for its paltry and unheroic constraints.

European fascism produced its own odd assortment of political athletes, while fascist or quasi-fascist intellectuals produced short hymns in prose to celebrate the political athlete as a fascist type. Eugen Weber's prototype of the fascist leader finds its "classical" antecedent in a sportive image from Spengler's *Decline of the West*:

How does one *do* politics? The born statesman is above all a knower, a knower of men, situations, things. He has the "look which, without a moment's hesitation and with absolute

certainty, grasps the circle of possibilities." The master equestrian assesses the bearing of the horse with *one* look and
knows its prospects for the coming race. The sportsman
[*Spieler*] casts a look at his opponent and knows what his next
move will be. To act correctly without "knowing," the sure
hand, which imperceptibly tightens or eases the reins—this is
the opposite of the theoretical man's talent. The secret pulse of
all becoming is in him and in the substance of history. They
sense each other, they are there for each other.[21]

Spengler's fantasy of the athletic statesman is Mosley's fantasy
of himself. Writing of his mother, Mosley states: "Our friends by
reason of her background were almost entirely concerned with agri-
culture and sport, and this was perhaps her chief anxiety: to enable
her sons to take part in the sports of the field which she and all her
friends felt were the only possible training for a man, and to which
almost from infancy we were ardently addicted."[22] Mosley, too, has a
high opinion of this sort of training, convinced that it promotes the
development of "a higher type of statesman":[23] "Action is possible
in crisis because men of intelligence and realism are prepared to set
dogma aside and to face facts as they exist."[24] Spengler, too, describes "the born statesman" as "the man of facts" (*der Tatsachen-
mensch*),[25] a type for which Mosley—who was much impressed with
Spengler—had his own (characteristically awkward) term, with
which even he is not entirely comfortable: "The 'thought-deed' man
described in *The Alternative* [1947] was the need of the hour. It is
not an attractive phrase, and I am not in love with it myself, but it
expresses concisely the prime necessity of the modern world: men
who can both think and act. So far from thought and action being
antithetical . . . they are essential complements in a creative whole:
their union is indispensable, vital to a new birth." For both men it is
the miraculous canceling out of the contradiction between thought
and action which permits them to distill the political figure down to
an athletic one, the real meaning of this reduction being the elimi-
nation of ethical obligation in favor of instinctive action requiring
no reflection whatsoever. For both Spengler and Mosley, the issue is
virility of style. It is for this reason that the latter writes of "my
strongly held opinion that men in office ought to live like athletes,
not dine out, go to banquets and dinners, but only see people relevant to business. If an athlete lives like that before a world championship, why should not a Prime Minister live in the same way?"[26]
Mosley's narcissism is evident in his identification with a superior
human type evoked by Nietzsche in *Twilight of the Idols*:[27]

Goethe conceived of a strong, highly cultured human being, skilled in all physical accomplishments, who, keeping himself in check and having reverence for himself, dares to allow himself the whole compass and wealth of naturalness, who is strong enough for this freedom; a man of tolerance, not out of weakness, but out of strength, because he knows how to employ to his advantage what would destroy an average nature; a man to whom nothing is forbidden, except it be *weakness*, whether that weakness be called vice or virtue.[28]

One of the many vulgar Nietzscheans of the fascist epoch, Mosley distinguishes himself by taking the doctrine of the superman and inflating it into a more athletic idiom than any of his contemporaries. And indeed it is probable that, of all the European fascisms, the British variant turned out to be the sportiest of the lot.

Continental fascism offers its own examples of the statesman-athlete, though none who takes athletic culture quite as seriously as Mosley does. The great political athlete of the fascist period was undoubtedly Mussolini. "The governing class [of Italy]," an observer writes after a night at the opera in 1933, "is well-built, well-fed, dark and athletic. One usually associates a governing class with a class of intellectuals. But here physical fitness and a commanding presence are the first requisites."[29] Mussolini, who dreamed of having his ministers hurdle through flaming hoops while newsreel cameras rolled,[30] was, as John Diggins has phrased it, "written up as a hero of sport," and his sense of the dynamism of sport extended into the field of aviation during its heroic age. To celebrate Lindbergh's feat he proclaimed: "A Superhuman will has taken space by assault and has subjugated it."[31] This is the futurist element in Mussolini, and one closely in tune with a fascination with speed which was widespread during the 1920s. The technological dynamism celebrated by Mussolini in 1927 would in 1930 be provided a philosophical and historical justification by the very sport-minded José Ortega y Gasset in *The Revolt of the Masses*: "It was a question of honor for man to triumph over cosmic space and time, which are entirely devoid of meaning, and there is no reason for surprise at the fact that we get a childish pleasure out of the indulgence in mere speed, by means of which we kill space and strangle time."[32] By its very nature, a "dynamic" age is ripe for the imagery of sport, even if it is motor sport, just as it is ripe for leadership in the fascist style. This is a thematic coincidence of major significance for understanding why the sporting style, as a political idiom, is a primarily fascist style. For speed is an intoxicant, and its natural fulfillment is paroxysm: in a word, an apotheosis of irrational experience. Stalin, too, as we shall see, was a sponsor of daring aviators, but a sponsor who made a point of taming the intoxication on behalf of rational praxis—an example of genuine ideological differentiation. "The aviator disciplined an uncertain machine and the dictator an unknown movement."[33] As a fascist "political athlete," Mussolini hails the aviator as a superior being (analogous to himself), whereas it is precisely this sort of identification which Stalin disdains on an ideological basis—Lenin's rejection of "spontaneity."

The French fascist novelist and political writer Pierre Drieu la Rochelle employed sportive imagery of both leadership and the state on behalf of a standard theme of the French Right: the regeneration of the body politic. Like Spengler and Mosley, Drieu exhibits that penchant for the biological which has served as the primary stratum out of which notions of political athleticism have grown. In Jacques Doriot, ex-Communist and founder in 1936 of the right-wing (and eventually collaborationist) Parti populaire français, Drieu found an attractive object for a kind of adolescent *Schwärmerei*. A gifted and quintessentially dynamic political personality, Doriot "had always had," as Gilbert Allardyce has put it, "an inclination towards action and movement that seemed innate rather than acquired, an inclination that the enforced discipline of [Communist] party life had at times frustrated but never tamed."[34] Doriot's "sportive" identity is in part a product of Drieu's imagination:

> Doriot, the good athlete, stands before France not as a fat-bellied intellectual of the last century watching his "sick mother" and puffing at his radical pipe, but as an athlete squeezing this debilitated body, breathing his own health into its mouth. . . . Doriot has that peasant vigor which goes beyond games of words to reach the heart, he has good humour and solid simplicity. Doriot will create a France where thousands of young couples will be happy rushing each season to primitive pleasures, skiing, fishing, camping, swimming. With him the France of the camping expeditions will conquer the France of cocktail parties and congresses.[35]

A more self-conscious political athlete of the French Right is Pierre Poujade, an incendiary but ephemeral figure whose *mouvement Poujade* originated in 1953 as a taxpayers' revolt among elements of the petty bourgeoisie. Representing what René Rémond has termed a "meeting of antistatism with exasperated nationalism," Poujade's self-dramatization included tales from his athletic past.[36] Jean Plumyène and Raymond Lasierra have described Poujade's integration of the sportive element into his public persona:

> Poujade is popular. A cut-up, *sportif*, of Rabelaisian dimensions, there is in his personality a contagious vitality and a persuasive *rondeur*. Dress, body, temperament, voice, all combine in him to make a public personality. The traveling salesman's gift for banter works wonders at meetings. His dream is to abandon the petty bric-a-brac in favor of the most noble political experiences.[37]

In the last analysis, the fascist political athlete is as much an imaginary figure—a reverie of the intellectuals—as he is a historical one. He embodies, consciously or unconsciously, the sort of archetype on which the imagination seeking virility or regeneration can feed. "The body," says Zarathustra, "is a great intelligence, a multiplicity with one sense, a war and a peace, a herd and a herdsman." "Behind your thoughts and feelings, my brother, stands a mighty commander, an unknown sage—he is called Self. He lives in your body, he is your body."[38] As a phenomenon, the fascist political athlete is founded upon the unchallenged authority of the body, which is in turn invested with the virtually sacred authority of instinct. In this sense, the political athlete is an almost predictable manifestation of any political movement in which male leadership and appeals to irrational impulses are combined. In the next part of this book we will examine a political culture which, while preserving the first of these elements, has experienced real inhibitions about exploiting the second. Differing attitudes toward political use of the irrational constitute the basis here for what I have called "ideological differentiation."

Sportive Imagery and the Leader: Marxism's Renunciation of the Political Athlete

Different styles of leadership, expressing a range of personae, occur within a political genre such as "dictatorship." The persona of a leader is the objective (public) form of personality, a unified and one-dimensional version of personality which takes on the character of an essence. Such essences can be compared, and the nuances of their differences understood.

In his chapter on the nature of Nasser's charisma, Jean Lacouture identifies such a difference in essences which appears to derive from an ideological partition: "In the eulogy he delivered in March

1965, when his old friend Nasser was re-elected President, Anouwar el-Sadat spoke of the 'rare phenomenon that constituted our people's encounter with Gamal Abdel Nasser.' Rare phenomenon? Encounter? These are words that would never do for Fidel Castro or Ho Chi Minh."[39] Lacouture's final assertion would be more accurate if it were emended to read: "These are words that, *offered publicly by their respective regimes*, would never do for Fidel Castro or Ho Chi Minh." For both of these leaders were, if anything, "rare phenomena" whose personae must have made possible many "encounters." For reasons into which we are inquiring, the truth about personality could not be permitted to assume the form of public doctrine.

The key to this problem is the "cult of personality," termed by Lacouture "a perversion Marx had not foreseen."[40] Another source, however, credits Marx with a greater awareness on this point and quotes a letter of 1877 as follows: "because of aversion to any personality cult, I have never permitted the numerous expressions of appreciation from various countries, with which I was pestered during the existence of the International, to reach the realm of publicity, and have never answered them, except occasionally by rebuke. When Engels and I first joined the secret Communist Society, we made it a condition that *everything tending to encourage superstitious belief in authority* was to be removed from the statutes [emphasis added]."[41] Lacouture's account of Nasser's career makes it clear that the sort of restraint demonstrated by Marx does not necessarily require a Marxist rationale. He notes that Nasser had never indulged "in the extravagant rites of Nkrumah or Sukarno, not only because he [has] a good memory for recent events, but also because as a faithful Moslem he is forearmed against the temptation of self-deification, a terrible sacrilege. Puritanism offers no shield against this type of folly: witness Cromwell. But Islam, in this case, is a good antidote." Nonetheless, as the author concedes, "the cult of personality has assumed spectacular proportions in Egypt, and with legal blessing. . . . Yet it took a great deal of will power on the leader's part to prevent the sunny psychological climate in which he basked from turning him into a Caligula."[42] Restraining the cult of personality requires enforcing ideological discipline.

Marx's disapproval of personality cults has remained official doctrine even as it has been violated by most Communist leaders. A later version may be found in Georgi Plekhanov's "The Role of the Individual in History" (1898): "A great man is great not because his personal qualities give individual features to great historical events, but because he possesses qualities which make him most capable of serving the great social needs of his time, needs which arose as a re-

sult of general and particular causes. In his well-known book on heroes and hero-worship, Carlyle calls great men *beginners*. This is a
very apt description. A great man is a beginner precisely because he
sees *further* than others and desires things *more strongly* than others." It is interesting to watch Plekhanov's deft appropriation of the
Carlyle who, as Bentley puts it, "admired grandeur more than utility," and whose admiration was a symptom of an "attempt to infuse
aesthetic standards into history and politics." By emphasizing the
great man's innate capacities, and in particular the intensity of his
desire, Plekhanov comes perilously close to infusing an "aesthetic
standard" of his own into the historical process. Plekhanov remains
a Marxist by assigning to intensity of feeling a relative and not an
absolute value, and by rejecting the idea that the great man "makes"
history as an autonomous creator: "He is a hero. But he is a hero not
in the sense that he can stop or change the natural course of things,
but in the sense that his activities are the conscious and free expression of this inevitable and unconscious course. Herein lies all his
significance; herein lies his whole power. But this significance is co-
lossal, and the power is terrible."[43] But for the political narcissist,
the political athlete, for example, feelings about the self do take on
an absolute value, and a sense of grandeur may well eclipse the concerns of historical utility.

Lenin was Marxist culture's prime candidate for political-
athletic stardom, but he emphatically declined the role. In his two
excellent volumes of memoirs intended as "a contribution to the
portrait of the living, 'non-geometric' Lenin,"[44] Nikolai Valentinov
(N. V. Volski) describes Lenin's interest in sport and physical culture
repeatedly and in detail:

> Before the time when he developed a passion for reading and
> politics, he went through a number of hobbies: riding a sled
> down the snow-covered mountains, playing croquet, walking
> on stilts, gymnastics, in particular exercises on the trapeze,
> rowing, swimming, and skating. Various kinds of physical ex-
> ercises helped the young Vladimir Ulyanov develop a strong
> physique. Throughout his life Lenin preserved his love and
> taste for all kinds of sports. He gave great importance to daily
> exercises.
>
> Lenin really amazed me (how many times he amazed me!)
> when it turned out that he was very interested in sport and
> physical exercise. He told me that back in Kazan he had often
> gone to the circus to see the athletic turns. But he lost 'all
> respect' for them when he happened to find out behind the

scenes that the athletes' dumb-bells were hollow and empty, and so weighed next to nothing at all.[45]

Valentinov makes the point that "only a few people" knew that Lenin was in fact a "great sportsman,"[46] and it is unlikely that it ever occurred to Lenin that he might dramatize himself as a political athlete in the fascist style, even if he portrayed the revolutionary as a physically as well as morally heroic figure. Commenting on *What Is to Be Done?* (1902), Valentinov notes: "In place of the 'trade-unionist,' organizing strike funds and mutual help societies, he put forward the image of the 'professional revolutionary,' of a St. George the Dragon-killer, who takes up arms in 'all cases of injustice and brutality, whatever class of society is concerned.' We liked this. Lenin glorified the 'selfless determination,' 'energy,' 'daring,' 'initiative,' 'conspiratorial skill' of the revolutionary, and argued *that personality can work 'wonders' in the revolutionary movement* [emphasis added]." It could, of course, be argued that Lenin's treatment of personality here does not differ essentially from that of Plekhanov, that even a personality which can bring about "wonders" nevertheless remains a subordinate element in the revolutionary movement it serves. Valentinov, however, does not take so charitable a view: "It was only many years later that the full implications of Lenin's book became evident, but at that time in 1902–3, we had no inkling of them. There were some discrepancies in the book, but no attention was paid to them. It was shot through with out-and-out voluntarism and it was certainly based on a 'heroic view of history' quite alien to Marxism . . ."[47]

Lenin's position can, however, be viewed from a somewhat different angle. "It is a curious fact," Jean Lacouture writes, "that the concept of the leader, of leadership and its possible perversions, has a minor place in the whole span of Lenin's writing (only twenty-three references to it have been found in the thirty volumes of his complete works). It is remarkable that a revolutionary so preoccupied with the concept and exercise of power gave so little space to a problem that was to prove fundamental." By way of answering his own riddle, Lacouture makes the following observation: "In fact, Lenin presents the question almost always in relation to the Party, described as the vanguard of the proletariat," and cites a Plekhanov-like passage from a speech Lenin gave in March 1919: "History has long demonstrated for us that in the course of the struggle, great revolutions bring forward great men and foster abilities that until then seemed impossible." Lacouture's summing up of the Lenin question is notable for its insistence upon a crucial instance of ideological differentiation:

> It is apparent in all these statements that the leader is always mentioned in a collective sense, in reference to the word "incarnation" and the relation between "great revolutions" and "great men." It is also evident that the founder of the Soviet system refused to pave the way for the cult of the hero, confining himself to the concept of the vanguard, however reduced to its simplest terms. The leader is not isolated from the group: he is ahead of it but linked to it. He represents an acute state of the collective revolutionary spirit, *but is not a prophet launching his appeal from the mountaintop* [emphasis added].[48]

There is a crucial difference between being an "acute state" of a larger spirit and being a prophet. In terms of nineteenth-century intellectual history, it is the difference between Hegel and Nietzsche, between the "World-Historical persons" of the *Philosophy of History* and the prophet Zarathustra. "Such individuals," according to Hegel, "had no consciousness of the general Idea they were unfolding": "Their fellows, therefore, follow these soul-leaders; for they feel the irresistible power of their own inner Spirit thus embodied. If we go on to cast a look at the fate of these World-Historical persons, whose vocation it was to be the agents of the World-Spirit—we shall find it to have been no happy one. They attained no calm enjoyment; their whole life was labor and trouble; their whole nature was naught else but their master-passion."[49] Hegel ascribes to these "Heroes" an agonal fate which recalls that of Bolívar's republican magistrate, the martyred symbolic "athleticism" of a Prometheus or a Hercules. Neither hero or magistrate is given time out to contemplate his own strength, while Zarathustra lectures against the "despisers of the body." As the Nazi sport theorist Alfred Baeumler states: "Der Leib ist ein Politicum [The body is a political space]."[50] A fundamental ideological differentiation separates the human instrument of history (Hegelian or Leninist) from the body-as-*Politicum*, a differentiation which observes Lacouture's distinction between the representative of an "acute state" and the prophet; for both body and prophet rely upon the absolute authority of an (ahistorical) autonomous instinct or inspiration.

There is a further piece of evidence bearing on the relationship between Leninism and the idea of "political athleticism" which, however arcane it may appear, makes perfect sense in terms of the argument presented so far. In *The New Course* Trotsky makes the following statement: "Leninism as a system of revolutionary action presupposes a mentally seasoned and experienced revolutionary intuition which is the equivalent in the social realm to muscular sensation in physical labor."[51] Displaying the labor fetishism so characteristic of Marxist theory, Trotsky presents a figure who is the perfect ideological refutation of the "political athlete": the laboring revolutionary. Uninfected by the rightist notion that politics and war are forms of play, Trotsky imagines an ideal revolutionary whose muscles register that sensation which is precisely opposed, ideologically, to the sportive urge: to wit, labor.

Stalin did not have Lenin's potential for political athleticism. "Less childishly carefree than most of his schoolmates, he would occasionally go off and apply himself with single-minded persistence to such enterprises as mastering the ascent of a high cliff or distance throwing with stone markers by the riverside." "He began to view himself as a person for whom it would be natural to excel in whatever activity he chose to pursue, whether wrestling or cliff-climbing or studies in school." Stalin's youthful interest in physical games apparently had a utilitarian, goal-oriented aspect very much reminiscent of Lenin's attitude, but unlike the latter he seemed to lose this interest entirely after entering the Tiflis theological seminary in 1894 at the age of fifteen. It is possible, however, to discern in certain of Stalin's remarks a taste for political athleticism. "When he came to the Tammerfors conference in 1905, where he was to see Lenin for the first time, 'I was hoping to see the mountain eagle of our party, a great man, *great not only politically but, if you like, physically too*, for Lenin had taken shape in my imagination as a giant, stately and imposing. What then was my disappointment when I saw the most ordinary man, below average height, in no way, literally in no way, different from ordinary mortals.'" In his speech to the Central Committee plenum of 1929 Stalin states: "The situation is that we live according to Lenin's formula of '*kto kogo*': either we shall pin them, the capitalists, to the ground and give them, as Lenin expressed it, final decisive battle, or they will pin our shoulders to the ground"—an image Robert Tucker calls a "metaphorical depiction of the Soviet situation as a great wrestling match of opposing classes."[52] These quotations are significant because they are virtual exotica: rarely do longings for a body image or sport metaphors find their way into the public idiom of a Marxist leader. It is all very well for a Hitler to refer to great men (in *Mein Kampf*) as "the marathon runners of history,"[53] but, as Lacouture puts it in another context: "These are words that would never do for Fidel Castro or Ho Chi Minh." It is a question of ideological style, and Stalin's "violations" of its canons would seem to grow directly out of the strong and relatively undisciplined feelings about Lenin emphasized by Tucker in his study of Stalin's personality.

Such remarks were clearly arbitrary utterances rather than elements of a sportive public persona. Stalin's affiliation with two kinds of applied athleticism during the mid- and late 1930s, on the other hand, was a truly public phenomenon and an authentic expression of the Stalinist ideology of that period. Rather than assume the role of political athlete, Stalin in effect created two types of para-athlete who were both in the service of the state and toward whom he comported himself as a paternal sponsor: the Stakhanovite worker, the heroic record breaker who vastly overfills the production quota, and the daring long-distance aviator who brings glory to the Socialist state.

In an ingenious study, Katerina Clark has demonstrated how these two para-athletic types mark the transition from the "fraternal" social ideal of the Bolshevist 1920s to the "hierarchy" of Stalinism. Both types exemplify a dramatic surpassing of the ordinary: "The Stakhanovite was not merely to be *greater* than all previous model men, but to represent a *qualitative* leap forward in human anthropology, as the rhetoric of the times claimed."[54] Wilhelm Reich terms the Stakhanovites "a small minority of work-athletes,"[55] and that is exactly what they were. The Stakhanovite, however, was only the best-known example of a type:

A typical 1935 list of "new men" comprises "heroes of the stratosphere and the Cheliuskin [Arctic] expedition, the inventor Tsiolkovsky, the *bogatyr'* [fantastic Russian epic hero] parachutist, the participant in a 9,000 km. ski marathon and the worker who drives a shaft for the new Metro." . . . If one were to characterize their achievements in general one would say that all had to do with advancing the norms for man's performance in the physical world: "higher," "farther," "deeper."[56]

In terms of the overall thesis of this chapter, there are two major points to be made about Stalin's renunciation of the sportive style. First, despite his need for adulation, Stalin did not attempt to dramatize himself as a figure of sport. (President Ceausescu of Romania has recently posed as a big-game hunter; like virtually all Soviet leaders, Stalin hunted, but he resisted any narcissistic temptation to put on virile airs.) In Stalin's case, the athletic roles are instead assigned to subordinate figures who owe him a virtually filial loyalty. Second, the very fact of this filial status requires of these para-athletes public acquiescence to a crucial kind of emotional self-censorship, amounting to deference, which will bring their emotional states, however heroic, into conformity with ideological norms: "in Leninist terms, the Stakhanovite represented a qualitative leap forward in *spontaneity*: he was a man of superior energy, daring, and initiative. The model guarantees that he will always be son: he will always need some representative of higher 'consciousness,' some father to guide that 'spontaneity.'" And in a similar vein: "All the pilots testified in their memoirs to the marked influence Stalin had in tempering their 'spontaneity.'" "These gifted but high-spirited children needed greater discipline and self-control ('consciousness'). And their main source of it was none other than Stalin himself."[57] Cracking down on "spontaneity" means interdicting the para-athlete's emotions before they begin to feed on themselves and become intoxicating for the self or others: charismatic personae are nipped in the bud. None of *Stalin's* aviators will succumb to the dreamy, vaguely fascist musings of a Lindbergh or a Saint-Exupéry. Ideological discipline—not ecstasy—will have the last word.

There are two serious challenges in the annals of Communist leadership to the thesis that Marxist leaders have consistently renounced political athleticism. Mao Ze-dong's legendary swim down the Yangtze River on July 16, 1966, would appear to be a spectacular exception to the rule. Mao supposedly covered a distance of about ten miles in sixty-five minutes—about the speed of a world-class racing shell. What is interesting is that Mao did not hesitate to create a cult of a mythic exemplary act requiring an impossible degree of gullibility on the part of his audience. It is the miraculous quality of Mao's political athleticism, even more than his advanced age, which negates the athleticism itself. The element of vanity is lacking; there is no hint of narcissistic pride, because the performance is pure pedagogy. The miraculous dimension of the achievement suggests that Mao's body was unreal; only "swimming for the revolution," a disembodied act of inspired instruction, remains. The physical effluvium of the fascist political athlete is nowhere to be found.

Lacouture maintains that "rare phenomenon" and "encounter" are words "that would never do for Fidel Castro." Never, that is, in an official sense; in fact, Castro is a rare phenomenon who presents the most charismatic image of the statesman-athlete since Mussolini: his physical charisma and passionate interest in sport are legendary. The irony is that Castro is a political athlete in fact but cannot be permitted to be one in doctrine. The marathon speeches constitute a verbal athleticism which must take the place of a literal one. The nature of the constraints operating here may be clearly seen in a critique by the Argentine Marxist Jorge Abelardo Ramos directed against Ernesto (Ché) Guevara's interpretation of "that telluric force called Fidel Castro." "The Cuban Revolution," Abelardo writes in 1964, "has unleashed a wave of indiscriminate admiration by Latin American leftists. Substantially healthy in origin, *this adulation threatens to paralyze the functioning of Marxist thought* [emphasis added]." He describes the paralysis in the following manner:

> The domineering personality of Fidel Castro is, for Guevara, the first "exceptional" characteristic of the Cuban Revolution. Castro's personality is explained by Castro's virtues. Had Guevara not proclaimed himself a Marxist, this tautology would only injure Guevara. But, since he is at the same time a Marxist and an important leader in the Cuban Revolution, *it is also Marxist ideas that turn out to be definitely jeopardized by this poor statement.* If Guevara had told us that Fidel Castro personified his people, he would have been telling the truth. No person can be explained intrinsically, except in terms of the idealistic view of history. *To explain Fidel intrinsically and his personality by his intrinsic virtues is tantamount to removing him from the historical process, to overestimating the personal factor, and to transforming him into a sacred product* [emphasis added].[58]

It is hardly coincidental that the world's most sportive political figure should give rise to a cult of personality, but this is precisely what Abelardo confronts in his indignation. For there exists no Marxist interpretation of the human "telluric force" other than to proclaim it a harmful illusion. This is the principle which underlies Marxist renunciation of political athleticism. Similarly, renunciation of intrinsic human qualities implies a ban on sportive leadership, since the body is a paramount symbol of the intrinsic *per se*. It cannot derive its authority from anything other than itself.

In summary, Marxist abstinence from what has been termed "political athleticism" reflects an implicit doctrinal disapproval of narcissistic traits in the persona of the leader. The argument presented here emphasizes appearances: manifest pride or pleasure taken in the experiencing of the self, including the body, has never been a virtue in any society which claimed to be Marxist. "His force," Malaparte says of Mussolini, "is a specifically natural phenomenon, entirely physical, instinctive and human."[59] These are words that "would never do" for any Marxist leader history has known.

Sportive Images of the State: Toward a Fascist Style

The idea of an athletic nation-state has evolved from a primitive anthropomorphic conception to a peculiarly modern notion made possible by the intensive sport-consciousness of the twentieth century. It is an image which still retains its primitive character and appears frequently in fascist writings and almost never in the rhetoric or the political literature of Marxist societies. It presents a striking example of what has been termed "ideological differentiation."

"The idea that human societies are like so many 'big men,'" Donald MacRae has observed, "is very ancient, embodied in myth, poetry and philosophy from the earliest times of which we have knowledge." Herbert Spencer puts it as follows in an essay titled "The Social Organism" (1860): "A perception that there exists some analogy between the body politic and a living individual body, was early reached: and has from time to time re-appeared in literature. But this perception was necessarily vague and more or less fanciful. In the absence of physiological science, and especially of those comprehensive generalizations which it has but lately reached, it was impossible to discern the real parallelisms."[60] Bruce Haley has pointed out that Spencer's faith in "physiological science" was typical of his age:

> Physiological models have been in use since the beginning of philosophy, when man first began to consider his body separately from his mind and to speculate on the relation between the two. One's body—what he can know of himself through his senses—is a natural vehicle for envisioning what he only knows subjectively: mind or spirit. In this way "health" has long been used analogically to represent various kinds of perfection or excellence. Several factors, however, coincided to give the healthy body a special conceptual prominence in nineteenth century thought.

Haley describes these factors as the emergence of physiology, physiological psychology, and a holistic approach to education, commenting: "it is remarkable how many Victorian writers used some sort of physiological model to explore and relate the issues of man's place in nature, man's place in society, and the mind's place in the body."[61] In an age of high-performance sport, it is a short step from the physiological model in general to the superior athletic physiology in particular.

Otto Gierke has described a crucial development in the history of the organic state concept:

> The idea of the State as an *organic whole*, which had been bequeathed by classical and medieval thought, was never entirely extinguished. But the natural law tendency of thought was hardly qualified to achieve the construction of an organic theory, or to crown it by the discovery of an immanent group-personality. The comparison of the State to an animate body regularly continued to be drawn. . . . A distinction was made between the head and the members of the 'body politic': descriptions were given of the structure and functions of its internal organs: the differentiation and the harmonious connection of the several parts were shown to issue in a living unity of the Whole.

For Gierke, however, this is still not a sufficiently organic conception:

> But the thinkers of our period [1500–1800], like those of the Middle Ages, never took the really decisive step. While they recognised an invisible unity as the internal principle of life in the body politic, they never conceived it as being the true Ruling personality. The organic theory was never applied to the problem of the 'Subject' of sovereign power. The organic being of the State stopped short, as it were, at the neuter gender. . . . An organism of this nature, destitute of any Ego, was after all only a simulacrum of a living being. In spite of all assertions to the contrary, it was no more than a work of art, counterfeited to look like a natural body; a machine, invented and controlled by individuals. Here again Hobbes—anticipated, it is true, by similar suggestions in previous writers—only pushed the premises of the natural-law school to their ultimate logical conclusions. He began by comparing the State, that great Leviathan, to a giant's body; he proceeded to expound, in the minutest of detail, its analogies with a living being; but he ended by transforming his supposed organism into a mechanism, moved by a number of wheels and springs, and his man-devouring monster turned into an artfully devised and cunningly constructed automaton.[62]

Hobbes had recognized the charismatic appeal of "Forme"—a combination of physique and bearing; and he had conceived of "that great LEVIATHAN called a COMMON-WEALTH, or STATE" as "an Artificiall Man."[63] But he does not combine these images in such a way as to come up with the athletic state; this image exists here only as a possibility which was eventually seized upon by the (predominantly fascist) political imaginations of a more consciously athletic age, imaginations which, as we shall see, would eventually condemn the Hobbesian notion of a machinelike state as a dead and despicable product of "liberal democracy."

Fascist objections to Hobbes's Leviathan are already visible in Gierke's impatient reference to "his supposed organism" and in the critique of the dead "mechanism." What, then, does Gierke—"a Germanist of the Germanists, nurtured in the tradition of the Folk and instinct"[64]—really want from the notion of the organic state? The substance of his critique of Hobbes is stated as follows: "In this position of affairs, it became impossible to vindicate unity for the personality of the State except by vesting it exclusively in *one or other of the constituted parts* of the body politic [the People, or the Ruler]."[65]

With this conclusion, Gierke deposits us on the doorstep of the political age in which either "the Ruler" or "the People" can be metaphorized into athletic figures, and Hegel is the first political theorist to avail himself of the opportunity. It should be noted that Hegel's dream of the heroic corporealized nation-state is of Hellenic rather than "modern" inspiration. The "modern" age of the body-as-*Politicum* would be inaugurated a century or so later by Nietzsche and Spengler.

Hegel actually offers both decrepit and heroic corporeal images of the state. In the *Philosophy of Right*, he compares the state to a physically defective man: "The state is no ideal work of art; it stands on earth and so in the sphere of caprice, chance, and error, and bad behavior may disfigure it in many respects. But the ugliest of men, or a criminal, or an invalid, or a cripple, is still a living man. The affirmative, life, subsists despite his defects, and it is this affirmative factor which is our theme here."[66] The "premodern" characteristic of Hegel's use of the body image is that he does not interpret physical deformity as a definitive curse. Fascist attitudes toward physical perfection and imperfection were, on the other hand, quite ruthless, especially since they were usually combined with racial theory. Even Hegel's heroic body image is free of chauvinistic overtones. In the section of *The Phenomenology of Mind* titled "The Living Work of Art," the "finely built warrior" incarnates the state but does not symbolize its racial superiority:

In the place of the statue man thus puts himself as the figure elaborated and moulded for perfectly free movement, just as the statue is the perfectly free state of quiescence. If every individual knows how to play the part at least of a torch-bearer, one of them comes prominently forward who is the very embodiment of the movement, the smooth elaboration, the fluent energy and force of all the members. He is a lively and living work of art, which matches strength with its beauty; and to him is given, as a reward for his force and energy, the adornment . . . and the honour of being, amongst his own nation, instead of a god in stone, *the highest bodily representation of what the essential Being* of the nation is [emphasis added].[67]

The "highest bodily representation" denotes not force but "perfectly free movement," and rather than glorying in his own image he is an expression of "the Festival which man makes in his own honour." Hegel goes on to make of this noble physique precisely the opposite of what modern nations make of him:

The finely built warrior is indeed the honour and glory of his particular nation; but he is a physical or corporeal individuality in which are sunk out of sight the expanse and seriousness of meaning, and the inner character of the spirit which underlies the particular mode of life, the peculiar petitions, the needs and customs of his nation. In relinquishing all this for complete corporeal embodiment, spirit has laid aside the particular impressions, the special tones and chords of that nature which it, as the actual spirit of the nation, includes. Its nation, therefore, is no longer conscious in this spirit of its special particular character, but rather of having laid this aside, and of the universality of its human existence.[68]

Hegel understands the cultural poverty of the body, and that its universality is achieved when spirit, in seeking "complete corporeal embodiment," is forced to sacrifice "the expanse and seriousness of meaning" which are the substance of culture. From Hegel's point of view, there is nothing more futile than seeking national identity in that nation's corporeal embodiment, from which "seriousness of meaning" and "the particular mode of life" have flown. The glory of the body is its universality, but it is universal only because it is a cultural vacuum: this is the point the sporting nationalists never fathom.

As we have seen, Otto Gierke's critique of Hobbes's Leviathan set an animate principle against what he believed to be a dead and "mechanical" one. This is a classical opposition within political theory and of self-evident importance to the idea of the athletic nation-state. A classic (and often misunderstood) presentation of this polarity is Ferdinand Tönnies' *Gemeinschaft und Gesellschaft* (Community and Society), first published in 1887. Pitirim A. Sorokin speaks of "two different modes of mentality and behavior,"[69] one of which—or so this book holds—will accommodate the notion of the state-as-body while the other will not. This question will be resolved below. First we must examine the basis of Tönnies' dichotomy: "All intimate, private, and exclusive living together, so we discover, is understood as life in Gemeinschaft (community). Gesellschaft (society) is public life—it is the world itself. In Gemeinschaft with one's family, one lives from birth on, bound to it in weal and woe. One goes into Gesellschaft as one goes into a strange country." It is not long before Tönnies sounds a familiar note: "In contrast to Gemeinschaft, Gesellschaft is transitory and superficial. Accordingly, Gemeinschaft should be understood as a living organism, Gesellschaft as a mechanical aggregate and artifact." And toward the end of the book, Tönnies resolves the question of which of these "two different modes of mentality" will tend to anthropomorphize the state: "The idea of the social body,"[70] we are told, is purely embodied in the *Gemeinschaft*.

In *Spießer-Ideologie* (The Cultural Roots of National Socialism), Hermann Glaser blames the notion of *Gemeinschaft* for having "blocked the acceptance of a reasonable concept of society in Germany."[71] Arthur Mitzman has pointed out that the notion of *Gemeinschaft* came to have a life independent of Tönnies' intentions, that "Tönnies attacked at its foundation the view of the state as an organism, a super-*Gemeinschaft*," and that "any conception of a return to *Gemeinschaft*—such as the Nazi version—was something Tönnies could never have accepted. The Nazis' *Volksgemeinschaft* represented a total perversion of Tönnies' ideas." Tönnies' critique of the organic theory of the state stresses the difference between a volitional community and an organism which is essentially subhuman: "What gives a quasi-organic character to a human group can be only the perception, the feeling, the *will* of the grouped men themselves. Through this foundation, my theory sharply distinguishes itself from the otherwise current 'organic' doctrines, which do not notice that, insofar as their biological analogies have any basis, they remain within even an expanded biology, and lack the specific character of sociological facts."[72]

Employed as a polemical device, the polarity to which Tönnies gave a classical formulation has flourished in the hands of political theorists of the extreme Right. The Italian fascist Alfredo Rocco describes society (in 1918) as "a real organism" and claims that his views are precisely opposed by those of "liberal-democratic ideology": "our conception of the state is organic, dynamic and historical, whereas the liberal-democratic conception is mechanical, static and anti-historical."[73] The Spanish Falangist José Antonio Primo de Rivera uses the term "body politic" and invokes the standard invidious comparison between the mechanical and the vitalistic: "No machine has ever managed to produce anything authentic, eternal and exacting such as government; it has always been necessary in the long run to turn to what has, from the beginning of time, been the only apparatus capable of governing man, namely man himself. That is to say: the leader, the hero."[74] In their "Nationalist Programme" of 1904, Giovanni Papini and Giuseppe Prezzolini injected a vaguely athletic note by contrasting "the robust organism of our nation" with a bourgeoisie depicted as "flabby and apathetic."[75] The truly athletic nation-state appeared in Italy as a product of the imagination of that brilliant futurist of fascist sympathies, Filippo Marinetti. "Everything of any value is theatrical," Marinetti writes in 1915, and particularly striking is the degree to which Marinetti's idea of the theatrical draws upon the inherent dynamism of sport. "If prayer means communication with the divinity, running at high speed is a prayer," he writes in "The New Religion-Morality of Speed" (1916). "The intoxication of great speeds in cars is nothing but the joy of feeling oneself fused with the only *divinity*. Sportsmen are the first catechumens of this religion." It was only natural for a man who dreamed of "bridges that stride the rivers like giant gymnasts" to anthropomorphize the state into a giant athlete: "The Italian people can be compared to an excellent wrestler who wants to wrestle with no special training and is unequipped with the means to train. Circumstances force it to win or to disappear. The Italian people has gloriously won. But the effort was too much for its muscles, so now, panting, exhausted, almost unable to enjoy its great victory, it curses us, its trainers, and opens its arms to those who counsel it not to fight."[76]

The idea of the sportive, agonistic state appears a few years later in *The Decline of the West*. At the beginning of his chapter on "The State," Spengler envisions the dynamic aspect of history as "movement": "A movement *has* form, and that which is moved; the State is 'in form,' or, to use another sporting expression, when it is 'going all out' it is in perfect condition. This is equally true for a racehorse or a wrestler and for an army or a people. The form abstracted from the life-stream of a people is the 'condition' of that people with re-spect to its wrestle in and with history."[77] The interpretation of the state as a body appears twenty years later in the writings of Alfred Baeumler, a respectable academic philosopher and the only Nazi sport theorist of note. In "The Political Training of the Body" (1937), Baeumler speaks of "the collective body of the *Volk*" and criticizes liberalism for having "disembodied" politics as a whole. At the same time, however, Baeumler distinguishes himself by disparaging the "pure sports team" (die reine Sportmannschaft) as inferior to the au-thentically political "team," which is nothing less than "the sym-bolic representation of its people." Baeumler's objection to the sports team is that, as a mere "technical association," it offers the individ-ual experiential impoverishment. Once the performance is achieved, Baeumler claims, this kind of team disintegrates, because it does not find its ultimate purpose in the life of the team itself.[78]

Baeumler is more fastidious about making such distinctions than the French fascist intellectual Robert Brasillach, who was exe-cuted in 1945 for having collaborated with the German occupiers. Brasillach's notoriety derived in part from well-publicized submis-sive fantasies about the Nazis; even as an adult he demonstrated a certain passionate adolescent interest in questions of virility. It is this sort of hyperbolic enthusiasm which accounts for Brasillach's claim that "a nation is *one*, in exactly the same manner that a sports team is *one*."[79] Baeumler knew better than that, even if his own ar-gument, which relies on intuition, is quite unsatisfactory. In general, the French fascists who pursue the body-state metaphor spend no time on ponderous theories of *Gemeinschaft*. Their interest is in virilizing the nation and in rejuvenating it—an echo of nineteenth-century French concerns about fertility and the lessons of Sedan. In a body-oriented meditation titled "A propos d'une saison de foot-ball" (1921), Pierre Drieu la Rochelle depicts the French nation as a body in the throes of fatigue and offers the following lament: "Yes, I have known the feeling of shame. I had to live for years bearing within myself this onerous thought: I was part of a body which was being drained of life . . ."[80] Drieu's rhetorical device is to make the borders of the state almost palpably coterminous with the surface of the skin; panic about the national health is experienced in the most immediate sense. The postwar neofascist Maurice Bardèche eschews Drieu's sentimentalism for a straightforward, somewhat brutal, ap-peal on behalf of the virile virtues of ascetic hardness, health, and energetic muscle. Bardèche is an admirer of Sparta who dreams of the "blood and musculature" of the state, which "loves to behold it-self muscled and raging."[81]

The corporeal state, as the fascist imagination has dreamed it, can inspire either pathos or awe. On the one hand, there is Drieu's lament at the sight of degeneration, on the other, the muscular, and merciless, behemoth of Bardèche. What is more, this is a specifically fascist genre. As Winfried Joch has pointed out: "It was Goebbels above all who recognized the popular effect of sport-metaphors and who exploited them. To sum up the battle of Stalingrad he employed an image from boxing: 'We wipe the blood out of our eyes so that we can see clearly, and when the next round comes we are still on our feet.'"[82] The fundamental principle of this doctrine was enunciated by Oswald Mosley during the 1930s: "Our policy is the establishment of the Corporate State. As the name implies, this means a state organised like the human body."[83] As we shall see, this image has been shunned by Marxist ideologists for demonstrable reasons. What accounts for its appeal to fascist thinkers?

First, we may assume that, particularly since Nietzsche, the body has signified a domain of the irrational, in that it has been interpreted as the sphere of instinct and as the tangible, if illusory, embodiment of racial substance. When Alfred Baeumler complains that liberalism has "disembodied" (entleiblicht) politics, his complaint, in effect, is that liberalism has forced the body politic to think, to relinquish its ties to racial instinct and its unspoken wisdom, thereby inflicting upon this body a crippling malaise by cutting it off from the wellsprings of action.

Second, we may assume that all organicists, such as the fascists, require special assurances that the body politic is not in danger of degenerating into an amorphous state. A clue to this anxiety may be found in Herbert Spencer's essay *The Man versus the State* (1881), which is particularly useful in that the author makes a point of identifying the ideological viewpoint he considers to be precisely contrary to his own. "The communist," Spencer writes, "shows us unmistakably that he thinks of the body politic as admitting of being shaped thus or thus at will; and the tacit implication of many Acts of Parliament is that aggregated men, twisted into this or that arrangement, will remain as intended." This, Spencer asserts, is the consequence of assuming that society is a "manufacture" rather than a "growth," leading to "this erroneous conception of a society as a plastic mass instead of as an organized body."[84] The implication is that right-wing biologism confronts left-wing environmentalism as a primal opposition, that people must make a fundamental choice between plasticity and organization. It is the belief in the absolute character of such choices that gives rise to what I have called "ideological differentiation."

A third way of accounting for the appeal to fascists of the anthropomorphic, embodied state emphasizes what may be called the sportive style of manhood, an ethos in which states, like men, may participate, and which is based upon a heroic ideal of constant self-testing. "The nation as the state," Mussolini writes, "is an ethical reality which lives and exists in so far as it develops. To arrest its development is to kill it. . . . Thus it can be likened to the human will which knows no limits to its development and realizes itself in testing its own limitlessness." The fascist state turns out to be as narcissistic in this personified version as the fascist "political athlete." As Bardèche puts it, such a state "loves to behold itself muscled and raging." In Mussolini's phrase, the fascist state is "the highest and most powerful form of personality."[85] It should be noted that this sportive, Spenglerian vision of the state in its fateful wrestling match with history sacrifices a certain notion of human progress. For it relinquishes that species of hope which bases itself on rational praxis rather than an exuberance in sheer risk and chooses to find inspiration in the blind energy of the life process itself. As Donald MacRae has pointed out regarding one major organic thinker: "Spencer did not think that the progressive development of any given society was at all likely. . . . To Spencer human history is a charnel house, heaped with the cadavers of evolutionary failure."[86]

"It is not too much to say that his organic analogy is Spencer's surrogate for that historical culture the lack of which was perhaps the single largest defect of his intellectual equipment." Is the organic style, then, a sign of arrested development? MacRae offers two answers which correspond to the intellectual and ethical consequences, respectively, of Spencer's organic doctrine. "The organic analogy may be ultimately empty; its heuristic value has been considerable." The ethical issue arises in that Spencer promulgates an "ideology that reduced society to the merely biological, approved 'struggle' *per se*, and denied the humane possibilities of human societies."[87] On balance, we are justified in concluding that the cult of the body in any of its forms is hostile to ethics in that it effectively precludes experiences like reflection and empathy. For this reason the idea of the sportive, agonistic state is a specifically fascist reverie.

Marxism's Renunciation of the Sportive (Organic) State

As Melvin Rader has shown, Marx by no means rejected organic images of society. In the preface to the first edition of *Capital*, Marx remarks that "the present society is no solid crystal, but an organism capable of change, and it is constantly changing." Marx also employs in *Capital* organic metaphors such as "cell-forms" and "metabolism," and in 1864 he went so far as to suspend his writing on economics in order to study anatomy and physiology, where such imagery could be found in abundance. Nevertheless, as Rader demonstrates, there is an absolutely crucial factor which separates Marx from virtually the entire organic tradition: "[Marx] concurs with Hegel's main concept that the state is an 'organism.' 'It is a great advance,' he says, 'to consider the political state as an organism . . .' But there is a fundamental contrast between Hegel and Marx. The former regards the state-molded society (at least in pure concept) as healthy, the latter regards it as diseased. This at once distinguishes Marx from all who extol the state as an organic unity. Both in this period and later Marx is concerned with organic *disunity* . . ." For this reason, says Rader, Marx "avoids the overemphasis upon organic unity or homeostasis that characterizes organicists of a conservative or reactionary bent."[88]

Marxism's renunciation of the sportive state may be traced to several factors. First, there is the fact that Marx "is mainly bent on disclosing the *pathological* elements in the 'social organism,'"[89] an interest which clearly precludes a depiction of the state as a physically heroic figure. Second, Marx does not even accept the idea of a "healthy" state; a theorist who calls for "the withering away of the state" is not likely to anthropomorphize it into a statuesque body. Third, Marx's aversion to nationalism led him to present as heroic not the state, but a class (the proletariat) which did not present a very sportive aspect. His "image of the proletariat as the living, breathing, suffering expression of self-alienated humanity" is far removed from the sportive euphoria of the body.[90]

It is unlikely, however, that Marxist forfeiture of sportive imagery is entirely due to concerns about Marx's attitude toward the state. It is not, after all, an attitude to which the Communist movement has paid much heed. More important ideological restraints have probably been old Socialist ideas about the "frivolous" nature of sport,[91] and Marxist condemnation of the racial doctrines which constitute one version of the cult of the body. When the Frankfurt Marxist Leo Lowenthal refers to "the morally insensate body-beautiful ideal of the racial hero,"[92] he speaks for modern Communist doctrine as well as colleagues like Theodor Adorno, Max Horkheimer, and Herbert Marcuse, all of whom published disparaging commentaries on the cultic male body. For Soviet psychologists, too, "Any suggestion of 'improving the race' by eugenic selection is attacked as the epitome of 'bourgeois racism.'"[93] For the fascist, racial substance is a fundamental principle of philosophical anthropology; from the standpoint of Marxist doctrine, it is a superstitious curse.

"The fatherland," Marinetti writes in "Beyond Communism" (1920), "is the greatest extension of the individual, or better: the largest individual capable of living at length, of directing, mastering, and defending every part of its body."[94] The dramatic appeal of such an image is obvious; equally evident is its incompatibility with the idiom of the Left. The refusal of Marxist political culture to make use of such body imagery—and, consequently, sportive images of leadership and the state—represents an act of doctrinal asceticism implying, in turn, the renunciation of irrational appeals which a propagandist like Goebbels was only too happy to exploit.

Fascist doctrine expresses urgent feelings about the body which Marxist doctrine does not: Marinetti's cult of "body-madness" (fisicofollia) is only the exaggerated form of a basic fascist preoccupation. What the study of sportive imagery can verify is that charismatic and narcissistic ideals of leadership and the state are doctrinally contrary to the spirit of Marxist culture, and that the Marxist proscription of physically narcissistic self-display by leaders has been a historical reality. For, as Jorge Abelardo Ramos points out, there is an adulation which "threatens to paralyze the functioning of Marxist thought." Narcissistic leadership—and physical exhibitionism in particular—directs precisely this kind of threat at the integrity of a Marxist culture. Even a genuine sportsman like Walter Ulbricht never dared—or perhaps never wished—to promote himself as an athletic hero (whereas his paternalistic interest in sport, like Stalin's, was well publicized). Such self-display would have amounted to an individualistic heresy; it would have demonstrated an immature "spontaneity" in the Leninist sense of the word; and it would have been too reminiscent of fascist notions about the biologically perfect specimen. My conclusion, then, is that the body is indeed an ideological variable, that only fascism possesses a self-conscious doctrine of the body, and that political psychology must account for the two temperaments which do or do not employ the body as a political metaphor. Marxist culture will never produce a narcissist like Oswald Mosley, because no Marxist leader can permit himself to become a virtual caricature of the (fascist) myth of virility. To understand why is to penetrate to the origins of ideology itself.

4. The Political Psychologies of the Sportive and Antisportive Temperaments

Fascism and the Sportive Temperament

"I, puny and ridiculous little man, unloosed upon the world a power extracted from the pure and clear beauty of athletes and hoodlums."[1] So speaks Adolf Hitler in Jean Genet's novel *Funeral Rites* (1953). This fictional soliloquy is uncannily accurate: Hitler did in fact preside over the glorification of a male ethos which combined the athlete and the hoodlum into the dread figure of the SS man (see below), and his personal endorsements of the hardened body appear with striking frequency. At a gymnastics festival held at Stuttgart on July 30, 1933, Hitler held up to contemptuous review the sorry fruits of "the so-called Age of Reason, stamped with its characteristic liberal outlook, with its half-knowledge and half-culture . . ." "The over-valuation of knowledge," he proclaims, "led not merely to a disregard of the bodily form and bodily strength, but in the end to a lack of respect for bodily work. It is not chance that this age, propagated and protected by sick persons, necessarily led to a general sickness—not only to sickness of the body but also to sickness of the mind. For he who despises bodily strength and health has already become the victim of a malformation of the intellect."[2]

Hitler's endorsement of the body is a specifically fascist one. We should not be misled by the disapproving reference to "a lack of respect" for physical labor, which is wholly secondary here and not to be confused with a Marxian interpretation of labor. The real substance of this passage is its overt anti-intellectualism and the invocation of the body's authority in that context. No other modern political culture has produced a doctrine of physicality for its own sake. As Susan Sontag has pointed out, "fascist art has characteristics which show it to be, in part, a special variant of totalitarian art. The official art of countries like the Soviet Union and China is based on a utopian morality. Fascist art displays a utopian aesthetics—that of physical perfection."[3]

The dream of dynamic virility, prominently featuring the perfected body as a symbol of force, has been a theme of every fascist culture. Fascism has always incorporated a cult of virility. It is well known that the Nazis promulgated a "virile" ideal of the Aryan warrior, and that Nazi art demonstrated a fascination with an "ideal" body type. What has been less noted is the relationship between fascism and a "sportive" male style, the degree to which sportive values coincide with fascist values, and how a sportive style featuring quasi-athletic self-dramatization in the form of the self-inflicted ordeal became a special province of the fascist imagination. This is an example of ideological differentiation, and it is in this sense that sport may be said to be "haunted" by fascism. For why was it the fascists who celebrated the aesthetic of the body with such passion and sincerity? Why was it that only fascism paid court to the body, ostentatiously and without the shame occasioned in others by the insistent restraints of reason and conscience? "The Communists," says Hans Buchheim, "placed in the foreground the imparting of knowledge, the National Socialists the shaping of a particular mentality. And their ideal—typically fascist—was the heroic fighter for the fight's sake, who 'after the victory fastens his helmet all the tighter.'"[4] The latter ideal can accommodate—indeed, demands—dramatization as a physical style of action.

Up to this point we have confirmed that the ideological differentiation of Left and Right can be expressed in terms of a dichotomy of (historically verifiable) ideal types: *homo ludens* versus *homo laborans* (see chapter 2), and fascist "political athleticism" versus Marxist renunciation of the narcissistic body (see chapter 3). Our task now is to establish the reality of characterological ideals which are "sportive" and "nonsportive," respectively, the essential point being to associate these categories with the ideological positions of Right and Left in a consistent way.

How, Wilhelm Reich asks in 1933, "is the nature of the Comsomol's heroism to be differentiated from that of the Hitler youth or an imperialistic warrior?"[5] Are there really ideologically specific forms of dynamic virility ("heroism")? Does ideological differentiation occur on this deep a psychological level? The crux of the problem is that "sportive" or "virile" temperaments occur within every political culture; and virtually every political culture rewards its successful sportsmen. For this reason, the notion that Communist athletes are distinguished by a uniform mentality of ideological origin can only derive from a cloud-cuckoo land of political psychology, particularly if they are contrasted with "bourgeois-democratic" athletes of equal uniformity. (The doctrine of the German workers' sport movement of the 1920s did, in fact, claim that sport unleased qualitatively different emotions in "Socialist" and "bourgeois" athletes.)[6] What we can say is that, while all cultures include such people, not all of them promulgate ideologies which encourage and incorporate as doctrine the characterological traits peculiar to the (idealized) sportive temperament: competitive aggressiveness, self-conscious physicality, ascetic indifference to pain, and an indifference to ethical concerns, or what the psychologist W. H. Sheldon once termed "psychological callousness." In fact, Sheldon's *somatotonic* (assertive, athletic) character type is as close as empirical psychology has come to defining the sportive temperament,[7] which corresponds in turn to a fascist ideal of manhood. The question now arises as to how virility itself is differently interpreted by the ideologies of the Right and Left.

Ideologies offer, in effect, different "personalities" which derive from different political anthropologies which offer competing models of the ideal man. A comparison of fascist and Marxist models leads to two important conclusions: first, fascist, and not Marxist, ideology accommodates—and even apotheosizes—elements of the sportive temperament; second, Marxism—notwithstanding the successes of Communist athletes—cannot accommodate some basic impulses of this temperament without violating the norms of its own official anthropology. These conclusions reiterate a finding reported in chapter 3, which distinguished between Marxist and fascist ideological "personalities" by pointing out their contrary attitudes toward "narcissistic" male leadership and the persona of the sportive political figure.

The sportive syndrome is not, then, founded on an interest in sport *per se*, though it may well find symbolic expression in sport. It is, rather, a temperament, a category defined by Sheldon as "the level of personality just above physiological function and below acquired attitudes and beliefs."[8] By emphasizing "virile" forcefulness, this syndrome places a premium on spontaneity and action, thereby effectively depreciating the world of reason and moral deliberation. Its implicit source of inspiration and authority is the body itself.

In the course of his own search for "a basic taxonomy of human beings," Sheldon does not shrink before the challenge of matching body structure and character, or of offering a typology which includes "the athletic (somatotonic) face."[9] Beyond such impressionism is a more complex one which interprets the body as an ideological variable. Communism, Rebecca West writes in 1947, "is fascism with a geographical and glandular difference." The difference between ideological types is not physical, but rather concerns subconscious attitudes toward the body: "There was a significance in the manner of speech adopted by the Communist-Fascists. The Nazi-Fascists shouted as if their lungs and more were in superb condition. When heard over the air their voices suggested tall, stout, virile bodies, under perfect control, which were either richly invested with sex or lack it because it had been replaced by some fiercer daemon. These Communist-Fascists spoke thinly and with a hesitancy that seemed to be assumed, that was exaggerated at times to a stutter, as if to make it plain that they renounced the body as unimportant and based all their claims on pre-eminence of intellect."[10] As noted in the previous chapter, there is much evidence which confirms Dame West's judgment that communism implies—on the level of doctrine—a renunciation of the body. Unlike Sheldon or the German psychiatrist Ernst Kretschmer—whose works include *The Personality of the Athlete* (1936)—she does not try to link body structure and character. At the same time, her observation conforms to a stereotype in that the idea of the decorporealized leftist radical had been circulating in Europe for many years. "The leanness of the 'fanatical agitator,'" Harold Lasswell writes in 1930, "figured in the popular mind long before Kretschmer gave it his scientific blessing. . . . The notion of a lean and bitter agitator is not entirely a static, cross-sectional description of a fortuitous juxtaposition of traits, but a hypothesis that bodily irritations operate dynamically to foster the selection of forms of activity which enable the individual to give rather free vent to his animosities."[11] This image explains why the (sport-minded) French fascist Robert Brasillach talks of *le maigre conspirateur judéo-socialiste*.[12] Needless to say, the somatic characterologies of Kretschmer and Sheldon are very dubious. But the antisomatic bias within Marxism is a matter of historical record, as is documented later in this chapter.

The physically endowed man of action is not, of course, an originally fascist type. The mythic stature of the "para-athletic" warrior, rooted in prehistory, is the true paradigm. But at what point does this charismatic figure become a modern one and therefore identifiable as a type of sportive character? By the end of the nineteenth century, certain authors are describing, with critical detachment, specific forms of a sportive temperament which combines athleticism with aggressive and even sadistic impulses. But only in the last of the cases cited below can one speak of a genuinely prefascist sportive type (in Rolland's *Jean-Christophe*). The other texts from this period stand outside the fascist tradition *per se*, even as they indict a puerilism of which fascism, as Huizinga noted, is one example.

The best-known of these polemical texts is Thorstein Veblen's *Theory of the Leisure Class* (1899). Veblen offers a characterology with two major categories: ethnicity and "temperament." The "three main ethnic types" to be found in industrial civilization are "the dolichocephalic-blond, the brachycephalic brunette, and the Mediterranean"; the "two main directions of variation" within the ethnic type are "the peaceable or ante-predatory variant and the predatory variant." Predictably, Veblen combines the first ethnic type with the second variation to produce a blond predator: "the dolicho-blond type of European man seems to owe much of its dominating influence and its masterful position in the recent culture to its possessing the characteristics of predatory man in an exceptional degree." More interesting, however, is Veblen's interpretation of "the predatory temperament" as a sportive one. Males who reach maturity, he says, "ordinarily pass through a temporary archaic phase corresponding to the permanent spiritual level of the fighting and sporting men" who—"punctilious gentleman of leisure" and "swaggering delinquent" alike—show "marks of an arrested spiritual development." Sporting activities present an opportunity for "histrionic" displays which Veblen obviously feels are inane and unredeemed by any compensatory function.

> Sports—hunting, angling, athletic games, and the like—afford an exercise for dexterity and for the emulative ferocity and astuteness characteristic of predatory life. So long as the individual is but slightly gifted with reflection or with a sense of the ulterior trend of actions—so long as his life is substantially a life of naive impulsive action—so long as the immediate and unreflected purposefulness of sports, in the way of an expression of dominance, will measurably satisfy his instinct of workmanship. This is especially true if his dominant impulses are the unreflecting emulative propensities of the predaceous temperament.

Veblen views "the sporting character" as "a rehabilitation of the early barbarian temperament." At the same time, however, this archaic mentality has been stripped of "the redeeming features of the savage character" which assist in human self-preservation. "The culture bestowed in football gives a product of exotic ferocity and cunning," qualities which "are of no use to the community except in its hostile dealings with other communities."[13] For this reason the cult of the sportive (predatory) temperament finds its ideological fulfillment in fascism. For it was Hitler who called war "the most powerful and classic expression of life."[14] "War alone," says Mussolini, "brings up to their highest tension all human energies and puts the stamp of nobility upon the peoples who have the courage to meet it."[15] But the fascist cult of the insensate warrior was specifically disavowed by the Bolsheviks. At the first All-Union Congress of Soviet Writers held in 1934, Karl Radek treated his audience to a quotation from a novel by one Mario Carli, titled *An Italian of the Times of Mussolini*, which had won a prize and been published under the auspices of Mussolini himself: "War represents a really valuable phenomenon, for it compels all people to make the choice between courage and cowardice. . . . It is, of course, a rude phenomenon—man against man, character against character, nerves against nerves; but this phenomenon divides the hysterical folk, the worms, the whiners, the spoilt children from the courageous, wise idealists, from the mystics of dangers, from the heroes of blood." Radek regards these sentiments as a form of debased ranting.[16] With less acuity, he also regards them as politically ineffectual—a signal instance of the Bolshevik hyperrationalism which, translated into Comintern policy, had already helped pave the way for Hitler. But this disapproval of the cult of war is an excellent example of ideological differentiation.

For his "sweeping though catchy speculations," as César Graña has pointed out, "Veblen has sometimes been accused of bogus and opportunistic scholarship. Such a view humorlessly misses the point. Veblen's accounts are really theoretical evocations aimed above all at uncovering the symbolic content of our social heritage." The sportive temperament is one form of this symbolic content. As Graña notes, the enormous influence of "Byronic" heroism, and its "symbolic content," is "inseparable from the figure of *the magically powerful male adventurer*, a figure so durable that one may say that in a variety of banal manifestations, including banal brutality, the romantic hero is still the hero of popular literature [emphasis added]."[17]

A second critique of the sportive temperament, virtually identical to that of Veblen, is found in J. A. Hobson's *Imperialism: A Study* (1902). Like Veblen, Hobson finds the essence of sport in an archaic predatory instinct: "The animal lust of struggle, once a necessity, survives in the blood, and just in proportion as a nation or a class has a margin of energy and leisure from the activities of peaceful industry, it craves satisfaction through 'sport,' in which hunting and the physical satisfaction of striking a blow are vital ingredients." Imperialism is, therefore, sport writ large. Jingoism, which is "merely the lust of the spectator" who applauds militarism, finds its sporting analogue in "the ideal excitement of the spectator" who watches professional athletes. Both kinds of spectators sacrifice the integrity of participation to the vacant gratifications of detachment; the jingo is more venal and more extreme, in that he remains "unpurged by any personal effort, risk, or sacrifice, gloating over the perils, pains, and slaughter of fellow-men whom he does not know, but whose destruction he desires in a blind and artificially stimulated passion of hatred and revenge."[18] Hobson understands that the ancient notion that war as a kind of game (analyzed by Huizinga in *Homo Ludens*) is present here only in the degenerate form of a will to exterminate.

A decade before Pierre de Coubertin was assuring his readers (in 1910) that the sportsman had nothing in common with the "refined ferocity" of Nietzsche's superman,[19] Veblen and Hobson were demonstrating precisely the reverse. A year or two after Coubertin's remarks were published, Romain Rolland introduced a representative of the younger generation in France whom he described as "full of joie de vivre, superficial, enemy of all spoilsports, passionately in love with pleasure and violent games, easily duped by the rhetoric of his time, inclined by the vigor of his muscles and the laziness of his mind to the brutal doctrines of the [fascist] Action Française, nationalist, royalist, and imperialist."[20] It is characteristic of Coubertin that, having mentioned (in a tone of horror) the body narcissism of the Nietzschean "monster," he simply banished it from his mind. But as we shall see, this is not where sport's affiliation with fascism ends, but rather where it begins.

In conclusion, it is important to recall that the sportive temperament does not always assume an overtly political identity. Graña's "magically powerful male adventurer," whom I have called the "para-athlete," may be a soldier, an explorer, an aviator, or a sportsman who represents, in Graña's words, a "symbolic content of our social heritage"—even if, in this case, he symbolizes an essentially antisocial (predatory) type. One example of this type of sportive temperament is "the new type of popular hero, the professional player or sportsman" described, without enthusiasm, by Lewis Mumford in 1933: "He is as specialized for the vocation as a soldier or an opera singer: he represents virility, courage, gameness, those talents in exercising and commanding the body which have so small a part in the new mechanical regime itself: if the hero is a girl, her qualities must be Amazonian in character. The sports hero represents the masculine virtues, the Mars complex, as the popular motion picture actress or the bathing beauty contestant represents Venus. He exhibits that complete skill to which the amateur vainly aspires."[21] Only in a superficial sense is the sports hero a nonpolitical type, for the "Mars complex" is the core of the fascist ideal of manhood.

Nietzsche and the Authority of the Body

In 1938 the Parti populaire français, a fascist movement founded by the ex-Communist Jacques Doriot, issued a program which included an explicit endorsement of the sportive body: "Our social and economic program is directed in its entirety toward the athletic transformation of man."[22] The fascist doctrine of the body finds its most important antecedent in Nietzsche's call for the "masculinization of Europe."[23] *On the Genealogy of Morals* (1887) refers repeatedly to the "physiological" aspect of being human: "the *majority* of mortals" comprise "the physiologically deformed and deranged," whose envy and resentment of "physiological well-being" is a mark of their morbidly ascetic outlook. This asceticism is to be contrasted with a "chastity" which does not derive from "any kind of ascetic scruple or hatred of the senses, just as it is not chastity when *an athlete or jockey* abstains from women: it is rather the will of their dominating instinct, at least during their periods of great pregnancy [emphasis added]." Nietzsche's idealized body is a vehicle of "*robust health*": "The knightly-aristocratic value judgments presupposed a powerful physicality, a flourishing, abundant, even overflowing health, together with that which serves to preserve it: war, adventure, hunting, dancing, war games, and in general all that involves vigorous, free, joyful activity." It is this physicality which links "the noble races" to "the beast of prey, the splendid *blond beast* prowling about avidly in search of spoil and victory." The body is the seat of "this hidden core [which] needs to erupt from time to time . . ."[24] Nietzsche does not propound an athleticism *per se*, but rather a vitalism for which the healthy and dynamic body is an effective metaphor. It is "dominating instinct," not the performance of the athlete or jockey, which really counts.

Nietzsche's doctrine of the body reappears, oddly enough, in Jean-Paul Sartre's essay on anti-Semitism (1946), and not as a target for enlightened refutation. Sartre claims that "inauthentic" Jews, in response to the anti-Semite's hostile emphasis upon "Jewish" physical characteristics, "deny the body that betrays them," thereby estranging themselves from their own "vital values." Like Nietzsche, Sartre identifies two distinct attitudes toward the body. While the "inauthentic Jew" flees his body, the "Aryans" manifest "a certain blossoming, a certain biological style that seems to be a manifestation of the intimate functioning of the organism": grace, nobility, vivacity.

> Hence the Christian, the Aryan, feels his body in a special way. He does not have a pure and simple consciousness of the massive modifications of his organs; the messages and appeals that his body sends him come with certain coefficients of ideality, and are always more or less symbolic vital values. He even devotes a portion of his activity to procuring perceptions of himself that correspond to his vital ideal: the nonchalance of the elegant, the vivacity and "stir" which characterize the stylish manner in certain epochs, the ferocious air of the Italian fascist, the grace of women—all these seek to express the aristocracy of the body.

In flight from the stigmata of his distinctive physicality, the "inauthentic" Jew "conceives of a sort of *universal and rationalized body*" from which he withholds the veneration the Aryan naturally accords his own organs. The irony of the argument is that, despite his profound hostility to fascism, Sartre winds up endorsing indirectly "the ferocious air of the Italian fascist" while chiding the Jew for treating his body as a "mechanism" and for having no feeling for "the vital values."[25] Nietzsche's invidious distinction between the knightly-aristocratic and priestly modes, between "powerful physicality" and "impotence," has survived nicely—attenuated but intact. Both authors, in effect, propose the body as an "ideological variable," and both pay homage to its authority.

Fascist Style and Sportive Manhood

"Sportsmen," Oswald Mosley's biographer has noted, "figured prominently in the galaxy of fascist types." And he adds: "There was a strong link between fascism and aviation with its 'fascist' combination of individual daring and futuristic technology."[26] It is by now widely recognized that fascism was, as much as anything else, a political aesthetic and therefore a phenomenon of style.[27] Mussolini—offered by Mosley to the British public in 1932 as an alternative to "statesmanship in skirts"[28]—was the most exuberant stylist of them all, and one who prominently displayed a twentieth-century sense of the sportive. One strategy was to have himself photographed on a horse soaring over small hurdles, "which by a judicious tilt of the camera could be given for publicity purposes the appearance of quite formidable obstacles."[29] Christopher Isherwood recalls that at Cambridge during the 1920s the Italian leader was accorded a certain virile modishness by the sportier undergraduates: "Mussolini was enjoying a certain popularity: rugger and rowing men, at this epoch, frequently named their terriers 'Musso.'"[30]

Mussolini described his own public technique as the perpetuation of an "electric" and "explosive" atmosphere. "Italy, he used to say, was a land of theatre and its leaders must orchestrate their public contacts."[31] Mussolini did this in the most self-consciously athletic way possible. Whether posing for cameras while brandishing a sword, arriving at Locarno by speedboat, or boasting of fisticuffs with his boxing instructor, Mussolini cultivated the image of "a man virilely conscious of the difficulties that exist in action and ready to face them."[32] "Every kind of sport was said to be close to his heart, and especially those involving danger. His horse-riding became legendary, as did the speed at which he drove a car. . . . Occasionally he invited foreign journalists to see him fence, play tennis or ride, and told them he hoped they would report how fit and expert he was; sometimes their honesty as reporters was sorely taxed." This conspicuous athleticism was not simply a publicity trick: it derived both from Mussolini's sense of showmanship and from a profound physical narcissism which fed energy into the public display. Mussolini hated the aging process and shaved his head to conceal it. The apotheosis of this body narcissism was a project conceived by the Duce in the 1930s but never completed. The idea was that "this *foro Mussolini* should be dominated by a great bronze colossus symbolizing fascism: a half-naked figure of Hercules, one hand holding a truncheon, the other raised in a Roman salute, the face bearing Mussolini's features."[33]

Ernst Nolte has captured the flavor of Mussolini in his account of the dictator's temperamental impatience with Marxist doctrine. Mussolini's defection from Marxism was a gradual process during which he carried on flirtations with blatantly anti-Marxist ideas, all the while displaying a keen sense of where ideological boundaries could not be crossed. The point of no return was reached "when Mussolini claims that what divides the parties is not a table of laws but their mentalities"—the original source of style itself. Nolte interprets Mussolini, in effect, as a restless Marxist whose dissatisfaction focuses on what Nolte calls the "dryness" of Marx:

> Where Mussolini does augment Marx's outline with some
> vivid colors, it is to express a keen sense of the dawning world

of technology. He enthusiastically greeted the first attempts at flight by Latham and Bleriot because they proclaimed a "quickening of the rhythm of our life." Although he interpreted the event from a strictly Marxist point of view as being a "sign of peace" and as proclaiming the end of the "fratricidal domination of man over man," a strange new note becomes audible when in the same breath he praises the pilots as a future *razza di dominatori* and *spiriti inquieti*. In many places it is possible to detect a shift in emphasis which seems to lead away from Marx's fundamental humanistic feeling to an enthusiastic recognition of the new technical world as such. Mussolini no longer speaks of man's domination of the machine; instead he describes socialism as a society "in which life will become more intense and frenetic, ruled by the rhythm of machines."[34]

It is astonishing to hear a world-historical figure fantasizing in the mode of the futurist lunatic Filippo Marinetti, but this kind of stylistic boldness is a crucial element of sportive fascist charisma. "If prayer means communication with the divinity," Marinetti writes, "running at speed is a prayer. . . . The intoxication of great speeds in cars is nothing but the joy of feeling oneself fused with the only *divinity*. Sportsmen are the catechumens of this religion." The virile Mussolini was Marinetti's kind of sportsman, as is clear from the following excerpts from his "Portrait of Mussolini" (1929), a fervent appreciation which demonstrates *inter alia* that Marinetti, like Nolte, had seen through the Duce's leftist veneer to the somatotonic sportsman who dwelled within:

Mussolini has an exuberant, overwhelming, swift temperament. He is no ideologue. Were he an ideologue he would be held back by ideas that are often slow, or by books that are always dead. Instead he is free, free as the wind.

He was a Socialist and internationalist, but only in theory. Revolutionary yes, but pacifist never. He necessarily had to end up obeying his own kind of patriotism, which I call physiological.

Physiological patriotism, because physically he is built *all'italiana*, designed by inspired and brutal hands, forged, carved to the model of the mighty rocks of our peninsula.

Square crushing jaws. Scornful jutting lips that spit with defiance and swagger on everything slow, pedantic, and finicking. Massive rock-like head, but the ultra-dynamic eyes dart

with the speed of automobiles on the Lombard plains. To right
and left flashes the gleaming cornea of a wolf.[35]

"Style," says Nolte, "is the visible essence of a political phenomenon." Mussolini is the perfect illustration of this principle in
that his case illuminates the struggle of contrary essences: "physiological patriotism" eventually breaks the Marxist mold. What is
more, style becomes an end in itself. As Nolte points out, "That
which for Marx and Lenin had been an obvious, unspecified element
in the cause—bravery and strength, courage and heroism, vitality and
separateness—becomes for Mussolini independent and self-aware."
The qualities of action are distilled out of the substance of action
and are given cultic importance—as clear an example of the "ideological differentiation" of Marxism and fascism as history can provide. For the "vital" style is a fascist preoccupation, as Mussolini
was well aware: "Democracy has deprived the life of the people of
'style': that is, a line of conduct, the color, the strength, the pictur-
esque, the unexpected, the mystical; in sum, all that counts in the
soul of the masses. We play the lyre on all its strings: from violence
to religion, from art to politics."[36]

In his virile flamboyance, Mussolini was the prototype rather
than the exception. "Nationalist and pre-Fascist propaganda," Adrian
Lyttelton writes of Italian fascism, "made much use of appeals to
the aesthetic sense. Sorel's myth was defined as a 'body of images';
the contrasted physical images of the New Man—young, virile, and
athletic—and of the old representative of the democratic order—
paunched, short-sighted, slow-moving—were highly effective. The
aesthetic and the biological view of politics reinforced each other."[37]
Jean-Paul Sartre, too, commented just after the war that the "ferocious bearing" of the Italian fascist signified a commitment to "the
aristocracy of the body."[38]

But for every style there is an antistyle; and if the style is athletic, its antithesis must represent the body which is weak or deformed. "It seems to me," Oswald Mosley writes in 1931, "that Britain in her crisis is being asked to turn her face to the wall and to give
up *like an old woman* who knows that she has to die. I want to see
this country at least make an effort. I do not believe and never have
believed in the cure of fasting, but in the cure of effort. I believe that
the way out is not the way of the monk but *the way of the athlete*
[emphasis added]."[39] Other fascist spokesmen were less oblique. In
"An Aristocracy of Brigands," Giuseppe Prezzolini calls for a "programme of men and not cripples."[40] José Antonio Primo de Rivera
calls the arrival of his father's Spanish dictatorship "an assertion of

health" and compares its political adversaries to "cripples." José Antonio was much taken with the notion of a physical health which served to indicate ideological health, as well. The "sickly" Rousseau is dismissed for this reason, and "those who call themselves intellectuals" either speak with "strangled voices" and "puckered eyebrows" or are "so very, very exquisite that they cannot go out into the street for fear that a whiff of air might kill them."[41] In Sheldon's terms, this is a visceral repugnance felt by the "somatotonic" for the "cerebrotonic" type—the characterological equivalent of racialism.

The irony of the "somatotonic" ideology of force is that it is very often the compensatory squawk of frustrated "cerebrotonia." For all his heroic rhetoric, José Antonio declined the role of hero: "To be a true leader, one must be something of a prophet, one must have such faith . . . health . . . enthusiasm and such anger as is incompatible with refinement. I personally would be suited to anything but the role of a fascist leader."[42] It was the club-footed Joseph Goebbels, not Max Schmeling, who offered sport metaphors to his public. It was poets like Stefan George and William Butler Yeats who celebrated athletic grace. It is, in short, the intellectuals who dream of athletes—never the reverse.

But what of those intellectuals who never dream of athletes at all? If for every style there is an antistyle, then what constitutes the antithesis of the sportive temperament? Let us continue our investigation of this temperament, and its fascist affinities, by attempting to define its characterologically, and ideologically, opposite forms from two fascist points of view, and then by examining three fascist ideals of sportive manhood.

The Marxist Lacks Virile Instincts. The French neofascist Maurice Bardèche writes that, while both Lenin and the novelist Henry de Montherlant held that a man should have neither wife nor children, Lenin advocated this doctrine "out of regard for a system," while Montherlant did so "out of regard for the dignity of the male."[43] The evident strategy of this comparison is to suggest that there is something subtly but profoundly wrong with Lenin, while praising Montherlant as a man who lives on the best of terms with those instincts proper to manhood. Bardèche has no reason to feel troubled by Montherlant's notorious misogyny—not surprising given Bardèche's admiration for the hard, virile ethos of Sparta (and the fine specimens of Hitler's SS)—and he is undoubtedly aware that Montherlant was the most distinguished literary sport-cultist in France during the 1920s. Lenin, unlike Montherlant, actually played a violent role in history, even going so far as to recommend that revolutionaries become physical culturists so as to harden themselves for the coming struggle. But this is irrelevant in light of his deficient sense of what it is to be a male, for he has replaced instinct with ideology.

The Marxist Lacks Dynamism and a Taste for Risk. "You cannot escape these two idea-feelings," the eccentric fascist Marinetti writes in "Beyond Communism" (1920): "*patriotism*, or the active development of the individual and race, and *heroism*, or the synthetic need to transcend human powers, the ascensional force of the race. All those who are tired of the stormy-dynamic variety of life dream of the fixed, restful uniformity promised by Communism. They want a life without surprises, the earth as smooth as a billiard ball."[44] The Communist temperament, being the antithesis of the futurist temperament, is also the antithesis of the sportive temperament. As we shall see in the second section of this chapter, Marinetti's image of the mentality of the Left conforms to a persistent twentieth-century stereotype: "we are reproached," Maurice Merleau-Ponty writes in 1947, "with wanting to curb men under the law of a 'transcendental *praxis*' that would eliminate human freedom with its spontaneity and risks"[45]—reproached, in short, for a quintessentially antisportive disposition.

The "political athlete" is one version of the risk-taking nationalist who is denied authority by the Marxist tradition. José Antonio, for one, found such ideological hostility to nationalism politically stupid almost beyond belief: "It is impossible to imagine a coarser political approach; when one offends against one of those primary feelings rooted in the depths of a people's spontaneity, there is bound to be a basic reaction of anger, even amongst those who least incline towards nationalism. This is almost a biological phenomenon."[46] "National narrowmindedness," Marx and Engels write, "is everywhere repellent,"[47] thereby discarding one of Marinetti's two cardinal "idea-feelings," and the one on which he built sportive images of both leadership (Mussolini built *all'italiana*) and the state (Italy as "an excellent wrestler"). His idea of heroism is equally alien to both Marx and Engels, who had nothing but ridicule for Carlyle's hero worship,[48] and the ideologists of Eastern bloc sport. The "hygienic," health-promoting, risk-avoiding attitude which is deeply rooted in Communist sport theory and practice is precisely that temperament for which Marinetti felt only disdain, and his implicit contempt for "hygienism" was shared by Nazi sport theorists, as well.[49] A recent East German treatise on risk management would have driven Marinetti into a state of apoplectic sarcasm had he lived to see it.[50] In its emphasis on the rational mastery, rather than the cultivation, of risk, it is a precise fulfillment of Marinetti's nightmare world worn "smooth as a billiard ball." For the sportive temperament, as Marinetti well understood, is impulsive and prone to the stylish gamble. Like the infinitely more staid Johan Huizinga, Marinetti interprets play as freedom, thereby ennobling that sportive style which represents nothing less than "the ascensional force of the race." In fact, it is Marinetti's attitude toward the dignity of the sportive style which puts him in respectable intellectual company—compare Ortega's paean to speed in *The Revolt of the Masses*.[51] On the other hand, Marinetti is most "fascist" in the implicit brutality of his technophilia (machines as superimages of bodily forces) and in the loving inspection of Mussolini's body which justifies "physiological patriotism."

Nazism, Athleticism, and the SS Warrior. In a 1981 preface to *The Crisis of German Ideology*, George Mosse remarks that, were he to write this famous book over again, he would "place increased emphasis on the role of the male stereotype in the myths and symbols of Volkish thought. I had not yet realized that in the age of mass politics, symbols and political liturgies were of central importance in making abstract ideas effective and concrete."[52] As we have seen, it was fascism which appropriated the symbolic male body as its own political territory. But the symbolic male body and the athletic body are not necessarily the same thing. The "idealized Nordic manliness" whose lineage Mosse has traced cannot be reduced to an athletic ideal. This is one of several distinctions which must be enforced if we are to understand the relationship between nazism and athleticism. More specifically, such distinctions illuminate the myth of the most notorious of all the fascist para-athletic types: the merciless warrior of the Waffen-SS.

The coalescence of the warrior and the athlete into a single figure is natural and yet misleading. On the one hand, every foot soldier must have athletic abilities. But these abilities are really incidental to a vocation which is more complex than that of the athlete, who is spared both moral and mortal peril. From a functional point of view, however, these vocations do tend to merge. The British military historian B. H. Liddell Hart, for example, describes modern foot soldiers as "athletes engaged in a contest of skill—the supreme form of test." "The modern infantry soldier must be *tria juncta in uno*—stalker, athlete, and marksman."[53]

Plato, too, called soldiers "athletes in the greatest contest."[54] But an ominous note is sounded when Liddell Hart equates his "carefully picked and highly trained *elite*" with German "storm-troops," albeit of 1918 vintage. The ruthless, marauding *alte Kämpfer* these storm-troops became do not constitute a moral issue for this military thinker. In retrospect, however, the "cat-like agility" of Liddell

Hart's modern infantryman is not entirely separable from the sadism it may serve. It is all very well for Liddell Hart to deplore, sarcastically, the "cult" of the bayonet. But the more serious cultic possibilities which reside in his delectations over "picked infantry" appear to have passed him by.[55] This is why his enthusiastic depiction of the military "athlete" needs qualification, for it suppresses the difference between athletic muscularity and psychopathic muscularity, between the sportsman and his distorted image, "the 'Unknown SS Man,' the muscular but frankly heartless and brainless hero forever tearing chains apart and smashing barriers," as Joachim Fest has put it. Yet Fest himself terms the SA "a kind of wrestling club with a political bias" and refers to its "athletic taste for violence."[56] This casual confusion of the athletic and the violent is worth avoiding, if only to prevent the violent from appropriating the role of the athlete, and its special charisma.

What was the SS ideal of manhood, and what were its origins? The "standardised SS man, the nordicised master-race type" of Himmler's imagination is a combination of body structure and character. Himmler insisted that the SS man be "of well-proportioned build: for instance there must be no disproportion between the lower leg and the thigh or between the legs and the body; otherwise an exceptional bodily effort is required to carry out long marches." Candidates of "inadequate" physique were given an opportunity to present a more subtle kind of physical evidence. "The point," he says, "is that in his attitude to discipline the man should not behave like an underling, that his gait, his hands, everything, should correspond to the ideal which we set ourselves."[57]

As a character type, the SS man was supposed to exhibit what Hans Buchheim has called "a certain specific *mentality.*" "So the SS man learned that: his basic attitude must be that of a fighter for fighting's sake; he must obey unquestioning; he must be 'hard'—not only inured but impervious to all human emotions; he should be contemptuous of 'inferior beings' and arrogant toward all those who did not belong to the Order; he must show comradeship and 'camaraderie'; the word 'impossible' did not exist." The concept of "hardness" is the absolute center of this mentality. SS-Obergruppenführer (General) Reinhard Heydrich solemnly told one visitor: "Abroad they take us for bloodhounds, don't they? It is almost too difficult for some people but we must be hard as granite."[58] To the Einsatzgruppen, the mobile squads of mass murderers who terrorized Eastern Europe, Heydrich counseled "unparalleled hardness."[59]

"Hardness," in turn, was in the service of an ethic of pure achievement. What Buchheim calls "the extreme subjectivism of the heroic fighter" was appropriated for an organizational objective: the SS man was "conditioned to heroic action in a criminal cause." As Heinz Höhne puts it: "Such an ethic, with no specific aim, opened the door to concentration upon achievement for achievement's sake and this became the focal point of the SS mentality described by Himmler with classic simplicity: 'The word "impossible" must never be heard in the SS.'"[60] As we shall see, both hardness and the cult of achievement are ambiguous ideals with sportive overtones. In addition, it should be understood that such quasi-sportive ideals, as Liddell Hart's comments on infantry clearly demonstrate, possessed—and continue to possess—an appeal which transcends the milieu of the SS. For example, the appeal of the British Fascist movement, which—thanks to the athleticism of Oswald Mosley—was more self-consciously sportive than any other fascist party, "broke through class barriers from the start. However, among middle- and upper-class recruits certain types predominated. They were, typically, ex-soldiers, marginal professional men dissatisfied with what life had to offer, and sportsmen."[61] By the late 1920s, the same recruitment process had been underway in Germany for several years, the first SS units having been formed in 1925. Whereas the founders of the SS had been of lower-middle-class origins, "now men from another level of society were flooding into the SS—the lost souls of the middle and upper-middle classes. The SS attracted these newcomers by its philosophy of 'hardness' and its attitude of bellicosity *per se*, basically unconnected with ideology." In a word, the appeal of the masculine ethos which characterized the SS as a community of "fighters" transcended both class and national lines. As Höhne points out, although the SS troops had been trained as ideological fanatics in the service of National Socialism, "in their own eyes they were no different from the American 'leathernecks' or the later French 'Paras'—surrounded by an aura of toughness and masculinity, inspired by a sense of belonging to an aristocratic minority, a closed community with its own rules and loyalties."[62]

Unlike Fascist Italy, the Third Reich could not display political athleticism at the top. Mussolini's physique was promoted as an unofficial ideal. But Hitler disapproved of Mussolini's "posing with bare torso among the peasants" on the grounds that it was undignified.[63] Göring enjoyed being called "the Iron Man," but it was his "beefy hedonism" which caught the attention of most observers. And as for Goebbels: "As a man with a physical deformity and an intellectual, he was something of a provocation to a party that regarded, not intellectual ability, but muscular strength and racial heritage, fair hair and long legs, as qualifications for genuine membership."[64]

The athletic ideal of the SS was Reinhard Heydrich, who by 1936, at the age of thirty-two, had risen through the SS ranks to become head of the Gestapo, the Sicherheitsdienst (SD), and the Criminal Police. In 1939, he organized the Reich Central Security Office (RSHA), thereby becoming the most powerful figure in the security services. At the time of his assassination in 1942, he was deputy Reich protector in Prague. Heydrich was a tall and athletic man whom his subordinates sometimes called "the Blond Beast."[65] According to Höhne, "Heydrich had a passion for all forms of sport; he was a fencer, a horseman, a pilot, a skier and modern pentathlon competitor; he was also SS Inspector for physical training . . ."[66] But here, as in the SS ethos as a whole, athleticism *per se* played a secondary role within a larger charismatic persona. Eloquent testimony to the cultic role of Heydrich's image appears in a memoir by an ex-SS cadet:

> My account would not be complete without a reference to the "blond God" Reinhard Heydrich. At that time Heydrich was already almost a mystic figure. There was hardly a room in the Cadet School without his picture—many more than of the *Reichsführer.* I cannot repeat all the qualities attributed to him, but one was outstanding—his "hardness." There can be no better proof of the iron discipline to which he subjected both himself and his body than the moments immediately after he had been attacked when, mortally wounded and in agonizing pain, he still mustered the strength to reach for his holster, open it and send five shots after his attackers. It is significant that almost without exception his pictures showed him as the winner of the "Reich Route March."[67]

It is clear that Heydrich's athleticism must be understood as emblematic of a physical superiority which is ultimately of racial significance. Here the body of the SS hero is both the unflinching instrument and the martyred victim of "hardness."

The SS warrior as a type had been evolving through several phases in Germany for over a century. The cultivation of the body in a nationalistic spirit dates from the beginning of the nineteenth century, when Friedrich Ludwig ("Father") Jahn, a professor at the University of Berlin, founded a gymnastics movement which would prepare the bodies of German youth to wage war against Napoleon. Jahn is also a seminal figure in the history of the "Volkish" tradition which eventually took the form of Nazi ideology.[68] "Volkish" thought is a mystical, integral nationalism founded on the racial doctrine of a transcendental German "essence," and Jahn was an early and important prophet of *Volkstum* and *Deutschheit*.[69] "A state without a people," Jahn writes, "is nothing, a soul-less artificiality; a people without a state is nothing, an airy, disembodied abstraction."[70] And the counterprinciple to such an abstraction was the physical, racial substance of the *Volk* itself.

Like Pierre de Coubertin, the French baron who founded the modern Olympic movement, Jahn saw himself as a pedagogue in possession of a "healing doctrine" required by the body politic.[71] Although profoundly anti-intellectual, Jahn's doctrine did not incorporate a conscious brutality. But the aggressive, fascist body is nonetheless present in embryonic form. "The Greek ideal of beauty," says Mosse, "was prominent here as well; it identified a hardened, lithe male body, whose contours were made particularly visible by the uniform Jahn invented for the gymnasts." The memorable content of history, Jahn claimed, required "the spectacle of masculine power."[72] In the course of the nineteenth century, the Volkish peasant stereotype came to include an element of brutality in the service of Volkish thought's antimodern, antiurban bias, "a primitivism which alone had strength enough to strip off the artificial veneer of manmade civilization."[73] In the twentieth century, too, a deep hostility toward modernity, toward "civilization" itself, would provide the rationale for a "spectacle of masculine power" of which its forbears could scarcely have dreamed.

As a virile community or order, the SS had two important precursors. The first was the Youth Movement or *Wandervögel* (Roamers), who flourished during the two decades preceding World War I and incorporated Volkish concerns about the shallowness of liberal bourgeois society and Germanic racial unity. "In a very real sense," Robert G. L. Waite points out, "there was no single German Youth Movement—there were dozens of separate groups which display a bewildering complexity and a range of programs which included everything from open homosexuality and sexual excess to extreme self-abnegation; from vegetarianism to epicurianism; from atheism to religious fanaticism; and from pacifism to folkish nationalism."[74] Notwithstanding its heterogeneity, there remained, says Mosse, a "note of physical and emotional toughness [which] permeated the ideal of the Youth Movement and helped shape the concepts of physical beauty which, in turn, were given functional roles in the ideal of German youth."[75] With its *Führer* cult, its glorification of pure action for its own sake, and its doctrine of the *Volk*, the *Wandervögel* constituted a reservoir of recruitment into the Free Corps legions of 1919–1920 and later the SA and the SS. The Free Corps, in turn, provided a charismatic model of "masculine power" for the postwar nazified youth groups. Gerhard Rossbach, a sadist, murderer, homosexual, and one of the two most admired heroes of nationalist German youth, puts it bluntly: "We purged from the old established youth movement all purely intellectual elements and attracted all the most activistic elements around us." The elite Storm Troopers gave preference to former athletes.[76]

Ernst Jünger, commander of a Storm Battalion during the First World War and, in his later writings, the great glorifier of the Free Corps mentality, described his comrades as endowed with an "insatiable restlessness, a determination to burn themselves out; they felt the primeval male urge permanently to court danger."[77] These were the "unknown, crazy fighters" many postwar youth would worship as "the very type and model of a soldierly dare-devil (Draufgänger)."[78] As Höhne puts it: "Himmler's elitist Order offered these men a real home."[79]

Although less important than racial doctrine, the athletic ideal had a useful function within the SS mentality. It was practical: boxing and jiu-jitsu, said Hitler, make the man.[80] It was a perfect vehicle for racial aesthetics. And it provided a stylish way to demonstrate the dynamic essence of the killer. At the same time, it is important to recognize that the athletic ideal and the characterological ideal of the SS are not identical. This discrepancy can be traced to the inherent ambiguity of "hardness," of the cult of achievement, and of the Volkish concept of male beauty.

"Hardness" is ambiguous in that it may be directed inward or outward; that is to say, its demands may be inflicted on the self or others. In the case of the athlete, the martyrdom of hardness is suffered alone; interaction with others takes the form of competition rather than annihilation. In the case of the SS warrior, hardness means submersion in a suffering which legitimates the cruelties inflicted on others. Here we encounter an intoxicated sadism which does not belong to the athlete's emotional repertory.

"Achievement" (Leistung) is ambiguous in that its meaning may be primarily subjective or objective. As Buchheim and Höhne point out, the doctrine of "heroic realism," derived from Jünger's philosophy of war by SS-Obergruppenführer Werner Best, produced a fighter who "was not merely a moralist in his own way but also an extreme individualist, even a subjectivist"; he is therefore "an independent personality, a true subjectivist responsible only to himself."[81] Such subjectivism is also characteristic of the high-performance athlete. The SS fighter, on the other hand, is essentially an organization man who is not entitled to formulate the meaning of his own deeds. The ordeal which the self voluntarily undergoes is finally claimed by the bureaucracy to which fealty is sworn. This is not to say that a subjective auto-intoxication cannot find a place within a bureaucracy like the SS. "The extreme subjectivism of the heroic fighter, who regarded any objective purpose as a matter of unimportance, can be made to serve any end whatsoever, always provided that care is taken to provide adequate subjective salve for the hero's conscience."[82] The conscience of the athlete, however, is rarely surrendered to the authority of a bureaucracy and its ideology.

Finally, there is an important ambiguity which inheres in the idealized male body itself. As George Mosse has pointed out, the "Aryan" concept of male beauty "combined ideas taken from racial thought, an idealization of ancient Germanic strength, and echoes of the Greek ideal of physical beauty. It exalted a primitive strength, which, as we have seen, often acquired a twist of cruelty; while the Greek ideal of bodily proportions supplied an indispensable harmony to the Germanic form."[83] This combination of "Germanic strength" and "the Greek ideal of physical beauty" is an unstable one. The first element suggests dynamism and the aggressiveness which is its ideological corollary; the second suggests stasis and the tranquil lunacy of racial aesthetics. The essence of SS athleticism is neither, but rather a reciprocal relationship between a mentality which points to an ideal body and this body, which points back in turn to a characterological ideal implying the dynamic, psychopathic muscularity which is capable of "unparalleled hardness." For it is the triumph of racialism to reduce character to flesh.

The Paratrooper as Fascist Para-Athlete. In April 1961, as the Algerian calamity moved France to the brink of civil war, the loyal citizens of Paris gazed anxiously up at the skies for signs of *les paras,* the notorious airborne commandos who were rumored to be on the way from Algiers. How, General de Gaulle's government asked itself, could French civilians defend themselves against a legendary corps of paratroopers? "A few hundred men were hastily assembled in the courtyard of the Ministry of the Interior and provided with ferocious-looking helmets, an assortment of ill-fitting uniforms and vintage guns. The photos of that scene portray a tragicomic eagerness and vast confusion. Fortunately, this improvisation did not have to meet the test of history."[84]

The "test of history" in this case would have been the dreaded confrontation with a warrior caste, a "sect" which has been expertly interpreted by one of its former members. The *parachutiste* we meet in the pages of Gilles Perrault's account is a being in whom the generic temperaments of "youth," "fascism," and the sportive type coincide. "Nos paras," an officer told his men in 1957. "En faire des véritables hommes: sains, sportifs, humains, bien élevés."[85] The paratrooper is what may be called a para-athlete: a man of action who, like a fighter pilot or an explorer, is charged by society with a serious mission, but whose style of action prominently includes both athletic and aggressive components which lend a sportive aspect to his feats.

Perrault's meditation on the paratrooper mentality, which is nothing less than an ethos, a world of its own, is an exemplary dissection of a sportive temperament (indeed, of its most significant historical form) into its psychological, sociological, and political factors. Perrault's point of departure is the wave of adolescent violence which took on worldwide dimensions during the late 1950s. From this "rebellion with a cause" he derives a basic character type—the adolescent male—for whom ideas of class consciousness or family loyalty pale when matched against the one thing which really matters: "the taste for violent action and for risk" acted out within the fraternal order of the "gang" (clan). Perrault's prototypical young male is not, however, an insensate thug; he is rather a "privileged and intolerable being whose vigorous body is poised for action and whose head is filled with vast projects"; he sees himself "as a unique being, irreplaceable, profoundly original."[86] He is, in short, a young, volatile, and politically unformed militant in search of a role.

Perrault's most interesting proposal, however, is that the violent idealism of this sportive militancy is not politically unformed at all. There is, he states, a political ethos which signifies both "the festival of youth" and "the festival of the body"—fascism.[87] "In the simplicity of the commands and imperatives of Hitler's nazism, in the romanticism of the adventure of war and death, in a vitalism which deifies impulse at the expense of reflection, in the cult of hardness, the love of tumult, the visionary, and the collective, in the communion with nature and the out-of-doors, there is a natural conformity with the essential outlines of adolescent psychology. One could say without exaggeration that there exists, between youth and national socialism, a kind of pre-established harmony."[88]

Many observers have commented on the emergence of a hard, "male" style in fascist Europe. Robert Paxton has noted the appearance of this style in France during the period of Nazi occupation: "Never had so many Frenchmen been ready to accept discipline and authority. A kind of jack-booted toughness had been part of the Fascist Leagues' appeal to the young in the 1930's, and a cult of outdoorsy muscularity was already a form of youthful rebellion against the Third Republic. 'Thanks to us, the France of camping, of sports, of dances, of voyages, of collective hiking will sweep away the France of aperitifs, of tobacco dens, of party congresses, and long digestions.' Cultists of virility like Henry de Montherlant renewed the call for spartan values."[89] The cult of hardness, of *la dureté*, was a specifically fascist style; what Bruce Mazlish has called "the psychological appeal of Marxism's steellike quality" is a generically different appeal which is based upon an intellectual or doctrinal hardness which, while it may well lead to emotional hardness, is not a cult of emotional hardness *per se*.[90] The fascist cult of hardness, on the other hand, bypasses the intellectual stage altogether. This is not to say that Marxism does not draw in its own way upon the aggressive instincts which fascism treats as the source of male virtue: "Indeed, Marxism is far from being unwarlike, unheroic, tenderhearted, philanthropic. But it will never become an ideology of victors, of heroes, of the hard, of the young."[91]

The disturbing feature of Sheldon's typology of "temperaments"—disturbing, at any rate, to a culture raised on the universal anthropology of Freud—is its almost racialistic differentiation of human types. Every such characterology retains an odor of the primitive, of interpreted stigmata and the dooming of misshapen souls; and it is precisely this odor, and the merciless dichotomy which emits it, which calls forth from Perrault's *parachutiste* a fanatical allegiance. "The first jump is a rendezvous the young soldier has with himself. He is going to find himself facing his own truth. At the conclusion of this test, he will be classed among the men or among the others. . . . He can refuse the opportunity of discovering his own intimate value, in which case he will dissolve into the asexual mass of all those who do not know if they are really men." The *para* "knows that at the stage of the jump a *race* is formed."[92]

But the ethos of the paratrooper is more than an intimate communion with the state of his maleness—it is, as well, a fearsome doctrine which exterminates in accordance with the dictates of its own "racialism," its inherent aesthetic:

On one side, force and beauty, purity; on the other, the obese ones and skinny ones, the aperitif drinkers, men who are vile and impure.

Here is where Dachau and Buchenwald, Maidanek and Ravensbrück begin.

For those who *live* the fascist glory cannot help but profoundly despise, and despise *physically*, those who stagnate in the somber valleys of life, the old ones, the ugly ones, the ones who would never march thirty kilometers at a stretch, who would never jump with a parachute, the ones who think, gossip, and have it easy—the subhumans.[93]

There is, however, another dichotomy as profound as that which divides the parachutists from the nonparachutists, and that is the ideological divide which separates those who jump for mundane reasons from those for whom parachuting is a cult of the masculine spirit. Perrault says:

> To jump with a parachute, it is both necessary and sufficient to make the same movement as is required for descending a flight of stairs. The rest follows of itself. . . . here, then, is one of the simplest of exercises and one which does not require any character resources which are out of the ordinary. For the Soviets, parachuting is, moreover, a mass sport practiced by hundreds of thousands of young people who jump on a regular basis without making anything of it.
> But, as is the case for so many things, one finds in the act of parachuting what one chooses to bring to it. One can choose to make it into a banal sporting exercise. But one may also decide that it will be the test on the basis of which humanity will be divided into two categories: those who jump and those who don't.

In their "banal" quest for an activity with both recreative and military value, the Soviets turn parachuting into a profane, as opposed to a cultic, practice. The difference, according to Perrault, is that, while the civilian jumper may choose to disengage himself from the challenge at any time, his military counterpart faces certain disgrace—and the calvary of the pariah—if he loses his nerve at the last moment. Ideological differentiation in this sphere turns on a crucial point of interpretation, and the same principle applies to the body itself. It may, says Perrault, be interpreted (by sportsmen) as an instrument, as a means to another end; or the exercising of the body may be interpreted as "an intimate matter: each discovers therein his own truth. The body is deified. It is the criterion of all superiority."[94]

Yukio Mishima: The Fascist as Body-Builder. The literary apotheosis of the fascist cult of the body is Yukio Mishima's *Sun and Steel* (1970), an elegant and deeply pathetic treatise and memoir on body-building by the gifted Japanese novelist whose ritual suicide in November 1970—the last gesture of a political reactionary's despair—achieved worldwide publicity. Mishima's body-consciousness is pathetic because it represents a desperate attempt to smother the mental agonies which attended his literary gift: a counteraesthetic he consciously opposed to the literary aesthetic which made him suffer. On the altar of the body Mishima offered the sacrifice of both his art and the very individuality whose natural expression that art had been. That he ended by fashioning a literary masterpiece out of his obsession with muscles is a comment on the inevitability of his tragic development.

Mishima's career as an extraordinary type of sportsman began as a decision to leave behind the complications of mind and language so that he might find an essentially monotonic consciousness of beauty—and surcease: "since my own, abnormal bodily existence was doubtless a product of the intellectual corrosion of words, the ideal body—the ideal existence—must, I told myself, be absolutely free from any interference by words. Its characteristics could be summed up as taciturnity and beauty of form." Possessed by a heroic imagination, Mishima sought a style which, while hardly "somatotonic" in temperament, shares with somatotonia the fascist's unquestioning acceptance of the authority of the body:

> Somewhere within me, I was beginning to plan a union of art and life, of style and the ethos of action. If style was similar to muscles and patterns of behavior, then its function was obviously to restrain the wayward imagination. Any truths that might be overlooked as a result were no concern of mine. Nor did I care one jot that the fear and horror of confusion and ambiguity eluded my style. I had made up my mind that I would select only one particular truth, and avoid aiming at any all-inclusive truth. Enervating, ugly truths I ignored; by means of a process of diplomatic selection within the spirit, I sought to avoid the morbid influence exerted on men by indulgence in the imagination.[95]

Much as Perrault offers a triangular unity composed of the body, fascism, and adolescence, so Mishima conjoins the body with the hero and the group. His notion of the hero, as we see in the following passage, reiterates his rejection of mind: "the conditions necessary for becoming a hero must be both a ban on originality and a true faithfulness to a classical model; unlike the words of a genius, the words of a hero must be selected as the most impressive and noble from among ready-made concepts. And at the same time they, more than any other words, constitute a splendid language of the flesh." The hero "speaks" through the flesh: "For the cult of the hero is, ultimately, the basic principle of the body . . ." And it is flesh which conjoins the hero and the group: "The intuition of my infancy—the intuitive sense that the group represented the principle of the flesh—was correct." If the group represents "the principle of the flesh," then it is the siren song of the flesh which calls on Mishima to give up his very self: "Only through the group, I realized—through sharing the suffering of the group—could the body reach that height of existence that the individual alone could never attain. And for the body to reach that level at which the divine might be glimpsed, a dissolution of the individuality was necessary." For the sacrifice of his individuality, Mishima is granted a para-athletic identity which makes possible a glimpse of the divine: "The group must be open to death—which meant, of course, that it must be a community of warriors." "The goal of my life was to acquire all the various attributes of the warrior."[96]

Mishima's fantasy of the warrior and his heroic torso is hardly unique. The remarkable feature of his doctrine of the well-developed body is the precise description of its rationale, which is both anti-intellectual and mystical. When has the house of intellect been renounced so tranquilly and so convincingly? When has the body taken such elegant revenge upon the mind, and in the language of the mind itself?

The ideological significance of Mishima's inspired tract lies in its equating of style with musculature. Only the fascist can hear—let alone accept—the "language of the flesh." By the same token, only the fascist (among the political types) can find nirvana through the suppression of mind. Communism, as Hans Buchheim points out, overburdens the minds of those it holds in thrall; but it does not lower itself to the point of substituting muscle for mind. For Marxists, who condemn themselves (and others) to live out "the pathos of the Enlightenment," this is an unthinkable heresy. For them, the musculature is an instrument. It cannot be a source, because it is reified instinct, or—at best—a metaphor of instinct.

Mishima is, therefore, a sportive temperament, if virtually *sui generis*. His uniqueness lies not in the choice of a physical style, but in the refinement with which the choice was made. He is also unique in the pathos which attended his cultic devotion to the development of the body: "The exercise of the muscles elucidated the mysteries that words had made." A literary genius substituted for mind the musculature which signifies dumbness, for it is "a special property of muscles that they [feed] the imagination of others while remaining totally devoid of imagination themselves." And worst of all: "[W]hat I found in muscles [was] the triumph of knowing that one was the same as others."[97] In the end, Mishima entered into the sinews of his body so as not to be alone.

Sport and the Left Intellectuals

Is the Marxist tradition somehow hostile to sport? However improbable this may seem, there is both anecdotal and doctrinal evidence which suggests that the enormous successes of Communist sport establishments are at variance with a long-standing disdain for sport which appears, or is referred to, with conspicuous frequency in the political literature of the Left. What follows is an attempt to document and explain an elusive bias which certain French leftists of the 1960s, newly awakened to the possibilities presented by a radical critique of sport, condemned as *le gauchisme anti-sport*.[98]

This bias, which has usually taken the form of a principled neglect, is by no means unique to Marxists. The American sport historian Allen Guttmann has pointed, and with good reason, to "that instinctive dislike of physical activity which has traditionally characterized a number of intellectuals."[99] What is more, this peculiar warp in the sociology of knowledge has acquired a reputation of its own. The French sporting newspaper *L'Equipe* once claimed that French failures in sport could be ascribed in part to "the defeatism of the so-called enlightened intellectual circles,"[100] and this idea may have some merit. "Remember, gentlemen," the legendary French teacher Alain once told his pupils, "that each true idea is a rejection of the human body."[101] Hostility to the body has not been monopolized by the intellectual Left. Rather, left-wing intellectuals have, for discernible reasons, been strikingly consistent in their bias.

On at least two occasions Communist parties have been accused by their own members of neglecting sport. At the conclusion of the 1924 Paris Olympiad, the French Communist party (PCF) daily *L'Humanité* complained that the party was overlooking the political importance of sport. "It is time that it renounce this attitude and open its major publications to the preoccupations which at this very moment are absorbing the attention of millions of young men around the world."[102] Forty years later the same complaint appeared in, of all places, the German Democratic Republic, long after the intensive development of sport in the GDR had begun (see chapter 9). When in 1964 an East German sport historian was permitted—for the first and last time—to publish an essay in the official philosophical journal of the GDR, he took the opportunity to criticize his fellow Marxist-Leninists for their lack of interest in sport.[103]

As we have already seen in chapters 2 and 3, Marxian thought does not lend itself to sportive themes. As John McMurtry has pointed out, sexuality and play—in a word, the province of the body—are themes about which "Marx says very little and, furthermore, he talks of the former only in terms of species-reproductive acts, and the latter only in terms of constructive leisure. Though his narrowness of purview here may be by constraint of his era, which tended to regard eros and playfulness as wicked, we judged this narrowness to be a cardinal limitation of his concept of man."[104] As devoted a Marxist as Sebastiano Timpanaro makes the same point: "Physical and biological nature is certainly not denied by Marx, but it constitutes more a prehistoric antecedent to human history than a reality which still limits and conditions man." The result of this attitude has been neglect of "that biological nature of man which Marxism, and particularly contemporary Marxism, tends to disregard."[105] If Marxism ignores the issue of human physical limits (or what Timpanaro, with unsportive pathos, calls "man's biological frailty"), it can hardly be expected to show much interest in the symbolic contests which challenge them.

The most important factor underlying the antisportive attitude of the Left is the sheer intellectualism which characterizes the Marxist tradition and which differentiates it, as an ideology, from fascist thought.[106] The "psychological appeal of Marxism's steellike quality" derives from the apparent rigor and consistency of its intellectual procedures. The Marxist dialectician does not share the fascist's "self-image as a man impervious to rational conviction";[107] whereas the fascist finds virility in an immunity to reason, the Marxist finds it in the training of rational faculties which aim for an intellectual, rather than physical, superiority. When R. Palme Dutt, a founder and for many years the leading theoretician of the British Communist party, was asked by the *International Who's Who* to list his leisure interests, his reply was "anything except sports."[108] As "an ideologue of Jesuit-like subtlety," and "the scholastic rationalizer of the Kremlin's decrees,"[109] Dutt simply had more urgent matters to attend to. The same attitude could be found in the European workers' sport movements of the twenties and thirties: "For a variety of reasons the labour movement had initially been reluctant to deal with sports. Workers had more important things to do than engage in such frivolous pursuits. . . . Workers would do better to make use of movement libraries and improve themselves intellectually even if those who did seldom read what the theoreticians prescribed." As a result, Robert Wheeler has pointed out, "the compulsory political lecture or discussion at the outset of a practice . . . probably had a way of repelling the very people the movement was seeking desperately to attract, namely the young."[110]

Not all Socialist intellectuals succumbed to the temptation to dismiss sport as politically innocuous. Fritz Wildung, leader of the German workers' sport movement, ascribes this particular myopia to the "historical conditions" which had formed the Socialist movement in Germany: "A political party is an intellectual [geistige] movement; it appeals naturally to the alliance and to the feelings of the masses, not to the muscles. There are, of course, people and parties which are only too happy to appeal to the muscles in the political arena, but that usually results from an intellectual deficiency."[111] The Social Democratic party, having ignored muscles, had arrived late, but not too late. Wildung's Socialist contemporary Helmut Wagner equated a "deficient understanding of sport" with a "deficient understanding of proletarian reality."[112] This is advanced thinking for its time (1931). During the 1920s, Trotsky, too, had acknowledged a "proletarian reality" which party intellectuals could not simply tamper with at will. The state, he warns in 1923, "must use great caution in its incursions into family life; it must exercise great tact and moderation . . ." Similarly, and more to Wagner's point, Trotsky asserts that the "longing for amusement, distraction, sight-seeing, and laughter is the most legitimate desire of human nature." The dream of creating an artificial "proletarian culture" had foundered.[113] The Left would have to take "proletarian reality" as it found it.

The picture which emerges is one of neglect, even to the point that one British Marxist, apparently unaware of a half-century of Marxist sport theory, has recently chided the Left both for its neglect of a (potentially) important issue and for its attachment to preconceived ideas about the invidious political consequences of having an interest in sport. Ralph Miliband asserts that "there is an important amount of what might be described as cultural fall-out from the sports industry and spectator involvement. The nature of this fall-out is not quite as obviously negative as Marxists are often tempted to assume. The subject lends itself to simplistic and prim-sounding attitudes, which are often over-compensated by hearty demagogic-populist ones. In fact, the sport culture deserves, from the point of view of the making and unmaking of class-consciousness, much more attention than it has received." This issue will not, however, be getting the necessary attention from Miliband: "The elaboration of a Marxist sociology of sport may not be the most urgent of theoretical tasks; but it is not the most negligible of tasks either."[114] As we shall see, the task of creating a critical Marxist theory of sport was left primarily to young Marxist radicals in France and West Germany, whose period of intense activity dates from 1968.

Apart from neglect, intellectuals are sometimes vulnerable to an automatic, even visceral, dislike of athletics *per se*. This hostility appears on the Left in two forms which correspond to the pre- and postfascist eras, respectively. The first is a reflexive prudishness with psychopathological overtones. Lenin's friend and chronicler Nikolay Valentinov recalls the chaste disapproval of a political colleague named Alexander:

> There were things in my room which made him turn away with unconcealed disgust: heavy dumb-bells and weights. He was unable to understand how a man calling himself a Social Democrat, or simply any intelligent man, could take any interest in athletics, in such rough 'circus' business as weightlifting. In his opinion such a man could not be a serious revolutionary. 'Read through the biographies of all the famous revolutionaries in the world and you won't find a single one who would even have thought of swinging dumb-bells.' Once, when he found *Thus Spake Zarathustra* on my table, Alexander asked me: 'Do you read even this?' and gingerly, as if it were an obscene book, he pushed it away. To tease him I started to tell him that there was a chapter in Nietzsche all about people like him: 'Of the despisers of the body.' He undoubtedly despised the body.[115]

It should be remembered that this mentality would eventually make a career for itself in the Soviet Union after 1934 in the form of Zhdanovism, the official aesthetic doctrine of the Stalinist period usually referred to as Socialist Realism: "here, the body and its innate drives disappear from Soviet Marxist aesthetics altogether, sublimated into a spirituality worthy of the Counter-Reformation itself."[116] Stalinist political culture actually includes two ideologies of the body: Zhdanovism represses it in the name of an antisexual puritanism, while Stakhanovism industrializes it in the name of heroic labor. It is for this reason that, in his classic anti-Stalinist novel *Darkness at Noon* (1941), Arthur Koestler gives the body itself a prominent role as the repository of conscience and decency, while at the same time making it the symbolic victim of Stalinist sadism.

The second type of hostility to the athletic body is a more sophisticated critique which responds directly to the fascist cult of the body. This attitude is prevalent among the Frankfurt Marxists. Leo

Lowenthal castigates "the morally insensate body-beautiful ideal of the racial hero."[117] "Physical exercises," Herbert Marcuse growled at a Hegel Congress in 1970, "the very word contains so much repression it makes you shudder."[118] Max Horkheimer and Theodor Adorno offer a complex, but finally contemptuous, meditation on the body in the form of an examination of civilization and the discontent which results from its impossible relationship to the body:

> The love of nature and destiny expressed in totalitarian propaganda is simply a veiled reaction to failed civilization. Men cannot escape from their body and sing its praises when they cannot destroy it. The "tragic" philosophy of the Fascist is the ideological party which precedes the real blood wedding. Those who extolled the body above all else, the gymnasts and scouts, always had the closest affinity with killing, just as the lovers of nature are close to the hunter. They see the body as a moving mechanism, with joints as its components and flesh to cushion the skeleton. They use the body and its parts as though they were already separated from it. Jewish tradition contains a disinclination to measure man with a foot-rule because the corpse is measured in this way for the coffin. This is what the manipulators of the body enjoy. They measure others, without realizing it, with the gaze of a coffin maker. They betray themselves when they speak the result: they call men tall, short, fat or heavy. They are interested in illness and at mealtimes already watch for the death of those who eat with them, and their interest is only thinly rationalized by concern for their health.[119]

This argument combines a theory of fascism's inherent necrophilia with a Freudian interpretation of musculature. Philip Rieff looks at "totalitarian ceremonial" as an essentially muscular "aesthetic experimentalism on the level of mass politics": "Coordinated movement—marching, saluting, chanting in unison—expresses the muscular imagination of the garrison state's ceremonial forms. A rhythm is a promise and, as such, a full alternative to political rhetoric. It moves the subject from one state of feeling to another. There remains only to notice that Freud thought that the aesthetics of muscular movement must always describe the movement from life toward death. The musculature, he wrote, was the origin of death."[120] Jewish tradition, the influence of Freud, and disgust with the fascist cult of musculature coalesce into an essentially anticorporeal doctrine. In Germany, as these German Jews were surely aware, the cultic—even anthropological—approach to the gymnastically trained body dates back to the mid-nineteenth-century doctrine of Friedrich Ludwig Jahn, which—its friendly reception in East Germany notwithstanding—is a fascist precursor if only because of its mystical and racialistic elements. Thus, for the Frankfurt group, the very worst aspects of *Deutschtum* were already visible in an exaltation of the muscular body ante-dating the rise of Hitler. The next step was to view fascism itself as the ultimate doctrine of the body.

Virility and the Left

"Fascist ritual," as Adrian Lyttelton has put it, "can be read at one level as a complex of virility symbols." As we have seen, the Marxists' renunciation of "political athleticism" signifies, in addition, a rejection of fascist virility, the extreme example of what Marcuse calls "false virility."[121] Sartre, for example, openly cedes to the fascists that doctrine of "the aristocracy of the body" which manifests itself as a flaunting, aggressively physical style. Sartre's friend Maurice Merleau-Ponty writes condescendingly of "the pitiable joy of being strong."[122] Marxists, in a word, have tended to flaunt not the body, but the mind. Henri Lefebvre's claim (in 1946) that "Only Reason is virile!" is symptomatic in this respect, recalling Trotsky's reference to "the physical power of thought."[123] Sartre's statement (in 1965) that "We must find a rational violence" calls implicitly for an alternative to fascist violence: "fascism," he once said, "is not defined by the number of its victims, but by the way it kills them," an idea which partakes of what David Caute has called "the comforting notion that the Right traditionally resorted to murder because the Left had a monopoly of intelligence."[124] Fascist virility, in short, is a sadistic virility. But is there another ideologically specific virility to be found on the Left?

"There are times," Raymond Aron writes, "when one wonders whether the myth of the Revolution is not indistinguishable from the Fascist cult of violence."[125] This is an interesting point. Is what Renee Winegarten has called "the cult of the tough proletarian" so different from the cult of the fascist tough? What about Sartre's fascination with revolutionary violence and the attraction of "dirty hands"?[126] Or the "eroticism of masculine virility," the "embryo of fascist romanticism" found in poems by the left-wing W. H. Auden?[127]

The case of Sartre is particularly instructive and illustrates the subtle ideological differences which make Aron's suggestion finally untenable. When Simone de Beauvoir—who once criticized Sartre for ignoring his body—told him that his *oeuvre* contained "traces of *macho*, even of phallocracy," his reply was: ". . . I did not assume that my *macho* arose from the fact that I was male. I took it to be a characteristic trait of mine."[128] Sartre concedes that "ferocious air" to the Italian fascist without one iota of envy or regret; his personal style completely eschewed the physical effluvium of manhood so prevalent on the Right. At the same time, Sartre turns on its head the myth of what George Orwell called "the pansy Left." In his novella "The Childhood of a Leader" (1939) and in "What Is a Collaborator?" (1945), Sartre gives the fascist personality a homosexual core. Despite his long career as a fellow-traveler with Stalinism, Castroism, and Maoism, Sartre was never feminized in the manner of a Robert Brasillach, even if—as Jean Plumyène has pointed out[129]— there are some interesting similarities between them.

The fascist critique of the physically deficient Left intellectual exploits an older stereotype of the decorporealized radical. Alberto Moravia offers the following portrait: "Quadri's anti-fascism, his unwarlike, unhealthy, unattractive appearance, his learning, his books, everything about him went to make up in Marcello's mind the conventional picture, continually pointed at in scorn by Party propaganda, of the negative, impotent intellectual."[130] "I despised the sloppiness of the Leftists," says Drieu la Rochelle, "their scornful attitude toward any sort of pride to be taken in the body."[131] Roland Barthes offers a lucid analysis of this mentality in "Poujade and the Intellectuals":

> . . . it is through his corporeal mediocrity that the intellectual is condemned: Mendès-France looks like 'a bottle of Vichy water' (double scorn, addressed to water and to dyspepsia). Sheltering in the hypertrophy of a fragile and useless head, the entire intellectual being is stricken by the gravest of physical flaws, *fatigue* (corporeal substitute for decadence): though idle, he is congenitally exhausted, just as the Poujadist, though hard-working, is always fresh and ready. We touch here upon the profound idea of any morality of the human body: the idea of race. The intellectuals are one race, the Poujadists are another.[132]

Oswald Mosley, too, makes a point of insulting the physiques of politicians who are more "heavily middle-aged"—and more successful—than himself.[133] In the last analysis, fascist contempt for the decorporealized leftist signifies a nostalgia for racial purity combined with a nostalgia for the asceticism of Sparta, its dooming of deformed infants, its merciless ethos of war.

What Marx Did Not Know

"A certain manichaeism of reactionary origin," Jean Duvignaud writes in 1956, "situates 'amusement' on the right, while it situates thought, and therefore boredom, on the left."[134] In one sense, this "manichaeism" is one form of the aristocratic, or religious, anti-utilitarianism of Ortega or Josef Pieper. It stamps the Left as terminally ascetic and, therefore, terminally dull. But it is important to remember that essentially the same indictment has often been directed at the Left by Marxists who recognized both the limitations of Marxist thought and the tactical propaganda failures such limitations produced, particularly during the Stalinist period. "A curse upon all Marxists," Trotsky writes, "and upon those who want to bring dryness and hardness into all the relations of life."[135]

Viewed in retrospect, Trotsky's analyses of the various aspects, and even the minutiae, of everyday life suggest the inevitability of his rupture with Stalin, who did not always wait until his opponents (e.g., the kulaks) had been properly seduced by cunningly formulated appeals. Trotsky placed a much greater emphasis on such appeals, although his writings are vitiated in part by a naive optimism which history has thoroughly discredited—his claim (in 1924) that democracy and the Soviet dictatorship "drove the unconscious out of politics" is a case in point.[136] Despite such ambitious gaffes, Trotsky did not succumb totally to the euphoric, and often dogmatic, collectivistic ideal of the early Bolshevik period. "Human psychology," he writes in 1923, "is very conservative by nature";[137] it is self-defeating to ignore the inertia of tradition and habit. At the same time, Trotsky's approach to what he calls "meaningless ritual" is essentially hostile, a combination of paternalism and utopianism. We shall encounter Trotsky's views on the body in a later chapter.

The rise of nazism made the whole area of irrational appeals, and their political exploitation, an urgent matter. The Left in general, however, was unprepared. The Marxist intellectual Ernst Bloch writes in 1930 that "the vulgar Marxists are not keeping watch on what is happening to primitive and utopian trends. The Nazis are already occupying this territory, and it will be an important one."[138] Marxism had always been hostile to the idea of a timeless "human nature,"[139] and now the resulting psychological shortcomings, both theoretical and tactical, attracted a lot of attention. The problem for

Marxist thinking was human irrationality. "For Marx," as David Caute has pointed out, "irrationality was a symptom of the decadence and desperation of a declining ruling class; for those who . . . continued to carry the torch of an earlier Enlightenment, irrationality represented a kind of innate mental curse comparable to the Calvinists' conception of original sin."[140] "I know full well the clarity of diagnosis the communists have," Harold Laski writes in 1937, "I admire their courage and their devotion. But they are often bad psychologists."[141]

In 1934 the renegade psychoanalyst Wilhelm Reich offered his fellow Communists a morale-boosting thought in the wake of Hitler's decimation of the German Left: "The juvenile tendency toward bondage to leaders and ideas is politically nonspecific; it can be exploited either way. . . . Love of sport, the attraction of men in military uniforms (which please the girls, and vice versa), marching songs, etc., are generally, under the conditions obtaining in the proletarian movement today, antirevolutionary factors because the political reaction has far greater possibilities of satisfying the demands they create. Football, in particular, has a directly depoliticizing effect and encourages the reactionary tendencies of youth. Yet these tendencies are, in principle, reversible, i.e., they can be used to the advantage of the Left . . ."[142]

Reich's proposal overlooks, however, a historical fact of real consequence. The Communists and, in particular, the Social Democrats had abundant opportunities during the 1920s to "satisfy the demands" for sport, choir singing, and other activities favored by German youth. But the popular culture served up by the Social Democrats—prominently including an antibourgeois sport movement—had not been able to hold its own against the appeals of "bourgeois" entertainments. Had Reich actually studied the reception of Socialist popular culture, he might have reconsidered the "political nonspecificity" of irrational appeals. That he apparently did not is curious in light of the fact that his well-known *Mass Psychology of Fascism* (1933) spends a good deal of time taking "vulgar Marxists" and the revolutionary movement in general to task for their ignorance of nonrational appeals. Yet even here Reich demonstrates a naive persistence in the idea that such "tendencies are, in principle, reversible" and convertible to exploitation by the Left. This notion of the political neutrality of popular culture is evident in the following passage, which also mentions sport: "Freed of its bonds and directed into the channels of the freedom movement's rational goals, the psychic energy of the average mass of people excited over a football game or laughing over a cheap musical would no longer be capable of being fettered."[143] Reich does not perceive an incompatibility between nonrational appeals and the Marxist project; it does not occur to him that such a strategy "threatens to paralyze the functioning of Marxist thought."

The German Socialists' attitudes toward nonrational appeals have been examined more empirically by George Mosse in his study of the "national liturgy" which developed in Germany during the nineteenth century. Festivals, male choir societies, sharpshooting societies, and gymnastic associations constituted "a familiar and congenial tradition" upon which the Nazi ceremonial style would eventually build, but which Socialist leaders were understandably reluctant to embrace. Rationalistic in outlook and hostile to the cultic nationalism associated with such liturgy, they tended to resist the use of myths and symbols as a political strategy even if they were tempted:

> The urge toward liturgy, however, remained only an urge and certainly never dominated the workers' movement. The French 'Society for People's Festivals' produced a 'hymn to reason,' but it was, naturally, the rational component of Socialism which proved hostile to such festivals. It may well be significant that in 1927 some five hundred rank-and-file members of the Social Democratic and Communist parties rejected all religious liturgy, though some had remained members of a Christian Church. None of these Socialists showed any sensitivity toward the psychological structure of liturgy. . . . Still, on the right we find a general appreciation of liturgical forms and no segment would have lacked sensitivity toward its psychological application. They did not suffer from such a handicap.[144]

Henning Eichberg, while confirming that German Social Democrats and Communists did not exploit liturgical speech forms, makes it clear, however, that the workers' sport movement did demonstrate an awareness of nonrational appeals. "This 'new festival culture' was regarded as one aspect of a 'socialist shaping of feeling' which was contrasted with the 'overestimation of formal knowledge.'" The workers' Olympiads of 1925 and 1931, he says, represented nothing less than a "cultic exaltation of sport" which pointed forward to the pageantry of the Berlin Olympiad of 1936.[145]

A systematic inventory of Marxist culture's failed appeals to the nonrational dimensions of human experience is among the unaccomplished major works of our century. This is the larger context in which Marxist "renunciation of the body" finds its place. At the origin of these failures is the sociologism bequeathed by Marx to his inheritors. As Wilhelm Reich puts it in 1933: "The character structure of active man, the so-called 'subjective factor of history' in Marx's sense, remained uninvestigated because Marx was a sociologist and not a psychologist, and because at that time scientific psychology did not exist."[146] As a consequence, Melvin Rader points out, a long series of critics "have said that Marx was not sufficiently aware of the irrational elements in human motivation: folk traditions, nationalistic sentiments, racial prejudices, group neuroses, unconscious or semi-conscious impulses."[147] The long and often clumsy Soviet campaign against religion is one result—although Marx and Engels would certainly have criticized Lenin for his naive outrage.[148] As for Marxist aesthetics, even as sympathetic an observer as Henri Arvon acknowledges that it "shares the extreme intellectualism of Marxist doctrine as a whole and thus tends to be very stiff and wooden"[149]—unwilling, in short, to accommodate "bourgeois" notions of beauty which may well be fundamental experiences rather than secondary and perverse. One thinks of the musical asceticism which drove Lenin to foreswear the Beethoven sonatas he so much admired.[150]

How does the severely circumscribed character of so much Marxist thinking about basic human experiences bear on sport and the body? We have already seen that the renunciation of the body effectively precludes sportive imagery of both leadership and the state. We may also ask whether the psychologically complex appeal of athletic performance *per se* is susceptible to definition—and thus humane manipulation—by Marxist social engineers. For example, Havelock Ellis refers to "the sexual enjoyment aroused by the spectacles of graceful, skillful, or athletic movement" as *ergophily* (love of motion).[151] But is there a political grammar of movement any more than there is a political grammar of music? A mass gymnastics display is, to be sure, the corporeal chant of the body politic; but it has no ideological specificity. A Marxist society can neither name it nor abjure it.

Marxist objections to nonrational appeals are not, however, invariably naive. One example of a highly sophisticated argument in this vein is Roland Barthes's analysis of a popular French magazine's coverage of a voyage into darkest Africa undertaken by a young couple and their months-old baby, Bichon: "*Match* goes into ecstasy over the courage of all three."

Barthes's primary target in "Bichon and the Blacks" is the celebration of sham virility and false sport:

> First of all, nothing is more irritating than heroism with-
> out an object. A society is in a serious situation when it under-
> takes to develop gratuitously the *forms* of its virtues. If the
> dangers incurred by baby Bichon (torrents, wild animals, dis-
> eases, etc.) were real, it was literally stupid to impose them, on
> the mere pretext of doing some painting in Africa and satisfy-
> ing the dubious ambition of getting on canvas 'a debauch of
> sun and light': it is even more reprehensible to disguise this
> stupidity as a piece of bravery, all quite decorative and moving.
> We see how courage functions here: a formal and empty ac-
> tion, the more unmotivated it is, the more respect it inspires;
> this is a boy-scout civilization, where the code of feelings and
> values is completely detached from concrete problems of soli-
> darity or progress. What we have is the old myth of 'character',
> i.e., of 'training.' Bichon's exploits are of the same sort as the
> more spectacular feats of mountain climbing or balloon ascen-
> sion: demonstrations of an ethical order, which receive their
> final value only from the publicity they are given. In our cul-
> ture, there frequently corresponds to the socialized forms of
> collective sport a superlative form of star sport: here physical
> effort does not institute man's apprenticeship to his group, but
> instead an ethic of vanity, an exoticism of endurance, a minor
> mystique of risk, monstrously severed from any concern with
> sociability.[152]

Barthes's idiom is Marxist in its ideals ("solidarity," "progress")
and in its critical vocabulary ("myth," "mystique"). His objection to
this sort of adventure is Marxist in its utilitarian premise, in its hostility to action-as-display and to the meaningless risks which turn
out to be the "real" point of the entire enterprise. The "political athleticism" of the fascist is no more or less than "an ethic of vanity, an
exoticism of endurance, a minor mystique of risk." Small wonder
that elsewhere Barthes lights into Poujade and "the legend of his
own physical strength."[153] Once again we encounter that quintessentially Marxist proscription of narcissistic self-display. This is an important passage because it represents a point at which Marxist "naiveté" turns into a more precise kind of principled disapproval—in
this case, disapproval of a fraudulent public rite. Not all critiques of
nonrational appeals, after all, are of comparable quality: Lenin's critique of religion ("unutterable vileness") is likely to be inferior to

Barthes's critique of the publicity stunt, if only because religion is more complex than the appeal of adventure. Barthes's target is small—indeed, his objection is that much ado is made about nothing—while Marxist naiveté is quixotic in that it ignores the dimensions of, or challenges only weakly, the nonrational phenomena it denounces. Finally, Barthes criticizes not the origin of this kind of charisma (respect for courage *per se*), but its alleged perversion into the form of an unedifying spectacle.

5. From Amateurism to Nihilism: Sport, Cultural Conservatism, and the Critique of Modernity

Sport and the Intellectuals

In 1935 the (exiled) German sociologist Karl Mannheim published a volume titled *Man and Society in an Age of Reconstruction*. The purpose of this learned manifesto is twofold. First, it analyzes "the crisis of liberal democracy" (Mannheim watched the Weimar Republic fail) in an attempt to find "the various sociological factors which could explain why civilization is collapsing before our eyes." Second, it advocates the application of sophisticated social planning to the problems of the European democracies: "We have now reached a stage where we can imagine how to plan the best possible human types by deliberately reorganizing the various groups of social factors. . . . Even though much still remains obscure and very many assertions problematic, nevertheless this approach has reached such a point that we can, logically at least, foresee our goal, which is the planned guidance of people's lives on a sociological basis, and with the aid of psychology. In this way we are keeping in the foreground both the highest good of society and the peace of mind of the individual." One of Mannheim's topics is sport, described *inter alia* as a "centralized means of influencing human beings" which is capable of effecting "emotional integration on a large scale."[1]

The same year Mannheim's treatise was published, the Dutch historian and cultural critic Johan Huizinga gave an address in Brussels later published as the somber polemic *In the Shadow of Tomorrow* (1936), which directs yet another warning to contemporary Europe: "Everywhere there are doubts as to the solidity of our social structure, vague fears of the imminent future, a feeling that our civilization is on the way to ruin. . . . We see forms of government no longer capable of functioning, production systems on the verge of collapse, social forces gone wild with power. The roaring engine of this tremendous time seems to be heading for a breakdown." But if the indictments sound similar, the minds which formulated them are not. Huizinga refers disapprovingly to "the politically Left-thinking sociologist Karl Mannheim" as one who endorses "the amoral character of the State"² —a gross distortion of Mannheim's position which derives from the categorical nature of Huizinga's "Christian fatalism" (see discussion below). Huizinga does, however, agree with Mannheim that sport is relevant to the crisis of culture as a potential vehicle for social hygiene. To a much greater degree than his "Left-thinking" antagonist, Huizinga also interprets sport as an index of cultural health, as a type of social life which can assume perverse or healthy forms.

Mannheim and Huizinga are only two of many distinguished European intellectuals who offered public commentaries on the mass sport phenomenon of the 1920s and 1930s. For it was during the interwar period that sport emerged as nothing less than a modern style in which an ideologically diverse collection of temperaments found an issue of sociological significance and, in not a few cases, a locus of value in a value-starved world. During this period diagnoses of European civilization proliferated to the point that they came to constitute a virtual genre. If Spengler's *The Decline of the West* (1919)— which employs sportive imagery (see chapter 3)—and Freud's *Civilization and Its Discontents* (1930) are the best known of these analyses,³ there are a good number of lesser-known manifestos which mention sport with surprising frequency. Martin Heidegger, Max Scheler, Karl Jaspers, Gottfried Benn, Bertolt Brecht, Robert Musil, Georg Kaiser, Jean Prévost, Henry de Montherlant, Paul Morand, Pierre Drieu la Rochelle, Paul Valéry, José Ortega y Gasset, T. S. Eliot—all offer commentaries or remarks on the cultural significance of sport. Invariably, sport is seen as an index of, or as a curative for, the European crisis of values.

The response of the intellectuals to the prospect of salvation through the sportive body may, in turn, be counterpointed to a less cerebral, more passionate one which nevertheless represents a reaction to the same crisis. As Walter Laqueur points out, the members of the German youth movements of the first few decades of this century, the so-called *Wandervögel*, "did not read Marx and Kierkegaard, or even Tönnies and the vitalist philosophers; but they certainly felt some deep disquiet about the society in which they found themselves—the society of Wilhelmine Germany at the dawn of this century." Then and later during the Weimar Republic, "they did try spontaneously, if often awkwardly, to alter the human condition at a time when philosophers and sociologists were writing about the 'alienation of man,' the 'atomization of society,' the lessening of contact between human beings; when the anonymity and impersonality of life in modern societies, a loss of vitality in individuals and a growing social torpor, were already themes of contemporary social criticism." Laqueur juxtaposes the *Wandervogel* movement and the sport movement in Germany in the following way: the youth movement, he claims, "was wider in its appeal and more ambitious in its scope than a sports club. It was concerned with the whole human being, it stood for revival and reform, not merely in one particular section of life, but in life whole and entire."[4] It will be noted that Laqueur sees only the intellectually limited clientele of the *Sportsvereine*, the whole purpose of which was an unreflective indulgence in the pleasures of sport, while overlooking the sport-minded intelligentsia whose cultural concerns are at least as encompassing as those of the *Wandervögel*.

The critique of sport which emerged during this period is one facet of a general critique of bourgeois civilization. It should be emphasized, however, that the interpretations of the bourgeois crisis of values offered by the thinkers listed above actually constitute an ideological middle ground, from the eccentric Marxism of Brecht on the Left to the eccentric fascism of Drieu la Rochelle on the Right.[5] For there are actually four critiques of the European bourgeoisie at this time: a Marxist critique comprising Communist and Socialist positions; a fascist critique which originates in Italy and eventually becomes a pan-European ideology; the neoliberalism of Karl Mannheim emphasizing "rational social control"; and the cultural conservatism represented in its variants by Huizinga, Ortega, Benn, Eliot, and others. What is more, all four of these critiques employ sport as a metaphorical representation of culture.

It is easy to overlook the fact that the term "bourgeois" has not been exclusively an epithet of the Left. The Italian bourgeoisie, the (eventual) Fascist Enrico Corradini writes in 1903, are

the sink into which sentimental socialism drains. Their truths become the lies which socialism discards when it genuinely turns to action. Like some old sewage barge they go to every sewer outlet discharging its lethal effluent and load it until they founder. They have been deeply affected by the contagion of the sociologies, the philosophies, the policies, the atheistic, secular, cosmopolitan mysticism which are the well-manured soil in which the weeds of socialism have grown and prosper. Every sign of decrepitude, sentimentalism, doctrinairism, outmoded respect for transient human life, outmoded pity for the weak and humble, utility and mediocrity seen as the criteria for wisdom, neglect of the higher potentialities of mankind, the ridiculing of heroism, every foul sign of the loathsome decrepitude of degenerate people can be found in the contemplative life of our ruling and governing class, the Italian bourgeoisie.[6]

The fascist critique of the bourgeoisie has an unmistakably sportive aspect. Italian fascists, in particular, have a tendency to employ imagery intended to represent the "virile" alternative to bourgeois "decrepitude" and "flabbiness." Giuseppe Prezzolini, for example, dramatizes political engagement as a form of physical prowess: "But in political and social studies it is impossible to free oneself from personal aims. . . . we feel a certain desire to come down into the arena and take sides with one of the combatants. A hefty punch leading to a decision in favour of our actions causes us pleasure; whilst a blow which not only knocks down the wrestler but also our hopes of winning our bet is as unpleasant as if it had knocked us out ourselves."[7] "Mussolini's historical function," Curzio Malaparte writes, "has been to give back to the nation the physical sense of heroism." Unlike the physically and spiritually complacent bourgeois, whose unvital image was promoted during the nineteenth century by hostile literati, Mussolini is "a modern hero, sick with unrest and bowed down with certain convictions, urged on more by the force of his natural qualities than by the course of events or the suasions of chance, continually oppressed by that obscure fear of time that is a sure sign of humanity in heroes."[8] The bourgeoisie, Giovanni Papini writes in 1904, "are flabby and apathetic and have no thought of how to save themselves."[9]

The fascist critique of the bourgeoisie coincides with the Communist position in one important respect. Both accuse bourgeois politics of depoliticizing whole areas of public life, like sport, which more aggressive ideological factions feel obligated to colonize. During the interwar period the idea that sport can constitute an apolitical island within the body politic was denounced by Soviet ideologists, by the propagandists of the European workers' sport movement (*Arbeitersportbewegung*), and by Nazi sport theorists. But in another important respect the fascist denunciation of the bourgeoisie differs markedly from the Marxist critique. The fascist sees the bourgeoisie as less exploitative than passive (when offered the banner of nationalism), acquiescent (to the demands of the Left), and lacking in virility (hence its "ridiculing of heroism"). "The word power [*Kraft*]," a Nazi sport philosopher writes, "gives the bourgeois chills; it sig-

nifies something which does not occur in his ready-made world.
. . . Bourgeois thought does not understand that power is not just
one phenomenon among others, but rather the root and source of
everything."[10]

This chapter is devoted to those "centrist" critiques of bourgeois sport culture which derive from the bourgeois intelligentsia itself. These are not revolutionaries; they have a definite stake in the
tottering European edifice. And the idea of a deep cultural malaise,
within which the interwar critique of sport developed, was hardly
without its precedents, nor has it ended. "Of the existence and scope
of the pessimistic movement," Alfred Cobban writes in 1960, "which
sapped the foundations of the Enlightenment, there can be no doubt."
To account for the origins and power of modern pessimism, Cobban
finds a "deeply seated cleavage in the modern mind [which] goes
back behind the nineteenth century to the very beginnings of the romantic movement. The essential principles of romantic thought can
be summed up in the terms, primitivism and subjectivism—back to
nature and back to human nature. The most marked features of the
development of modern society, on the contrary, have been an increasingly complex and 'artificial' social life, and an increasing reduction of the individual to a mere unit in a vast industrial system."[11] This is precisely the dialectic to be found at the heart of so
much theorizing about sport during the interwar period: civilization
harboring within itself a somatic discontent bent on exacting its
due. It is for this reason that Nietzsche, creator of Zarathustra's doctrine of the body and the propounder of a fierce *Zeitkritik* of his
own, is often mentioned (or imitated) by the sport-minded intellectuals of this period. Cobban's interpretation of modern pessimism—
of which Nietzsche is a spectacular example—is developed further
in Judith Shklar's *After Utopia* (1957), an elegant meditation on the
exhaustion of modern political thought. "The sense of cultural disaster," she writes, "is not entirely new, though the extent to which it
is now felt is unprecedented. Even during the last century romantic
and Christian thinkers felt alienated from the social life about them,
and the representatives of these philosophies are today the most impressive exponents of the various theories of social decay. For the romantic, then and now, civilization has become mechanical, crushing the individual and drowning in mediocrity."[12]

But there are different "romantic" responses to the sport phenomenon. Gottfried Benn, for all his interest in the body, sees a cultural exhaustion sport cannot heal. Ortega y Gasset, who became famous as a philosopher of cultural crisis, actually refuses pessimism
and promotes "the sense of life as a sport and as a festivity."[13] Karl

Jaspers conforms perfectly to the "romantic" response to modernity when he portrays contemporary man as "engaged in sport as a man who, strapped in the strait-waistcoat of life, in continuous peril as if engaged in active warfare, is nevertheless not crushed by his almost intolerable lot, but strikes a blow in his own behalf, stands erect to cast his spear."[14] Yet Jaspers' "romantic" dramatization of the modern predicament in a sportive idiom is integrated into a sociological rationalism which resembles that of Mannheim. This can be explained if we keep in mind that it was against an "analytical fragmentation of man, rather than against reason itself, that romanticism protested. From the first outbursts of the *Sturm und Drang*, romanticism was dedicated to the ideal of human totality, the integrity of the entire personality. . . . Life was not just identified with energy; the inner unity of man's powers was sought, instead of their departmentalization into 'feeling' and 'reason.'"[15] It is not too much to say that the twentieth century has been haunted by the competing versions of the "total" or "integral" individual which have been promoted by Marxism and fascism alike. But the "total" person incorporates the somatic person. It is for this reason that an ambitious political ideology must include a doctrine of sport. Both of these doctrines respond to a (nineteenth-century) critique of modernity which is "romantic" in origin, and to its idealized (often neo-Hellenic) human type.

The interwar critique of sport takes its place within the post-Enlightenment critique of modernity. But what about specific precedents for the use of sport as an index of cultural health? A logical point of departure would appear to be the ancient Roman spectacles, to which the sporting spectacles of this century are so often compared. The irony is that the—comparatively speaking—utterly benign sporting exhibitions of the modern period have been subjected to an often unambiguously hostile criticism,[16] which, according to Roland Auguet, has no real counterpart during the Roman age. The familiar critique of these spectacles, he says, is essentially a retrospective creation, and he cites a passage by the nineteenth-century French writer Chateaubriand as an example.[17] "However," Auguet adds, "the possibility of such censure scarcely ruffled the spirit of the Romans. If they passed judgment on the gladiatorial combats, it was rather in the manner in which a modern philosopher might pass judgment on motor races: casually, and because he happened to find in them, and in the behaviour of those taking part, material illustrative of this or that theory." Cicero and Pliny actually found value in the gladiatorial combats (if not, perhaps, in the more elaborate atrocities), because they provided slaves and criminals with a forum in which they could elevate themselves by demonstrating nobility of character; they could thus be seen not as victims, but as beneficiaries of these spectacles. "On the other hand, an attitude of ostentatious contempt for the spectacles and especially the *munera* as manifestations of a stupidity and vulgarity typical of the masses was probably more widespread at Rome than has generally been allowed." But ostentatious contempt is not necessarily principled contempt; indeed, Auguet's point is that we must "start from the idea that such disapproval was out of the question."[18] The age of sport, by comparison, has been far more self-reflective and, therefore, self-critical.

An early modern reference (1843) to the athlete as an unwholesome public figure appears in an attack on "blasé" education by the Left Hegelian Arnold Ruge: "The jokes and stale humor of great cities which always lie in wait for a suitable opportunity to break forth and sparkle, the idolization of all genius and fame, empty enthusiasm for dancing girls, gladiators, musicians, athletes—what does all this prove? Nothing more than a blasé education, lacking all sense of real labor toward great goals . . . nothing more than the frivolousness of formal knowledge and formal talent. A man must be able to despise all these gifts and all this skillfulness if he is not to be caught up in this same senseless maelstrom, insipid and lifeless."[19] Unlike his contemporary, the nationalistically minded gymnast Friedrich Ludwig Jahn, Ruge does not see the body as a *Politicum*; he is not a vitalist in this sense. For him, the athlete is just one more example of all that glitters in the public sphere.

There are two other critiques of sport which antedate the interwar period but are not cited by the theorists of the 1920s and 1930s. In Victorian England an "athletic mania," as Bruce Haley terms it, and the issue of professionalism provoked criticisms which anticipate certain twentieth-century reservations about the "rationalization" of sport. In 1870 an influential sporting magazine comments: "Many do not like to see athletics made so artificial. Instead of casually walking into a cricket-field, you now pass a policeman, and show a season ticket, or pay for entrance, into a ground furnished with a path of cinders, and fenced in with grim barriers, in order to look at athletes who have been training systematically, instead of runners who take off their coats, and go in with glorious uncertainty as to who's going to win what. Many look back with a sort of regret to the more primitive athletic times . . ."[20] This essentially nostalgic argument differs in several important respects from those of the interwar critics. Certain of these writers, for example, look upon sport's affinity with a (post-Victorian) modernity favorably or, perhaps, with some ambivalence. Even a cultural conservative like Huizinga recommends a "veneration of the past,"[21] rather than a recovery of the past; and the recovery he promotes has to do with values, not deceased cultural forms. In addition, the awareness of sport's relationship to industrialism, its alleged compensatory functions within modern individuals and societies, references to Nietzsche, and widespread symbolic interpretation of the record performance all separate the interwar theorists from the Victorian critics of the sport of their epoch. The second "early" critique of sport, that of Pierre de Coubertin, founder of the modern Olympic movement, does address these issues even as it borrows much of its philosophy of sport from the Victorians. But despite its greater complexity, Coubertin's analysis does not amount to a critical sociology of sport; its motives are too rooted in nationalism and social anxiety, and its intentions are too practical. The social analysis of sport still awaited its first real step beyond anglophilia.

An Early Sociology of Sport

Heinz Risse's *Soziologie des Sports* (1921) is the first systematic, deliberately "sociological" treatment of sport to appear in any language. Although it is by no means a "value-neutral" piece of writing, Risse's book distinguishes itself from its more significant predecessors simply by emphasizing social science rather than encomiums to sport or schemes to achieve national rejuvenation through the body. Like most works on sport and society published during the period 1900 to 1940, Risse's *Soziologie* offers both a sociocultural diagnosis and a conception of sport's therapeutic potential; and in the last analysis, Risse, too, confers upon sport unique curative powers. What makes his treatise unusual is the thematic diversity which results from applying a genuinely sociological imagination to a new social phenomenon. His work presents, even if it did not originate, what has become a standard agenda of themes.

Risse's book may be compared, for example, with another early German interpretation of sport's social significance. Robert Hessen's *Der Sport* (1908), which appeared in a social psychology series edited by Martin Buber, represents less the work of a sociologist than that of an admiring observer of the sport culture of Victorian England.[22] Hessen is a straightforward proponent of using sport to promote national vitality. The author's main purpose is to persuade his compatriots that sport practices along English lines would have an invigorating effect on the nation as a whole and thereby serve the national interest. In addition to articulating the conjunction of sport and nationalism, Hessen advances several arguments which are of interest. He moralizes over the notorious homosexual English aesthete Oscar Wilde, who, he says, would have better resisted falling into blithe effeminacy had he been a practicing sportsman; there is no better preventive measure against such degeneration, he insists, than open-air sport. Hessen invokes the *mens sana in corpore sano* ideal, ascribed to Aristotle, the ancient Romans, and the Victorian educators who made sport into an element of national pedagogy. And it is interesting to see him regretting the cultivation of technical perfection in fencing at the expense of a lustier match. The emphasis on style reminds the author (unfavorably) of a higher stoicism recalling, he says, the Japanese *harakiri*. The monograph ends with a passage which, in retrospect, may seem to contain the seed of things to come. "Our race," he declares, "has attained too high a stature in world history to end up as a menagerie of coughing, stunted weaklings with withered arms and potbellies."[23] Its Hitlerian idiom notwithstanding, this passage in fact contains less parlor Nietzscheanism than the frank ebullience of a nationalism which had not yet lost its innocence. In summary, Hessen endows sport with two major functions. First, it promotes a "respect for the dignity of the body" which will ultimately strengthen the body politic; second, it promotes a "limiting of competing interests" and a "respect for an opponent's rights" within the body politic. This, in effect, is the scope of Hessen's social theory: nationalistic (and racialistic) chauvinism combined with a vague notion regarding the capacity of the sport ethos to mitigate social conflict. Most of the issues which would later preoccupy the numerous (and in some cases distinguished) European sport theorists of the interwar period (1920–1940)—the relationship of sport to industrial society, the professionalization of sport, the problem of the spectator, sport as an index of cultural decline, the record performance—are absent here. What is more, Hessen's book conspicuously fails to associate sport with a conception of modernity and the unique demands of a new age.

All of these issues are addressed in the writings of Pierre de Coubertin, a Frenchman whose work as a social theorist of sport seems to have remained unknown to the interwar sport theorists in Germany. Coubertin (1863–1937) is best known as the *rénovateur* of the Olympic Games and as the founder of an international sport culture which survives to this day. Less well known is the fact that Coubertin was also a prolific author (some sixty thousand pages) whose interests embraced pedagogy, history, current politics, and most aspects of private or social life which had some bearing on sport.[24] It was, in fact, this preoccupation with sport which made Coubertin a social theorist, one of those "Third Republic conservative Liberals" who offered practical advice to public authorities confronting a mass society they did not really understand. Like his more famous contemporary Gustave Le Bon, author of *The Crowd* (1895), Coubertin considered himself a social engineer, an "applied psychologist" in Le Bon's phrase, who could make a contribution to what Coubertin once called *la bonne humeur sociale*.[25]

Like the French sociologist Frédéric Le Play (1806–1882), who was his principal intellectual mentor, Coubertin's ruling obsession was what the former called "the reestablishment of social peace in my country" through the influence of "non-ideological" institutions (Le Play's Unions de la Paix, Coubertin's Olympic committee).[26] Having appointed himself to this mission, Coubertin saw himself as a social physician who could import to France the healing influence of contemporary British sport of the public school variety. What is more, a popularized medical idiom flowed effortlessly from his pen.

In this sense, Coubertin may be seen as a contributor to the "hygienist" doctrine of his time. If hygienism in late-nineteenth-century France is defined in terms of its best-known concerns—a declining birthrate, increases in crime rates, mental pathologies such as suicide (see Durkheim), the spread of venereal disease, and the fear of racial degeneration—then he is not one. Coubertin's writings do not address these issues. It may be argued, however, that these alarming social phenomena were actually symptoms which could be accounted for within a more comprehensive hygienic doctrine, and that any organismic interpretation of society at this time was also a hygienic one.[27]

Interpreted physiologically—that is, anthropomorphically—the body politic became a sentient organism whose needs, psychic and organic, could be served by hygiene. If the dominant figures in the hygiene movement were doctors, then Coubertin was an ambitious paramedic, an auxiliary whose therapeutic ideas stressed the psychological rather than the physical. It is in this sense that one can, as Robert Nye has pointed out, "make a good case for the continuity between the work of the hygienists and the aims of the less medically oriented figures in the French sporting movement such as Paul Adam and the founder of the Olympic movement, Pierre de Coubertin."[28] In fact, Coubertin found the medical community insufficiently vigilant. He complained that the doctors were all too ready to condemn sport therapy out of ignorance, that they preferred their prejudices to empirical study, that their inclination to oppose muscular exertion to cerebral effort led them to ignore the nervous system, and that they exaggerated the expenditure of nervous energy occasioned by muscular fatigue, thereby discrediting an effective remedy for "neurasthenia."[29] Coubertin criticizes the doctors, in effect, for being ineffective hygienists, and in particular for neglecting the psychological dimension of health. It was this concern with mental well-being which made his version of hygienism an approach to culture as a whole rather than an essentially medical concern with organic disorders.

Coubertin's hygienism was primarily a philosophy of culture with implicit conceptions of cultural sickness and health. "Our existence," he writes, "is contrary to good health [hygiène] to such a degree that we will almost never be able to enjoy ourselves as the Greeks could." Such a hygienism addresses the total state of a culture, amounting to a judgmental phenomenology of cultural experience. As for the Greeks, "their civilization made the state of health [santé] more perfect and the state of disease more pitiful than is the case for the current generation."[30] Needless to say, this idealizing nostalgia amounted to a wholly unoriginal comparison of the ancient and the modern. More than a century earlier, Friedrich Schiller had offered similar arguments in On the Aesthetic Education of Man (1795). For Schiller's aesthetics Coubertin substitutes his own rather fanciful neurology. Coubertin, in a word, was an inheritor, not the inventor, of the athletically minded philo-Hellenism which was eventually adopted even by the Socialist sport movement in Germany during the 1920s.[31] But even more than the Socialists, Coubertin greeted modernity with an ambivalence which forms the very basis of his social doctrine.

Coubertin's version of the hygienist gospel emphasized the precarious emotional health of his contemporaries. By establishing "the correlation between psychology and physical movement," the reformer established sport as the social therapeutic required by modern life, which had given rise to what he calls "the universal neurosis." Two chapters of the Essais de psychologie sportive are, in fact, titled "Can Sport Stem the Universal Neurosis?" and "Sporting Remedies for Neurasthenics." "Sport," Coubertin writes, "is an incomparable psychic instrument and, we may note, a dynamic to which one can profitably appeal in the treatment of many psychoneuroses. For, very often, the psychoneuroses are distinguished by a kind of disappearance of virile feeling, and there is nothing like sport to revive and maintain it."[32]

Coubertin's idea of the "modern" disorder did not, however, focus on anything as specific as the issue of virility. "The term 'universal neurosis,'" he writes, "is not scientific. Nor can it be claimed to be specific in any real sense. Everyone, however, will understand the sense in which we are using it here, and will recognize that it clearly describes the current state of affairs. Modern life is no longer local or particular; everything has an influence on everything else."[33] "The tendency today," he writes, "is toward a total culture. It is not just democracy which is pushing in this direction, but especially the transformation of labor, the industrial character of the epoch, the almighty goddess Activity who already reigns uncontested."[34] It should be remembered that Coubertin was a Third Republic "democrat" who listed "the triumph of democracy" as one of four *faits nouveaux* history would have been better off without.[35] His ideology, accordingly, represents an effort to adapt reactionary instincts to certain features of an emerging mass society he deemed both undesirable and irreversible.

The internal tensions which characterize Coubertin's ideology are expressed most significantly in two of his major themes: the nature of democracy and the search for social and psychological equilibrium in an increasingly feverish civilization. Coubertin's somewhat reluctant endorsement of "democracy" should be viewed against the background of his deep distaste for the revolutionary impulse and for socialism, which he saw as unlettered and, worst of all, as the most formidable adversary of *l'enseignement supérieur*.[36] Coubertin's second theme, which plays the central role in his hygienist response to the "universal neurosis," assumes that sport functions both as a social stimulant and as a soporific. In Coubertin's terms, there exists a dynamic relationship between "equilibrium" and "excess." "One point at which sport bears on the social question," he writes, "is its pacifying character. Sport relaxes the [coiled] springs which have been stretched by anger"; and elsewhere he calls for an educational system capable of producing a "collective calm." The idea of *calme* plays a major role in the *Essais*, Coubertin's explicitly hygienist text. Sport is viewed as a tranquilizing therapy on both the individual and social levels, and they are presumably interrelated. "Precisely because, in the modern world which is emerging, sport can play an eminent role in promoting progress and social *rapprochement*," Coubertin writes, "we wish it to be purer, more chivalric, more transparent, more calm."[37] Sport is needed to mitigate what he calls the "intensive character" of "a pulsating [*trépidante*] and complicated" civilization: "Considering the expenditure of nervous and mental force demanded of people by modern civilization, they need an equivalent dose of muscular force" by way of compensation. "Total repose of the limbs," he continues, "should be extended to the brain. But it is perfectly apparent that the excessive

aspect of civilization, in destroying in part its equilibrium, has falsi-
fied the relations between [limbs and brain]. Thus it becomes necessary to re-establish this equilibrium artificially . . ."[38]

An important theme which preoccupied Coubertin was that of
the crowd (la foule). Although he does not mention Gustave Le Bon,
author of The Crowd, Coubertin's admirer Paul Adam does. Like
Coubertin, Adam is interested in finding "the correct remedy to heal
our public sickness," and he refers to the criminologist G. de Tarde
as "the excellent crowd psychologist."[39] Coubertin refers to "haste"
and "the crowd" as the "two vampires of contemporary civilization"
and speaks of "a population in which the irrational is the general and
obligatory law."[40] "Unfortunately," says Adam, "the politicians do
not peruse books on psycho-physiology,"[41] and this is also Coubertin's point. It is the "applied psychologist"—a Le Bon, a Coubertin,
an Adam—who will warn politicians of the "irrational" lurking
within the masses they rule. Nor is contemporary sport culture
wholly innocent of certain rabble-rousing tendencies of its own. One
manifestation of the crowd phenomenon, says Coubertin, is the
sporting press, which spreads a noxious influence by virtue of its hy-
perbole and sensationalism. But political authorities can also use
sport to defuse the irrational through a hygienic equilibrium.

For all their intellectual substance, Coubertin's writings on
sport remain primarily an attempt at a pragmatic social strategy. He
is, as a Third Republic establishmentarian, far more inclined to ex-
orcise the issue of social class than to analyze it. His conception
of sport's compensatory effects is both rudimentary and fanciful.
His critique of "degenerate" forms of sport is inhibited by his self-
appointed mission to promote sport as an international movement.
Similarly, his instrumental approach to sport precludes a critique of
the (passive) spectator and the "star" phenomenon. His pronounced
distaste for the political Left causes him to ignore (save for one diplo-
matic reference) the important Socialist sport movement of Western
Europe. Risse's Soziologie des Sports broadens the sociological frame
of reference by dealing with these themes, and others, in greater detail than Coubertin does.

There is, however, an interesting exception to this rule, and that
is the issue of "modernity." It is evident that Coubertin offers the
social therapy of sport in response to what he sees as a dramatic, and
potentially dangerous, historical transition. Risse, too, situates sport
within a modern age which has given rise to the phenomenon of
sport both as a symptom of and as a response to itself. The crucial
difference between Coubertin and Risse is that, while the former
fears the new age, the latter welcomes it even as he acknowledges its

negative features. Like Coubertin, Risse speaks of "the unhealthy life of modern man."[42] But, unlike Coubertin, Risse divorces this hygienic issue from his ultimate evaluation of the age itself, which stresses its dynamic potential. This important difference in outlook may be due, in part, to different intellectual milieux. Unlike Coubertin, who found "the superman of Nietzsche" both distasteful and a threat to social stability,[43] Risse praises Nietzsche and calls the "will to power" the fundamental characteristic of the modern age, which he calls the age of capitalism. A second, more hypothetical source of influence is German expressionism, a thematically diverse artistic and literary movement whose apogee coincided with the publication of Risse's book. The following passage is striking in this regard. Risse calls the marathon runner "a strange expression of our entire world-view [*Weltgefühls*], which wants to establish its dominion backwards and forwards, for which there are no limits and which is constantly reaching beyond itself. We are at all times men of the day before yesterday and the day after tomorrow. Temporally and spatially we are at every moment standing with one foot in the beyond. Into this world-view sport fits perfectly. It is only one form of escape sought by the fettered individual."[44] In its extreme subjectivism, its urgent need to escape the confines of everyday existence, its ideal of a New Man, and its intoxication with sheer dynamism, this passage is quintessential expressionism. Risse's idiom may be compared with that of the expressionist playwright Georg Kaiser. "The purpose of being is the attainment of record achievements. Record achievements in all areas. The man of record achievements is the dominant type of this age . . ."[45] Risse interprets the record achievement as an expression of the "will to power," dismissing those who condemn record-seeking as a distortion of sport.[46]

An unusual aspect of Risse's book is its caustic denunciation of the contemporary German intelligentsia—"those people with streaming hair and wide collars and questioning eyes and the light vibration in a beautiful voice; this whole impotent species we designate our intellectuals." Risse's contempt for the intellectuals derives from two factors. First, he establishes an invidious comparison between the "aesthetic vaporings" of the intellectuals and the willpower which is formed "not in the literary café or in the cabaret," but on the sports field. "Intellectualism" is pitted against a Nietzschean "education of the will." Second, he accuses the intellectuals of a virtually effeminate ineffectuality which has estranged them from the masses. The influence of sport has replaced the leadership of the intellectuals, who have proceeded to dismiss the sport movement as a subject unworthy of their interest.[47]

This is an important issue, and an assessment of Risse's claim is in order. Did the intellectuals of the Weimar Republic in fact disdain sport? Wolfgang Rothe has concluded that "talk of a regular hatred of sports on the part of the intellectuals is probably a fable as far as the twenties are concerned. On the contrary, enthusiasm for sports, uncritical lionization of sports activities, prevails in the books of this period."[48] It is true, of course, that Risse's book appeared on the threshold of the new age of sport, before many commentaries had been published. Still, Risse's indictment anticipates a similar one published six years later in *Die Neue Rundschau* by the prominent literary critic Frank Thiess: "The republican state put playgrounds at the disposal of this [sport] movement; but what did the intellectuals within the state do to interpret this movement and to lead it into a culturally fruitful channel? Nothing. In spite of this the possibility of exercising a truly significant effect upon the body politic should have been considered; all it would have required was the insight of those who, as the administrators of the country's intellectual resources, have also assumed responsibility for observing and analyzing all new phenomena. Only the Leftist party member, who more instinctively than deductively recognized the bourgeois aspect of the sport movement, has taken an interest." The crisis of sport, Thiess writes in 1927, is that it has been ignored by the intellectuals.[49] This is also Risse's complaint: "The movement is being labeled anti-intellectual. It is coarse, it is suitable for peasant boys, it is a children's game and of no significance whatsoever."[50]

As Rothe demonstrates, Weimar intellectuals of the 1920s did not simply ignore sport; many were aficionados or even athletically active. The real issue, as Risse and Thiess suggest, is whether sport is taken seriously as a sociological factor and, therefore, as a potential instrument of policy. Even the adherents of the German workers' sport movement (Thiess's "Leftist party member") do not begin publishing their better known manifestos until about 1930.[51] It is only during the 1930s that thinkers like Karl Jaspers and Karl Mannheim begin to look at sport as an instrument for the (psychologically astute) social engineer in the manner of Coubertin.[52]

Risse divides the sociological theory of his sport sociology into two parts, which he terms "positivistic" and "metaphysical," respectively. The first part is "the doctrine of sport's socializing effect," which examines not the social effects of specific sports but rather "the forms in which people who are linked by sporting ties react and relate to each other, and the extent to which old class formations are discarded and new ones produced." The second meaning of "sociology," Risse says, represents an extension of the first: "The interrelatedness of all of the elements of a culture . . . its origin in an entirely specific human community [*Menschentum*], its derivation from a definite spiritual disposition [*Seelenrichtung*], and its place within a wholly individual cultural sphere which emanates from this spiritual identity [*Seele*]—all of this means nothing other than an extension of the interpretation of the forms we have analyzed to what these forms contain . . ." What is essential is not the content (the sport) itself, but the manner in which it expresses a specific outlook or "sense of life" (*Lebensgefühl*). On this level the sociologically relevant factor is whether sport somehow fits into a "cultural sphere" or, similarly, whether a social structure gives rise to specific values.[53] It is in this sense, Risse says, that Marxist materialism derives ideologies from economic conditions, and that Max Weber calls Judaism the religion of a pariah race.

Sport takes the form of ideology, first, as it derives from a social structure (e.g., industrial society) and, second, as it expresses itself (e.g., in the record performance) in a manner which refers back not to economic circumstances, but to an "original" outlook (*Lebensgefühl*). Risse's assertion that ideology does grow out of an "economic foundation" shows that he agrees with this doctrine of "Marxist materialism."[54] Elsewhere, however, it becomes clear that Risse's own ideology is a kind of Nietzschean individualism, and that the adoption of this much "superstructure" theory in no way makes the author a Marxist. In one passage Risse makes a point of refuting Marx in the following way: "What is fundamental is not the fact that the means of production are not owned by the workers, but rather that the means of production determine the principle of the division of labor, and that this principle never permits the worker to complete the assembly of a finished product instead of parts of products." The conclusion he draws from this is that the division of labor precludes "creative individual activity."[55]

Risse proposes for his sport sociology two "genuinely sociological" questions. "First: Which social classes generally participate in the different types of sport, and according to which criteria do they choose precisely these types of sport? Second: To what degree is sport, as a form of socialization, capable of forming classes, i.e., on the basis of which principles do cliques, for example, form within [sport] clubs?" Responding to the first question, Risse points out that "class ideology" plays a role in selecting specific sports for participation; what is more, he suggests that the higher classes do not need sport for the "expansion of their individuality" as much as the lower classes do. As for the second question, Risse finds "sociologically interesting" the fact that talented athletes, irrespective of their social class or position, constitute a "new upper crust" both within the world of sport and in society at large. His critique of the "star" syndrome, however, stops at the point of observing that the public shows a curious interest in the private lives of celebrated athletes.[56]

It is apparent that the "genuinely sociological" content of Risse's *Soziologie* remains at a rudimentary theoretical level and actually takes up very little space. And yet it is the most explicitly sociological study of sport of its time. This curious circumstance can be accounted for if we recognize how closely sport has been associated with cultural criticism since the second half of the nineteenth century. For Risse—and, indeed, for virtually all of the interwar commentators on sport—the central issue is not social science *per se*; it is rather the critique of European culture and its values. Many sociological issues are raised, but few are treated in the spirit of academic sociological inquiry. It is instructive in this regard that Risse identifies the crisis of modern sport as the buying and selling of professional soccer players. His *Soziologie*, in short, is the product of a polemical age.

One of Risse's characterizations of this period is that it is an age of "mechanization." The fundamental contradiction of modern capitalism, he states, is "the contradiction between man and machine, i.e., the destruction of human individuality." He proceeds to make a historically important distinction between gymnastics (*Gymnastik*, or the more Teutonic *Turnen*) and sport, the specifically modern form of physical culture which has triumphed in the public sphere. Regimented group gymnastics expresses the unfreedom of existence in an industrial society; sport, on the other hand, is the antithesis of this kind of existence, since it emphasizes the body of the individual. Sport has flourished in England, the first of the industrialized societies, as a reaction to *Maschinentechnik* and the capitalist system as a whole[57]—one version of a compensation theory of sport's social function which has appeared in the writings of Arnold Toynbee, Lewis Mumford, Karl Mannheim, and many Marxist authors.[58]

Referring to the industrial working class, Risse talks of "the expropriation of man by the machine." The modern age bears within itself a "tendency toward rationalization." At the same time, however, Risse draws two dichotomies which give his analysis some interesting nuances. For one thing, he distinguishes between the bureaucratic rationality of the age (in the Weberian sense) and the "rationalization of training," the "rationalization of the body," and the "rationalization of sport equipment." One is a mass—the other an individual—phenomenon. The second point is that Risse sees the "rationalizing" tendency of the age challenged by irrational factors which inhabit the individual athlete—"the psychological elements." "The [sport] movement as a whole is, of course, thoroughly rational. But the limitless number of moments in which feeling and will assert themselves in the sporting life of the individual are irrational."[59]

Risse associates this irrational element with both sport and the theme of individuality: "The feeling of a free, creative activity is something the individual acquires only from competition in the sporting sense: from a contest." Risse's notion of individuality embraces Nietzsche's Zarathustra as well as heroic types like Napoleon and Cecil Rhodes. It is a path to a "new corporeal ideal" which leads, not through the old body-denying asceticism, but through the asceticism of the athlete. The problem of the individual in modern society is "his ability to demonstrate his creative will, in the end to find himself, without his self-expression being bound by mechanical forces." This is, of course, a standard aspect of the conservative critique of industrial society; Risse, however, draws from this familiar portrait of modern unfreedom an unusual conclusion: "Mechanized man has only one form in which he can express this will in everyday life: the domain of physical culture."[60] For the "mechanized" industrial worker, sport is the only path of self-realization. This is the most radical sociological premise of Risse's book.

Throughout the interwar period, the critique of modern sport is offered from every ideological standpoint. An interesting feature of this criticism is its relative uniformity, ideological differences notwithstanding. If, for example, the Nazi sport philosopher Alfred Bauemler expresses concern over passive spectators, sensationalism, the "reintegration of man," the decline from ancient Greek athletic culture, and the pursuit of record performances,[61] he is covering an agenda common to virtually all of the interwar theorists, prominently including the Socialists of the workers' sport movement. Risse's *Soziologie* anticipates these and other concerns raised later during the 1920s and 1930s.

Risse is hardly the first European cultural critic to invoke the example of Hellenic antiquity to the disadvantage of his contemporaries. The Greeks had seen "the human body in its highest perfection, as an ideal type," a model which accentuates the disproportions of the specialized modern athlete's body. Greek sport had found its "deeper sense" not in its economic foundations or in some sort of ideology, but in "the joy taken in the beautiful body." Risse's assertion that the Romans had perverted the Greek idea of sport is a standard formula; it can, for example, be found in one of Friedrich Schiller's famous texts.[62]

Risse introduces the issue of professionalism by claiming that this is one example of how Roman physical culture signified "a distortion of the Greek ideal."[63] The historical inaccuracy of this remark is less important here than Risse's unequivocal condemnation of professionalism *per se*, which he traces to the Roman technique of *panem et circenses.*[64] The prize awarded to a professional represents only a "material value" and has thereby lost contact with its "aristocratic" origins, having surrendered its integrity to "the democratizing element of money"; it is "in a genuine sense the correlate of the masses."[65] These judgments derive from a frankly "aristocratic," and wholly unoriginal, outlook. Risse's argument against professionalism includes, at the same time, two themes which seldom occur in social commentaries on sport during this or any other period. First, he anticipates an idea which would appear in a better-known manifesto by Johan Huizinga, *In the Shadow of Tomorrow* (1936).[66] His point is that professionalism creates a situation wherein "sport becomes a profession and professional activity turns into farce,"[67] an injunction against a confusion of categories (labor and play) which antedates Risse. As Bruce Haley points out, "Many Victorian intellectuals insisted on carefully distinguishing work and play, the two expressions of the healthy nature."[68] Huizinga, for reasons discussed in chapter 2, makes this dichotomy nothing less than an index of cultural health. Second, Risse raises the question of whether the professional athlete is somehow comparable to the professional artist; his answer is that these are distinct types, a conclusion from which the West German sociologist Christian Graf von Krockow has dissented in his recent study of sport and the performance principle (1974).[69]

Risse offers two arguments. First, the athlete engaged in a contest is bribable in a way that the artist is not. Second, and more important, "sport as a profession appeals to the lower instincts." This claim, in turn, raises the issue of sensationalism in its various aspects. Sport, as Risse points out, can attract because it is modish, because it offers a stage to the coquette (e.g., the tennis court), or because it offers spectators a perverse gratification of their blood lust (e.g., the boxing match).[70]

These arguments, and the same key terms (*Sensation, Nervenkitzel*), begin to appear at the end of the 1920s in Socialist sport manifestos.[71] Risse, however, is anything but a Socialist, and his political identity, if somewhat vague, is in fact most clearly defined by examining the values he rejects. Risse's several references to the working class are progressively less sympathetic. He begins by interpreting "the spiritual as well as physical degeneracy of the working class" as a result of the "expropriation of man by the machine." The workers' sport clubs, he later says, "arise out of socialism's attempt to strictly segregate itself from the other classes in every area of life"—an observation which is basically correct.[72] "It is difficult to say," he notes, "which is more important here: the idea of class struggle or sport." It eventually becomes clear that Risse views socialism as a pathology whose deliberate attempts to inject the ideological issue into sport compete with sport's inherent capacity to reconcile the classes. The worker who joins a bourgeois sport club, he notes without sympathy, will feel like a foreigner surrounded by social and intellectual superiors. "He feels rejected and arrives through the feeling of resentment at the idea of class struggle. At that point he is ripe for the workers' sports clubs."[73]

Risse's hostility to socialism does not, however, make him (doctrinally, at any rate) a bourgeois. He maintains that the bourgeoisie, "lacking piety," has succeeded only in producing the "industrial apparatus of a technical civilization" and is no longer capable of "the inner mastery of a culture." The conservative segment of the bourgeoisie is "utilitarian" and "phlegmatic." Capitalism itself demands of the individual that false asceticism based upon "the inferiority of the body." Having separated himself from the Socialists and the bourgeoisie, Risse chooses a "third way"—the way of Nietzsche, whose "new form of asceticism" must replace the old one. "Zarathustra, that is the new ideal, the attempt to reach beyond the limits of the self. And Zarathustra must become for the masses the expression of that feeling in them which strives for individuality." Risse's Nietzscheanism provides an important clue to his political outlook. For in his Zarathustra worship, his anti-intellectualism, his contempt for "the shallow amusements of the metropolis,"[74] and his substitution of idealistic abstractions for political thought, Risse recalls the *Wandervogel* youth movements of the pre-1914 period in Germany. As Walter Laqueur has observed:

> We tend to look back on the world that ended in 1914 with a nostalgia mixed with a certain amusement. It is true that the great crisis of 1900 seems somewhat unreal, if not artificial, in comparison with the problems of the twenties and thirties. But for those who lived then, the cultural crisis was real enough; it turned some towards socialism, others toward an attitude of aristocratic disdain of the masses and hostility to bourgeois society and its culture or lack of culture. Politically, this rejection of society and its values could lead to either left- or right-wing extremist solutions. The German youth move-

ment was an unpolitical form of opposition to a civilization that had little to offer the young generation, a protest against its lack of vitality, warmth, emotion, and ideals.[75]

A curious aspect of Risse's *Soziologie* is that it represents a prewar mentality which has survived into the postwar period, by which time the vogue of Nietzsche had largely passed.[76] The sense of crisis, the "aristocratic disdain," the "unpolitical form of opposition," the doctrine of "vitality"—all of this is central to Risse's book. Small wonder, Robert Wohl comments, that the *Wandervogel* types "listened with approval to men outside the movement, like the educational reformer Gustav Wyneken ["this Platonic athlete and educator"] and the publisher Eugen Diederichs, who told them that they represented a 'new generation' and that they bore within them a revolution of the body against the exaggerated rationalism and the smug self-satisfaction of a soulless epoch."[77] Risse, like André Gide in *The Immoralist* (1902), understood that Nietzscheanism did in fact imply "a revolution of the body"; it is Zarathustra who condemns the "despisers of the body."[78]

Risse's *Soziologie*, then, is less a sociology than an antimodernistic tract. That he considered it a sociological document in 1921 tells us something about the arrested development of sport research over many years. None of the great social doctrinaires of the nineteenth century foresaw the age of sport, and Risse and Thiess are correct in faulting German intellectuals of the 1920s for their neglect of sport as a topic of sociological and political interest. At the same time, we must acknowledge that Risse's notion of sociology is essentially the practice of cultural criticism in the context of which sociological concepts appear as "scientific" ornaments. It is easier, after all, to speculate about "the total social-psychic disposition of our age" than to establish the sociology of sport,[79] which has eluded social science to this day.

Ambivalent Liberalism: Sport and Rational Planning

If it is legitimate to segregate Karl Jaspers and Karl Mannheim from other contemporary thinkers who address the subject of sport, this is due to the primacy of their secular liberal values and the consequent tone of detachment from sport as a cultural issue. This is not to say that Jaspers, in particular, has renounced the practice of cultural criticism. On the contrary, his *Man in the Modern Age* (*Die geistige Situation der Zeit*, 1931) is a classic polemic of existential sociology in a tradition which originates in Kierkegaard's *Two Ages* (1846).

"What is to-day common to us all," Jaspers writes, "is not our humanity as a universal and all-pervading spirit of fellowship, but the cosmopolitanism of catch-words in conjunction with the spread of world-wide means of communication and the universalisation of certain pastimes," for example, sport.[80] Like Kierkegaard and Heidegger, Jaspers interprets the public sphere (and what fills it) as a realm of inauthenticity. Unlike these primarily negative cultural critics, however, Jaspers lacks the great normative symbol (Christ and the ancient Greeks, respectively) against which an unambiguous decline can be discerned. The result is a curiously noncommittal, and therefore evenhanded, manifesto which treats sport in precisely this way. Lacking irony, Jaspers presents the sport phenomenon with naive detachment and with few judgments.

Jaspers approves of sport for three basic reasons. First, it promotes "the self-preservative impulse as a form of vitality": "Through bodily activities subjected to the control of the will, energy and courage are sustained, and the individual seeking contact with nature draws nearer to the elemental forces of the universe." Here Jaspers' discourse has sunk to the level of vitalistic jargon. Second, "Sport as a mass-phenomenon, organised on compulsory lines as a game played according to rules, provides an outlet for impulses which would otherwise endanger the apparatus. By occupying their leisure, it keeps the masses quiet." Jaspers' view of this compensation effect appears to be neutral; like Kierkegaard and Heidegger, he is not a partisan of the masses. Third, "we discern, we feel, in the sport movement, something that is nevertheless great. Sport is not only play and the making of records; it is likewise a soaring and a refreshment. To-day it imposes its demands on every one." The "soaring element" constitutes "a defiance to the petrified present. The human body is demanding its own rights in an epoch when the apparatus is pitilessly annihilating one human being after another. Modern sport, therefore, is enveloped in an aura which, though the respective historical origins differ, makes it in some ways akin to the sport of the ancient world."[81] Like Risse and others hostile to the claims of the proletariat, Jaspers concedes that the industrial revolution ("the apparatus") has made inhuman demands upon the human body, which is now "demanding its own rights" in the form of sport.

Jaspers' endorsement of modern sport coexists with a critique consisting of two major points. First, Jaspers invokes the Roman analogy to make the point that the appeal of sport is contrary to "the clarity of rational thought"; it is rather a form of "the human urge towards the alluring contemplation of eccentric possibilities," "the pleasure that is felt in witnessing the danger and destruction of persons remote from the spectator's own lot. In like manner the savagery of the crowd is also manifested in a fondness for reading detective stories, a feverish interest in the reports of criminal trials, an inclination towards the absurd and the primitive and the obscure." This is the voice of Jaspers the psychiatrist. The second objection to sport comes from Jaspers the philosopher, who suddenly states that sport "lacks transcendent substantiality": "But even though sport imposes one of the limits upon the rationalised life-order, through sport alone man cannot win to freedom. Not merely by keeping his body fit, by soaring upward in vital courage, and by being careful to 'play the game,' can he overcome the danger of losing his self."[82] By the standards of the time, this criticism—directed at sport itself rather than at its misappropriation by a vulgar public—strikes a discordant note. For although it is true that, in his *Psychologie des sports* (1927), Alfred Peters effectively attacked sport as a truncated mode of experience (see below), the critique of sport as experience becomes prominent only in the neo-Marxist sport theory of the 1960s (see chapter 11). Jaspers' sense of sport's limitations also emerges in another context: "What is to-day obvious to all is a decay in the essence of art. Insofar as in the technical mass-order art becomes a function of this life, it approximates itself to sport as an object of pleasure." Like sport, a debased art "cannot further the selfhood of the individual."[83] Of the two "secular liberals," Jaspers is the cultural critic who exposes the threats to "selfhood"—like spectator sport and the cinema—which occur in the public sphere.

Nor is Jaspers a friend of social engineering. "Sociology, psychology, and anthropology teach that man is to be regarded as an object concerning which something can be learnt that will make it possible to modify this object by deliberate organisation. In this way one comes to know something about man, without coming to know man himself . . ."[84] For Karl Mannheim, as we have seen, this position is untenable, since his goal is "the planned guidance of people's lives on a sociological basis." Mannheim is essentially a democratic liberal who is forced to announce, without pleasure, the passing of nineteenth-century liberalism as a viable doctrine for "late liberal mass society."[85]

For Mannheim, cultural criticism is a peripheral issue. Like Jaspers, he criticizes a "constantly increasing hunger after ever new sensations"; but, unlike Jaspers, who accents the threat to "selfhood," Mannheim looks at "the craving for variety" sociologically and even in a managerial fashion: "This unbridled craving for variety is not ingrained in human nature but is the product of the constant stimulation aroused by anarchic competition." An advertising campaign, he suggests, could control public demand for staple products—a benign suggestion Jaspers would certainly condemn as manipulation. Mannheim's lack of interest in pursuing a cultural critique of sport is apparent in his consigning these issues to a footnote in which he acknowledges that "sport in itself may be based on many different psychological gratifications. It may, for instance, deteriorate from a social game with an agreeable sense of team work into a mania for records. These are psychological processes of degeneration which are common in a mass society and which can be set right if one consciously teaches people to enjoy the genuine pleasures of community pastimes."[86]

Mannheim's view of sport, then, is one of clinical detachment; but "different psychological gratifications," far from remaining private, have distinct social consequences. Mannheim points out that "liberal capitalism" encourages "the mania for competition, which springs not from the desire for objective achievement and community service, but from sheer self-centredness and very often from neurotic anxiety." On the other hand, competition does not have to be a mania: "Deflection of the so-called fighting instinct occurs, e.g. when, as in the Greek legend, the angry Ajax massacres sheep instead of men, or when the lust for fighting is converted into competitive impulses. Examples of such sublimation are to be seen in such organizations as the militant order of the Jesuits, the Salvation Army, and the Boy Scouts, which subordinate this instinct to socially useful goals." For Mannheim, the legitimacy of social engineering, or what he calls the "centralized means of influencing human beings— radio, propaganda, mass meetings, sports, cinema, etc." resides in its being employed by democratic planners; it is "the dictatorial societies" which "try to neutralize the desire to take part in the decision [regarding public affairs] by making use of every technique for diverting public opinion by pageantry and sport . . ."[87] Mannheim is one of the very few commentators on sport during this period for whom the corruption of sport as a subculture is not an issue.

Radical Disillusion: Sport and the Spiritual Vacuum

Radical disillusion with sport during the interwar period can emphasize the utter inability of sport to redeem a mediocre world and/or the vacuous character of sport as a particular kind of experience. Unlike Risse, Jaspers, or Mannheim, these critics see sport not as ambiguous in its effects, but as futile or worse. Lewis Mumford's treatment of sport, for example, is unrelievedly bleak, not least in its interpretation of modern sport as little more than a variation on the

Roman spectacle. Mumford also emphasizes that sport has already been corrupted by the civilization it is meant to improve: "there is within modern civilization a whole series of compensatory functions that, so far from making better integration [of "romantic" and "mechanical" elements] possible, only serve to stabilize the existing state—and finally they themselves become part of the very regimentation they exist to combat. The chief of these institutions is perhaps mass sports." "Thus sport, which began originally, perhaps, as a spontaneous reaction against the machine, has become one of the mass-duties of the machine age."[88] The idea that sport had been thus "infected" also found its way into Arnold Toynbee's *A Study of History* (1939).

Critics like Mumford and Toynbee who observe the failure of sport to fulfill a "compensatory" function are certainly disillusioned. But there are more "radical" forms of disappointment which appropriate sport for polemical purposes during this period. One of them stresses, like Jaspers, the relative barrenness of sport as experience, and the ancient dichotomy of spirit (*Geist*) and body (*Körper*). This type of scepticism permeates the sport essays (1931–1932) of the Austrian novelist (and ex-athlete) Robert Musil (1880–1942), whose original infatuation is haunted by doubts. "One can hardly contest today the fact that we have a physical 'culture.' But whose spiritual child [*Geisteskind*] is it?" Musil senses, and is disturbed by, an abdication by the mind of its rightful position of surveillance: "In the experiences of sports the core of the self shines out of the darkness of the body, and illuminates thereby the darkness all around; but what I would like to know is, how many sportsmen would condescend to ask about such things or listen to such questions at all?!" Musil finds danger in that "spiritual vacuum" (*Geistesabwesenheit*) which lasts longer than the ephemeral sportive struggle, in which behaving "like an animal" is actually desirable. And "if art which aims to show us a body finds nothing deeper or more beautiful than the bodies of athletic specialists—or of athletes, period—then this is without a doubt a great triumph of sport over spirit [*Geist*]."[89] Finally, Musil addresses the social dimension of sport with a detached irony: "One feels a vacuum into which sport plunges. One doesn't quite know exactly what it is that takes the plunge, but everyone talks about it and so it must be something: that is how everything that has been called a high value has come to power."[90] Musil's "radicalism," then, is his critique of sport's limited character as experience unqualified by the familiar vitalistic doctrine.

The Prague expressionist Paul Kornfeld, in an essay titled "Sport" (1930), pursues the critique of the body with greater stridency:

The spiritual characteristic of this age is that it has none, for it has all the characteristics there are. . . . And so, nothing is certain, there are no values, the scale of values disappears, the world of the spirit disgraces itself, and only the visible remains in the life of the nation—the economy; in the life of the individual—the superficial, his external success; and in the phenomenon of man, the expressions of his vitality and the unambiguously perceivable, controllable, measurable achievements of his body.

The body, like the economy, is only positivistic evidence of vitality; its tangible character is its inferiority, corresponding to Jaspers' claim that sport lacks a "transcendent substantiality." And Kornfeld, too, addresses the mass character of sport:

It's a matter of the worship of the body torn out of all contexts, of the worship of its achievements, which by any human standard are not achievements at all, of the worship of muscles and sinews. But this is not the onesidedness of which we have just spoken; it is the plunge into idiocy, the outbreak of mass insanity. And those who perhaps, if only they wanted to make use of it, might have brains enough to contain the madness, to protest against it, go along, cheer along, for they are all afraid of losing their contact with their age.[91]

What Kornfeld does not realize is that it is possible to combine "the worship of muscles and sinews" with a contempt for "the plunge into idiocy." Gottfried Benn, the German poet and essayist, physician, brilliant nihilist, and—for a time—spiritual ally of the Nazis, is a case in point. Benn is fascinated by the body: "always there is this body, its mysterious role, the soma, bearing the secrets, primeval, strange, opaque, wholly turned back upon the origins . . . the principle of Nietzsche's orgiastic philosophy . . ."[92] But when it comes to idealizing the athletic body, Benn's taste is strictly classical Greek.[93] His critique of modernity is severe, and it is typical of Benn to offer his readers a spectacle of degeneration for which no therapeutic can suffice.

"As for the present-day phenotype," Benn comments with a deliberately (perhaps the physician's) excessive naturalism, "its *moral* factor has largely been shed and replaced by the legislative factor and hygiene. . . . Nor has *Nature* for him any longer the lyrical quality and tension that it had . . . it has been dissolved by the sporting, therapeutic medium: toughening of the body, ski slopes, ultra-violet rays on mountain-peaks . . ." For Benn, the cultivation of sport is not only untherapeutic, it is actually a part of the cultural disease. Echoing Jaspers, Benn points out that "the vast existential emptiness of today's German man" will not be filled by "a vacuum of historic twaddle, crushed education, bumptious political forgeries by the regime, and cheap sports."[94] Benn's critical faculties precluded an endorsement of the Nazi sport which, like all sport, had become both antinature and one part of a lame and vulgar attempt to heal an enormous spiritual wound.

It is this sense of an enormous, even unfathomable, cultural disaster which links Benn with Martin Heidegger's critique of modernity. "The spiritual decline of the earth is so far advanced," Heidegger writes in 1935, "that the nations are in danger of losing the last bit of spiritual energy that makes it possible to see the decline . . . and to appraise it as such." Europe, he says, "in its ruinous blindness forever on the point of cutting its own throat, lies today in a great pincers, squeezed between Russia on one side and America on the other. From a metaphysical point of view, Russia and America are the same; the same dreary technological frenzy, the same unrestricted organization of the average man." Like Benn, Heidegger associates sport with "the plunge into idiocy": this is an age "when a boxer [presumably Max Schmeling] is regarded as a nation's great man." And, like Benn, Heidegger pays cautious but sincere homage to the "beauty of the body," though he, too, is thinking of ancient Greeks rather than modern Germans. Nowhere does Heidegger condescend to find the prospect of renewal in a sport-based vitalism. True, he is willing to rank "healthy physical activity" over the Marxists' conception of intelligence, but this is a highly qualified endorsement, since Heidegger disdains Marxism and insists that all vital qualities (for example, "all sureness and boldness in combat") are "grounded in the spirit and rise or fall only through the power or impotence of the spirit."[95]

"Christian Fatalism": Sport and the Decline of Values

In 1926, T. S. Eliot describes the French novelist Marcel Proust as "a point of demarcation between a generation for whom the dissolution of value had in itself a positive value, and the generation which is beginning to turn its attention to an athleticism, a training, of the soul as serene and ascetic as the training of the body of a runner."[96] Why, one might ask, does Eliot offer this abrupt endorsement of the athletic spirit? Like his fellow poet Paul Valéry, Eliot found in what Valéry calls *l'idée sportive* an ideal of self-discipline,[97] an ascetic

principle which Eliot opposes to a perceived dissolution which is oc-
curring within Western civilization. For example, Eliot defines the
waning ideology of liberalism as "something which tends to release
energy rather than accumulate it, to relax, rather than to fortify."[98]
This is a tendency which the sportive ideal, by its very nature, should
be able to correct.

The ideal of athletic discipline can serve a variety of doctrines.
Valéry's doctrine is an aesthetic one: "*Le sport intellectuel* consists,
then, in the development and control of our interior [mental] acts,"
Valéry's paragon being the musical virtuoso.[99] The French stage director Antonin Artaud presents an analogous case. "The actor," he
writes in his famous manifesto, "is like the physical athlete, but
with this surprising difference: his affective organism is analogous
to the organism of the athlete, is parallel to it, as if it were its double,
although not acting upon the same plane. The actor is an athlete of
the heart."[100] Here, too, the ideal is of aesthetic origin. Eliot, however,
invokes the sportive ideal on behalf of Christian self-discipline:

> A Christian society only becomes acceptable after you have
> fairly examined the alternatives. We might, of course, merely
> sink into an apathetic decline: without faith, and therefore
> without faith in ourselves; without a philosophy of life, either
> Christian or pagan; and without art. Or we might get a "total-
> itarian democracy," different but having much in common
> with other pagan societies, because we shall have changed step
> by step in order to keep pace with them: a state of affairs in
> which we shall have regimentation and conformity, without
> respect for the needs of the individual soul; the puritanism of a
> hygienic morality in the interest of efficiency; uniformity of
> opinion through propaganda, and art only encouraged when it
> flatters the official doctrines of the time. To those who can
> imagine, and are therefore repelled by, such a prospect, one can
> assert that the only possibility of control and balance is a reli-
> gious control and balance; that the only hopeful course for a
> society which would thrive and continue its creative activity
> in the arts of civilisation, is to become Christian. That pros-
> pect involves, at least, discipline, inconvenience and discom-
> fort: but here as hereafter the alternative to hell is purgatory.[101]

Eliot is a "Christian fatalist." The term belongs to Judith Shklar,
who uses it to denote an attitude toward history which has been embraced by a distinguished group of adherents of both the interwar
and postwar periods. "Many Christian thinkers," she writes in 1957,

"both Catholic and Protestant, today subscribe to the idea that civilizations live and die with their traditional religious faiths, and that ultimately all social events are the expression of some religious attitude. . . . Moreover, it is the historical fatalism implicit in a theory that makes cultural life dependent upon one factor—religious faith—that unites so many Christian social theorists today. War, totalitarianism, in short, the decline of European civilization—all are inevitable results of the absence of a religious faith in the modern age."[102] Eliot is a Christian fatalist in just this sense, maintaining that "a wrong attitude towards nature implies, somewhere, a wrong attitude towards God, and that the consequence is an inevitable doom." Eliot then pronounces judgment upon the present age: "For a long enough time we have believed in nothing but the values arising in a mechanised, commercialised, urbanised way of life: it would be as well for us to face the permanent conditions upon which God allows us to live upon this planet. And without sentimentalising the life of the savage, we might practise the humility to observe, in some of the societies upon which we look down as primitive or backward, the operation of a social-religious-artistic complex which we should emulate upon a higher plane."[103]

Eliot's invocation of a primitive "social-religious-artistic complex" points, once again, in the direction of Johan Huizinga, whose critique of modern sport is the most detailed and sophisticated treatment by any of the cultural conservatives. Huizinga's relationship to Christian fatalism is curiously problematic. On the one hand, as noted in chapter 2, Huizinga frequently uses the terms "sacred" and "holy," as in the following passage from *Homo Ludens*: "In the form and function of play, itself an independent entity which is senseless and irrational, man's consciousness that he is embedded in a sacred order of things finds its first, highest, and holiest expression."[104] It is play, the realm of the *ludique*, which fascinates Huizinga; sport is important because it is a form of socialized play, and it too is accorded a "spiritual" significance: "But sport is not just the strictly physical development of skills and strength; it is also the giving of form, the stylizing of the very feeling of youth, strength, and life, a spiritual value of enormous weight."[105] Such formulations, however, beg the question of what the "sacred order of things" or "spiritual value" really mean for Huizinga. Is he, like Eliot, a Christian? Certain passages seem to indicate that the answer is yes: "When the generally held convictions of to-day regarding good and evil are tested by the Christian principle or from even a platonic point of view, it appears that in theory the fundamentals of Christianity have been abandoned along a much larger front than that of its official or semiofficial abjuration."[106] In the last analysis, however, the element of personal religiosity is missing from Huizinga's writings. He may well praise the medieval cleric John of Salisbury for having "visualized the ideal of a society combining the purest of faith with the highest of civilization,"[107] but this faith is not his own. Where, then, is the Christian content of Huizinga's Christian fatalism to be found?

In the Shadow of Tomorrow was reviewed unenthusiastically in 1936 by a young Frankfurt Marxist named Herbert Marcuse. "He wants to be on the right side," Marcuse observes, "he wants to oppose reaction; but he opposes it with weapons which are more likely to wound its opponents. Again and again he works with concepts which belong to the rigid character of the Weltanschauung of the totalitarian state and whose present function can only be a psychic and intellectual subordination to that state."[108] This is, in fact, a mistaken judgment which probably derives from Huizinga's open disapproval of Marxism, a position which can only have provoked Marcuse's worst suspicions. Like the other Christian conservatives, Huizinga is resolutely antitotalitarian. Why, then, does Marcuse align Huizinga with the totalitarian position? What Marcuse apparently finds unacceptable is that to the totalitarian absolutes Huizinga opposes a Christian one: "These are strange times. Reason, which once combated faith and seemed to have conquered it, now has to look to faith to save it from dissolution. For it is only on the unshaken and unyielding foundation of a living metaphysical belief that the concept of absolute truth, with its consequence of absolute validity of ethical norms, can withstand the growing pressure of the instinctive will to live." For Huizinga, the real function of Christianity is to provide a "Christian code of ethics" which can resist the variable, and seductive, claims of political ideology.[109] It is rarely noted that even Homo Ludens concludes with an eloquent paragraph which pays profound obeisance to morality itself, to "the sphere of ethics," and to the dignity of conscience. Given the choice between the intoxications of play and the moral order, Huizinga chose the latter.

But the idea that play has "no moral function" coexists with play's relationship to "the very core of comparative religion: the nature and essence of ritual and mystery." "The Platonic identification of play and holiness does not defile the latter by calling it play, rather it exalts the concept of play to the highest regions of the spirit." The significance of play is, at the deepest level, a "religious" one, although the precise character of this religiosity is never specified. It is enough for Huizinga that "play is still bound up with the sacred emotion of the sacramental act," and this is its significance for sport:

"In modern social life sport occupies a place alongside and apart from the cultural process. The great competitions in archaic cultures had always formed part of the sacred festivals and were indispensable as health and happiness–bringing activities. This ritual tie has been completely severed; sport has become profane, 'unholy' in every way and has no organic connection whatsoever with the society, least of all when prescribed by the government."[110]

Huizinga's cultural philosophy of sport is, in part, an elegant apologia for the Victorian ideal of amateurism, the rationale for which is no longer the class prejudice which disdained professional athletes, but rather a respect for the "ritual tie" which once bound ancient sport to the realm of the sacred, an affinity which is now threatened by the decline of amateurism. The play phenomenon can infuse itself into many cultural forms, but the two in which Huizinga is most interested are sport and sacred ritual. ". . . why is a huge crowd roused to a frenzy by a football match? This intensity of, and absorption in, play finds no explanation in biological analysis. Yet in this intensity, this absorption, this power of maddening, lies the very essence, the primordial quality of play."[111] The primordial, in turn, embodies the authority of an ultimate (religious) value. Huizinga's next step is to formulate a culturally conservative critique of sport which will define the degenerative (compromised) forms of play.

Huizinga views sport as an important element of Western civilization: "Without competition there can be no culture. That our time has found in sport and sporting events a new international form of gratifying the ancient agonistic impulse is perhaps one of the factors which may contribute most towards the preservation of our culture. . . . Sport gives vitality, zest for life, balance and harmony, all of inestimable worth for culture."[112] This passage appears in the cultural polemic of 1935. *Homo Ludens* (1938), however, ascribes to sport a fallen state: "Ever since the last quarter of the 19th century games, in the guise of sport, have been taken more and more seriously. . . . Now, with the increasing systematization and regimentation of sport, something of the pure play-quality is inevitably lost." For example, Huizinga is unimpressed by the ability of "modern social techniques to stage mass demonstrations with the maximum of outward show in the field of athletics." Why should this kind of mass sport not remind him of Nazi pageantry? At the same time, however, there is little originality in Huizinga's critique of sport. His discussion of the Roman games is a standard item; the idea that "business becomes play" and "play becomes business" had been anticipated both by Risse (p. 38) and by the Victorian doctrine which insisted that work and play be preserved as separate categories. Even

Huizinga's claim that the game of bridge represents "a sterile excellence"[113] finds an antecedent in Lewis Mumford, who laments certain "feats of inane endurance: the blankest and dreariest of subhuman spectacles,"[114] both representing a surrender to the absurd expenditure of human energies. Huizinga's originality lies in the highly developed (if essentially polemical) doctrine of play and in the concept of "puerilism," which he defines as "the attitude of a community whose behaviour is more immature than the state of its intellectual and critical faculties would warrant, which instead of making the boy into the man adapts its conduct to that of the adolescent age."[115] It is "that blend of adolescence and barbarity which has been rampant all over the world for the last two or three decades." On one level, puerilism is Nuremberg rallies, "the whole rigmarole of collective voodoo and mumbo-jumbo," "the insatiable thirst for trivial recreation and crude sensationalism, the delight in mass-meetings, mass-demonstrations, parades, etc."[116]—in a word, it is the public style of fascism. On the less momentous level of sport, it is "present wherever athletic rivalry assumes proportions tending to push intellectual interests into the background, as is the case at some American universities. It threatens to creep in with over-organisation of sport and with the disproportionate place which the sporting page and the sporting magazines have come to occupy in the mental diet of untold numbers. It shows itself in a particularly striking form where national passions impede the observance of fair play in international contests."[117] On this level, puerilism is an aggregate of modern vices: bureaucracy, inane amusement, and chauvinism, phenomena Huizinga lamented rather than analyzed with the rigor he brought to the *ludique*.

Aristocratic Vitalism: Culture and the Sportive Style of Life

Max Scheler's treatment of sport is characterized by the ambivalence which is at the heart of the conservative critique: an instinctive sympathy for a vital subculture which has been corrupted by modern conditions. Scheler differs from Huizinga in two major respects. First, Scheler's pronounced—even provocative—vitalism is far too Nietzschean for Huizinga's temperament. Huizinga would have considered unholy a statement like this: "A thing that gives pleasure to a vitally valuable being is preferable to one that gives pleasure to a vitally less valuable being."[118] Scheler's "scale of vital values" is very different from Huizinga's "Christian code of ethics." Second, Scheler's hostility to "utilitarian civilization" is both more categorical than Huizinga's and based on different premises. The foreword to *Homo Ludens* claims that *homo ludens* belongs next to *homo faber*, not in his place. It may also be noted that Huizinga's indictment of "rationalism and utilitarianism" holds that they have "killed the mysteries and acquitted man of guilt and sin,"[119] not that they have suppressed a "noble" heroic type. The depth of Scheler's indignation over the idea that "the *'noble'* is being subordinated to the *'useful'*" is evident in his assertion that "the propelling motive of the hard-working modern utilitarian is *ressentiment* against a superior capacity and art of enjoyment, hatred and envy of a richer life that can enjoy pleasure more fully."[120] Scheler's paean to the "art of enjoyment" contrasts sharply with Huizinga's emphasis on duty and conscience.

Scheler finds value in both ancient and modern sport. First, he claims that the "races, games, and the Gymnasium of ancient Greece," the "knightly games and tournaments of the Middle Ages," and "the training of a Japanese Samurai," represent "vital techniques" for "the intensification of vital forces." Ancient Greek sport had been one expression of "the principle of the 'agon,' the ambitious contest for the goal, which dominated Greek life in all its aspects—from the Gymnasium and the games to dialectics and the political life of the Greek city states."[121] In the late 1920s, too, Scheler finds a vital core in sport. In a brief preface to the *Psychologie des sports* (1927) by his doctoral student Alfred Peters, he acknowledges the sheer force of this "abrupt, explosive reactive phenomenon" and endorses "this self-conscious conversion and rechanneling of vital instinctual energy away from spiritual sublimation and into the development of the body and maximal physical performance."[122] Scheler makes the same point in the convocation address he delivered in November 1927 at the German Institute for Politics in Berlin, titled "Man in the Era of Adjustment." At this late stage of his intellectual career, Scheler is promoting a deliberately anti-intellectual notion of "re-sublimation," two political expressions of which are Bolshevism and the fascism of Mussolini. But Scheler does not explicitly endorse these movements. His point is that they are manifestations of a *"systematic instinctual revolt"* against centuries of hyperintellectualism and the ascetic renunciations which had led to this overvaluation of mind. Other symptoms of this worldwide revolt are the American eugenics movement, the new sexual mores of youth, psychoanalysis, the global dance craze, panvitalistic doctrines—and the enormous international sport movement.[123]

Scheler's penchants for vitalism and for dressing his admiration of force in the raiments of theory did have their limits. As John

Staude has pointed out, "Scheler's Bavarian Catholic background gave him a Catholic corporatist perspective that prevented him from ever accepting racialist nationalism, the cult of blood and soil, cosmic pantheism, and glorification of chthonian vitalism which provided the pseudo-religious background of the conservative revolutionaries [such as Paul de Lagarde, Julius Langbehn, and Moeller van den Bruck]." As late as January 1927, in a lecture to an assembly of officers at the Reichswehr Ministry, "Scheler lit into the romantically minded militarists among the Stahlhelm and the Nazis who insisted that war was necessary to the cultivation of heroic virtues and to the preservation of national unity."[124] In *Ressentiment* (1915), Scheler defends Christianity against Nietzsche's critique: "The idea of goodness cannot be reduced to a biological value, just as little as the idea of truth."[125] At the same time, however, Scheler propounds a vitalism which, if not as straightforwardly biological as Nietzsche's, nevertheless treats physical prowess as a virtue, and the mind as an inferior faculty. "As it is," Lewis Coser has noted, "his emphasis on the vigor of biological drives, his assertion that the vital sphere is in some way more 'real,' than the others . . . are based on a number of assumptions that have repeatedly been used by modern apologists of irrationality as engines of revolt against reason."[126]

Scheler's critique of modern sport focuses on its alleged crypto-utilitarian and pseudo-vitalistic aspects. "Bodily training in all its forms," he says "is nothing but 'recreation' from work or the gathering of strength for renewed useful labor—it is never valuable *in itself* as a pure play of vital forces. . . . Even modern 'sports' are nothing but recreation from work, and by no means a manifestation of free vitality at whose service work itself should be."[127] In the preface of 1927, Scheler largely agrees with Alfred Peters that modern sport has become "a narcotizing overcompensation for feelings of exhaustion and spiritual emptiness."[128] It is further striking that in both texts Scheler interprets the record performance not as an expression of vitality, but as a surrender to utility. To set a "record," Scheler says in *Ressentiment*, is to participate in the fraudulent notion of "progress"; and in the preface, he refers to an "infantile record-fever."[129] Nevertheless, Scheler is not willing to endorse the full scope of Peters' unsparing critique of the modern sporting mentality.

Peters' *Psychologie des Sports* is a genuinely radical document. By comparison, the sport manifestos of his Socialist contemporaries are often superficial in their naive assumption that "Socialist" sport represents a new kind of experience which is immune to the seductions and defeats of "capitalist" sport. By the same token, "conservative-pessimistic" argument goes beyond the conventional conservative critique by offering a relatively detailed portrait of the mental life of the sportsman.[130]

Scheler's influence is evident in Peters' ambivalence toward the doctrine of vitalism. "Sport is—despite its profound separation from life—somehow filled with a primal force, and gives birth to values which are higher than 'merely' vital ones." Sport is a bastardized manifestation of force, "not really struggle [*Kampf*] and not really play [*Spiel*]," but includes both in distorted form. "Somehow there is always something 'decayed' in the vitality in which sport finds its roots." The "higher, genuinely 'human' sphere" should not be put in the service of "purely vital functions." Peters differs from Scheler in that for him, as for Huizinga, the genuinely "vital" phenomenon is play. And, like Huizinga, Peters maintains that modern sport fails to give expression to "the authentic values of play."[131] Peters seems to suggest that there is a vitalistic principle for which sport is not adequate, but, unlike Scheler, he does not take its existence for granted.

It is this sceptical attitude toward the "vital" sphere which accounts for the sharpness of Peters' attack on sport: for if, *pace* Scheler, sport is not a positive vitalistic phenomenon, then it is a degraded one, as Peters repeatedly claims: sport is a "parasitic phenomenon" which gives only the "sensation" of struggle. But the heart of his critique is that modern sport represents a flight from introspection and self-knowledge. The sportsman flees from "his own emptiness," he is "at bottom a nihilistic type," "closed off" from others. He is "the typical 'pushy' type [*Ellenbogenmensch*]" who at the same time is "in his innermost soul timid and tired." He shows an "absolute indifference to God."[132] Originally printed as a dissertation in 1925, Peters' essay—like Risse's—anticipates Huizinga's emphasis on the degradation of play, as well as Jaspers' insistence upon sport's ultimate superficiality *qua* experience. Peters' clumsy syntax and his turgid, pseudo-philosophical jargon have no doubt cost him readers he otherwise deserves.

A better-known thinker whom Scheler may have influenced is the Spanish philosopher José Ortega y Gasset (1883–1955), who "became friends with Scheler between 1923 and 1928," the year of his death. Ortega refers to Scheler as phenomenology's "first man of genius" and writes: "The death of Scheler left Europe without the best mind it possessed."[133] It is characteristic of Ortega's (well-founded) touchiness regarding his own originality that he denied any direct influence from Scheler. This disclaimer notwithstanding, Ortega shows a great deal of interest in both vitalism and antiutilitarianism after 1923.[134] Like Huizinga, and unlike Scheler, Ortega was genuinely fascinated by sport, which is mentioned in several of his books. In *The Revolt of the Masses* (1930), Ortega pursues the standard conservative strategy of interpreting sport as a potentially "vital" subculture which exists in a fallen state. He is also one of the interwar writers who uses sport as a metaphor to suggest an expanded or dynamic consciousness: "To be surprised, to wonder, is to begin to understand. This is the sport, the luxury, special to the intellectual man. . . . This faculty of wonder is the delight refused to your football 'fan' . . ." Like Scheler, Ortega was temperamentally an elitist who chose democracy over dictatorship *faute de mieux*—"it is well known that I uphold a radically aristocratic interpretation of history." Referring to the "aristocrat," Ortega notes with disapproval "how many of his characteristic traits, in all times and among all peoples, germinate in the mass-man. For example: his propensity to make out of games and sports the central occupation of his life; the cult of the body . . ." Ortega claims that "the reality of history lies in biological power, in pure vitality, in what there is in man of cosmic energy . . ."[135] But by 1933, as Robert Wohl points out, "Ortega was careful to distinguish his views from those of the vitalists. The biological metaphors had disappeared. Life, he made precise, was not a simple biological fact." By then vitalism had fallen into conspicuously ugly hands. Europe, he complains in 1930, "persists in the ignoble vegetative existence of these last years, its muscles flabby for want of exercise . . ."[136] But by 1933 the athletic nation-state was clearly a Nazi ideal.

Prior to this change of heart, Ortega had written of sport with much imagination. In *The Revolt of the Masses*, for example, he focuses less on decline than on a modern "plenitude" of which sport can be one expression. Like Huizinga, he offers a "diagnosis of our times," but the emphasis is on the vitality of the modern era: "our life as a programme of possibilities is magnificent, exuberant, superior to all others known to history." What is more, this vitality has its own distinctively sportive form:

> . . . for the man of the middle classes who lives in towns—and towns are representative of modern existence—the possibilities of enjoyment have increased, in the course of the present century, in fantastic proportion. But the increase of vital potentiality is not limited to what we have said up to this. It has also grown in a more immediate and mysterious direction. It is a constant and well-known fact that in physical effort connected with sport, performances are "put up" today which excel to an extraordinary degree those known in the past. It is

not enough to wonder at each one in particular and to note that it beats the record, we must note the impression that their frequency leaves on the mind, convincing us that the human organism possesses in our days capacities superior to any it has previously had.[137]

In *The Modern Theme* (1931), Ortega writes in praise of "vitality" and "the vital Ego" while cautioning that the philosopher must not permit himself "to be carried away by [life's] movement toward the ultra-vital." Nevertheless, Ortega's chapter titled "Vital Values," which eulogizes Napoleon's "dazzling perfection of vitality" and "the 'noble' animal," emulates, however respectably, the spirit of fascist hero worship. This volume, too, employs a sportive idiom metaphorically and, in contrast to Ortega's infatuation with biological vitalism, most benignly. The "vital function" called desire "resembles a tireless archer, despatching us endlessly to the targets that excite our emotions." The author calls "the sense of life as a sport and as a festivity" one aspect of "the new reaction to existence." "The poet will manage his art with his toes, like a good footballer." Even Einstein is "advancing directly upon problems with the gestures of a young athlete and, by employing the method readiest to hand, catching them by the horns."[138] Such images put Ortega in tune with the age and gave his penchant for "vitality" a wholesome outlet.

As early as *The Modern Theme*, Ortega pronounced his hostility to the category of labor. Work, which Ortega calls "compulsory effort" and which, he strongly implies, is always drudgery, is "balanced by another kind of effort which does not arise from any kind of imposition, but is a perfectly free and hearty impulse of vital potency: this is sport." The "cheerful, hearty and even slightly waggish air that is peculiar to sport" is contrasted with "the morose expression of the worker who alleges the justification of his toil in pathetic reflections on the duty of man and the sacred labour of culture."[139] This antisocial and potentially nihilistic doctrine is eloquently presented in the *Meditations on Hunting* (1943), a carefully argued work of real conviction from which Ortega's dilettantish discussions of philosophy are refreshingly absent.

Ortega's antiutilitarianism in the *Meditations* takes three forms, the most direct being a devaluation of work; Ortega claims that "life used for work does not seem to us to be really ours, which it should be, but on the contrary seems the annihilation of our real existence." He sees "the human being suspended between two con-

flicting repertories of occupations: the laborious and the pleasing."
Human activity is characterized by an absolute dichotomy which
severs work from the vocation, which represents the real point of
being alive. And for the aristocrat, the highest vocation is hunting.
Ortega's second point is that the hunter secedes from the sphere of
history and progress into the infrahistorical realm of the biological;
hunting is "*a contest or confrontation between two systems of instincts,*" it "occurs throughout almost the entire zoological scale," it
is an imitation of nature and of the animal itself. Hunting is "neither
utilitarian nor sporting"; it "cannot substantially progress." "Pushed
by reason, man is condemned to make progress, and this means that
he is condemned to go farther and farther away from Nature, to con-
struct in its place an artificial Nature. Now it is clear why I said earlier that, far from hunting's being a 'reasoned pursuit' of the animal,
the greatest enemy of hunting is reason." Finally, hunting is essentially hierarchical in that it is "irremediably an activity from above
to below"; "the universal fact of hunting reveals to us the inequality
of level among the species—the zoological hierarchy."[140] As a cultic
celebration of the fact of domination itself, hunting is a perfect expression of that aristocratic self-confidence which confirms his disdain for the process of production, for "progress."

In summary, Ortega views hunting as a consummate expression
of "vitality" which, like sport, is susceptible to corruption—for example, "photographic hunting, which is not progress but rather a digression and a prudery of hideous moral style."[141] With his final
phrase, Ortega sounds an authentically ideological note, repudiating
the "humane" adversaries of hunting on their own ground of moral
feeling. The *Meditations* is in this sense a profoundly revanchist
document, both in its hostility to Enlightenment values and in its
exaltation of instinct. It is a species of cultural conservatism which
must be distinguished from the ethically based doctrine of Huizinga
and from Christian fatalism in general. It is not surprising that Huizinga explicitly dissociates himself from Ortega's elite/mass dichotomy in *The Revolt of the Masses.*[142] For while they are both sportive
temperaments, Huizinga reacted viscerally to talk about "the progressive descent of vitality" and "the biological potency of the
type."[143] For Huizinga, the play impulse is not an instrument of force.

The Critique of the Spectator

"The entire mankind of antiquity is full of tender regard for "the
spectator," as an essentially public, essentially visible world which

cannot imagine happiness apart from spectacles and festivals.—And, as aforesaid, even in great *punishment* there is so much that is festive!"[144] So speaks Nietzsche in 1887.

The critique of the spectator, as we have seen, does not derive from classical antiquity. Ancient Rome provided its future critics with the spectacle, but not with a critique of the spectacle. Yet, by the twentieth century and the interwar period in particular, critical and even contemptuous attitudes toward the sport spectator reach across the ideological spectrum, even if in some cases the point is to distinguish between wholesome and unwholesome types of spectatorship. Nor is the spectre of the Colosseum dead; on the contrary, it remains to this day the classical nightmare of its type. As Allen Guttmann has pointed out, at least one modern critic of "dehumanization" in the stadium "writes as a Christian moralist in the tradition of Tertullian and the other Fathers of the Church who turned their patristic wrath against the circus and gladiatorical games of imperial Rome."[145]

But there are more recent historical phenomena, as well, which underlie the condescension so often accorded the sport spectator. In *The Government of Poland* (1772), Rousseau recommended to his sponsors "numerous public games" on the model of Sparta and early Rome, whose citizens partook of "public spectacles that, by keeping them reminded of their forefathers' deeds and hardships and virtues and triumphs, stirred their hearts, set them on fire with the spirit of emulation, and tied them tightly to the fatherland—that fatherland on whose behalf they were kept constantly busy."[146] This, however, is a technique which was adopted on a large scale by the totalitarian societies of the twentieth century, not by the authoritarian or parliamentary societies of the nineteenth. As George Mosse has pointed out, "the fascist style was in reality the climax of a 'new politics' based upon the emerging eighteenth-century idea of popular sovereignty."[147] Nineteenth-century liberals and conservatives united in their disapproval of mass political movements, including nationalist ones. The notion of a tyrannical and amorphous "public"—a classic treatment of which appears in the Danish thinker Søren Kierkegaard's polemical *Two Ages* (1846)—was born. Behind it stood the howling mobs of the French Revolution, the "spectators" in attendance at the guillotine. In short, mass politics tended to give the image of the spectator a barbaric aspect, that of the "mob."

It is only apparently paradoxical that the emotionally violent spectator came to be viewed as a passive type. The most famous example of French counterrevolutionary literature, Gustave Le Bon's *The Crowd* (1895), makes a point of emphasizing—in addition to its "barbarian" and "impulsive" aspects—the crowd's "stupidity," "suggestibility," and "feminine characteristics"; it is a phenomenon in which "conscious personality vanishes."[148] A second nineteenth-century antecedent of the passive spectator is the cultural philistine. The striking fact for the French poet Alfred de Vigny "was that society was divided into two hostile camps, the culture creators and its countless, mediocre, uncomprehending consumers. . . . and that a society controlled by sterile, parasitic audiences was corrupt."[149] Nietzsche attacks the quality of nineteenth-century theatre audiences in *The Genealogy of Morals* (1887)—but refers approvingly to the Roman games.

During the interwar period, the mass character of European societies became the paramount sociological theme. Karl Mannheim attacks "the plebiscitary element in democracy" as a manifestation of "crowd psychology," basing his argument on a conception of the spectator which combines the political and aesthetic critiques reviewed above: "A modern plebiscite treats the individual as a spectator, whereas in the smaller democratic groups he was an active and co-operative member of the commune. The spectator is known to be completely irresponsible; he is simply there to see the show, and has no intention of weighing the facts or grasping the implications of the spectacle."[150] This distinction between participating and spectating had been applied to sport spectators in 1902 by J. A. Hobson, as one of the "moral and sentimental factors" conducive to the insensate mentality of imperialistic ambition.[151] During the interwar period, the critique of the passive, indiscriminate, sensation-hungry sport spectator becomes ubiquitous. Risse (1921) portrays this attachment to sport as being merely modish and motivated by a need to appear up-to-date.[152] Frank Thiess (1927) speaks of "a sheer desire to gape" (*bloßer Schaulust*).[153] Ortega (1930) disparages the football "fan."[154] Lewis Mumford (1933) defines "mass-sports" as "those forms of organized play in which the spectator is more important than the player."[155] The Nazi Alfred Baeumler (1935) and the German Socialist Helmut Wagner (1931) criticize the passive and sensation-seeking types of spectator, respectively, implying that there are alternative (and superior) forms of spectatorship.[156] It is worth noting that Bertolt Brecht, who made the consciousness of the spectator a primary issue of his "epic" drama, actually saw the sport spectator as superior to contemporary patrons of the theatre.[157] The idea that the sport spectator possesses unusual expertise has recently been revived by Christopher Lasch.[158]

6. Nazi Sport Theory: Racial Heroism and the Critique of Sport

The Doctrine of the Body

Unlike Mussolini, Hitler had no genuine interest in sport apart from its use as a form of political expressionism, such as the Olympic spectacle of 1936 in Berlin.[1] In fact, according to Albert Speer, Hitler's view of sport could be decidedly unheroic: "His dislike for snow burst out repeatedly, long before the catastrophic winter campaign of 1941–42. 'If I had my way I'd forbid these sports [mountain climbing and alpine skiing] with all the accidents people have doing them. But of course the mountain troops draw their recruits from such fools.'"[2] *Mein Kampf* (1925), however, tells a rather different story. Here Hitler conjoins the formation of his "first ideals" with "my association with extremely 'husky' boys";[3] and there are some twenty favorable references throughout the book to sport and the cultivation of the body. The primary significance of the body for Nazi ideologists lay in its racial rather than its sportive properties, which were officially interpreted as evidence of racial superiority.[4] If National Socialism meant *inter alia* "a bombastic pedagogy incorporating the primacy of the body," this was directly attributable to Hitler's demand for "bodies which are healthy to the core."[5] Second in ideological authority to Hitler was Alfred Baeumler, an academic philosopher and the only sport intellectual of consequence produced by the Third Reich.

The body is the core of the Nazi political anthropology. The body of the Aryan is the tangible and vital evidence of racial virtue, of the "new human type" that National Socialism had brought into being.[6] The culmination of this racial doctrine is achieved in the "human breeding institutes" whose purpose was to produce "the aristocracy of the future." Extending this policy even further, Himmler planned at one point a search for the "Chosen Women," possessed of "athletic grace and cultured intelligence, delicacy of feeling and subtlety of expression," whom SS leaders would be required to marry after having taken "honorable" leave of their wives.[7] On this level, the body is valued for its biological (and aesthetic) qualities *per se*.

But in a racial community, the body (*Leib*) is, as Baeumler puts it, *ein Politicum*, a public rather than a private entity; the *Volk* itself is a "collective body" (*Gesamtleib*).[8] Physical exercises (*Leibesübungen*) are "a public matter."[9] It is Baeumler's emphasis on "the political education of the body" (*die politische Leibeserziehung*) which compels him to resist the apotheosis of the body *athleticum* in favor of the body *politicum*: "Recognition of the political character of our bodies rules out any absolute conception of the body. . . . The honor of the body is one part of the collective honor of the nation."[10]

The ideological preoccupations of Nazi sport theory are prefigured in, and in some respects derive from, the doctrine of Friedrich Ludwig Jahn (1778–1852), founder of the gymnastic movement in Germany in 1811. It was Jahn who first seized upon the concept of *Volkstum* to denote a cultic and racial nationalism which would require little improvisation on the part of the Nazis.[11] As Hajo Bernett has commented, "The 'fascistoid' spirit of the national [*völkischen*] movement is evident."[12] "Jahngeist ist Hitlergeist," one contributor to the *Deutsche Turnzeitung* proclaims in 1933, and the *Führer* was happy to agree.[13] It is worth noting that Alfred Baeumler, who along with Edmund von Neuendorff of the Deutsche Turnerschaft was one of Jahn's principal promoters during the Third Reich, felt obliged to claim that Nazi sport ideology actually surpassed Jahn's doctrine in three ways. First, it ascribes a "deeper significance" to Jahn's racial mysticism (*Volkstümlichkeit*) than even the master himself; second, it has a deeper appreciation for adolescence as an "initiation into manhood"; and third, Nazi doctrine presupposes "the reawakening of the sense for public life"[14]—the body as a *Politicum*. These improvements notwithstanding, the three fundamental themes of Nazi physical culture—the feeling of racial superiority, the health of the *Volk*, and military education—are all present in Jahn.[15]

The aesthetics of the body is another theme which connects Jahn's cult of the body with that of Nazi ideology. As George Mosse points out, Jahn "condemned the departure from that noble simplicity of form which his gymnasts should symbolize: 'the bigger the stomach, the more unsteady and turbulent man's looks, the emptier is his soul.' The student fraternity movement, from its beginning in 1810, worshipped a similar beauty, and this continued into the Youth Movement which began at the end of the nineteenth century. The constant reiteration that the true German must have a beautiful body repeats the worship of the Greek models."[16] In his controversial *Spießer-Ideologie*, Hermann Glaser denounces "an exaltation of the physical which became a part of common culture" during the latter part of the nineteenth century. "This was reflected in such tasteless metaphors as 'sublime body' and 'divine bosom' and from the very beginning exalted the artistic, and later the real, cult of the body to the highest level in the hierarchy of values, as a kind of aesthetic myth."[17]

Glaser's objection to this kind of aestheticism is that it is inherently mendacious—"a literally maniacal craving for beauty which was coupled with the repression of truthfulness." The National Socialists "endowed the 'Greco–National Socialist' body with a 'grace' which really spelled brutality, and with a form of dignity which reflected racial arrogance. Anatomy was trump. . . . Classicism was cancelled out in the name of classicism: man was beautiful not to be true and free, graceful or ennobled, but rather to entice to race-conscious copulation." A neoclassical worship of the body, however degenerate, could conquer through the prestige of ancient Greek art, whose most famous exponent had been German art historian J. J. Winckelmann (1717–1768). The crucial difference is that Winckelmann's admiration for ancient Greek bodies specifically ruled out a cultic approach to modern German ones: "The most beautiful body of ours would perhaps be as much inferior to the most beautiful Greek one, as Iphicles was to his brother Hercules."[18] For Winckelmann, "political athleticism" is literally unthinkable, "the Nazi Tarzan" (Glaser) a biological fantasy of the future, and the notion of the "Greco–National Socialist" body an absurdity.

Corporeal aesthetics was also an element of racial doctrine. The basic racial categories are the nordic and eastern types, the former being characterized by coolly superior emotions and a heroic outlook, while the latter shows warmth of feeling, excitability, and a less martial disposition: the steel-hard muscles and firm flesh of the German, writes Bruno Malitz in 1934, contrast with the softness and effeminacy of the Jew.[19] The Jews, another author states, lack the "heroic body-frame."[20]

A particularly insulting axiom of this attempt at a racial anthropology claims that Jews do not have control over their own bodies: "Observing the movements of a Jew, one has the feeling that his limbs are fitted in their joints in a manner which differs from that of the German. Legs and arms dangle, their movement apparently uncontrolled, as though they were to some extent independent of the will of their bearer." This principle is occasionally applied to dancing, which has allegedly given rise to racially distinct styles. The nordic type dances "with a cool and clear self-mastery," in unison with others and in harmony with traditional forms, whereas the eastern type dances with the "intoxicated virtuosity of the solitary dancer." The nordic (male) dancer should preserve a soldierly, austere bearing.[21] Alfred Baeumler claims that he cannot take seriously anyone who finds "fulfillment" in a state of dancing frenzy.[22] It may be noted that the theme of self-control appears frequently in Nazi sport texts.[23]

Nazi sport doctrine is consciously anti-intellectual. In this sense it presents a vulgar imitation of the aristocratic disdain for the intellect endorsed by body-conscious thinkers like Nietzsche and Ortega y Gasset.[24] In his address to the German Gymnastics Festival (1933), Hitler declares, "Life will not be protected by weak philosophers, but by strong men." The youth leader Baldur von Schirach calls for a "decision between the soul and the cold intellect." Physical education for women is endorsed as a "counterweight to the one-sided development of those mental tendencies which lead to a solitary existence and to estrangement from the racial community."[25] Sport is a prophylactic against "one-sided intellectualism."[26] There is a warning against tolerating the unwholesome inhibitions of "sport illiterates."[27] Jahn, too, emphasized the limitations of human understanding,[28] and it is interesting to see that Jahn's disciple Baeumler, who in 1934 crowed about "the triumph over intellectualism," demonstrates a greater caution three years later, if only to reject the total denigration of "intellectual workers" like himself.[29]

The Nazi Critique of Sport

No less than their Communist adversaries, the Nazis insisted on "committed" culture. It is for this reason that the Nazi critique of sport is, in the last analysis, a critique of "unpolitical" or "bourgeois" sport. Like other types of culture, Nazi sport fulfills a political role which precludes its being an end in itself.[30] The body, in short, requires a political education. Baeumler, somewhat paradoxically, suggests that "unpolitical" sport is both politically innocuous and politically noxious. Sport as a mere "formalism"—that is, sport without political content—does not affect the individual "deep inside"; but he then goes on to claim that the "unpolitical character" of sport is really a mirage: "Nothing is more instructive in this regard than the philosophical and political 'neutrality' of the sport associations. To the practical internationalism of the Olympic Games there corresponds an inner internationalism: here as everywhere, neutrality is just the word for a concealed political position staked out on the path of least resistance . . ."[31] The "unpolitical character" of sport, another commentator states, is a figment of the "bourgeois" sport clubs.[32] From a totalitarian standpoint, the "unpolitical" or "neutral" position is equivalent to dissent, being a perverse refusal to conform to ideological norms.

One such Nazi norm was sheer aggressiveness. Boxing was Hitler's idea of a politically wholesome sport—an antidote to "peaceable aesthetes and bodily degenerates"—and one which Baeumler too could endorse.[33] International sport, on the other hand, was a "pacifist-international" plot concocted by the Jews to soften up the German male and substitute sport for war on behalf of global reconciliation.[34] Baeumler considers the forced adherence to "international rules and norms" alien to Nazi praxis.[35]

The Nazi critique of sport must also, by virtue of its collectivistic ideal, take a deeply ambivalent position vis-à-vis high performance sport and attempts to set records. On the one hand, record seeking is an expression of undisciplined individualism, of an "abstract," "unpolitical" technical effort which is divorced from the community at large.[36] On the other, the crowning performance of Nazi athletes are a positive expression of the vitality of the state. Alfred Baeumler, as usual, takes the most nuanced position. It is too easy, he says, to reject "record mania" and the objective standards which make records possible; these belong to the essence of sport and prevent the degeneration of sport into "mere play." But record mania and an "industrial" approach to sport lie on sport "like a curse" once "the early phase, the first tests of courage and conquests of space, has been left behind."[37]

Incorporated into the Nazi critique of sport is a selective critique of modern ("liberal") civilization strongly reminiscent of (non-fascist) cultural conservatism. For example, the claim that "our civilization is characterized by an excess of nervous tension" is pure Coubertin; but to associate this condition, as one Nazi author does, with "an effeminacy of body and spirit" suggests the Nazi infatuation with virility *per se* which Coubertin never shared.[38] It should be clear that National Socialism itself, far from being a palliative for the hyperbolic character of modern life, was rather an extreme example of it; for the genuine cultural conservatives, Nazi Germany was a horrific and inhuman spectacle despite its flights into "conservative" nostalgia.

A second conservative issue is the fragmented or incomplete condition of the modern individual, for whom the secular state is a poor substitute for the loss of an organic religious culture. This is a problem any totalitarian government must claim to have solved, and associated with this "solution" is a critique of inauthentic existence. Alfred Baeumler offers the diagnosis that "modern man inhabits a world devoid of earthbound symbols and secure footholds," a world which will be redeemed through nazism. What Baeumler has to offer is "the re-integration of man" in a Nazi context. "The newly awakened sense of the importance of physical culture [*Leibesübungen*] in our epoch is a historical phenomenon of the first rank, a sign that the re-integration of man, the recuperation of space, has begun."[39] For the relationship to God or ethics Baeumler substitutes the relationship to "space," which has taken on a new and eccentric dimension. Once again a Nazi ideologist offers the form, but not the substance, of cultural conservatism.

A third conservative theme, and another adopted by Baeumler, is the critique of the passive spectator, which as a Nazi theme actually derives from a more basic critique of "the individual" (*der Einzelne*), the passive "experiencer" who has refused integration into the body of the nation. The Olympic festivals of ancient Greece, for example, were not "a production put on before a feverish mass." Jahn envisioned a human type superior to the "mere spectator." It is high-performance sport, focused on the achievements of the individual athlete, which creates "the public as a crowd of passive, more or less expert spectators."[40] But here, too, appearances are deceiving, since the Nazi idea of passivity differs from that of the cultural conservative. For Baeumler, "passivity" is really the refusal to participate in the political whole, whereas for the conservative it is rather a lack of autonomy or energy (e.g., Ortega) which tends to massify the individual. Both conservative and Nazi ideologies express a concern for the quality of human experience, and for this reason both offer critiques of the modern age. However, as we have seen, different values give rise to essentially different criticisms of "modern" civilization. In this sense, nazism is indeed a pseudo-conservatism.

A Comparative Perspective

How does Nazi sport ideology fit into the theoretical framework of this book? First, let us examine its use of sportive imagery. It is ironic that, due to Hitler's unsportive physique and disposition, the most important of the fascisms was not in a position to exploit the essentially fascist theme of "political athleticism." The idea of the corporealized nation-state, on the other hand, encountered no such impediment, and Alfred Baeumler employs it in two ways. On the one hand, there is "the collective body of the people": "The honor of the body constitutes one part of the collective honor of the nation"; on the other, a "genuine team is the symbolic representation of its people."[41] The nation may be one body or a coordinated collective of bodies. This is imagery which the Nazis, unlike the Marxists, had no reason to renounce.

We should also examine Alfred Baeumler's views on the labor-leisure dialectic, since he appears to be the only Nazi author who accords it serious attention. Hermann Rauschning quotes Hitler as endorsing what the "play-impulses" (*Spieltriebe*)—rather than the intellect—have to teach, but this is not the spirit of Schiller. In his next breath Hitler calls upon youth to learn the art of domination. Nazi sport texts in general emphasize self-mastery rather than playful spontaneity; Hajo Bernett points to Nazi ideology's tendency to "denature" play.[42] But Baeumler, as Winfried Joch points out, stresses the noninstrumental character of physical culture, thereby severing himself from Nazi doctrine in this as in certain other instances.[43] Baeumler speaks of a "spontaneous joy" without which gymnastics loses its character. What is more, the critique of instrumental thinking is one aspect of his critique of modernity: "Modern man is divided by his practical goals [*Zwecke*] and no longer arrives at being. This is why our life is so joyless: the descent into gloom is the mark of modern culture." Baeumler emends the labor-play dichotomy by introducing the physical exercise (*Leibesübung*) as a third factor denoting the mode in which the body "works" for itself. The gymnast walks a fine line between sacrificing the strenuous factor (*Übung*), which results in the body's indolent self-enjoyment, and the danger that performance *per se* may become the goal of the exercise, with the consequence that the animate body (*Leib*) is devalued to the status of a carcass (*Körper*).[44]

Another anti-instrumental aspect of Baeumler's sport doctrine is his hostility to the interpretation of sport as a hygienic measure. It need hardly be pointed out that Baeumler, like every ideological interpreter of sport, has certain hygienic goals of his own. (As Bernett has pointed out, Nazi ideologists considered the renunciation of high-performance sport a "humane" measure.)[45] The difference is that Baeumler's hygienism is holistic and focused on the existential well-being of the German citizen, whereas the hygienism he attacks is deficient in its narrowly medical outlook.[46] It cannot be an accident that the medically hygienic approach to physical culture is the basis of early Bolshevist sport doctrine. It is likely that here, as elsewhere, Baeumler is mimicking the conservative anti-Marxist (e.g., Huizinga), in this case his distinction between the banality of Marxist "materialism" and the transcendence contained in "spirit." This dichotomy is interpreted by another author as the difference between "material accumulation and calculation" and "the courage to take risks"[47]—in short, a defiantly antiutilitarian *Heroismus*.

The larger context in which Nazi sport ideology may be interpreted is that of "totalitarianism" itself. Both Nazi and Soviet sport doctrines promulgate a new human type to replace the mediocre or venal "bourgeois."[48] Both must deal (ambivalently) with the contradiction between the star performer and a strict collectivistic ethos. Both exhibit what Hajo Bernett has called the "utopian initial phase,"[49] which—in the name of a collectivistic principle—scorns competition before this phase, too, is sacrificed to sport's inherent expressionism, its cult of force.

7. The Origins of Socialist Sport: Marxist Sport Culture in the Years of Innocence

Early Soviet Sport Ideology

The Critique of Bolshevism. Eventually, every revolution casts an indulgent, but disabused, look back upon its euphoric origins. The 1920s, a Soviet sociologist writes in 1976, "had no shortage of the most fantastic proposals for instantly smashing the old life-style, destroying existing morals, customs, and traditions, and introducing a new revolutionary morality at a single leap, so to speak. It was forgotten that daily life, which contains a very powerful charge of banality and self-isolation, conceals an elemental capacity to resist all attempts to change it . . . "[1]

The Soviet and Maoist versions of Communist sport culture both began as revolutionary (visionary) sport cultures—so revolutionary, in fact, as to have devalued sport as we understand it. (The sport culture of East Germany represents the transplanting of Stalinist sport onto the soil which had produced the visionary, antibourgeois workers' sport movement of the 1920s, whose heritage is claimed—if not entirely deserved—by the sport doctrinaires of the GDR.) All three of these Communist sport cultures, judged by their original ideals, have degenerated. The dream of an alternative to "bourgeois" sport, its ruthless competitive ethos, its unscrupulous appeals to the lowest appetites, and the cult of the star performer, has died a grotesque death in the sport factories of the East, where "bourgeois" vices have hypertrophied into "Socialist" ones. This chapter examines the early phases of the two European Marxist sport cultures. As we shall see in later chapters on Soviet and East German sport, the values which characterized the idealistic early periods did not wholly succumb to the massive revisionism of the later years. In some cases these values have been enshrined as party doctrine, and as such may be respectfully disregarded: one thinks of the recurrent Soviet analogy between sport and labor. In other cases, they may live on as bizarre (albeit humane) anachronisms, such as the Soviets' proscription of certain "dangerous" or "alien" sports. Patronized, preserved, or distorted almost beyond recognition, the early doctrines have survived even if they have not prevailed.

Early Bolshevist Sport Culture. For about a decade after the Bolshevist Revolution there were really three important sport ideologies in the Soviet Union, although the term "sport" is something of a misnomer. James Riordan calls the 1921–1929 period "the years of *physical culture* rather than sport, the dividing line between the two being in the presence of an element of competition. . . . Competitive sport bred, in some people's minds, attitudes alien to socialist society."[2] The first school may be called the utilitarian. That the early period of War Communism and the New Economic Policy (NEP) did not produce a flourishing leisure culture is hardly surprising. Times were very hard, and the emphasis was on austerity and practicality. "As Soviet life is essentially Spartan in character," an American observer writes during the 1920s, "so physical culture assumes an essentially Spartan hardness and utilitarian purpose. . . . There is undoubtedly a seriousness about sport that is apt to daze an outside observer even though he may be thoroughly cognizant of the seriousness that may animate Western teams as they contend for the championships and public glory."[3] A premilitary training program, the so-called Vsevobuch, was formed on May 7, 1918; while tolerating competition, its primary concern was the application of sport to human hygiene.

A second group, actually called the "hygienists," added to public health *per se* an ideological dimension—hostility to competition and political disapproval of certain types of sport—which is no longer acceptable in the light of modern Communist sport doctrine, even if traces of these attitudes still persist. "Such pursuits as weightlifting, boxing and gymnastics were, in their opinion, irrational and dangerous, and encouraged individualist rather than collectivist attitudes and values—and, as such, were contrary to the desired socialist ethic."[4] One remnant of the hygienist ideology still present in Soviet sport concerns the game of chess: "In Russia today," an observer notes in 1977, "it's illegal to play simultaneous blindfolded chess, because too many good young players went insane doing it."[5] The Polish sport sociologist Andrzej Wohl, a representative of the modern Soviet school, criticizes the hygienists for their cultural myopia, in that they "actually wanted to make the program of the 'Vsievobuch' permanent in this narrowed down form. In such a Utopian way they intended to eliminate all the other functions of sport, with the exception of its prophylactic functions and those that were important for health. They wanted to turn their one-sided professional knowledge into a principle, on which was to be based the entire rich and all-round practical aspect of physical culture."[6] Phrased somewhat differently, the point is that purist hygienism did not stand a chance against the Stalinist cult of sheer performance which was enforced throughout Soviet society beginning in the early 1930s.

The allies of the hygienists were the "Proletkultists," who

> demanded the rejection of competitive sport and all organized sports that derived from bourgeois society, as remnants of the decadent past and emanations of degenerate bourgeois culture. A fresh start had to be made through the 'revolutionary innovation of proletarian physical culture,' which would take the form of 'labor gymnastics' and mass displays, pageants and excursions. Gymnasiums and the 'bourgeois' equipment would be replaced by various pieces of apparatus on which young proletarians could practice their 'labour movements.' The Proletkul'tists therefore went much further than the 'hygienists' in condemning all manner of games, sports and gymnastics 'tainted' by bourgeois society.[7]

It is a matter of some urgency to Andrzej Wohl to show why this extreme antibourgeois ideology simply could not last. The Proletkultists, he says, "demanded [the] rejection of competitive sport and sports events as remnants of the past and signs of the degeneration of bourgeois culture. They rejected all the achievements of world sport, thinking that one can be completely detached from the past and begin to create physical culture from scratch."[8] The "Proletkult" literary movement, too, had wanted to sever all connections with the past: "In the name of our future we are burning Raphael, destroying the museums, and trampling on the flowers of art . . . " Lenin, however, saw the Proletkult heresy as cultural vandalism: "Proletarian culture is not something that suddenly surfaces without our having any idea of where it comes from, it is not the invention of people who claim to be specialists in proletarian culture. All of that is preposterous. . . . All the culture that capitalism has left us must be carefully preserved and it is on this basis that Socialism must be built, otherwise it will be impossible for us to create the life of Communist society."[9]

Wohl, like Lenin, is very impatient with these short-sighted ideological purists, and he is relieved to be able to tell us that on July 25, 1925, the party, in addition to adopting a resolution supporting the hygienist and other practical roles for sport, "also expressed itself in favor of top-level performances in sport, provided there is the necessary medical and pedagogical control and also in favor of competitive sport as a means to reveal collective achievements as well as individual ones." Wohl's impatience with the purists, and his eagerness to see "top-level performances," is one aspect of his revisionism, which is wholly in tune with modern Soviet sport ideology. The key to his opposition to the early purists is his observation that they were people "who had no understanding whatsoever for the emotions of the athlete, for the fight in sports, to put it in a nutshell: for the culture-creating functions of sport." The problem with the early theorists, from Wohl's standpoint, is "a quite far-reaching lack of orientation regarding further perspectives of development for sport."[10] Back in the 1920s the chairman of the government-sponsored Supreme Council of Physical Culture, Nikolay Semashko, was even more blunt about the matter: "If you keep the populace on the semolina pudding of hygienic gymnastics, physical culture will not gain very wide publicity." He need not have worried: the leaders of the hygienist and Proletkult movements did not survive the Great Purge of 1936–1938.[11]

The Transformation of the Body. In *The Possessed* (1872), Dostoyevsky's crank nihilist Kirilov dreams of "the new man." The goal of history, he insists, eyes flashing, is "the physical transformation of man and the earth. Man will be a god and he'll change physically and the whole world will change. Man's preoccupations will change; so will his thoughts and feelings. Don't you think man will change physically then?"[12] A half-century later (in 1924) Trotsky's answer to this question is an unqualified yes: "Even purely physiologic life will become subject to collective experiments. The human species, the coagulated *homo sapiens*, will once more enter into a state of radical transformation, and, in his own hands, will become an object of the most complicated methods of artificial selection and psycho-physical training. This is entirely in accord with evolution." What is more, this transformation promises to be aesthetically improving: "Man will become immeasurably stronger, wiser and subtler; his body will become more harmonized, his movements more rhythmic, his voice more musical." Trotsky is not ashamed to speak of "a higher social biologic type, or, if you please, a superman." While predicting lively ideological debate concerning "a best system of sports,"[13] Trotsky does not envision for his readers a superathletic type. Indeed, his alleged ties to the hygienists suggest instead a utopian, anticompetitive orientation.[14]

Trotsky's vision of somatic transformation is essentially euphoric. Yet a very different sort of physical ideal is also relevant to this period, though it is more a crypto-ideal than a publicly acknowledged one. A literary prototype for the "Spartan hardness" of Bolshevist physical culture is Rakhmétov, the hero of Nikolay Chernyshevsky's famous novel *What Is to Be Done?* (1864), a type which has been described as "the revolutionary ascetic." "Rakhmétov's asceticism, we are told, was not from personal desire but from a temporary, functional necessity of being 'hard' in order to carry out the needed tasks. Meanwhile, although it was also necessary to refrain from 'useless expenditures of time,' physical exercise was essential. Starting with gymnastics, Rakhmétov proceeded to search for work requiring strength (chopping firewood, forging iron). Adopting the diet of pugilists, 'he ate food known exclusively as strengthening, especially almost raw beefsteak.'" [15] (Kirilov, too, has a regimen of physical exercises.) [16] Rakhmétov's reincarnation in revolutionary history is Lenin, who adopted in addition to his physical asceticism the very title of the book in which Rakhmétov appears. Lenin's friend Valentinov has described Lenin's virtually obsessive devotion to physical sports, [17] but he makes it equally clear that this devotion was firmly based upon a functionalism antithetical to the sort of emotionalism or aestheticizing which sport so often generates in less ascetic temperaments. This is not to argue that Lenin did not enjoy the strenuous physical regimen he imposed on himself. He undoubtedly did enjoy it; but it was the functionalism rather than the enjoyment which became social policy.

A third interpretation of the body took as its point of departure what René Fueloep-Miller calls in 1926 the "imitation of the machine":

> Just as pious mystics once strove to make themselves into an image of God, and finally to become absorbed in Him, so now the modern ecstatics of rationalism labour to become like the machine and finally to be absorbed into bliss in a structure of driving belts, pistons, valves and fly-wheels. People began eagerly to investigate the mechanical elements in man himself, the technical foundations of the bodily organism, which must in the future be encouraged and religiously developed; they tried to schematize as mechanical functions all the organic movements, to arrive, finally, at the conception of every vital manifestation as a partial function of a regularly pulsing world of automata. [18]

The sportive expression of this "machine-cult of the Bolsheviks" and its reverie of an artificial "homunculus" appears in a famous novel by Yuri Olesha. *Envy* (1927) is a meditation on the transition from the old bourgeois values to the new Soviet utopia; its primary spokesman is a Dostoyevskian antihero whose fecklessly subversive attitude toward the new order makes him a significant reincarnation of the Underground Man. Olesha's innovation as an antiutopian writer is to employ the body as an ideological variable. Kavalerov, the antihero, is physically timid and assures the reader that "I'll never be either handsome or famous. . . . nor a sprinter, nor an adventurer." His ideological opposite, Volodia Makarov, is both the protégé and symbolic stepson of a powerful Soviet bureaucrat and a star soccer player who is described as "a completely new human being" by his sponsor.

Olesha finds in sport a profoundly ambivalent quality. On the one hand, there is its nonrational dimension, its "magical" realm. Volodia's spontaneous, innate athleticism expresses itself as an "athletic jauntiness" and as wondrous physical ability: "Volodia would get hold of the ball when it seemed physically impossible to do so"; "Volodia would grab the ball, tearing it out of its line of flight, transgressing the laws of physics, for which the indignant elements tried to retaliate." But Volodia's acquired (and political) conception of himself in effect renounces his natural gift. "I am of the new generation," he declares. "I have become a human machine. . . . I want to be proud of my work, to be indifferent to everything outside it. So I have become envious of the machine; why am I not just as good? We invented, designed and constructed it. It turns out to be much harder than we are." Volodia is also a utopian psychologist who cannot fathom why human relations do not obey a law of harmony: "Such people don't understand our times. Time is also a technical concept. If everyone was a technician, wickedness, vanity, and other petty feelings would disappear."[19] Long before its real flowering in the Soviet bloc, Olesha foresaw the fusion of sport and technocratic optimism. For this reason, the real import of his critique of sport is less the idealism of his contemporaries than the scientific realism of the future.

If revolutionary innovation in early Bolshevist Russia called for the arts to be more dramatic and spectacular, revolutionary logic also demanded, as we have seen, that physical culture be reduced in large measure to a socially oriented functional role. But what about the "theatrical-utopian" element? "As soon as the Bolsheviks recognized the great importance of the theatre for purposes of propaganda," Fuelœp-Miller writes in 1926,

they made increasingly strenuous efforts to extend the suggestive force of the stage to the greatest possible number of people. . . . They tried, by the introduction of great festive mass-performances, to make the streets themselves the arena for dramatic events, and to link up parades, processions, and national festivals, so as to form an ordered and systematically organized total effect. In the slogan 'Theatricalize life,' the dictators of revolutionary art saw a possibility of evolving with scenic means a propaganda such as could never be attained within the theatre itself. By this means the 'collective man' was also to celebrate his glorification in a solemn and magnificent way. It was no wonder that the Bolshevists began to regard the 'theatricalization of life' as a task of high political importance.[20]

At one point the "theatricalization of sport" had been criticized as a Proletkultist heresy.[21] But this theatrical-utopian style, too, would eventually be appropriated by its destroyers. The mass gymnastics displays and parades have survived, thanks to the adoption of Stalinist monumentalism as a state aesthetic. Fueloep-Miller has described the more refined early phase of the "theatricalization of life," including a "mass festival performance" which the great director Vsevolod Meyerhold planned in order to celebrate the third congress of the Communist International but which was never carried out, apparently for nonpolitical reasons. In Fueloep-Miller's account: "After a great parade of troops, the gymnastic associations on motorvans were to have shown the people of the future engaged in throwing the discus and gathering the hay into sheaves. . . . Rhythmic movements performed by the pupils of the public training schools were to have symbolized the phrase, 'Joy and Strength—the victory of the creators.'"[22] One contemplates Meyerhold's "people of the future" with the anthropologist's gentle awe at the thought of a vanished race. The symbolism conjoining images of labor and play point forward with a naive charm to the communism of the future, which would eventually insist on the fusion of labor and leisure; and it points backward to a Hellenic ideal derived, no doubt, from a bourgeois civilization's dream of Winckelmann's Greece and the perfections of its athleticism—all of this, of course, in the service of the Revolution. Meyerhold, who did not survive Stalinism, took his utopianism seriously: "In the past," he writes in 1922, "the actor has always conformed with the society for which his art was intended. In future the actor must go even further in relating his technique to the industrial situation. For he will be working in a society where labour is no longer regarded as a curse but as a joyful, vital necessity." "How do we set about moulding the new actor?" he asks. "It is quite simple I think. When we admire a child's movements we are admiring his biomechanical skill. If we place him in an environment in which gymnastics and all forms of sport are both available and compulsory, we shall achieve the new man who is capable of any form of labor. *Only via the sports arena can we approach the theatrical arena*"[23]—an idea which posits nothing less than the synthesis of labor, sport, and art. We recall that Trotsky, too, aestheticizes physical culture in a way that is less revolutionary than utopian, and one can trace this Proletkultist aesthetic element forward to the sport culture of East Germany. As a young man, the sport-minded Walter Ulbricht and his friends "met regularly in the Socialist Leipziger Volkshaus (People's House) to practice calisthenics and to rehearse for club parties, at which they liked to present so-called living statues—'three-dimensional compositions under colored lights.'"[24] This fusion of aesthetics and physical culture later became known in the GDR (and in the Soviet Union) as "sports acrobatics," and it is an athleticism with an ideological message: "Stage acrobats sell their act and that is the difference between professionals and ourselves. They go on with props, apparatus, dazzling costumes and a bit of gimmick to catch the interest and imagination of their audience. We sports acrobats, on the other hand, do without all that."[25] Even in the context of physical aestheticism, the spartan element of early Soviet sport lives on.

The Workers' Sport Movement in Germany, 1893–1933

The Concept of Socialist Sport. "Is there really no antidote to whatever our class dreams up?" Hans Magnus Enzensberger asks in "On the Irresistibility of the Petty Bourgeoisie" (1976).[26] The workers' culture movement (*Arbeiterkulturbewegung*), which in Germany dates from the last decades of the nineteenth century, was an attempt to provide working-class people with an alternative to, and an "antidote" for, the dominant culture of the bourgeoisie. Music, theatre, pedagogy, and even photography were—at least in theory—given "Socialist" content and thereby incorporated into a larger ideological project.

Workers' sports movements existed throughout Europe during the 1920s and 1930s, the oldest (German and British) having been founded during the 1890s.[27] In 1913 representatives of the Belgian, British, French, German, and Italian workers' sport federations met in Ghent to form the short-lived Socialist International of Physical

Education. In 1925 it was refounded as the Socialist Workers' Sport International (SASI) with a membership of 1.3 million. "The aim of the workers' movement," Robert Wheeler writes,

> while it might vary moderately from group to group, was basically the same everywhere. It tried to provide working people, especially the young, with the opportunity to participate in healthy, enjoyable physical activity and to do this in a positive working-class atmosphere. Workers' sports were to be consciously different from 'bourgeois' sports in that they were open to all—the classic example being the 'Workers' Wimbledon' championships of the 1930's. But beyond presenting equality of opportunity to all workers, the labour sports movement set itself up as a humanistic *alternative* to the excesses of 'bourgeois' athletic competition. Not only did workers' sport seek to remove the class line from participation, it also sought to substitute socialist for capitalist values in the process and thereby help to lay the groundwork for a uniquely working-class culture. Such thinking contributed to the tendency within the movement prior to 1914 to emphasize less competitive physical activities, such as gymnastics, cycling, hiking and swimming.[28]

This struggle against a dominant bourgeois culture was a heroic enterprise, which would have lasted much longer than it did had it not been crushed by the Nazis. But could it have survived the era of television, consumerism, and the cult of immediate gratifications?

For Helmut Wagner, author of *Sport and Workers' Sport* (1931), sport has two components: a "biological-psychological core" and "a specific social, historical form." Every sport has "a healthy core" which can be preserved (by "Socialist" sport) or forfeited by social-historical conditions ("bourgeois" sport). Wagner emphasizes that no specific type of physical culture is unhealthy in and of itself; it is rather the basic "disposition" (*Gesinnung*) with which it is practiced that is decisive.[29] This view is endorsed by the most prominent of the workers' sport ideologists, Fritz Wildung, who sees sport either as a means of self-regeneration or as the body-deforming obsession.[30] Socialist sport is not "militarism in the guise of sport, professionalism, passive spectatorship, sensationalism, record-chasing." Nor is it "muscle foolishness," uncritical admiration of star athletes, or anti-intellectualism.[31] It is worth noting that both Wildung and Wagner disapprove of the cultic approach to sport, which can produce apoliticism or a purist sectarianism. Wildung dismisses as "one-sided fanatics" those who think that "the social issue" can be solved by gymnastics—or music, or theatre. Wagner criticizes the "sport sects" (primarily nudists and gymnasts) who insist on "a purely socialist attitude to sport" and want to banish competition and high-level performances.[32]

The issue of competition created problems for an essentially fraternal mentality. A fundamental tenet of this sport ideology is that, under capitalist conditions, competition is easily hypertrophied and converted into a predatory spectacle. Wagner goes so far as to compare record-setting athletes with religious fanatics and the insane.[33] Wildung's approach to the competitive spirit is more dialectical. "Competition [Kampf] as such is not an asocial [asozial] principle. But competition needs to be disciplined by society; it must be put in moral chains so as not to decline into decadence." The ambition to improve performance must not become "antisocial" (unsozial); it is only among the "intellectually inferior" that athletic ambition degenerates into egotism and its "social instincts." The essential criterion, says Wildung, is whether watching such a contest produces the "catharsis" which permits an abreaction of undesirable instincts, in the manner of Aristotelian tragedy. Competitive sport must have an edifying (erzieherisch) effect.[34]

Having inherited Marx's dream of an enriched and rehabilitated labor, Wildung mingles labor and play in suggestive but inconclusive ways: children treat work as play, inventive work is "creative" play, sport and games represent "enjoyable labor."[35] Wagner defines sports as "the body laboring on its own behalf."[36] This implicitly utopian synthesis is contemporary with Soviet analogies between sport and labor which appear during the Soviet "cultural revolution" of 1928–1931,[37] on behalf of a notion of euphoric labor.

If Wildung and Wagner interpret play itself (Spiel) with differing degrees of ideological militancy, neither accords it the almost cultic dignity conferred by cultural conservatives like Huizinga and Pieper—both Socialist writers insist on the eventual utility of play. Wildung, however, comes rather close to the conservative position by stressing the association of play with purity and spontaneity. "Every type of physical exercise," he writes, "is a pure and unfalsified activity so long as it remains play in the purest sense of the word." He speaks of an "innate play-impulse" (Spieltrieb) and quotes Schiller with approval. "Play," he states, "is the springtime of life, the source of the purest joys and the noblest happiness."[38] Such rhetorical flourishes make it evident that Wildung is no labor fetishist. Nevertheless, his frequent allusions to the fusion of labor and play constitute the sort of Marxist signature which is anathema to the conservative temperament.

Wagner approaches the play issue with more ideological self-discipline. "Play," he says, "is the application of the urge for movement and activity in the form of exercising inherited and acquired psychosomatic traits and abilities." Wagner's ideological vigilance expresses itself most pointedly in his insistence that the "impulse to movement" (*Bewegungstrieb*) and the "play-impulse" (*Spieltrieb*) are not "some sort of mysterious 'spiritual forces,'" but are rooted in the physiology of the body: "The impulse to movement"—the fount from which sport flows—"is nothing other than the response to a variety of chemical processes within the body which are caused by glandular secretions." Wagner wants to refute the "philosophical-idealistic" interpretation of the "impulse to movement," which would make it an "independent psychical trait" and, therefore, an offense to Marxist materialism.[39]

The Challenge of Nonrational Appeals. The crucial issue for workers' sport culture was the power of nonrational appeals. Let us return for a moment to the East German "sport acrobat." Implicit in this athlete's invidious comparison between "dazzling costumes" and "gimmicks" and the spartan style of his own troupe is a moral judgment of ancient vintage, the condemnation of all that glitters, and its power to distract people from the path of righteousness, be it a religious calling or—in modern times—a political one. In this sense, the cultural revolutionary and the missionary perform the same function: they attempt to substitute a "virtuous" or "progressive" system of values for "sinful" or "reactionary" ones. Trotsky in particular was interested in techniques which might bring about this sort of conversion, and he understood that "progressive" and "reactionary" cultural institutions compete for human loyalties at a virtually subliminal level. In a lecture titled "Vodka, the Church, and the Cinema" (1923) he says:

> The elements of distraction, pleasure, and amusement play a large part in church rites. By theatrical methods the church works on the sight, the sense of smell (through incense), and through them on the imagination. Man's desire for the theatrical, a desire to see and hear the unusual, the striking, a desire for a break in the ordinary monotony of life, is great and ineradicable; it persists from early childhood to advanced old age. In order to liberate the common masses from ritual and

the ecclesiasticism acquired by habit, antireligious propaganda alone is not enough. . . . Meaningless ritual, which lies on the consciousness like an inert burden, cannot be destroyed by criticism alone; it can be supplanted by new forms of life, new amusements, new and more cultural theaters.

As noted above, Trotsky realized that sport would eventually become a significant cultural and political factor, and the same principle applied to play: "The character of a child is revealed and formed in its play. The character of an adult is clearly manifested in his play and amusements. . . . The longing for amusement, distraction, sightseeing, and laughter is the most legitimate desire of human nature. We are able, and indeed obliged, to give the satisfaction of this desire a higher artistic quality, at the same time making amusement a weapon of collective education, freed from the guardianship of the pedagogue and the tiresome habit of moralizing."[40] A decade later, Wilhelm Reich applies this principle to sport: "Football, in particular, has a directly depoliticizing effect and encourages the reactionary tendencies of youth. Yet these tendencies are, in principle, reversible, i.e., they can be used to the advantage of the left . . . "[41]

"The human brain," the Austrian Socialist Julius Deutsch writes in 1928, "is formed in such a way that it spontaneously strives for spiritual nourishment."[42] The crucial question, which Trotsky had already posed (and answered) for his Russian audiences, concerned the kind of nourishment people were going to get. Like Trotsky, Deutsch and other workers' sport theorists were cultural revolutionaries who knew that "the character of an adult is clearly manifested in his play and amusements," and that some amusements are more revolutionary—and perhaps less gratifying—than others. But unlike Trotsky, whose sheer intellectual exuberance seemed to displace the temptation to "moralize" much about cultural matters, the workers' sport theorists were not at all reluctant to make judgments which had the ring, if not the intentions, of Christian antisensualism. Like good churchmen, they understood both the power of temptation and the virtues of moderation. But unlike some churchmen, they tended to oppose, rather than adopt, the "elements of distraction, pleasure, and amusement [which] play a large part in church rites." Instead, the workers' sport leaders confronted what one of them called "the capitalist pleasure industry" (Vergnügungsindustrie) of modern society,[43] and offered in its place a wholesome temperance or, at the very least, healthier distractions. It was a heroically antimodern way to build the future.

"Socialist work in the cultural area," one of these authors writes in 1930, "confronts great difficulties which at first sight seem to be insuperable."[44] These difficulties are rooted in human nature, which, as Trotsky once pointed out, is "very conservative by nature."[45] "A person's world-view," this author continues, "grows out of his emotional structure. Feeling comes before knowledge." Enlightenment, therefore, will require a Freudian strategy: "Proletarian festivals go to work on those feelings which exist in the unconscious as class identity and which must be reformed into class consciousness; feelings must be turned into rational faculties." The obstacle to the "new life-forms" for which Socialists were struggling was bourgeois culture, and in particular its special genius for offering the masses all kinds of sensual gratifications which tended to dissolve class militancy: "The worker who wants to experience sensations . . . will alienate himself from the strivings of his own class."[46] The Socialist sport leader Fritz Wildung readily acknowledged an initial disadvantage: "The bourgeois tendency has the advantage of responding better to the tastes of the sport-enraptured public than the workers' sport movement. We are still living in the social order of the bourgeoisie, and to some extent we are still captives to its spirit. Public taste is not oriented toward finding serious educational benefits in physical exercises, but rather sensationalism in competitive sport; one need only think of boxing matches or six-day bicycle races. Very large numbers of workers are still devoted to these sensational sporting events and make up a large part of their spectators." What is more, the appeal of competitive sport reduplicates the nature of capitalist society and its perverse satisfactions: "This fighting and wrestling for success, for victory, this frenzied driving of performance up to record-breaking levels—isn't this a faithful reflection of modern capitalism with its brutal use of the elbows? Indeed it is! Competitive sport is the physical culture of the age of capitalism, which drains the last sparks of energy out of a man on behalf of success. It is an overrefinement of the performance principle, a race between the human body-machine and the motor, a wild competitive struggle." And what is the alternative, the physical culture of the future? "In gymnastics we have glimpsed the realm for which we yearn."[47] As in science fiction, the utopian future seemed to look a lot like the classical past.

Throughout the manifestos of the workers' sport theorists one finds the German word *Sensation* being used pejoratively on behalf of what one calls "a new socialist morality."[48] Its connotation is always negative: "the lust for sensation," "a greed for sensation," "a frenzy of sensation," "the constant search for new sensations," and so on. But this pillorying of "sensation" aims only at proscribing its corrupt forms, those forms of sensual pleasure which rob the individual of autonomy—and class consciousness. In fact, these thinkers see a profound ambivalence in the relationship between pleasure and the working class. On the one hand, every proletariat has been denied its share of pleasure and of the satisfaction of the senses. "The masses have begun to remember their rights to the joys and beauties of life."[49] Sport, says Julius Deutsch, represents a "conquest of the gloomy asceticism of the Middle Ages"; when a woman sheds her regular clothing for a lighter sport outfit, it is a victory for "the joy of life" over "a ridiculous prudery."[50] Sport offers the working class "a noble joy of the senses."[51] "For a long time," Fritz Wildung writes in 1929, "the proletariat has had little understanding of corporeal beauty, simply because it had no reason to be familiar with the idea."[52] It is time, he says, for working people to rediscover their senses and their capacity to experience wholesome pleasures; during the period of early capitalism, "animalized working slaves wallowed in the slime of alcoholism and sexual excesses,"[53] and these injurious diversions have by no means disappeared.

The Great War made a new relationship to the senses necessary.

> In many areas of proletarian cultural activity there were new and bold initiatives which represented reactions to the iron-hard constraints of the terrible war years. For four long years the human body had been abused. Despair, grief, and hunger had crushed the slightest longing for uplifting joys, for a fulfillment of one's free time which would have answered these deep needs. So it is quite understandable that, once the horror of the war had ended, the joys of life would be rediscovered and enjoyed. Sports, hiking, and other such activities attracted large masses, and especially working-class youth. Personal hygiene and physical exercises gave the lives of hundreds of thousands of proletarians a new content and achieved their great importance in the context of postwar social development.

But the war had not, in the long run, been an entirely healthy influence. On the one hand, it had provoked the workers into a healthy response to sensual privation. But at the same time, the senses were fickle, and they could not be relied upon to align themselves with the right sort of diversion:

> The war, which the nationalists have called a 'bath of steel,' has incubated homicidal and sexual passions on a large

scale. A growing generation of youth was left to its own devices. Hunger and insecurity destroyed all inhibitions. When the safety valves were opened after the war, everything that had been held back broke out into the open. The pleasure industry blew this up into a frantic greed for deadening sensations. As a special branch of the pleasure industry, the sensational sport of the bourgeoisie came to play, as it still does today, a very important role. In the shrill manner of the marketplace the bourgeois press—and not just the sensational press—praises every new top performance by some record-chaser as though it were a kind of wonder of the world.[54]

"Sensational sport," however, was only one aspect of the bourgeois cultural offensive. Paul Franken writes in 1930,

[the] capitalist pleasure industry takes every 'taste' into account, from the most primitive to the most refined. The search for new experiences and a thirst for sensations are awakened and heightened with ever newer methods. But the pleasure industry is not just interested in doing a good business. At the same time it is an instrument in the service of the ruling class, the purpose of which is to splinter the rising working class and divert it from its class duties. If all the responsible functionaries of the proletarian cultural organizations would recognize that it is precisely the capitalist pleasure industry which is choking and paralyzing the socialist will to action we would have taken a giant step toward our goals.

In this sense, the bourgeoisie uses sport as it does "new technical inventions" like radio and the cinema, which serve to distort reality and "to make the average person insecure and confused so as to put him at the mercy of constant mood changes."[55]

"Bourgeois" sport, says Julius Deutsch, creates spectators who are "full of feverish passion which is cunningly and artificially incited." It is an unnatural stimulant. "The more brutal and the more dangerous the type of sport, the greater is its power of attraction." Deutsch is agog at Johnny Weissmuller's "swimming tricks" because they, too, are somehow unnatural: "Man is not an amphibian, and he should not have the ambition to be one." A new world record in airplane somersaults leaves him with only a sense of its irrelevance to human affairs. "Tricks belong in the circus, to which, as the abode of pleasure, we naturally have no objection. But don't try to tell us that there is a connection between the circus and the popular hygiene of genuine sport."[56] Years later, Soviet ideologists—and the ideologists of amateurism like Avery Brundage—would make an analogous (and equally invidious) distinction between the "professional" entertainment of the circus and "amateur" sport.

"As everybody knows," Freud writes in 1905, "modern cultural education utilizes sports to a great extent in order to turn youth away from sexual activity; it would be more proper to say that it replaces the sexual pleasure by motion pleasure, and forces the sexual activity back upon one of its autoerotic components."[57] Freud views this kind of sublimation as a detached observer. But for the workers' sport theorists—not to mention the Church—this conversion of sexual energy into sportive energy was welcomed as an instrument of moral hygiene. "Play and sport," Fritz Wildung writes, "are a very healthy influence during the years of puberty, because they absorb impulses which otherwise push toward an untimely sexual discharge."[58] It should be emphasized, however, that the workers' sport theorists were not advocating a religious prudery regarding sex. Helmut Wagner writes in 1931,

> Christianity views sexuality not only as 'sin' but also as injurious in order to serve the aims of its persistent 'moral' campaign of terror. Christian morality, however, has never been able to hold its own before the tribunal of the sciences. Nor can it hold its own against biology, which demonstrates the necessity for life itself of the fulfillment of all the bodily functions. The sexual activity of man is not injurious. It is natural and therefore 'healthy,' as well as biologically 'useful.' the only thing that is harmful is sexual excess, in the same manner that persistent overexertion while working or overloading the stomach through overeating are also harmful.

Wagner even goes so far as to maintain that the "sport drive" is an expression of a (sexual) drive for the self-preservation of the species. And, unlike Wildung, he distinguishes between the sexual effects of sport upon adolescents and adults. For youth, sport is a useful distraction from sexual preoccupations; but for adults, it is "a stimulus to sexual functioning." Wagner goes out of his way to castigate the "sublimation" theory, presumably because it was giving sport a bad name among the sexually enlightened. He also argues that the "conditions prevailing in bourgeois society lead to an intense artificial exaggeration of the sex drive" which sport can moderate; sport is almost a necessity for achieving sexual equilibrium, given "the hysterical sexual influences of modern society."[59]

The bourgeoisie, however, cannot escape this perverse hysteria, and it has turned sport into an expression of its own sexual degeneration. "Capitalist flirt-sport," according to Wagner, is debased pseudo sport, the purpose of which is to exchange "serious physical exertion" for an opportunity to display oneself in the latest ski fashions and the like. The play factor is no longer taken seriously; everything now is vanity and appearances: "The sport of the upper ten thousand is as a rule nothing more than the undisguised opportunity to establish legitimate and illicit sexual relationships, and for the most part illicit ones. The sport of the bourgeois is in the service of 'flirting' and sexual game-playing."[60] It must be emphasized that Wagner is anything but a censorious prude. He opposes not sexual pleasure, but cynical or aimless thrill seeking, and in doing so he sounds very much like the notorious renegade psychoanalyst and maverick Communist Wilhelm Reich. "All reactionary types condemn sexual pleasure," Reich writes in 1933, "because it attracts and repulses them at one and the same time. They cannot resolve the contradiction between sexual demands and moralistic inhibitions in themselves. The revolutionary negates perverse and pathological pleasure because it is not *his* pleasure, is not the sexuality of the *future,* but *the pleasure born of the contradiction between morality and instinct;* it is the pleasure of a dictatorial society, *debased, sordid, pathological pleasure.*"[61] Like their more famous colleague, the workers' sport theorists view "pathological pleasure" not with a sense of scandal, but with contempt.

"The worker's recognition of the beauty of his own body," Fritz Wildung writes, "represents a turning point in the history of civilization."[62] The attitude of the workers' sport movement toward the beautiful body was marked by a humane ambivalence. Particularly around the turn of the century, when the movement was emphasizing gymnastics rather than competitive sport, it openly admired the classical Greek ideal of the beautifully proportioned body: "The Greek ideal of the perfected human body no longer belongs to the past, but has reappeared in our own era." "We want to democratize the aristocratic doctrine of the people of the sun and make it a part of the life of the masses."[63] This doctrine of the body is also present in the later phase of the movement, but it never degenerated into an amoral cult of the beautiful body. "Fascist art," as Susan Sontag points out, "displays a utopian aesthetics—that of physical perfection."[64] The humane aspect of the workers' doctrine of the body was to have disavowed this "utopian aesthetics" and its merciless exclusion of those who could not glory in their own "physical perfection." Instead, the workers' sport theorists emphasized the proletariat's

lack of physical self-confidence and recommended sport as a repara-
tive measure: "When one sees members of the working class together with people from the propertied circles, it is clear that the
worker, his body exhausted and deformed by labor, can scarcely conceal his sense of inferiority when confronted with the well-tended
and better-developed body of the bourgeois. This feeling of physical
inferiority can easily turn into a sense of intellectual inferiority. The
worker does not have confidence in his own abilities, because he
feels weaker than he really is. The harmonious development of
the body which is achieved through sport counteracts this sense of
inferiority, which is at the same time an impediment to revolutionary defiance."[65] In 1930 another movement spokesman stresses the
importance of offering physical culture to the entire human family:
"But what will happen to all those young children who have some
sort of physical defect? And there are so many of them. . . . The
schools have shirked their responsibilities in this area, in that they
excuse all of these children from gymnastics instruction without—
as is the case with the retarded—providing special activities. Nor do
the gymnastics and sports associations take them into consideration. But these people, too, will have to face the hard struggle of
life."[66] A humane and truly hygienic sport culture is respectfully
mindful of the physically handicapped. Years after the workers'
sport movement had been extinguished, this idea was realized in
East Germany in the form of special competitions for the physically
disabled (*Versehrtensport*).[67]

   Sport, Anti-intellectualism, and the SPD. "Sporting activity,"
Paul Franken writes, "should not lead to the suffocation of intellectual interests. It should assist the work of the mind. Daily newspapers and illustrated magazines frequently print pictures of sports
heroes. The faces of these 'public favorites' very often express spir-
itlessness and stupidity."[68] Wildung, too, warns against sport's tendency to produce anti-intellectual attitudes.[69] Franken also took
note of the fact that the general public paid more attention to heroes
of sport than to distinguished scholars and artists. His disillusion,
or disappointment, in this regard gives expression to yet another
unusual—even noble—aspect of workers' sport culture: its inspired
but finally unsuccessful attempt to fashion a rational culture out of
an essentially nonrational experience. Workers' sport culture was
the first—and last—intellectuals' sport culture; that was both its
triumph and the root of its inability to compete more successfully
with "bourgeois" sport. "For a variety of reasons," Robert Wheeler
has pointed out, "the labour movement had initially been reluctant
to deal with sports. Among movement ideologists there appeared to

188 The Origins of Socialist Sport

be a certain intellectual bias against sports. Workers had more important things to do than engage in such frivolous pursuits."[70] Lenin encountered the same problem. A genuine sportsman, he had only his friend Valentinov for discussions of sport. "To Lenin's other companions," Valentinov writes, "the subject made no more sense than embroidery or knitting."[71] The history of the Left is filled with this sort of naiveté about the nonrational modes of experience: art, sexuality, sport. But once the workers' sport theorists developed a genuine interest in sport, they began to make important observations, one of which pertained to the anti-intellectual bias of "bourgeois" sport culture.

It turned out, in fact, that this critique was too radical even for many Socialists. In 1931 the Swedish writer (and Socialist) Ivar Lo-Johansson had the temerity to publish a manifesto titled "My Doubts about Sport," in which he branded sport as a particularly barren form of culture responsible for arresting the intellectual development of the working class. This sort of daring produced indignant howls of pain from many Swedish Socialists, who cherished a more idealistic view of physical culture.[72] Fifteen years later Lo-Johansson republished the pamphlet, and this time it was the Norwegian Communist party which scolded him for negative thinking.[73] The "noble joys of the senses" had won again.

The rationalism of *Arbeitersport* had to defend itself on a dual front:[74] against the external threat presented by the "bourgeois" sports clubs, which always had more working-class members than the workers' clubs; and against the internal threat represented by the unwillingness of most Left intellectuals to direct against sport the same sort of critique which came naturally when applied to other aspects of modern society. A third problem, and one which is closely related to the Left's attitude toward sport in general, concerns the long and difficult relationship between the workers' sport movement and the German Social Democratic party (SPD).

From its origins in the 1890s, the workers' sport and gymnastics movement had been viewed by the Prussian state authorities as a creature of the SPD and for that reason a threat to state security.[75] The irony is that this perception, which led to two decades of state harassment ending only in 1914,[76] was false. In fact, the initial and long-persisting attitude of the SPD was one of indifference.[77] And when relations began to improve around the turn of the century this was due not to the integration of sport into the political theory of the SPD, but to the fact that the number of double memberships in the SPD and the Workers' Gymnastics Association (ATB) had shown a marked increase.[78] In 1908, at the party convention in Nuremberg,

SPD functionaries did issue a declaration of sympathy, instructing the membership to join the ATB rather than its state-approved "bourgeois" rival (DT). In general, however, recognition from the SPD came only gradually and was considerably retarded by the sport movement's lack of support for the Weimar Republic. The breakthrough occurred at the 1929 party convention, when a member of the SPD central committee called for close relations. A year later, Fritz Wildung jubilantly declared that the movement had "returned to the womb of the party,"[79] and the final identification with both the SPD and the Republic was achieved.

The intellectual failures which mark the history of this political relationship were the work of both factions. On the one hand, the Social Democrats looked down on sport as a "hobby" which could attract youth to the party, but which did not warrant further analysis.[80] Fischer and Meiners speak of the SPD's "theoretical indolence."[81] On the other hand, it was not simply the fault of the SPD that intellectuals as a group refused to be recruited into the workers' sport clubs,[82] or that the radical gymnasts of the 1890s never developed an independent didactics or methodology of gymnastics instruction. Unable to apply the Marxist classics to physical culture, they had no choice but to rely on "bourgeois" theorists like Jahn and Guths Muths.[83] Eventually, as we have seen earlier in this chapter, Socialist authors like Deutsch, Franken, and Wildung, editor of the *Arbeiter-Turnzeitung* and later "the spiritus rector of workers' sport,"[84] would produce a creditable, but largely unsophisticated, doctrine of sport. Both the party and the sport movement paid a price for this conceptual (and political) myopia and the failed alliance it produced. And this failure, among many others, played its part in the German catastrophe.

8. Sport in the Soviet Union: Stalinization and the New Soviet Athlete

Sport, Labor, and the New Soviet Man

"The leaders of Soviet Russia," readers of *Foreign Affairs* were told in 1956,

> have always considered sports to be a matter of primary importance to the state and have made their position clear in numerous Communist Party decrees and *Pravda* editorials. They have stated that there can be no "sport for sport's sake," that hunters, for example, must not merely look for game but consider themselves explorers with obligations to Soviet society. Their preoccupation with the utilitarian and sociopolitical aspects of sport is reflected in their definition of the term *fizkultura* (physical culture). . . . Thus, sports can have no independent existence in the U.S.S.R. and are merely a means to an end—the consolidation of state power through mass training and indoctrination.[1]

American impressions of this period emphasize the ubiquitous fervor and utilitarian sobriety of Soviet sport. First, sport is suddenly revealed to be a mass obsession. "Russia is building the greatest mass army of athletes the world has ever known" (1955).[2] "In fact, sports are everywhere. The ideal of physical fitness is symbolized in the countless statues of sport figures seen in every Soviet park. . . . More practically, the physical fitness ideal is evident in the huge stadiums and sports fields of the big cities and the numberless more modest but thoroughly efficient installations in smaller towns" (1957).[3] Second, the Soviet athlete seems to be fiercely tenacious yet curiously demoralized and devoid of élan. "By American standards," the Soviet sports program "is harsh and severe. It is both Spartan and puritanical. Most of the spirit of fun seems to have been bled from it, and it thrives on regimentation and fierce national pride" (1955).[4]

"Their athletes are deadly serious. . . . When Mikhail Krivonosov smashed the world hammer-throw record, he merely sat down on a bench and pulled a cap over his eyes. He had been given a job to do and he did it—that was all" (1954).[5] Here are the origins of the myth of the Communist athlete—the despiritualized automaton, the sportive alien. Such impressions, however, contain an important kernel of truth deriving from the close relationship between sport and labor that is already evident during the early Bolshevist period (see chapter 7). Modern Soviet sport culture, while preserving certain links to its "naive" origins, is, nevertheless, a creation of the Stalinist period and temperament.

How seriously have the major Soviet doctrinaires taken sport as an ideological issue? Lenin (like Marx and Engels), as James Riordan has pointed out, "wrote virtually nothing directly" on the subject of physical culture.[6] Stalin "hardly ever attended a game during his lifetime." When Nikita Khrushchev found it expedient in 1959 to come up with some evidence of the "withering away of the state"—an indication of the transition from socialism to full communism—he announced the dissolution of the state sport apparatus headed by the All-Union Committee of Physical Culture and Sport, a development which had been conveniently timed to occur the week before,[7] and one which suggests the marginal importance of sport in the larger political context. (On at least one occasion, however, the larger context did prompt Stalin to make a political, if not an ideological, issue out of sport—when the Soviet national soccer team lost an Olympic qualifying match to the Yugoslavs in 1952. This failure to vanquish representatives of the ideological renegade Tito infuriated Stalin, who disbanded the team and ordered that its members be interrogated as suspected Tito agents.)[8] This ideological indifference toward sport on the part of the major figures should not, however, dissuade us from investigating the ideological content of Soviet sport. The ideological apparatus of Soviet society exists independent of its nominal leaders. As Peter Ludz has pointed out: "Changes in the ideological sphere of an authoritarian Communist industrial society, besides being indicators of actual social conflicts, have a dynamic of their own and therefore can be viewed as independent variables in the processes of social change. This aspect of ideology is an important consideration in any systemic sociopolitical study."[9]

Stalinist sport culture has developed in the industrialized societies of the Socialist bloc, all of which share a basic sport doctrine of Soviet origin. The foundation of Stalinist sport is the promotion of competition as a socially useful way of life. The official turn toward sport "productivity" came in 1936, when the party ratified "a shift of emphasis from purely physical culture to physical culture combined with competitive sport as a means of politically socializing the population to the new prevailing norms, with emphasis on its utilitarian, 'applied' functions in preparing people for labour and defence. The cloud that had hung over the word 'sport' (implying competition) since the early 1920's was now officially lifted."[10] The Stalinist athlete may be seen as a sportive analogue to the Stakhanovite worker of the mid-1930s, the heroic record breaker who vastly overfulfilled the production quota to "build socialism."

The transformation of Soviet sport corresponds to a transformation of Soviet political anthropology. Katerina Clark describes this transformation as a change in the societal ideal: "fraternity" is devalued in favor of "hierarchy":

> A capsulized version of the major shifts in values which took place in the thirties would go as follows. Phase one (1928–31): A cult of the lowly man and the common garden fact (i.e., empirical knowledge). The age of the little. Transitional period (1931–35): Greater social differentiation and scepticism about the empirically verifiable. The age of the big-ger. Phase two (late 1935–37 and beyond): A hierarchy in the orders of both man and reality. The cult of the *extra* ordinary. The age of the biggest.[11]

The collectivistic ideal and, for a time, the cult of technology and the machine are replaced by a leadership ideal and a cult of individual performance which could take the form of a fantastic voluntarism. In fact, as early as about 1928, what Raymond Bauer terms "the Stalinist Center" faction is employing an idiom which anticipates the voluntarist intoxication of the Stakhanovites: "We are bound by no laws. There are no fortresses which Bolsheviks cannot storm. The question of tempos is subject to decision by human beings."[12]

The transition from a fraternal-collectivistic to a hierarchical-performance ideal can also be followed in the development of Soviet psychology. "Viewed in the light of psychological theories of the twenties, man was a machine, an adaptive machine which did not initiate action but merely *re*-acted to stimuli from its environment. Concepts like 'consciousness' and 'will' were suspect; they smacked of subjectivism, voluntarism, idealism. After all, man and his behavior were determined by antecedent social and biological conditions." But during the period 1930 to 1936 these theories were attacked and discarded (except for the notion of the unlimited plasticity of human nature). Throughout these years there is an increasing emphasis on the development of "will" as a human faculty. Consciousness and purpose become the dominant psychological motifs, though not, of course, in the "idealist" sense of a "free will" (the new Soviet freedom is "the recognition of necessity"). In the new Soviet psychology, says Bauer, "the dynamism of personality is of central importance. . . . Emotionality—in the pursuit of a consciously fixed goal—is a highly valued trait of the Soviet Man, as is a strongly developed will, whereby this emotional drive can be effectively channeled. Emotionality is in disfavor only if man becomes a victim of it, if his will and consciousness cannot retain control."[13]

It is in this context that the heroic cult of labor known as Stakhanovism may be understood. "The Stakhanovite movement represented a peak in the reaction to the plan years' lust for fraternity. The Stakhanovite was not merely to be *greater* than all previous model men, but to represent a *qualitative* leap forward in human anthropology, as the rhetoric of the times claimed." And it is of great interest that the "most characteristic epithet used for the Stakhanovite was *bogatyr'*, which places him in the tradition of fantastic Russian epic heroes who perform superhuman feats." Endowed with special innate powers, the Stakhanovite possesses the sheer "*daring* to discount established empirical norms and 'scientifically' determined limits of technology."[14] Here is a direct analogy to the record-breaking athlete, and one which points forward to the psychological discipline of East German sport culture and what Willi Knecht has called its "conviction that many barriers of human performance are of a predominantly psychological nature."[15]

But the modern East German or Soviet athlete is not a genuine Stakhanovite for two reasons. First, he or she does not symbolize a disdain for the limits imposed by scientific calculation and technology; and second, the athlete is not, as Katerina Clark puts it, "an extra-systemic figure" whose "ontological status in society" elevates him or her above all other citizens except an Ulbricht or a Stalin. After all, the Soviet concept of sport—of whatever period—has always been identified with labor in its less extraordinary aspect, while the Stakhanovite "para-athletes" were pilots and explorers. In 1930 a common slogan on factory walls was: "Every Sportsman Should Be a Shock-Worker, Every Shock-Worker—a Sportsman"[16]— but a shock-worker ranked lower than a Stakhanovite. In the early thirties the Komsomol spoke of a "*Kul'testafeta*, or cultural relay-race,"[17] to pass on the traditions of the industrial working class as a whole. David Caute has pointed out how at this time the films of the Soviet director Dziga Vertov "could pulverize Western audiences" and "create an audience of fellow-travellers mesmerized by pulsating energy symbols" by presenting labor expressionistically, as a euphoric struggle: "But of course it was not real work, not the steady, monotonous drudgery that Don miners or Welsh miners would have recognized from their own experience. Vertov offered the Western middle class romanticized work, work-as-dance, work-as-sport, work-as-prayer."[18] This, of course, is the celebration of Stakhanovism even before its time; for Stakhanovism is the great, essentially stylistic, temptation presented by the fantasized fusion of sport and labor—physical grace and visceral toil become one. As Perry Anderson has noted: "Utilitarian in its means and goals, the official utopianism of the Five Year Plans was Romantic in its iconography and rhetoric, hailing from every loud-speaker the creative pleasure of the shock-worker in his labour. The spell of these images lasted long . . ."[19] The "spell" of this myth resides ultimately in its pathos: the longing to transform heartbreaking toil into "the creative pleasure of the shock-worker." The pathos deepens when one contemplates how thoroughly, and horribly, this ideal was betrayed by Stalin.

The New Stakhanovites

The Athlete.   Stakhanovism as a cult has disappeared from Soviet society, but the problem of the extraordinary individual and egocentricity has not. Today Soviet sport ideology still faces a "dilemma that [the pedagogue] Makarenko was never able to resolve satisfactorily: the conflict between censure of individual overperformance and the encouragement of Stakhanovism."[20] What the Soviets can not and do not tolerate is an exacerbated "star syndrome": open conceit, exhibitionism, and the descent into an antisocial egomania. In 1958 the star soccer player Eduard Streltsov was expelled from the national team and sentenced to twelve years in a labor camp for rowdyism.[21] Anticipating the objection that Streltsov was one of the team's "stars," *Komsomolskaya Pravda* denounced this sort of "Hollywood terminology."[22] In 1978 an offending hockey player was banished for drinking and for displaying "too egotistical" an attitude.[23] This critique of athletic egocentricity takes its place within a broader condemnation of adolescent perversity encouraged by Western values. In 1966 the popular Soviet poet Yevgeny Yevtushenko, once something of a Khrushchev protégé, criticized the James Bond image for exemplifying "the seductive cruelty of the modern superman—an anti-Hamlet. Hamlet's question is: 'To be or not to be?' Bond's question is: 'To beat or not to beat?' And pimpled youths fidgeting on sweaty seats in packed theaters burn with the desire: yes, yes, we ought to be like Bond, just as strong—stronger than anyone else in the world. And they lift weights, and learn judo and boxing, infected with the disease of a 'supermanism' that stimulates their vanity."[24]

But the critique of athletic egotism, or what Yevtushenko calls "athletic narcissism," exists in a state of tension with the idea that the charismatic star is also an edifying figure, an "educator."[25] "The term 'star sickness,'" *Sport in the USSR* comments in 1979, "was rather widespread in sport at one time. It referred to the conceit of a person who rose to the summits of fame in the sports world. The word 'sickness' has basically vanished, but 'star' still remains. We feel that there is nothing wrong in this. Stardom is the watchword for many athletes. A star is a source of light, warmth, joy." As if to illustrate the degree to which earlier ideological scruples have been left behind, this author invokes an American hero of the cult of virility: "Hemingway contended that sport teaches us life. In this aphorism, which is as precise as a scientific formula, lie a wealth of interrelations between the sportsman and the world around him. Indeed, where else can one graphically see the crystallisation of such human qualities as courage, will-power, self-control, purposefulness, determination, selflessness. . . . Whence the tremendous social and educational effect of a big competition" and its charismatic models.[26] The cultivation of individualism can also have a pragmatic aspect. According to a Danish observer, the Russians abandoned a "collective" style of ice hockey in favor of individualism in 1971, the result being a world championship two years later.[27] It is somewhat ironic that, having been derided by Westerners as "machines and robots" in the late fifties, the Russian players eventually triumphed by adopting the Marxian-Hellenic ideal of "all-round development of the individual."[28]

The Cosmonaut. Just as the long-distance air pilot was the predominant para-athletic type of the twenties and thirties, in our own age it is the cosmonaut who is the quintessential para-athlete, representing (as did the pilot) the development of physical endurance and skill within the context of the "man-machine symbiosis." He or she is also an officially sanctioned inspirational figure. When a Soviet atheistic-literature official was asked in 1981 by a Baptist whom atheists believe in, he replied that it was "people with initiative such as Stakhanovites or [the deceased] cosmonaut Yuri Gagarin."[29] The cultic stature of this type is expressed by a sculpture which stands before the cosmonaut training institute near Moscow: "In the center of the clearing, facing the entrance, stands a statue of a heroic figure, larger than life. The face is modelled after Yuri Gagarin's, but the character—fearless cosmonaut, devoted communist, perfect father and husband, brilliant engineer, role model for the idealistic youth, charismatic leader—is a creature of legend."[30]

The Polish sport sociologist Andrzej Wohl, who is essentially a Soviet bloc doctrinaire, believes that sport plays an evolutionary role in the (historically necessary) development of human motor skills. The basic relationship here is that between human and machine, and it is a relationship about which Soviet bloc ideology is pointedly optimistic. The idea that the growth of technology threatens to overwhelm humans themselves is considered a myth. "This assertion," a Soviet sociologist writes in 1969, "is based essentially on the tacit assumption that in the course of progress it is only the machines that change qualitatively, while man remains the same, regardless of whether he lives in ancient, medieval or modern times."[31] Wohl, too, believes that people, like machines, can "change qualitatively":

> During each stage of the historical development of our civilization there existed the need to adapt the human motor apparatus to the needs and tasks resulting from the stage of development of their social life, but above all from the production and defence requirements. That is why there always existed certain universally recognized efforts to take care of the human body, and to increase its motor skill. These efforts were, however, as a rule of spontaneous, uneven nature. . . . The development of present-day technics nevertheless requires increasing rationalization of physical culture. . . . We have embarked on the era of cosmic flight, which has clearly shown how it is to improve the motor ability of human beings. In this situation improvement of the motor skill of people can no longer remain the private affair of individuals.

Wohl dreams of "a transformation of the human body, to adapt it to the human world we have created," and for this purpose record-breaking sport is "a priceless instrument."[32] In a later text, Wohl develops further the common mission of sport and technology, including the necessity of acrobatics for the development of aviators.[33] More so than in the United States, in the Soviet Union and in East Germany the cosmonaut is an official heroic sport figure and is celebrated in those terms.[34]

Haunting the sport-technology fusion, however, is a Soviet cybernetician's thesis "there is no difference between a cybernetic machine of a sufficiently high level of organization, and man."[35] What is more, the systematic approach to transforming human physiology can be traced back to the influence of I. P. Pavlov. As James Riordan points out, the official Soviet position is that "the principles of Pavlov's theory of the nervous system are fundamental to the formation of motor habits . . . establishing, maintaining and developing sporting form."[36] A Soviet colleague reported that after visiting one hospital patient, Pavlov remarked: "Machines . . . machines and nothing more. An apparatus, a damaged apparatus . . . "[37] The adoption of Pavlov by official Soviet ideology, however, is rather odd. As David Joravsky notes, "His explicit denials that his doctrine was materialist did not stop Bukharin and other Communist ideologists of the twenties from insisting that Pavlov's doctrine furnished an important weapon for 'the iron arsenal of materialist ideology.' Largely ignored or briefly dismissed by the sophisticated Marxists seeking a new psychology, Pavlov's doctrine appealed to Bolshevik ideologists."[38] "One often gets the impression," says Gustav Wetter, "that Pavlov was much more of a mechanist than a dialectical materialist. . . . The official theorists themselves admit that Pavlov often expressed himself in a thoroughly mechanistic fashion, but seek to 'interpret' such utterances somehow in the sense of orthodoxy." Given these important discrepancies, why is the appropriation of Pavlov important? Because Pavlov's doctrine seems to invite the use of "psychagogic moulding-processes," under the auspices of the notion that human nature is characterized by an unlimited plasticity, a doctrine which reached its ascendancy during the "fraternal-collectivistic" twenties. Pavlov's continued influence is, in effect, a Bolshevist relic which "sophisticated Marxists seeking a new psychology" would prefer to leave behind. What is more, since the Pavlov Conference of 1950, the "inadequate philosophical training" of some Soviet psychologists "has been leading them, by a mistaken application of Pavlovian physiology to psychology, into identifying the mental with higher nervous activity and into calling for a fusion of psychology with physiology."[39] Taken together, this kind of physiologized psychology, the notion of the cybernetic human, the "man-machine symbiosis," and the myth of the cosmonaut combine to yield a composite image of the technologized athlete of the future.[40] Nor is this type without precedent. Katerina Clark has analyzed a book published in 1934 to celebrate the White Sea–Baltic Canal project, in which there appears the idealized figure of an engineer named Magnitov. "The authors relate how, after Magnitov began to labor on the canal, he developed a quicker pulse and faster thought processes and nervous reactions: 'He begins to take on the new tempo, to adjust his reason to it, his will and his breathing.'"[41] Just ten years after Trotsky predicted that even "purely physiologic life will become subject to collective experiments," this dream came true—after a fashion—under the paternal auspices of his bitter ideological enemy and eventual murderer.

The Soviet Critique of Sport

Soviet hygienism proscribes—officially if not always effectively—three categories of sports: antirational games, exhibitionistic sports, and philosophically alien forms of physical culture. Soviet dogma stresses the rational utilization of time and human energy. But, as Riordan notes, "a number of games exist that clearly are at odds with notions of rationality—horse racing (as a spectator sport for gamblers), dominoes, lotto (bingo) and many card games. That they are tolerated is an indication that the authorities are willing to compromise with the strong personal desires of sections of the public on such matters—perhaps in order to gain compliance or at least the absence of active resistance in other, more important spheres. They are the equivalent in sport of such semi-tolerated or tolerated but non-approved actions as vodka drinking, tipping and religious observance."[42]

The proscription of "exhibitionist" sports applies to women's soccer, which allegedly "damages female organs" and "provokes unwholesome excitement,"[43] unarmed combat (sambo), and male body building. Riordan notes in 1977:

> The state has been concerned that "athletic gymnastics" should not step over the border into "culturism." With an eye to the "excesses" that exist in the West, the authorities fear it will become an excuse for exhibitionism and narcissism: "egotistic love and dandified culture of the body and one-sided, unhealthy development of the organism are alien to the Soviet system of physical culture." The sport has not been banned, but all the various "Gerkules," "Atlant," "Atlet," and "Anteus" studios up and down the country . . . have been officially warned (1970 and 1973) to keep their activities "strictly in accordance with scientific, medical, and hygienic recommendations, thus precluding all manner of contests and exhibitions that include posing and the judging of the body."[44]

There is evidence, however, that the "dandified culture of the body" is a persistent heresy within Soviet physical culture. In 1977 the Canadian founder and president of the International Federation of Body Builders responded to attacks on the sport in *Sovetsky Sport* by claiming that this criticism "was provoked, quite simply, by sheer jealousy" on the part of weight lifters. "The two sports attract a similar type of people, and weight lifters are angry at the rapid growth and popularity of body-building in the Soviet Union, both in terms of numbers participating and crowds attending competition."[45]

An example of a "philosophically alien" sport is yoga, which in 1973 "was roundly condemned as being potentially injurious to health, but particularly for two ideological reasons: first, 'yoga does not involve teamwork; it encourages individualism and advocates that "yogis" should lead a closed ascetic life outside of society and even of the family'; second, it is 'based on idealist philosophy and mysticism.' The latter accusation was also levelled at karate."[46] Karate, however, has struck its deal with the modern, and less scrupulous, hygienists of the USSR; by 1979 a more "hygienic" and less "alien" karate had won official approval: "Karate is only beginning to develop in the Soviet Union. We are, of course, speaking only of traditional, contact-free karate, as contact karate is strictly prohibited here, because it does not conform to the humane principles of the Soviet system of physical education."[47] Nowhere does this author even allude to what was previously condemned: karate as a "philosophically alien" discipline which has long been associated with the sort of introspection Soviet authorities interpret as antisocial defiance. Bridge, too, was deemed "socially harmful" by a USSR Sports Committee resolution of January 1973 titled "On Certain Facts Concerning the Incorrect Development of Some Physical Exercises and Sports."[48] "We cannot understand the reasons for creating bridge clubs," the Committee said. However, it approved bridge played in private by consenting adults.[49] In this respect, bridge is treated like art. "Art," says Alex Inkeles, "being expressive, is linked to affect. If it is produced privately for private viewing, it violates the principles of nationalization of affect and the communalization of communication. . . . Such expression, by virtue of being private, is, in addition, suspect. No less than in the case of conversation, the fact of its being private hints that it is a-communal, and more likely that it is anticommunal; else why should the artist seek to hide it?"[50]

The Soviet critique of sport derives, in the last analysis, from communism's salvational—and proprietary—attitude toward human time, which must be redeemed from the injurious and vacuous character of "bourgeois" experience.[51] The ideological requirement is that sport be both hygienic and edifying; indeed, these categories are dynamically linked, in that the absence of edification permits the growth of noxious habits requiring hygiene. This is why sport must not descend to the level of "entertainment" or "amusement," which is by definition culturally vacuous.[52] Instead, sport is put on a par with art,[53] leaving unresolved the question of whether such an amalgamation, in elevating one, may not debase the other.

9. The Sport Culture of East Germany: Optimism and the Rationalization of the Body

The Origins of East German Sport Culture

"Among other things," the Italian Marxist Sebastiano Timpanaro writes, "evolutionism posed again the question of the existence of nature before man, of the origin of mankind and of its future disappearance. To what extent would the 'second nature' established with the appearance of labour and what one might call the 'third nature' developed with the passage to communist society be able to push back the biological limits of man?"[1]

The sport culture of East Germany represents a very specialized kind of answer to this question. In fact, Timpanaro and the East Germans view "the biological limits of man" from antithetical viewpoints. For Timpanaro, the human relationship to nature is the story of a "biological frailty [which] cannot be overcome, short of venturing into science fiction"—which is precisely, in a sense, where East German sport theorists have ventured to go.[2] For Timpanaro, human "biological frailty" is mortality and comes under the heading of tragedy; for the East Germans, "the biological limits of man" pertain to human adaptation to technology and its symbolic analogue, sport. Where Timpanaro sees pathos, the East Germans see science.

The sport culture of East Germany, judged on a per capita basis, is by far the most successful in the world.[3] This demographically anomalous achievement has generated a notoriety which deserves some examination here, since it derives in part from Western assumptions about the effects of Communist ideology on the practice of sport. As we have seen, the Western image of the dehumanized or mechanical Communist athlete, reflecting a degree of envy as well as contempt, has been influential for about thirty years. As recently as 1979, the *New York Times* described an "Eastern European" style of soccer, "where fluidity, precision and technical production blend teams into machines. In Eastern Europe, such machines run more efficiently in low gear"[4]—that is to say, they cannot accommodate an excessively individualistic style. It is likely that such impressions combine accurate observations and received ideas which influence the interpretation of what is observed, one example being a pronounced tendency not to recognize the degree to which Western sports medicine is coming to resemble that of the "scientific" East. It might also be noted that not all of the comparisons offered by East German athletes who have defected to the Federal Republic reflect unfavorably on the sport culture they have left behind. In 1972 one soccer player commented on the superiority of East German sport medicine and in particular the hygienic scruples which make "unthinkable" the exploitation of an injured athlete; in the Federal Republic, he says, the (professional) athlete is kept functional at any price.[5] In 1977 another defecting soccer star stated: "There are egoistic methods here which you don't find in the DDR. Here the human element is pushed into the background."[6] Such testimonials, which serve no apparent self-interest, ought to be considered along with the more numerous reports of oppressive authoritarianism and medical abuse. (Such remarks are symptomatic of a broader critique of, and ambivalence about, the Federal Republic on the part of many émigrés from the East. In the GDR, one exile states, "at least you could never develop such a feeling of being lost and abandoned [as in the Federal Republic]. Of course it was a bit annoying because it was sometimes simply too much, and always politics . . . but all the same you were in a collective, and there was an ideological consistency to it, even when you differed with people. You were always discussing things. There was a chance for communication . . .")[7] As we shall see, East German hygienism—a genuinely Socialist doctrine rooted in early Bolshevism—is a profoundly ambiguous phenomenon which sometimes makes it difficult to draw a clear line between medical concern about and medical exploitation of the human body.

East German sport has been made possible by two historical factors. First, Walter Ulbricht, the dominant political figure in East Germany from 1945 until his retirement in 1971, was genuinely interested in sport both personally and as a vehicle for demonstrating the political superiority of socialism. Ulbricht, once a member of a workers' gymnastic club in Leipzig,[8] resolved just after the establishment of the GDR on October 7, 1949, to create an exemplary, performance-oriented sport culture that would serve as a model for other sectors of East German society. This has been achieved, in that East German social scientists now consider the sport establishment to be "the most highly developed subculture of the DDR."[9]

The East German investment in sport has been offered as a popular policy. One of its primary purposes, in fact, has been to offer an unusually youthful population the sort of activity it can be expected to enjoy; ubiquitous sport is one response to a demographic imbalance which resulted when a good part of the adult population of the GDR fled the country prior to the building of the Berlin Wall in August 1961. Westerners heard no dissenting voices on sport policy within the GDR until 1978, when a dissidents' manifesto (of unconfirmed authenticity) was released, supposedly by a "group of middle and higher level Socialist Unity Party officials . . . who call their group the Association for Democratic Communists in Germany."[10] This document states: "We demand an end to the irresponsible expenditures on competitive sports, for culturally illiterate pop song writers and TV dilettantes. What is the value of a gold medal which costs 25 million marks? Why does a soccer professional earn 2,000 marks while a highly qualified doctor earns 1,500, including all overtime?"[11] It is a small mercy that Walter Ulbricht, the original promoter of sport development in the GDR, was not alive to read this protest, even if he had heard much the same thing from his own Politburo in 1950.[12] Back in 1960, on the tenth anniversary of the founding of the now famous German University for Physical Culture in Leipzig, he had proclaimed: "In those days [1950]—as you will remember—there were still many people in the GDR saying: 'Do we have to spend so much money on sport? Don't we have more urgent tasks to carry out? Isn't all of this being planned on too great a scale?' . . . Today there is no one saying: 'We should have used the money for more practical goals.'"[13] As it happens, Ulbricht's sportive legacy has proven to be more durable than its creator. Two months after Ulbricht's death in 1973, Walter Ulbricht Stadium was renamed. "He's the nearest thing to an unperson that we have," the writer Stefan Heym commented in 1975.[14]

If Walter Ulbricht was the prime mover, the Soviet Union has been the doctrinal mentor of East German sport.[15] The official initiation of physical culture in the "Soviet Zone of Occupation" took place on July 1, 1946, in the context of a general reformation of the educational system. Given the official[16]—even privileged—pedagogical status of sport in the GDR, the evolution of its educational program is directly relevant to this discussion.

In 1952, the official organ of the Socialist Unity party (SED) published an article titled "Learn from the Scientific Physical Education in the Soviet Union!"[17] It is an essay which speaks with two voices, one representing the past while the other signals future developments. The first seems to be that of the workers' sport movement of the interwar period, denouncing record chasing ("a means of profiteering"), sensationalism, and "decadent manifestations" like mud wrestling, female boxing, and "other degenerate practices." This, of course, is the face of capitalist sport, which was the object of Soviet as well as German opprobrium. The second voice is an unmistakably Stalinist one, alien to the spirit of workers' sport. It speaks of managing the emotions of the athlete scientifically, of the importance of high performance, of the futility of the solo achievement compared with "collective performance," and of the Soviet trainer who is "both pedagogue and political educator."

Soviet influence on East German education or sport really means the hegemony of Marxist-Leninist ideology, not Russification in a more specific sense. If, for example, the German Left of the Soviet zone found the 1946 school reforms something to cheer about, this was because it saw in such measures the cultural and political fulfillment not of the triumphant Russian revolution of 1917, but of the tragic German revolution of 1918.[18] The authority of Marx antedates the authority of Lenin.

The relative importance of Marxian doctrine on the one hand and Leninism-Bolshevism on the other for pedagogical theory in the GDR may be gauged by examining its most important theoretical and practical concepts, respectively: "all-round human development" (allseitige Entwicklung aller Menschen) and "polytechnical education" (polytechnische Bildung). Both of these ideas are Marxian, and both figure prominently in Bolshevist pedagogical theory.

"All-round development of the personality," the pedagogue Helmut Klein writes in 1974, "is an ancient ideal of mankind. Marx and Engels consciously ally themselves with this tradition." As Klein notes, Marx and Engels call for "the totally developed individual" (das total entwickelte Individuum) to replace the alienated "partial individual" created by the specialized needs of modern industry; Lenin, Krupskaya, and Lunacharsky promote this ideal in the wake of the October Revolution.[19] And this ideal has persisted. The Third Program of the Communist Party of the Soviet Union (1961) includes a paragraph on "All-Round and Harmonious Development of the Individual."[20] In modern Communist societies the inclusion of physical development within this model has become a ritual requirement.

"Polytechnical education [polytechnische Erziehung]," Marx and Engels write in 1866, is a pedagogy "which imparts a knowledge of the general scientific foundations of all production processes, and which at the same time acquaints the child or the young person with the use and handling of the basic implements of all trades . . . " In

1919, Lenin employs this term in its Marxian sense.[21] In 1918, the Soviet educator Lunacharsky defines polytechnization as "the unification of the mental and the manual." For Anton Makarenko, a prominent Soviet pedagogue of the 1920s and 1930s, polytechnization "was something more than mere vocational training. It was a whole educational outlook which saw society based on shared, productive work and saw culture as the sum total of this productive work. Thus, through polytechnization, through the production of cultured, complete citizens, the Soviet educators hope to achieve a nice balance between the liberation of the individual and the necessary cohesion of society. . . . The whole cultural tradition of the communist era lay ahead of the people, not behind them. Education became the instrument for inventing and keeping in the public view the dreams or utopias."[22]

Both of these ideas—all-round human development and its practical correlate, the polytechnical ideal—are fundamental to Marxist political anthropology. The first can be traced, at least in part, to Marx's famous sixth thesis on Feuerbach, which states that "human essence is not an abstraction inherent in the single individual. In reality it is the ensemble of social relationships"—an assumption which reappears in Soviet psychology's notion of the plasticity of the human organism.[23] The polytechnical ideal appears in Marx's well-known passage about that unachieved "communist society . . . where nobody has an exclusive area of activity and each can train himself in any branch he wishes, society regulates the general production, making it possible for me to do one thing today and another tomorrow, to hunt in the evening, criticize after dinner, just as I like, without ever becoming a hunter, a fisherman, a herdsman, or a critic."[24] What these two themes share is the principle of almost unlimited adaptability, and it is left to the observer to decide whether they constitute a basis for Marxist "humanism" or a framework for "totalitarian" control. It will become evident that such "anthropological" principles are at the heart of Marxist sport ideology, which, to paraphrase Dieter Voigt, may well be the "most highly developed" ideology in the GDR.

A third, and somewhat more haphazard, illustration of the relationship between East German sport culture and that of the Soviet Union concerns the Free German Youth (FDJ) organization, which in the year of its founding (1946) took control of the new (nonschool) sport movement in the GDR.[25] In his history of the German Youth Movement, Walter Laqueur points out that the FDJ "owes a great deal (as the Hitler Youth did) to the traditions of the old youth movement—in its camps, excursions and war games; its songs, banners, camp-fires, sports competitions; and in its outward trappings in general. By a minor irony of history, this legacy from the *Wandervögel* and the *Bünde* reached the F.D.J. indirectly, via the [Soviet] *Komsomol*, which had taken it over from the German Socialist youth of 1910, who in their turn had copied it from the *Wandervögel*."[26] This example represents an inadvertent recourse to German tradition and is yet another (albeit unusual) example of how the ideological hegemony of Marxism-Leninism in the GDR has had to compete to an ever greater degree with an aggressive appropriation of the German past which wears only a thin ideological veil over essentially nationalistic ambitions.

Even prior to more specific inquiry into the role of German tradition in the sport culture of the GDR, the shifting balance between Sovietization and a German national consciousness can be discerned in the ideological evolution of the sport movement as a whole. Gerhard Engelhardt's (1965) chronology of the development of physical culture within the educational system identifies four stages: 1. demilitarization of (Nazi) sport (1945–1949); 2. massive politicization and systematic Sovetization (1949–1952); 3. completion of the "ideological breakthrough" among youth, introduction of a military theme into physical culture, further Sovietization of youth movement ideology (1952–1958); 4. introduction of patriotic consciousness, focus on eighteenth- and nineteenth-century German physical culturists (Guths Muths and Jahn), rehabilitation of "folk gymnastics" as Socialist culture, promotion of the parallel between high-performance sport and labor.[27]

Dietrich Martin's (1972) chronology of East German sport culture as a whole distinguishes five phases: 1. imitation of the Soviet model (1945–1952); 2. patriotic consciousness raising about physical culture (1952–1955); 3. emphasis on gymnastics, including a renaissance of Jahn's gymnastics movement (1955–1958); 4. sport competition with the Federal Republic (1958–1963); 5. promotion of all-round physical development on behalf of economic productivity (1963–   ).[28]

On November 14, 1954, the SED party organ *Neues Deutschland* reported that Manfred Ewald, then as now the leader of the GDR sport establishment, had returned with his delegation from Moscow, overflowing with humble thanks for the expert advice extended to them. Two decades later, it was the Soviets who were asking for advice.[29] Today the East Germans not only outperform their original sponsors but even show a certain ingratitude. "Sport medicine in the DDR," a West German physician has observed, "is subject to the same security measures as military or atomic secrets."

When the Russians ask for the results of secret research, they do not always get them. East German sport research has, after all, required huge expenditures by the state. This funding has produced a body of advanced knowledge which is exported (selectively) throughout the world and on behalf of which few stones have been left unturned. When the president of the West German Sport Federation toured the major East German sport research facility in 1975, he noticed in particular one unusual piece of equipment—a corpse.[30]

Sport, Play, and the Labor-Leisure Dialectic

East German culture is a "total" culture based on the ideals of a Marxist-Leninist "humanism" within which sport enjoys an official status.[31] The author of a 1961 treatise on the political nature of sport employs the potent combination of "humanism and optimism" to describe Marxist-Leninist philosophy.[32] A 1968 resolution of the GDR Council of State calls on sport to promote "everybody's participation in the development of a healthy, optimistic and creative way of life."[33] A text from 1971 states that "Physical culture and sport belong to the culture-rich, life-affirming and creative way of life of our socialist community."[34] The formulas change, but they are functionally identical. All of them represent the positive, "Socialist" alternative to the sterility and perversity of capitalist culture.

Socialist bloc ideology does not accommodate the idea of autonomous leisure, except as a negative category of experience encountered in capitalist society ("hobbies").[35] In the GDR, leisure (Freizeit) is integrated into that ideal of "all-round human development" which, as we have seen, is certified not just by Marx but by the cultural authority of ancient Hellas as well. "The world-view of the working-class allies itself with the ancient ideal of the active and engaged human being, who experiences his era intensively, helps to shape it, and is therefore able to discover and find pleasure in the joys of life." Aristotle and Marx join hands to define leisure as independent activity which, at the same time, is anything but mere idleness. The crucial difference is that Marxian leisure is not reserved for a privileged elite.[36]

Leisure is also conjoined with the theme of productivity. "The alpha and omega of a higher culture in the sphere of leisure is and continues to be the constant raising of the productivity of labor, since freedom for Marxism is not a realm of beautiful appearance but rather a real life-process." Productivity is the prerequisite for leisure and thus the privileged category. Any notions that leisure rather than labor is the soil from which the "Socialist personality" grows are dismissed as representing a "preindustrial cultural ideal" or as "utopian conceptions of a 'holistic' activity."[37] Sport, too, serves productivity as a symbolic expression of maximum effort. "Technique, tactics and training, the three big T's in sport, become 'basic forms of labor planning and organization,' because they 'contain the same basic elements which also constitute the basis of high labor productivity in production.' For between 'socialist physical culture' and 'socialist labor' there is 'ideologically' a complete parallel: both are 'a matter of fame and honor.'"[38]

Socialist "entertainment culture" (*Unterhaltungskultur*), of which sport is one type, offers plenitude where capitalist entertainment allegedly offers emptiness or worse. This is made possible by what one SED ideologist terms "the abolition of the contradiction between labor and leisure" in Socialist society, which in turn makes possible "an abundance of pleasures and relaxing activities which are based upon educational, moral, and aesthetic values." Under capitalism there is a qualitative gulf which separates art from entertainment, which has an "escapist, narcotizing function." This is the consequence of giving "the capitalist pleasure industry" free rein. Paul Franken's phrase from 1930 reappears forty-two years later in the organ of the Central Committee of the SED.[39]

As we saw in chapter 2, East German sport ideology denies the primordiality of play and confers upon labor the honor of historical precedence. Play (*Spiel*) exists, but only as a "dialectical moment" within the overall process of social development, where it is "historically mediated." Play is made into an "abstract category" by "bourgeois" sport science, which is itself "thoroughly *ahistorical*, that is, it abstracts from the social contingency of physical culture and thus from the social content of such categories as play, struggle, etc. In the process there arises the appearance of physical culture's independence in the sense of an *absolute autarchy*." What are the consequences of such an "abstract" sport science? First, it propounds the myth of "a polar opposition between 'homo faber' and 'homo ludens' (Huizinga) . . ." Second, and as a consequence of this false dichotomy, it refuses to rescue people from their state of fragmentation. Third, it devalues physical culture by construing it as a "mere expedient" which serves as an antidote to the experience of alienated labor. According to Willi Nitschke, director of the Institute of Social Sciences at Leipzig, the major villains are the "ideologues" Huizinga and Ortega y Gasset, who reduce physical culture to an indeterminate primal phenomenon originating in a vitalistic principle, both of which are inaccessible to rational analysis.[40] Dieter Voigt has pointed out that the sport historian Gerhard Lukas approaches the interpretations of Huizinga and Ortega by assuming that an (essentially nonutilitarian) "need for movement" was experienced by prehistorical humans.[41] Otherwise, Lukas' (1969) version of the origins of physical culture conforms to orthodoxy.[42] It is worth noting that as early as 1953, Lukas was attacking the pure Marxist-Leninist orthodoxy as "too narrow." To trace physical culture back to nothing but the labor process is, he says, a regression into "economic materialism: for it can hardly be denied that physical culture also derives from other roots which belong to physiology and psychology," such as "the joy of movement."[43] For this sort of theoretical daring Lukas was eventually dismissed from his position as director of the Institute for Physical Education of the University of Halle-Wittenberg.[44]

Marxist-Leninist orthodoxy is not the only schema which dissolves the "bourgeois" concept of autonomous play in a larger process. The cybernetician Georg Klaus, whom Peter Ludz describes as "an ideological representative of the institutionalized counter elite" within the GDR, posits society as "an intermeshed control system of gigantic proportions without either 'practice' or 'history' in Marx's sense."[45] It is hardly surprising that play as Huizinga defines it must be extinguished in such a utopia.[46] "By *homo ludens*," Klaus writes in 1965, "we understand, in a general cybernetic-cognitive sense, the player who plays with ideal or material models of the outside world." "In our schema the game [*das Spiel*] begins with a preconceived plan, namely to better prepare *homo faber* for his task."[47] By merging *homo ludens* and *homo faber* so perfectly—at least in theory—Klaus fulfills the ultimate dream of Marxist sport theory: the "abolition of the contradiction" between labor and leisure.[48]

No one in the GDR, Willi Nitschke writes in 1960, "has claimed that sport and labor are identical."[49] This comment, delivered in the course of a sarcastic rebuke to the West German sport historian Hajo Bernett, may well be correct, for this relationship is invariably treated not as an identity, but as an analogy. Nevertheless, a series of close analogies can easily take on the appearance of an identity. To define physical culture (*Körperkultur*) as "the social process resulting from the conscious improvement and perfection of the physical qualities of human beings [construed] as productive power" is to come very close to doing what Nitschke claimed no one did.[50] Prime Minister Willi Stoph, receiving the many East German medal winners shortly after the 1976 Olympic Games, unwittingly touched on this theoretical issue in the course of an address which attempted to defuse any latent hostilities directed at privileged athletes by the laboring rank and file. East German workers, he proclaimed, recognize the sacrifices and the strength of character required for an Olympic medal; the politically mature appreciate "performances in all areas of our social life."[51] The ellipsis of this statement is clear: the athlete is, in effect, a worker. What is interesting from an ideological standpoint is that the ellipsis—the analogy—is consistently retained.

In the GDR the "performance principle" (*Leistungsprinzip*) has become a basic social and political doctrine,[52] and one in which latent analogies between sportive and productive effort abound. Within the SED, as Peter Ludz has pointed out, "two groups that embody major strains of conflict have emerged: the leading political group, which remains bound to the traditions of a secret society, and is characterized as 'insulated' on the margin of East German society; and the party experts who exercise decisive, day by day influence on economic and social decisions. Even within the party apparatus these experts are relatively more open-minded toward modern organizational solutions and more committed to the criteria of pure 'performance' (*Leistung*) in the sense in which it is universally accepted within capitalist systems."[53] The point here is that sport in East Germany has been promoted by both factions as a dramatic demonstration of "pure performance": by Walter Ulbricht of the "secret society" and by the performance-oriented modernizers. Stakhanovism, in effect, is alive and well in the GDR.[54]

The Technological Human of the Future

Sport in the GDR has achieved a futuristic scientism—itself a repudiation of early leftist ideals about preserving sport from the "abnormal" effort—which has left some foreigners in a state of both dread and awe. "One question," a West German observer writes in 1976, "from the standpoint of a humanistic psychology, remains open: how far does one want and should one want to develop the combination of technology, medicine, training, and athletes in the area of sport, and where should the line be drawn?"[55] In 1970 *Le Monde* offered its impressions of an East German handball team, emphasizing "this feeling of tranquil power, of imperturbable calm which is exuded by a team *whose machinery seems tuned to perfection. Rarely has the comparison of a team to a machine been more appropriate; a steam-roller, the DDR team seems to be composed of tireless human robots* who can maintain the same rhythm for an hour; they are cast physically and mentally from the same mold: iron morale, nerves of steel, muscles of brass. *It is almost as though one were talking about a team that was virtually metallurgical in nature.*[56]

"Training in East Germany," a sport scientist who defected has stated, "is based on the concept that the human body is designed to adjust to the demands made upon it. However, great care is taken not to challenge the system to the point of breakdown."[57] Paradoxically, the scientific cultivation of high performance tends to confirm, as well as corrupt, hygienic ideals. Here is the profound ambiguity of East German hygienism: the body is pushed to limits which have been carefully determined—calculation is in, physiological bravado is out. East German sport physicians were accused of subjecting children to inhumane athletic regimens by certain critical outsiders until the latter came around to accepting the results of the physicians' research.[58] It should be noted, however, that the new sport medicine was for many years, and may still be, a bitterly contested matter within the East German medical establishment, where a faction representing traditional medical ethics watched with growing concern as children, in particular, became experimental subjects for the high-performance theorists. Eventually the SED itself intervened, transferring responsibility for sport medicine from the Ministry of Health to the sport research establishment, a clear endorsement of the high-performance faction.[59]

The ambiguity of advanced sport medicine is resolved in the notion of "athletic sickness." Despite all of the research, one observer has commented,

> critics of the GDR system still argue that the scientific procedures are inconsistent with traditional concepts of "sport." The GDR sport scientists counter by asking if it is sport to allow a cyclist to ride a hard road race when his hemoglobin level might be dangerously low and when the effort could set him back six months in training. Is it sport, they ask, to have a cyclist go on a 75-mile ride with no knowledge of his true physiological condition? . . . With this goes the concept of "athletic sickness," a theory that if a cyclist's blood or musculature is lacking in some essential element, then he is as sick as a person suffering from severe vitamin and mineral deficiencies. Doctors won't hesitate to inject or prescribe supplements for the "sick" athlete just as they wouldn't for a normal person.[60]

The East German idea of "athletic sickness" represents, in fact, a breathtaking inversion of traditional attitudes toward athletic conditioning: perfection is now considered not the exceptional but the normative state of the body. As early as 1964, an East German scholar refers to "health" and "physical perfection" as "synonyms."[61]

It has long been rumored that pharmacological technology has played a role in developing East German athletes; there are also credible reports (from 1972 and 1977) which suggest that such experiments have been terminated.[62] In 1974 French and Swedish sports physicians publicly stated that female swimmers in the GDR were being treated with male hormones in order to increase muscle bulk.[63] In 1978 Willi Knecht reported that the original doping procedures had been discontinued in favor of more advanced, and undetectable, methods.[64] Also in 1978 the East German sprinter Renate Neufeld defected to the Federal Republic carrying pills she claimed had been prescribed for her on a regular basis. She had been told they were vitamins; a chemical assay found them to be dehydrochlormethyl testosterone, male sexual hormones otherwise known as anabolic steroids. It is well known that these compounds are medically hazardous for both men and women.

Renate Neufeld also described psychological pressures to which developing high-performance athletes are subjected. The instructors at her special sports school required regular sessions of self-analysis. "They were called evaluations of one's own performance and goals, or presentations of one's own development." Pupils were required, in addition, to provide written evaluations of their parents' social behavior. Shortly after she began to take the prescribed "vitamins," Renate Neufeld noticed that her upper thigh was becoming thicker and ached, and that a light moustache had appeared on her upper lip. When she refused to continue medication, she was required to defend her decision before the Free German Youth (FDJ) collective, of which she was a nominal member. "They accused me of not striving to achieve my best performances. The pills were never mentioned." After warning that she would wind up as a factory drudge, her trainer sent her to a psychologist. "We never went to the club psychologists on our own," she said. "True, they could influence our precompetition emotional states and calm us down. But we knew that they were there primarily to get the last reserves out of you." Finally, the state security police interrogated her to find out "why I didn't want to join the SED, why I was refusing to take medication, and how I could become engaged to a foreigner [a Bulgarian]." Small wonder that students at the special sports schools are required to take a vow of silence.[65]

To what extent does the highly developed East German athlete represent a "bionic" creation? Athletes in the GDR, *Der Spiegel* claimed in 1972, are accorded medical attention in a manner comparable to cosmonauts.[66] Given the exotic aspect of this issue, it is important here to distinguish between what is intended and what is achieved, between what is imagined in the GDR and what is actually possible in the real world. There can be no question that current Socialist bloc sport ideology promotes the ideal of human adaptation to an evolving technology—for example, Andrzej Wohl (see chapter 8). This is known as "man-machine symbiosis." As Peter Ludz points out, the cybernetician Georg Klaus "not only assumes that in borderline cases men can behave like automatic machines, but that automatic machines can react like men. Indeed, Klaus is also convinced that human action, and consequently all behavior, can be algorithmically described and controlled." Klaus was at one time interested in "projected research in bionics."[67] A minor but revealing indication of the relationship between sport and technology in the GDR appeared in *Neues Deutschland* on April 11, 1979, when its sports editor rejected as "nonsensical" a proposal that sports employing any sort of mechanical apparatus be banned from the Olympic Games.

If East German sport culture has not become robotics, it nonetheless retains an alien and even disturbing ambiance. "The overestimation of 'physical culture,'" a GDR sport historian writes in 1956, "coupled with a contempt for intellectual development, was an essential characteristic of the 'philosophical doctrines' of German imperialism, which were in turn closely tied to a reactionary racial theory." The question is whether the GDR is not promoting an analogous overestimation of sport, even if the East Germans can hardly be accused of cultivating—like "German imperialism"—a "disbelief in the cognitive ability and social power of human reason"; after all, "technological pessimism" is an official ideological sin in the GDR.[68] The answer is that while the East Germans, like the Nazis, promote the authority of the body, they do not (consciously) do so for fascist reasons, but rather to serve the "man-machine symbiosis." The ideological basis for emphasizing the body is the theory that, from the earliest stages of human development, physical movement has played an important role in shaping intellectual and even artistic capacities. Kurt Meinel insists that "intellectual development and formation cannot and should not be separated from their sensomotor foundations." Both sport and labor employ movements which integrate mind and body in a "dialectical" rather than a "dualistic" manner. Nor does Meinel fail to mention the "optomotor coordination of millimeter precision" required by modern technological production.[69] The idea that "rhythmic gymnastics" in conjunction with music can develop "creative powers" appears as early as the pedagogical program of 1946.[70] Finally, sport is even equated with art.[71]

The Role of Tradition

In tradition there is legitimacy, and in the GDR there is much searching after legitimate tradition. "After the war," one East German historian states in 1975, "there was a certain radicalism, a kind of 'Proletkult' which maintained that nothing was of interest except what happened after the Russian Revolution."[72] German Proletkultism was, however, no more successful than its Soviet antecedent; a treatise on the concept of tradition published in 1975 describes such notions as "anarchism." Engels' rather lukewarm recognition of tradition as a historical factor and Marx's depiction of tradition as a burden which crushes the living are treated not as obstacles, but as stepping stones to a dialectical interpretation of tradition. "Marxism-Leninism does not recognize traditions *per se*. Accordingly, its relationship to traditions is concrete. It calls for, makes use of, popularizes, etc., progressive traditions, and it takes a broad and decisive position against all reactionary traditions." Dialectical flexibility also rules out drawing rigid dichotomies between "progressive" and "reactionary" traditions. "Negative traditions can under certain conditions be channeled and converted into positive ones. Progressive traditions can become petrified and thereby take on a negative character." A Socialist society offers "the possibility of creating new traditions and giving new content to old ones *through conscious instruction*." And as for Proletkultism: "An abrupt break with tradition is foolish and un-Marxist."[73]

The GDR lays claim to what Erich Honecker, who succeeded Walter Ulbricht as head of the SED in 1971, called "all the humanistic traditions of the German past within it." Ulbricht had

> devised a three-dimensional cultural formula. From the eighteenth century he synthesized the "Spirit of Potsdam," with its emphasis on military-bureaucratic authority, with the "Spirit of Weimar" and its embrace of German classicism in the written and performing arts. Out of the nineteenth century, Ulbricht sought to develop a pattern of ideological consistency capable of linking SED authority with the recent all-German past. While Marx and Engels were used to provide the foundation stones upon which party authority was to be presented to the people, Karl Liebknecht, Rosa Luxemburg, and

Ernst Thälmann were presented as contemporary, as well as German, expressions of SED legitimacy. Finally, the all-German past was integrated into the world of technology,[74] the modern world in which, as Ulbricht foresaw, sport could serve as a language of symbolic force.

East German sport has two principal historical exhibits. Friedrich Ludwig "Father" Jahn (1778–1852) presents problems for historians in the GDR, but none that cannot be dealt with "dialectically" or simply ignored, depending on the audience. "A leading ideologue of aggressive, muscular, German patriotism," as Richard Mandell has described him, Jahn "appealed for an upsurge in German national spirit to be based upon a submission to the ideals of militaristic, hierarchical Prussianism. Prussian pride was arrogant, uncultured, and at odds with the tolerant cosmopolitanism of the German literary figures. To base one's hopes for a German regeneration on the toughness and loyalty of German *Volk* was quite different from pride in the spiritual monuments of the *Aufklärung*."[75] The East German cult of Jahn is an overt, if unacknowledged, retreat from Enlightenment rationalism.

"I am too old and too stubborn to change," Jahn writes in 1848. "I'll never be a Red."[76] What Jahn could not foresee was that he would be adopted by the Communist descendants of his republican opponents within the German gymnastics movement. Heirs of the Enlightenment, the East Germans have absorbed the unenlightened Jahn, his racial chauvinism, and his religiosity, though not without editing his image to make it more ideologically palatable. Edmund Neuendorff's (1930) description of Jahn as "the *well-known National Socialist*" elicits from the sport historian Günther Wonneberger only scorn for this attempt "to make ideological capital out of Jahn's nationalistic weaknesses."[77]

In official texts Jahn has been presented in two ways. The wholly expurgated version, such as appeared in *Neues Deutschland* in 1978 on the occasion of his bicentennial, presents Jahn as a patriot and class-conscious social critic. Jahn "was one of the patriots who in word and deed contributed to preparing and carrying out the 'patriotic war' against the 'World Conqueror' Napoleon." And: "We honor in Jahn a champion of the antifeudal reforms and nationalist demands which were seen by the oppressing feudal powers quite rightly as an attack upon their class oppression."[78]

It should also be pointed out that in recent years SED authorities have been promoting an identification with the Prussian past. "In a key statement underlining the change of climate, Dr. Ingrid

Mittenzwei, a Communist historian, declared [in 1978] that 'Prussia is part of our history' and should by no means be regarded simply as 'reactionary.' The new stance seems to be part of an overall policy of trying to combat a national vacuum the Communists themselves created when they established the German Democratic Republic in 1949 and said it had no ties to the past."[79] In 1980 Erich Honecker ordered the once-banned equestrian statue of Frederick the Great, a symbol of Prussian nationalism, returned to its site on East Berlin's Unter den Linden boulevard.[80]

The second portrait of Jahn is more nuanced and apparently reserved for a limited audience of sport historians and others who peruse scholarly publications. In the first of three installments on the image of Jahn, Willi Schröder maintains that the ideas of Jahn can be "creatively" developed, "because we have critically evaluated them with the help of the doctrines of Marxism-Leninism and on the basis of the experiences of the international workers' movement."[81] The official East German history of physical culture in Germany points out that Jahn's antirevolutionary disposition was ineradicable, and that his nationalistic feelings degenerated into a "Teutonomania." At the same time, however, Jahn played a role in the formation of a "national consciousness." Even Engels, for all his scorn of the Teutonic fanatic as a type, conceded that the type represented by Jahn constituted "a necessary formative stage of our national spirit."[82]

The sport culture of the GDR stands in a somewhat contradictory relation to the German workers' sport movement of the twenties and thirties, from which East German officialdom claims a lineal descent. This assertion is made infrequently,[83] since the resemblances—ideological and otherwise—are few. The East Germans have turned most of this conspicuously humane doctrine inside out, and for this reason it is not a subject for party ideologists to dwell on. Nor did the "Ulbricht group" hesitate to slander and push aside former *Arbeitersportler* in its drive to establish its control over East German sport.[84]

The principal function of the workers' sport movement is to provide antifascist martyrs from the world of sport, German sportsmen (usually of working-class origins) who were executed by the Nazis for resistance activity. The most prominent of these martyrs is Werner Seelenbinder (1904–1944), six times wrestling champion of (Nazi) Germany and a fourth-place finisher at the Berlin Olympiad of 1936. Had he won, *Neues Deutschland* claimed in 1979, he was to have used the resulting radio interview to denounce the crimes of fascism before a world audience. It should also be noted that Seelenbinder is credited with having worked for "the restoration of unity

within workers' sport,"[85] a euphemism alluding to the poisonous
hostility which separated the Soviet-dominated Red Sport International (RSI) from the Socialist Workers' Sport International (SASI)
from the mid-1920s through the early 1930s. The RSI vilified its
rival as "the treacherous and iniquitous Reformist International of
Workers' Sport which under 'apolitical' slogans aspires to indoctri-
nate athletes in the spirit of nationalism and peaceful collaboration
of all classes."[86]

This feud and the implicitly subversive doctrines of workers'
sport have led East German commentators to ignore its theoretical
content and concentrate instead on heroic personalities and political
infighting.[87] A minor exception to this rule is Günther Wonneberger's dissertation from 1956, which makes a point of dismissing
with Stalinist contempt any critique of culture which cannot be reduced to militant class struggle. Slogans used in 1929 by a sport official of the German Social Democratic party (SPD)—such as the
"struggle against sexual misery" (cf. Wilhelm Reich), the "affirmation of life," and "feeling for human dignity"—are dismissed as
"petty bourgeois." Wonneberger's point that "back to nature" types
and tunnel-vision sport enthusiasts represented an apolitical mentality had been anticipated by the very Socialist sport theorists he
disdains.[88] Nor can the Socialists' protests against increasing an athlete's muscle bulk or competition mania be of much comfort to
modern East German historians bent on absorbing this period, no
matter how "dialectically" they go about it.[89]

The Critique of Capitalist Sport

"Music," the German Communist composer Hanns Eisler writes in
1932, "like every other art has to fulfill a certain purpose in society.
It is used by bourgeois society mainly as recreation, for the reproduction (re-creation) of labor power, to lull people and to blunt their intellect."[90] In 1928 Gorky ascribed the same function to "bourgeois
sport"; and his contemporaries in the workers' sport movement described the "sensational" sport of the bourgeoisie as only one branch
of a "pleasure industry" or "entertainment industry" (*Vergnügungsindustrie*) which appealed to people's least civilized feelings. In 1931
Eisler makes this point in relation to music: "The advantages of
classical music over entertainment music are clear, in that a certain
demand is made of working-class listeners to be attentive, while entertainment music makes no such demand and rather panders to
laziness and comfort."[91] "The concert form arose in the epoch of the
bourgeoisie and is useless for the purposes of the revolutionary

working class. It can only offer noncommitted pleasure and make the listener passive."[92]

Hanns Eisler is an interesting figure because he represents the continuity between the workers' culture of the interwar years and the modern East German state; a "revolutionary" composer of the 1930s, Eisler has been made a cultural hero in the GDR. One element of the continuity Eisler exemplifies is the critique of capitalist culture and its appeals to base and passive instincts. Like the workers' sport theorists before them, East German ideologists contrast the "decadent" cultural manifestations of capitalism with the wholesome cultural institutions of socialism. The difference is that workers' culture had to be built within the walls of the enemy camp; thus encircled, it was forced to compete with the unscrupulous appeals to primitive feeling launched by the media of the bourgeoisie. In the GDR, by contrast, Marxist culture has had the field to itself.

The critique of capitalist sport is based on that polemical Stalinist concern for "man's injury to man" pointed out by Czeslaw Milosz back in 1951.[93] East German criticism of professional boxing, for example, goes back at least as far as an issue of Neues Deutschland published three weeks after the founding of the GDR on October 7, 1949.[94] (Professional sport had been effectively abolished in the Soviet-occupied zone in 1948.)[95] In 1978 the death of an Italian professional gave Neues Deutschland an opportunity to remind its readers of the difference between "boxing as a sport" and "professional boxing." In fact, this commentator contented himself with reporting the remarks of Cardinal Benelli, archbishop of Florence, whose critique of this tragedy nicely anticipates the "Socialist" viewpoint. The cardinal criticizes professional boxing as a "commodity" which offers people an unwholesome form of entertainment ("gratification and titillation") and which, consequently, is a threat to human dignity. We may note the connection between the aesthetic critique (the commodity has lost its integrity as sport) and the moral one (the appeal of indecent excitement is a threat to human dignity).[96]

The same principle can be applied to a less depraved sporting milieu familiar to virtually all Americans: "Teams which play a kind of distorted basketball mixed with amusing comedy routines have traveled the world. Here the salary of the player depends on how well he entertains, like a show business artist, which is what in a certain sense he is . . ."[97] Workers' sport's emphatic distinction between the "circus" and "genuine sport" reappears as a component of East German ideology. And who has "distorted" basketball with their amusing routines? The Harlem Globetrotters, of course.

10. Purism and the Flight from the Superman: The Rise and Fall of Maoist Sport

The Origins of Maoist Sport

Chinese Communist sport culture comprises two historical phases: the orthodox Maoist (1950–1976) and the post-Maoist (1976 to the present). Seen as a single developmental process, these earlier and later doctrinal stages can be shown to recapitulate the evolution of Soviet sport ideology from an anti-competitive to a highly competitive doctrine. It should be emphasized, however, that Chinese sport, like Chinese Marxism, has diverged from the Soviet model. For example, Chinese sport ideology, even after Mao Ze-dong's death in 1976, has not promoted the "man-machine interface" theme which conjoins sport, technological progress, and an aggressively competitive sport culture.[1] As one historian has noted, the Soviet model only partially adopted by the Chinese after 1949 offered "a network of technological solidarity (between roles and structures rather than human beings)."[2] But a centralized technological apparatus was precisely what the Great Leap Forward of the late 1950s was meant to repudiate.[3] "In many ways," Frederic Wakeman, Jr., has pointed out, "the self was . . . more important to Mao than to Marx,"[4] and a conspicuous deemphasizing of technology in favor of a faith in boundless human powers was emblematic of Maoist ideology. That this faith did not lead Mao to promote high-performance sport is a matter which must be addressed in this chapter.

The origins of Maoist sport long antedate Mao's proclamation of the establishment of the People's Republic of China on October 1, 1949. Mao's first published writing, *A Study of Physical Education* (1917), is notable both for the total absence of Marxist or even pre-Marxist ideas and for its anti-Confucian promotion of physical culture as a virtue.[5]

In this essay Mao begins by lamenting the physical deterioration of the Chinese people. He proceeds to define the goals of physical education as the development of the body in a uniform manner, the prolonging of life, and finally the cultivation of the will and military heroism. He emphasizes that it is necessary to cultivate a "savage" disposition in pursuit of physical fitness.[6] In summary, the most prominent characteristics of the essay are its innocence of radical ideology (Mao did not consider himself a Marxist until 1920), its promotion of conscious asceticism, and, as Stuart Schram has pointed out, a certain fascination with violence.[7] There is, in addition, Mao's pronounced interest in the body *per se*. "If the body is perfect, then knowledge is perfect, as well."[8] Clearly, Mao's body-consciousness, which persisted into his old age, was not consistent with Marxist doctrine as a whole. At "the heart of Marxism," says Wakeman, "is the belief that knowledge is power."[9] It is evident that, as early as 1917, Mao had in an important sense equated knowledge and the body.

The origins of Mao's interest in the development of the body can be traced, at least in part, to three intellectual models. Mao's philosophy professor, Yang Changji (1870–1920) had taken a degree in Edinburgh and was, Mao said, "the teacher who made the strongest impression on me." Mao was one of a devoted circle of students who "almost literally sat at Yang's feet—visiting him frequently at home and following to the last detail his moral injunctions and Rugby-like insistence upon physical education, which included deep breathing exercises and year-round cold baths."[10] As we shall see below, Yang may also have influenced Mao's attitude toward competition.

Mao's interest in "savagery" may derive from his exposure to the writings of Chen Duxiu (1879–1942), editor of a journal titled *New Youth*, which began publishing in 1915 and of which Mao consumed every issue. One of Chen's essays "urged that the Chinese nurture the more physical and savage aspects of their nature just as the Japanese writer, Fukuzawa Yukichi (1835–1901), had suggested."[11] The hands of Chinese youth, Mao says, "do not have the strength to strangle a chicken, while their hearts lack the courage which befits a man. They have pale faces, puny frames, and are as flirtatious as young maidens; they fear both heat and cold; they are as weak as the infirm."[12] It is more than probable that Chen's text is the model for Mao's essay. If there is a difference, it is one of tone, in that Mao does not employ a rhetoric of insult to get results. Mao's use of "terror through rhetoric alone" would eventually be applied not to the physically but to the ideologically unfit.[13]

Mao's third source was Friedrich Paulsen (1846–1908), professor of moral philosophy at the University of Berlin after 1896. The Chinese translation of Paulsen's *System der Ethik* appeared in 1913, and the copy which Mao read at the First Normal School "contains 12,100 characters of Mao's personal comments." "What Paulsen offered Mao Tse-tung," says Wakeman, "was a rational justification for placing the will over the intellect," and it was the function of the body to be a vehicle of the will. For Paulsen was a staunch advocate of physical training, which he associated with nothing less than the survival of the species. He took satisfaction in the rise of the gymnastics movement, which was contributing, in his view, to the survival of Germany itself.[14] From the standpoint of ideological consistency, all of this is highly ironic, as the eventual ultraleftist Mao Ze-dong drinks from the cup of the mystical nationalist "Father" Jahn, whose gymnastic doctrine Paulsen clearly admires. But the irony is, in an important sense, merely formal in that both Mao and Jahn cast themselves in the role of the nation builder who takes seriously, if not quite literally, the metaphor of the body politic.

Here we detect a vague, but unmistakable, difference between Mao's position and the Marxist renunciation of the corporealized state described in chapter 3. Mao's affinity for body imagery is confirmed by his comparison, in 1968, between a human being and the Communist party: "A proletarian party must also get rid of the waste and let in the fresh, for only in this way can it be full of vigor. Without eliminating waste and getting fresh blood the party has no vigor."[15] Mao's use of the body-party analogy can, then, be traced to intellectual influences which antedate his conversion to Marxism.

Maoist Sport Ideology

The Chinese idea of "physical culture" comprises three types of activity: physical education (*tiyu*), sport and athletics (*yundong*), and fitness and conditioning (*duanlian*). Like Mao's 1917 doctrine of the body, this is an essentially utilitarian conception, within which the Western notion of sport plays a distinctly subordinate role. The hygienic emphasis is evident in "The Common Program," a blueprint for social development published in 1950, and in Mao's official endorsement of June 10, 1952, which called upon the Chinese people to "promote physical culture and sport, and build up the people's health." The emphasis on social utility makes Maoist physical culture comparable to the early Bolshevik programs of the 1920s. The Standards of the National Physical Training Program, revised in 1975, were originally based upon the Soviet "Ready for Labor and Defense" program of 1931.[16]

The myth of a burgeoning Chinese sports colossus has surfaced episodically over the past two decades. Even "the expert Russians,"

Sports Illustrated warns in 1961, "are impressed—and perhaps alarmed—by a crash program begun in Red China four years ago. Awesomely mammoth, it may soon vault Chinese athletes into the leading ranks of world sport."[17] In 1979 a well-traveled German soccer trainer predicted that the Chinese would dominate that sport over the coming century.[18] Such predictions, however, are easier for foreigners to make than for the Chinese to fulfill, if only because their physical culture is much more remarkable for its ideology than for the athletic performances it has engendered.

Maoist sport, which has been subverted in important ways since Mao's death in 1976, specialized in an etiquette based on the eradication of hostile or aggressive feelings toward an opponent. It is an etiquette for both winning and losing, and one which can leave non-Chinese competitors in a state of emotional disorientation. In 1977 it was reported that Chinese deportment, combined with Chinese domination of world-class table tennis, was causing psychological problems. "Table tennis stars, particularly the Europeans, are beginning to squawk. The Chinese policy of 'friendship first, competition second' has hurt their pride, mocked their skills and, they say, put the sport in jeopardy."[19] "One never knows if they are playing seriously," a Swedish world champion lamented, presumably concerned about the legitimacy of his title.[20] The Maoist athlete must also lose with imperturbable grace. A reporter for the French sporting newspaper *L'Equipe* was awed at the 1974 Asian Games in Teheran by defeated Chinese athletes whose faces seemed to be lighted by smiles of exquisite amusement. There is even an etiquette for boycotting ideological undesirables without being unnecessarily rude. To show their disapproval of Israel at the Asian Games, the Chinese refused to engage Israelis in fencing matches but had no qualms about swimming against them in a pool. "We are avoiding bodily contact and individual confrontation," a Chinese fencer explained.[21]

Reporting in November 1976 from the Sixth Asian Women's Basketball Championships in Hong Kong, the Chinese news service offered the following addendum to its report of a lopsided Chinese victory over a Japanese team: "During the tussle, the Chinese and Japanese players made only a few fouls because they fully displayed the spirit of 'Friendship first, competition second.' The players would rather miss the ball than harm each other."[22] Maoist sport culture is a hygienic sport culture. Deemphasis of competition, "sport for the masses," and a profound disinterest in breeding super athletes reflect a stage of development corresponding to the early Bolshevik period which fell victim to Stalinization during the 1930s. It also shares with the extinct workers' sport movement a determination to prevent sport from leading to what one ideological ally of the Swedish Socialist Ivar Lo-Johansson called "democratization on the basis of stupidity." Even during competitions Maoist athletes have been required to read political articles—precisely the sort of demand which drove prospective recruits from the ranks of the workers' sport movement in Europe. "He must study the latest techniques of other societies and must train himself well in basic skills. He must take hold of basic techniques and be good at making flexible use of them. He must learn humbly and dare to create things. He must look for the factor of success in defeat, and be able to perceive the defective aspects in success. He must, through practice and summing up things, continuously translate matter into spirit and spirit into matter, carrying out the revolution without interruption, and ceaselessly march forward."[23]

It is clear that Maoist sport, as expressed in its etiquette, places much less value on competitive struggle than its Western or Soviet bloc counterparts. This is certainly a natural bias for a collectivistic ideology which has to date refused to make the sport champion—except for Mao the inspirational swimmer—an exemplary or edifying figure. And here, too, one can point to early doctrinal influences on Mao which would have discouraged an acceptance of the competitive ethos. Yang Changji's ideal of the "kingly way," which encouraged the fit to aid the destitute, obstructed the path to a pure Social Darwinism. A second, and rather bizarre, figure who could have influenced Mao in this regard is Kang Youwei (1858–1927), a reformer whom Mao idolized as a youth and whose teachings he still remembered, at least in part, a half-century later.[24] Kang was a prophet, indeed a cultist, of universal harmony whose career and utopian blueprint for a worldwide Great Community have been described at length by Jonathan Spence. The substance of Kang's vision is evident from the following excerpt: "I was born on this earth, so I come from the same womb as humans in all countries, even though our blood types may be different. . . . It is as if we were all parts of an electrical force which interconnects all things, or partook of the pure essence that encompasses all things."[25] Not surprisingly, Kang describes competition as "an extremely evil thing for the whole world," and he is repelled by Darwin's portrait of competition between species.[26]

And yet the fact remains that Mao decisively rejected Kang's doctrine of terrestrial unity. "Struggle is absolute," he says in 1967, "while unity is relative." Kang, as Wakeman points out, "could hardly bear the notion of natural strife; Mao Tse-tung's entire structure of thought and action was based upon it." For Mao, "Darwinism preceded Marxism; it constituted the prime scientific discovery of his youth."[27] Why did Mao refuse, in effect, to let sportive competition symbolize historical struggle? First, because Mao—like the early Bolshevik sport doctrinaires and even Stalin—could not permit the ideal of sheer performance to gain ascendancy over the ideal of collectivism. As a *People's Daily* editorial put it in 1958, "Individualism and particularism will not be exterminated until every commune member possesses communist ideology."[28] Any Communist society is forced to circumscribe the stature, and thus the implicit authority, of the champion.[29] Or, placing this act of censorship within the conceptual framework of chapter 3, Mao refused to anthropomorphize the state. His willingness to use body imagery (noted above) simply did not go this far.

There is, in addition, a crucial difference between sportive and historical struggle. Mao's "one invariable principle—call it struggle, contradiction, or the dialectic—which explained all phenomena . . . tended to become a uniform and monistic principle,"[30] whereas sportive contests—excepting pursuits of the record performance—are not absorbed by a hypothetical metaprocess embodying a teleology. This (Hegelian) conception of sport is not required, apparently, by any sporting public.

Finally, Mao may have considered competitive sport too marginal, too gratuitous, a human activity to be symbolic of the historical struggle. Unlike Stalin, whose administrative model he adopted in the early 1950s,[31] Mao never promoted high-performance sport as a celebrated analogue of heroic labor. Even the famous Yangtze swim of July 16, 1966, as I have argued in chapter 3, was less performance than pedagogy, less Mao the athlete than Mao the "living exemplar" of good health, whose miraculous fitness was in the service of a hygienic ideal rather than a competitive one.[32] Mao did, in fact, have an ideal of high performance; but it was not abstract, not removed from the labor process as the purely sportive achievement has to be.[33] "Ultimately more humanistic [than Marx], he placed man squarely in the center of being, fulfilling himself by completing nature. And, because man's own struggle was the principle of the universe, anything was possible, nothing could not be done."[34]

This doctrine of potentially limitless human achievement is one interpretation of the term "ultraleftism," which "at a highly abstract level . . . signified an idealist faith in human capacity regardless of socio-economic constraints." Bill Brugger has compared "ultraleftism" and "fascism" in order to account for Lin Biao's transformation from "ultraleftist" to "ultrarightist." "Both tend towards individual discipline rather than organisational discipline. Both stress the power of human will and believe that history is made by great men. Both rate the 'hero' as more important than ordinary people and turn the masses into a metaphysical category."[35] It is obvious that Mao's own style contained much "ultraleftism" of this kind, and that he remained a singular and peerless "hero" until his death. In fact, the Maoist period saw a literal ban on certain kinds of superlative performances which connoted self-indulgence on the part of the performers. For example, the novelist Ding Ling, charged in 1957 with "advocating hero worship," was also accused of " 'one-bookism,' a complex intellectual crime that implied a writer was selfishly trying to produce a perfect literary work at the expense of the other demands of life and the party."[36] Even seven years after Mao's death, the officially approved hero type is a self-sacrificing person who often dies in the course of his or her supreme effort.[37] Mao's successors, like Mao himself, are not prepared to release the individualistic, and charismatic, forces which constitute the mythos of the champion.

The End of Maoist Sport

In 1976, the year of Mao Ze-dong's death, a Chinese sport magazine accused the disgraced Deng Xiaoping of being concerned merely with "raising the level of technical skills" while disregarding mass sport: "how do you measure success? According to Deng Xiaoping's approach, all the athlete has to do is win fame and [first] place in competition, make it to the championship, and then there will be 'heroes' [the metaphor is 'shining roosters,' or superstars]. But which line they will be following, which thoughts they will be guided by, how these successes will be attained, that is never asked. . . . This is capitalist utilitarianism, meritocracy, the trap of revisionism. These things have a 'corrupting' influence in their emphasis upon *individual* and small group accomplishments."[38] Less than three years later, in January 1979, the rehabilitated Deng, now deputy prime minister of the People's Republic, recalled at a White House dinner how Red Guards had denounced him at the beginning of the Cultural Revolution for his "decadent" fondness for playing bridge.[39]

During the period of the Cultural Revolution (1966–1970) competitive sport in China was harshly criticized and international sporting contacts were sharply reduced. The Physical Culture and Sports Commission was put under the control of the General Political Department of the People's Liberation Army.[40] Hostility to sport may even have lasted until Mao's death in 1976,[41] thus surviving the advent of "ping pong diplomacy" in 1971. It is interesting to note that some ideological enthusiasts of the Cultural Revolution encouraged a form of ersatz "sport" in the service of Maoist orthodoxy: "speed contests in reciting the 'Quotations' (some champions could give them not only in the right order, but also *backward*) and Quotation Calisthenics (where movements followed not the tune, but quotations from Chairman Mao: bend the arm on this phrase, flex the legs on that one, and so on . . .)"[42]

In the wake of Mao's death, the arrest of the vilified "Gang of Four," and the ideological turn toward "pragmatism" and productivity, Maoist sport became a target of "revisionist" policies. In late 1976 a purge of the Chinese bureaucracy extended into the Sports Commission. An article distributed by the Chinese press agency offered a cryptic indictment: "The gang of four labeled those who trained hard as practicing the revisionist theory of productive forces and those who failed to show good form in international competition as 'impairing national dignity.'"[43] It will be noted that, according to this report, the Gang of Four had actually taken opposing positions on the same question. It would seem that Mao's widow, Chiang Ching, and her purged cohorts had both discouraged and then encouraged top-level performances. But this technique was the essence of Maoist terror. "The *People's Daily*," Simon Leys points out, "may well give you the solution to a certain problem, but it also gives the *opposite* solution to the *same* problem at a *different* time. Maoist truth is essentially fluid and changing; to survive, one cannot miss the train, or the turn. Maoist propaganda may be one of the most monotonous, arid, and indigent creations in the world, but for this reason it is followed by millions with burning interest: their careers, their very lives depend on the changing ideological line, which must be read between the lines and whose message may sometimes be found in the most unexpected and out-of-the-way places."[44]

The decline and fall of Maoist values within Chinese sport culture can be followed with great precision in the official sport periodical, *Xin tiyu* (New Physical Culture). During 1975 and 1976 the Maoist line, which included the clear subordination of sport to larger ideological requirements, is unchallenged. Sport is "an integral element of the [social] superstructure," and major ideological documents unrelated to sport are reprinted to underscore the subordination of the athletic community to ideological orthodoxy. The leftist heretic Lin Biao is denounced for having promoted "the poisoning effect of 'medal-and-trophyism,'" for having promulgated the slogan "Skill is no. 1," and for finding inspiration in Confucius. The right-wing deviant Liu Shaoqi is accused of depriving "the poor and middle peasants of their right and ability to exercise their bodies" and of "wantonly encouraging athletes and instructors to block-headedly play the ballgame and not to study the principles of the revolution." Deng Xiaoping is reviled for counseling an ideologically unprincipled pursuit of athletic success, for following the line that: "no matter if white cat or black cat, the good cat is the cat that catches the rat," for being concerned only with "raising the level of technical skills."[45]

By 1977 the overt display of ideological pronunciamentos is being phased out; toward the end of 1978 and the beginning of 1979 there is a shift away from the use of sport to illustrate ideological principles to the presentation of sport features as such. The primacy of ideology is gradually replaced by an interest in sport in the Western sense of the term.

The post-Mao cult of disciplined productivity and the acquisition of technological expertise calls for a systematic competition-oriented athleticism. Hua Kuo-feng, Mao's immediate successor, issued a call for world-class performances.[46] The result has been an expansion of the sport school system, rewards for good performances, the introduction of scientific sport medicine, and even the importing of professional athletes from West Germany to serve as tutors.[47] The Gang of Four stands accused of having criminally neglected weightlifting and of "sabotaging the development of socialist sport."[48] Both the etiquette—a sign of ideologically based self-discipline—and the hygienic content of Maoist sport are on the decline. In January 1980 Deng Xiaoping lifted a 23-year-old ban on boxing so as to permit Muhammad Ali to help train Chinese boxers for the 1984 Olympic Games.[49] During the Asian Games held in Bangkok in December 1978, Chinese basketball players—who had been known to refuse scoring opportunities if an opposing player stumbled—became involved during a game in a brawl with their (South Korean) opponents, a fracas which required the intervention of fifty police.[50] The society which had virtually shut down sport during the period of the Cultural Revolution was leaving the civilized norms of Maoist sport far behind.

Since 1978 Chinese sport ideology has undergone some striking, and even shocking, reversals. Perhaps the most novel of these developments is the appearance of a para-athletic Stakhanovism strongly reminiscent of the Maoist cult of mind-over-matter and "revolutionary will-power."[51] In an article titled "Breakthrough into the 'Death-Zone'—The Truth Emerges from Praxis" (1978), an author named Weng Qingzhang writes of Chinese mountaineers who, due to the failure of their oxygen equipment, "were forced into the discovery that they could with proper preparation operate for up to 6 hours in the 'death-zone' (where, according to theory, one cannot survive) . . ."[52] This hymn to physical transcendence recalls both Mao's mythic swim down the Yangtze in 1966 and Stalin's arctic explorers of the 1930s. From this point of view, human progress is linear, limitless, and the result of penetrating barriers which are understood as primarily psychological in nature.

The Chinese revolutionaries' treatment of sexuality has been— and largely remains—rigid, repressive, and puritanical. "It is not so much that the Chinese Communists borrowed their sexual mores from the Russians, along with their ideology and party apparatus, but that many revolutionaries by nature see themselves as dedicated, ascetic souls."[53] There are, however, two ways in which the liberation of the body is taking place within post-Maoist sport culture. Maoist ideology already called upon women to break "feudalistic ideological fetters" by learning to swim, even if this required "a young wife to expose her arms and bare her legs . . ."[54] By 1981, even more delicate matters are being discussed for the purpose of removing obstacles to physical development. For example, a male gymnastics instructor may be required to give "timely assistance" to his female charges; but such expert guidance may also lead to "misunderstandings." This author points out that "the stage of puberty" involves "a sense of mystery about physiological phenomena," and that female students, "under the influence of antiquated thought," may resist athletics in general and thereby forfeit an opportunity to contribute to the "Four Modernizations."[55] Modesty must not impede modernity.

The drab and baggy revolutionary uniforms prescribed for both sexes by Maoist doctrine have long symbolized an ascetic renunciation of personal narcissism. But the hegemony of instinctual and aesthetic repression is wholly disregarded by an article which appeared in 1981, titled "You Wish Your Body to Be Healthy and Beautiful? Some Notes on Sports Aesthetics."

> Whether a person is tall, short, fat or thin depends to a certain extent on congenitally transmitted elements and postnatal conditions. Quite a few people are not one hundred percent satisfied with their own bodies, and the women comrades in particular painstakingly and singlemindedly invest much effort on their clothes—selecting the newest and sharpest fashions, matching all colors and materials and, using all of the different

components like the vertical, horizontal crossing and slanting cuts, correct their tallness, shortness, obesity or thinness by adjusting the 'line' properly. This is a method that uses optical illusion to make a less than ideal figure relatively more pleasing to the eye, and it definitely can 'cover the ugliness' and have a distinct aesthetic effect, even if it is hardly a method which gets at the root of the problem. The beautiful human body is what artists from ancient times until today have always dreamed of and sought after. The unprecedented pioneer in the veneration of the beauty of the human body was ancient Hellas. Those sculptors with their overflowing talent may have lacked systematic anatomical knowledge, but as early as 776 B.C., at the quadrennial Olympic Games, they had ample opportunity to observe naked athletes, to fully activate their formal sense and create innumerable images of healthy and beautiful human bodies.[56]

Even more surprising is this author's reference, without censure, to "the male beauty contests that flourished during the thirties in the countries of Europe and in America," and to "an international women's pageant" held in 1980, from which "one can form a rough idea of the aesthetic standards which apply to the human body." Figures 1 and 2 demonstrate the influence of aesthetic norms peculiar to Western "body building."

In 1978 *Xin tiyu* published the confessions of a self-proclaimed "sport nut" (*t'i yü mi*), a concept Maoists must have considered politically obscene.[57] "I am a sport lover [the Chinese word has an erotic tinge] and I particularly like to watch movies dealing with sports themes. Since the Liberation [1949], many good films with such themes have appeared. However, at the time when the Gang of Four held sway, this love of ours had to remain unfulfilled. Not only did feature films on athletic themes disappear, even documentaries hardly found grace. The great group of workers in athletics and the spectators long so much to see more athletic activities on the silver screen!"[58] An officially sanctioned outpouring of this kind represents a spectacular defection from the sensual asceticism of the Maoists. At the same time, it implies that concessions must be made to a certain kind of sensual-aesthetic appetite which existed in a state of chronic frustation during the Maoist period.

"The addiction to sports," Thorstein Veblen writes in 1899, "... in a peculiar degree marks an arrested development of [a] man's moral nature." Like the Maoists, Veblen interprets immoderate de-

FIGURES 1 AND 2. With the decline of Maoist sport ideology after 1976, the pursuit of high performance—and the developed bodies it required—became acceptable. These illustrations are from a 1981 issue of *Xin tiyu* (*New Physical Culture*).

votion to sport as an emotional barbarism: "The ground of an addiction to sports is an archaic spiritual constitution—the possession of the predatory emulative propensity in a relatively high potency. A strong proclivity to adventuresome exploit and to the infliction of damage is especially pronounced in those employments which are in colloquial usage specifically called sportsmanship."[59] Few observers have concluded, as Veblen did, that competitive sport is inherently a philistinism. Only Maoism succeeds in founding an entire sport culture on this principle, even if this achievement must be viewed in a much larger context: Maoism, after all, has also meant "a deliberate destruction of intelligence and culture, of arts and letters, of the cultural heritage of the past—all this seems to have been nearly swept away by a magical Ping-Pong paddle."[60]

Like the workers' sport movement of the 1920s, Maoist sport "asked too much" of those it attempted to transform: the renunciation of aggression (viz. the ban on boxing), partisan frenzy, egotism, and virile pride, and the cultivation of a sportsmanship which humbled and distressed the Western mind.[61] With the appearance of China's first "sport nut," Maoist sport had lost its struggle against arrested development. The anticompetitive sport cultures of the twentieth century were finally extinct.

11. Toward the Abolition of "Sport": Neo-Marxist Sport Theory

Historical Background

"Only sport," a West German neo-Marxist writes in 1970, "seems to move the masses in a really massive way."[1] There is a poignancy to this statement, an unspoken wish it were not so, and a corresponding determination to find out why it is. As we have seen in chapter 7, the Socialist sport manifestos which appeared between 1928 and 1931 had already posed this question, though less to answer it than to deal with its practical political implications. "What is it," Fritz Wildung asks in 1929, "that can carry away these ordinary people, that can whip up their passions to such a pitch? It is sport! If we take a somewhat closer look and try to find a basis for the psychology of this sporting public, we encounter two phenomena, two strong drives of the human soul: the play-impulse and the competitive spirit."[2] The real issue, these observers realized, was that of non-rational appeals and the ways in which such appeals related to the formation of political strategy. This was also Wilhelm Reich's message to the German Communist party, which expelled him in 1933. "It is unlikely," he writes a year later, "that a revolutionary organization will ever succeed in persuading the mass of women to adopt the austere appearance of Communist women.[3] A way has to be found between bourgeois glamour and Communist asceticism, satisfying both the demands of the class struggle and the natural healthy vanity of women. Our political leaders should not dismiss such matters as being unworthy of their attention."[4] Such issues would eventually be taken more seriously by the European neo-Marxists of the 1960s and 1970s.

It is the neo-Marxist sport critics of Western Europe, and not the East Germans, who are the legitimate heirs of the workers' sport movement and its theorists, even if they rarely acknowledge the debt. Heirs do not, of course, occupy the same historical ground as their ancestors, and this is likely to give rise to doctrinal differences. A Socialist leader like Wildung actually had a politically self-conscious working-class movement to write for, while his West German counterpart of the post-1968 era speaks to a less established radical minority. Consequently, the homely practicality one sometimes finds in Wildung's treatment of sport is utterly foreign to the modern European sport radicals who suddenly appear during the late sixties and early seventies. Wildung, after all, was more a reform-minded alternate establishmentarian than a "radical." Compared with the modern demythologizers of sport, he is an innocent whose critique is circumscribed by an idealist's faith in sport itself and by an intellectual range which, while admirable by contemporary standards, does not, for example, make use (in 1929) of psychoanalytic concepts which have helped make possible a more refined (and more hostile) anatomy of sport.

The differences which separate workers' sport theory from that of recent neo-Marxist criticism should not, however, be overestimated. What is striking, in fact, is the relative infrequency with which the moderns even mention their Socialist predecessors of the interwar period. In the case of the French ultraleftists, this is understandable if only because the workers' sport movement in France— unlike its German, Austrian, and Czechoslovakian counterparts— was not particularly significant.[5] But in the case of the West German radicals of the post-1968 generation, this lack of interest is more difficult to explain. Neo-Marxist critiques of high-performance sport, the cult of the record, the Olympic movement, moronic sport journalism, the sensation-hungry spectator, sport as a "mirror" or "reproduction" of capitalist labor, sport as compensation (*Ausgleich*) for debilitating labor, the deformation of the play-impulse by sport, and sportive anti-intellectualism[6]—all appear in the Socialist manifestos of the 1928–1931 period.

While several of the neo-Marxist authors mention the workers' sport movement,[7] only one volume investigates the reasons for its failure to reappear after 1945. It is notable that this look back upon an extinct political culture of sport also criticizes—from a leftist position not wholly disapproving of East German sport praxis—the failure of the New Left to create a "proletarian physical culture" in the Federal Republic, as well as its failure to transcend the "autonomous negative criticism" and "antiauthoritarian" position of the Frankfurt School.[8]

Proletarische Körperkultur + Gesellschaft (1973) makes clear why the workers' sport movement of the 1920s was not a particularly attractive model for the Left radicals of the 1960s. For one thing, the Arbeiter-Turnerbund (ATB), founded in 1893 as a revolutionary political organization for working-class gymnasts, underwent a gradual embourgeoisement for several reasons: 1. the absence of both proletarian tradition and the Marxist theoreticians who might have established and maintained one; 2. the indifference of Social Democrats regarding proletarian culture in general; 3. state persecution of the Socialist movement as a whole, and the consequent depoliticizing of its sport culture; and 4. the patriotic fervor of August 1914, which turned "the workers' gymnastics movement (and the workers' movement as a whole) into an integral component of the 'pluralistic' Wilhelminian system." (The workers' gymnasts did manage to distinguish themselves ideologically from bourgeois patriots by refusing to adopt a "romantic conception" of war.) A major factor adduced by these authors is the alleged intellectual barrenness of the workers' sport movement,[9] a claim chapter 7 shows to be exaggerated. That the worker gymnasts and athletes lacked a "theoretical concept of sport" is less important, given the contemporary context, than the fact that workers' sport incorporated a system of humane norms.

The neglect by modern radicals which derives, at least in part, from this pacific and compromised image has had consequences. A greater influence by the *Arbeitersport* ideology of the 1920s would undoubtedly have moderated the radicalism of the neo-Marxist sport critics. Such moderation would probably have been both an advantage and a disadvantage. On the one hand, it would have encouraged a more tolerant, more dialectical understanding of sport's relationship to themes such as discipline, narcissism, and sexuality. On the other hand, it might well have blunted the radicals' insights into sport's "irrational core" and the depth of sport's nonrational appeals.[10] As it happens, the void was filled by Frankfurt School doctrine (see below) and its seigneurial disdain for both sport and the body.

The appearance of radical sport theory in France and West Germany after 1968 was, of course, only one aspect of a larger revolt. The intellectual ferment which accompanied the French upheaval of May–June 1968, and in particular the attitude of total contestation, constituted a fertile milieu for this kind of oppositional thinking. At the same time, however, sport had not been on the agenda of the May insurgents. "The critical fire which had attacked all other institutions (University, Theatre, Family, Army, Arts, etc.) had spared, paradoxically, sport, that great absent event of events, even to the point where the reformist Left, led by Mendès-France, could hold a great assembly in the Charléty Stadium."[11] Daniel Cohn-Bendit, for one, was taken by surprise. "Even the football clubs," he emotes in 1968, "were taken over by their players!"[12] And as late as 1975, he calls himself *un fana de sport* without any hint of awareness that this might constitute an unrevolutionary kind of exuberance.[13]

The most important precipitating factor bearing on the new sport radicalism was the West German student revolt of the 1960s.[14] As Alfred Grosser points out in 1970, "the critical examination of society [in West Germany] became much more widespread in the late 1960s as education became 'democratized,' that is, as more young people were still at school at an age when they would formerly have had to be at work. The *Gymnasien* in particular have been the scene of unrest that was sometimes creative, at other times aimless or destructive."[15] The First Commune, an experimental youth collective, was founded late in 1966 in West Berlin. "It traces its historical antecedents to the youth communes of postrevolutionary Russia, with the condition that it proposes to improve on some of their structural aspects, notably those criticized by Wilhelm Reich, such as their rigid work orientation, and their repressive sexual morality."[16]

Rigid discipline was exactly what these communards did not want. As Reimut Reiche points out in 1968, "They opposed the 'Marxist alienation theory' with the concept of 'fun.'"[17] But high-performance sport demands not fun, but a "rigid work orientation" which opposes spontaneity, and this is the germ of the hostility which marks the neo-Marxist approach to sport. Nor is sport in this sense compatible with the cultivation of a neo-Reichian sexuality; here the notion of play (*Spiel, jeu*), construed as a way of life, addresses the body not as a vehicle of performance, but as the vessel of pleasure and fulfillment—an orientation which the staid (and sport-loving) French Communist party (PCF) associated, quite rightly, with the culture of the Right and its affinity for the irrational.

A third factor associated with radical sport theory in the Federal Republic was the meteoric rise of Frankfurt School theorists like Adorno and Marcuse as culture heroes of the New Left (see below). Göran Therborn has argued that it is the "function of Frankfurt theory as a developed reflection of anti-capitalist revulsion which explains the persistence of the School. The combination of institutional continuity and the freezing of a common attitude by the Nazi trauma has preserved it and its basic ideas despite all the changes of the last forty years. Hence it could suddenly re-emerge as something like a magical *anticipation* of the contemporary student movement."[18] Thus, 1969 saw the republishing of Horkheimer and Adorno's *Dialectic of Enlightenment*, representing the earlier radicalism, and the publication of Bero Rigauer's *Sport and Labor*, representing the later one. The fact that many young radicals were confusing Horkheimer and Adorno with the more radical Marcuse, or were simply unaware of their profoundly unrevolutionary attitudes, is termed by Paul Connerton one of those "historical errors at once painful and productive."[19] Or as Reimut Reiche puts it, one could not reproach the founders of the Unverbindliche Richtlinien (Nonobligatory Principles) groups of the early sixties "for not having correctly understood their mentors: Marx, Freud, Adorno. That would be a philological rather than a political criticism."[20]

Neo-Marxist social theory, French and West German variants of which are discussed below, represents Marxism's attempt to recover from certain intellectual consequences of Marxism-Leninism. "In the past," Richard Gombin writes, "any work which aimed at relaunching revolutionary thought came up against the totalitarian pretensions (in the etymological sense) of 'orthodox' Marxism, which presented itself as a closed, scientific and final system. Not only all social life but all the sciences were contained by this veritable *cosmogony*, with its holy writ, its official priesthood, its devotions and its heresies." As I have argued in earlier chapters, until very recently the Marxist tradition as a whole has demonstrated an inability to deal with the importance and complexity of nonrational experience, and this is certainly Gombin's view. Arguing on behalf of a French "leftism" which "excludes all authoritarian, centralist, interventionist, planned and ideological models," he introduces the theme of the irrational in the course of a digression into what I have earlier termed ideological differentiation: "The leftist intention, undoubtedly, is also a quest for the 'whole' man, who, to enrich the concrete nature of his real existence, brings the irrational into his experience. The irrational, as an added dimension, has traditionally been invoked, if not monopolized, by *reactionary* thinkers, as an obscure ('nature') justification for the existing state of things."[21] This is the warning Wilhelm Reich gave in *The Mass Psychology of Fascism* (1933), and forty years later it had lost little of its relevance. Henri Lefebvre, a Marxist philosopher who left the French Communist party in 1956 and who is an important source of the "leftism" analyzed by Gombin,[22] agrees with Reich that Marxists must recognize that the locus of the struggle against repression lies at a much deeper level than that at which its visible manifestations occur: "A study of the foundations of a repressive society must be far reaching; only a superficial anarchist or Marxist interpretation can restrict the significance of this concept to the police force and to class legislation, for as things now stand the repressive nature of any society is more deeply rooted than that."[23] Herbert Marcuse makes the same point on behalf of the liberating potential of art: "The universality of art cannot be grounded in the world and world outlook of a particular class, for art envisions a concrete universal, humanity (*Menschlichkeit*), which no particular class can incorporate, not even the proletariat, Marx's 'universal class.' The inexorable entanglement of joy and sorrow, celebration and despair, Eros and Thanatos cannot be dissolved into problems of class struggle."[24]

The next part of this chapter presents (very similar) French and West German neo-Marxist critiques of sport in a combined format. It should be pointed out, however, that neither the respective doctrines nor their intellectual origins are identical. Both ultimately derive in part from the young Marx and his critique of alienation in the "Economic and Philosophical Manuscripts of 1844." But the channels through which the original Marxian impulses have flowed are not the same, and this fact helps to account for differences which often have less to do with content than with tone and emphasis. On the French side, the most important sources of theory are Henri Lefebvre and the Situationist International (IS) group, which played a major role in fomenting the famous "Strasbourg University Scandal" of 1966–67, and which provided much of the ideological foundation for the tumultous events of May–June 1968.[25] As we shall see below, Lefebvre and the Situationists both offer the vision of a civilization in which play is the supreme activity, and one in which modern sport fares poorly when judged from the utopian perspective of ultraleftist cultural criticism. But this ludic ideal is not shared by the Frankfurt theorists, unless one includes the maverick Herbert Marcuse. The Frankfurt School—and its "left melancholy"—could not, in this sense, be further removed from Lefebvre and his "resurrection of the Festival."[26] This profound difference in tone and factors like the surrealist tradition in France, the euphoric French experience of 1968, the general unavailability of Frankfurt School writings in French until the early 1970s,[27] and the proximity of the Nazi past to West German youth have produced two culturally distinct neo-Marxist critiques of sport.

The Neo-Marxist Critique of Sport

Both the French and the West German schools stand in relation to Marxist-Leninist ideology, but in very different political contexts. The French group confronts, from its ultraleftist position, the calcified French Community party (PCF), which they outmaneuvered in spectacular fashion during the upheaval of 1968. Presented on this occasion with the opportunity to participate in an insurrection, the PCF allied itself with the Gaullists by appealing for calm, thereby underlining its establishmentarian sobriety. This schism between the PCF and its neo-Marxist adversaries also applies to their respective doctrines of sport. The PCF, rejecting the notion of "the so-called antisportive attitude of the French," endorses high-performance sport, the Olympic ideology, the "educative value" of sport champions, and French success in international competitions.[28] (It should be pointed out that all of these positions are compatible both with French official policy and with the Eastern bloc doctrine represented, for example, by the Polish sport sociologist Andrzej Wohl.) The neo-Marxists' condemnation of the PCF and its "social-chauvinist line" on sport is unsparing, and they take pleasure in reprinting PCF attacks on their alleged "cultural nihilism," "university idealism," and so forth. Nor do the French sport radicals demonstrate any ambiguity in their attacks on the "Stakhanovism," the "cerebro-affective Pavlovism," the *cosmonaute sportif*, or the totalitarian "humanics" (*l'humanique*) of Eastern bloc sport.[29] For their critique of what Jean-Marie Brohm calls "the sport robot," these writers could call upon Henri Lefebvre's *Vers le cybernanthrope* (1967) and its notion of the *cybernanthrope*, a new and de-complexified human type of the technological age with an affinity for both sport and the robot, and Roland Barthes's powerful short sketch, "The Jet-Man," in his famous collection *Mythologies* (1957), whose para-athletic subject is described as "a kind of anthropological compromise between humans and Martians."

The West German neo-Marxists stand in relation to a Marxism-Leninism, that of the GDR, which is neither entirely foreign nor entirely domestic. The sport radicals do not endorse what Jean-Marie Brohm calls "the cybernetic socialism of the DDR";[30] instead, they tend either to ignore it or to react in a defensive manner on behalf of the East Germans. Gerhard Vinnai, for example, rejects the idea that the sport cultures of East and West are essentially the same, although he declines to explain precisely why; the point, he says, is that in the GDR socialism is being held captive by its "capitalist past" and needs only to be liberated through a "fundamental democratization."[31] At least, one authors' collective maintains, the East Germans recognize that there is no such thing as "apolitical" sport.[32] Such evasions probably derive from the West German New Left's agonized fixation on the Federal Republic, which represents, in its failure to carry out real denazification, a deeply compromised image of the unrepentant father and his sins. "The applied psychoanalysis of the revolutionary students," Daniel Cohn-Bendit writes, "was clearly bringing on a general cure."[33] Both French and West German sport radicals employ psychoanalytic concepts. This is striking in that until about 1968 the Left intelligentsias of both countries—like the Stalinists—emphatically rejected psychoanalysis. In West Germany this change was largely due to the influence of thinkers like Wilhelm Reich, Theodor Adorno, and Herbert Marcuse; in France, the disillusionments of 1968 revealed the limitations of current radical social theory. But there was much resistance to overcome. "The present organized condemnation of psychoanalysis by neo-Stalinism, revisionism, and Maoism," the West German neo-Marxist Michael Schneider writes in 1973, "reproduces unchanged all of the anti-Freudian prejudices of the thirties."[34] In France, psychoanalysis fared poorly for this as well as other reasons. "Before World War II," Sherry Turkle has pointed out, "the French had rejected psychoanalysis as a German inspiration, an object of distrust . . . " Since 1968, however, "psychoanalysts have become deeply involved in radical social criticism, and French social criticism has become deeply involved with psychoanalytic thinking. In fact, psychoanalytic premises have become the common reference point shared by Communist party and nonparty Marxism, utopian and anarchistic *gauchisme*, and by the radical anti-Marxism which burst forth in France in 1977 under the name of 'the New Philosophy.'"[35] This is the context in which the French neo-Marxists of the *Partisans* group refer to sport and "the repression of erotic satisfaction," the "sado-masochistic relationship between the individual and his body," or "the ferocity of the muscular superego."[36] Sport's alleged role in suppressing sexual impulses is also addressed by a West German collective which (following Reich) portrays the sexually repressed individual as politically dominated as well.[37] Gerhard Vinnai sees sport as "characterized by its masochistic element," as a perverse asceticism.[38] Conspicuous here is a failure to transcend the pure rejection of asceticism by carefully analyzing its appeal to otherwise healthy people.

Both neo-Marxist schools reject what Vinnai calls the "absolutized performance principle" (*Leistungsprinzip*) which is sport's "purest expression."[39] For Jean-Marie Brohm, competition is "the very *essence* of sport," and an alienating one.[40] Christian Graf von Krockow has dismissed the critique of high-performance sport as "a type of 'late bourgeois' self-hatred," and the philosopher Hans Lenk has responded at length to the New Left critique of performance and competition.[41]

Both neo-Marxisms exalt the body as the sphere of pleasure and freedom. In a preface to the 1961 edition of *Eros and Civilization*, Marcuse speaks of "the release of the repressed body, instrument of labor and of fun in a society which is organized against its liberation."[42] In 1973 Jean-Marie Brohm calls for "a *new culture of the body* in the total sense of the word, a culture in which the body would rediscover all of its rights: aesthetic, ludic, erotic, and intellectual [!]"[43] As we have seen in earlier chapters, a profound interest in the body runs counter to Marxist tradition, and it is therefore not surprising that the PCF accuses its ultraleftist foes of cultivating "the old reactionary idea of a culture of the body." This criticism would be accurate were it not for the neo-Marxists' intellectualizing approach: "the body is an institution which merits analysis, and we refuse to give it a 'natural' image beyond the social reality which has established it; we refuse to mythify the body." There is "no neutral idea of the body" on which an unreflective "culture of the body" might be founded.[44] In a similar vein, Vinnai defines capitalism as hostile to the body, protests the "reification" of the body, and demands its "resexualization."[45] What should be emphasized here is how long it has taken for Marxist thought to develop a genuine consciousness of the body.

Both neo-Marxisms idealize the domain of play, of the *ludique*, and both see it subverted by modern sport. Sport, says Brohm, is "nothing but the *systematic perversion of the agonal ludic instinct* by competition."[46] Vinnai sees in modern soccer a loss of "playful charm" (*spielerischen Reiz*). It is the French, however, who have really developed the theme of the *ludique* as a utopian criterion, not only for sport, but for culture as a whole. (German authors like Vinnai and Eichberg, lacking a German Lefebvre, have a tendency to quote from the cultural conservative Friedrich Georg Jünger.)[47]

Lefebvre's interest in play (he does not mention Roger Caillois) derives from Charles Fourier, Sartre (see chapter 2), and Kostas Axelos, who was in turn influenced by Heidegger[48]—an unorthodox lineage by Marxist standards other than those of the new "leftism." In the first volume of his *Critique de la vie quotidienne* (1958), Lefebvre devotes several pages to leisure and sport. He interprets leisure as a "general requirement" of modern industrial civilization which is ambiguous in that it may be active or passive, enriching or impoverishing; like Huizinga before him, Lefebvre sees a further ambiguity in forms of leisure (e.g., gardening) which incorporate an element of labor. Modern leisure is basically a distraction from, and a compensation for, everyday life. Sport, too, according to Lefebvre, is ultimately both a cultural illusion and a compensatory stratagem. "As sport has developed, it has been presented as a culture of the body, of individual energy and team spirit: as a school of health. And what has been the result of these grand ambitions? A vast social apparatus (commercialized or not) and great dramas of competition which are sometimes spectacular to the point of magnificence."[49] This is the sport culture from which the *ludique* must be rescued. In *Everyday Life in the Modern World* (1968), Lefebvre envisions an urban environment which "will restore *adaptation* so that it prevails over compulsion and sets a limit to make-believe, restricting the imagination to style and works of art, monuments, festivals, so that play and games will be given their former significance, a chance to realize their possibilities . . . "[50] The Situationists, too, call for what Gombin terms "the *civilization of play*": "The liberated man will cease to be *homo faber* and will become an artist, that is to say the creator of his own works."[51] Raoul Vaneigem's Situationist manifesto of 1967 sees the entire social order conspiring against "authentic play" (*le jeu authentique*).[52] As the child of compulsion, sport must be exiled from this kingdom.

A more detailed exposition of neo-Marxist sport theory would necessarily treat, in addition to the five topics discussed above, sport's alleged depoliticizing effects, neo-Marxist hostility to the Olympic movement, the critique of the sport champion, and sport's alleged anti-intellectual essence.[53] "Sport passion," a West German radical claims, "is inherently regressive in nature: corresponding to it as an 'archaic state of consciousness' which is conserved by means of irrational social relationships."[54] If this is indeed the case—as Veblen claimed in 1899—then any "rational" social praxis of sport will be severely complicated by its hidden effects. This is one reason why neo-Marxist sport doctrine is more an adjunct to "critical theory" than a real program for the future.

The most detailed critiques of neo-Marxist sport theory have been formulated by Henning Eichberg (1973) and Wilhelm Hopf (1979).[55] One important objection to neo-Marxist procedure raised by both authors concerns the use of analogical reasoning. "One fancies oneself a Marxist," says Hopf, "on the grounds that one can make analogies between the labor process and sport. In so doing, however, one does not come to grips with the real problem, which is explaining the realm of sport."[56] Eichberg, too, speaks of "the prescientific leap from analogy to causality" which underlies, for example, Bero Rigauer's assumption that sport and industry employ "analogous methods of training and instruction."[57]

The sport-labor analogy is one of several metaphorical equations employed by the neo-Marxists. "This search for analogies," says Eichberg, "goes so far as to interpret and condemn the team principle as a reflection of the 'domination of collective labor criteria throughout all sectors of the economy'—an obvious misinterpretation of the preindustrial, then group and collective principle which the same social critics generally regard—and rightly so—as potentially emancipating."[58] Soccer may be interpreted as a machinelike activity, referees can be seen as police, and it can even be claimed that "the loss of the ball to an opposing player contains a symbolic castration."[59] Such analogies, however casuistical their use, are an authentic expression of the intellectual aggression cultivated by Marx and by so many of his later admirers (e.g., Lenin, Sartre) as a form of intellectual virility.

Neo-Marxist analogies between sport and labor prefigure the critique of sport's core ethos—the performance principle itself (*Leistungsprinzip*), which is seen as an enslaving and impoverishing, rather than liberating, discipline. But the critique of the performance principle, says Eichberg, overlooks the sheer necessity of such a standard to make sense of sportive contests or, for that matter, of social rank. What is more, it can have an emancipating influence by virtue of its inherently egalitarian ethos, or an implicitly critical function vis-à-vis a stagnant or rigid social structure which has suppressed the openness which derives from competition.[60] It should be noted that the sportive *Leistungprinzip* was not the first such principle to be subjected to criticism from the Left. In *Eros and Civilization*, Herbert Marcuse had already identified an invidious performance principle within the context of the labor-leisure dialectic:

> The performance principle, which is that of an acquisitive and antagonistic society in the process of constant expansion, presupposes a long development during which domination has been increasingly rationalized: control over social labor now reproduces society on an enlarged scale and under improving conditions. . . . Work has now become *general*, and so have the restrictions placed upon the libido: labor time, which is the largest part of the individual life's time, is painful time, for alienated labor is absence of gratification, negation of the pleasure principle.[61]

This is the larger concept into which the sportive performance principle fits as an object of opprobrium. Here one finds critiques of both alienated labor and alienated libido—a combination which proved irresistible to the Left radicals of affluent bourgeois Europe during the sixties. Within the world of sport, militant partisans of libido could find—in the very midst of everyday life—nightmarish examples of hyperdiscipline, monotony, pain, and mortification of the flesh which were all the more disturbing for being both voluntary and, apparently, masochistic. Eventually, neo-Marxist sport theory would exhaust its own resources because of this sort of diagnostic arrogance. It may be, however, that its achievements were in part contingent on that arrogance, and both can be traced to the influence of the Frankfurt theorists who came to prominence during the antiauthoritarian revolts of the late sixties.

The Frankfurt School on Sport and the Body

Frankfurt sociology, Theodor Adorno writes, can be defined as "insight into the essence of society, i.e., insight into what *is*, but in a critical sense. It measures societal reality against what it pretends to be, in order to explore in the contradictions the potentiality and possibility of the changing of the entire social structure."[62] The Marxian ambition of this project is evident. Yet, as Zoltán Tar has pointed out, the sociology of the most important Frankfurt theorists—Max Horkheimer and Adorno—is neither Marxist nor sociological in a strict sense. First, in its deviation from classic Marxist epistemology and ontology, its refusal to offer a synthesis of theory and praxis, and its radical critique of modern science and technology, Frankfurt theory—particularly during its last phase—is only tenuously "Marxist." Second, the work of these thinkers substitutes an essentially intuitional method for scientific sociology. (It should be noted that the most influential work by a Frankfurt theorist, Adorno's *The Authoritarian Personality* [1950], represents a fusion of the reflective method and empiricism.) Tar thus defines the Frankfurt Theory of Society as "an amalgamation of artistic reflections (*Kulturkritik*), combined with Marxian categories and elements, and a pessimistic philosophy of history."[63]

Frankfurt theory, based less on Marxist doctrine than on the personal histories, tastes, and preoccupations of its practitioners, is fertile (and simultaneously vulnerable) precisely because its heterogeneous sources preserved it from the cruder aspects of Marxist anthropology. This is why writers like Adorno and Marcuse have been so far ahead of more orthodox Marxist contemporaries in their studies of aesthetics, political psychology, and the nature of "domination" in the modern world. It was this originality, in conjunction with a perceived (but not always real) leftism, which made possible their enormous influence on the European "New Left" of the 1960s and which accounts for the frequency with which they are cited by the West German sport radicals of this period.

At the age of nineteen, Max Horkheimer writes of "a yearning for perfection, which cannot be attained *as long as we possess a body* and perceive it through senses [emphasis added]."[64] As we shall see, this demotion—or implicit denigration—of the body foreshadows a fundamental disdain which reappears thirty years later in *Dialectic of Enlightenment* (1944), which Horkheimer wrote with Adorno. However, it was the latter who, among the Frankfurt group, best recognized the body as an issue of cultural and political significance. And if it is true that Adorno saw the importance of the body and its sportive role only with his peripheral vision, the fact remains that the image registered sharply, and this in itself is unusual. What is typical about Adorno's response is the disinclination to make the body more than an incidental object of critical reflection.

The fundamental disdain for the vibrant or athletic body one finds in Adorno is both an advantage and a disadvantage. It is an advantage in that without this hostility he would not have seen the body at all. "Veblen's evil eye," Adorno writes, "is fertile,"[65] and the same principle applies to his own. But this disdain is a disadvantage in that Adorno seems literally unable to imagine sport as something other than a complex of pathological attitudes and instincts.

Adorno's critique of the body is better described as a critique of the body-beautiful, of the body as narcissistic object, of the body from which a perverse virility is actually estranged. In *Dialectic of Enlightenment*, Horkheimer and Adorno write of

all the werewolves who exist in the darkness of history and keep alive that fear without which there can be no rule—all these men stand for the love-hate relationship with the body in its crudest and most direct form; they pervert all they touch, they destroy what they see in the light and this destruction is their rancor for reification; they repeat in their blind anger against the living object all that they cannot remake: the division of life into spirit and its object. They are irresistibly attracted by man: they want to reduce him to a physical substance; nothing must be allowed to live.

Physical culture is a fraud in the most basic sense: "The body cannot be remade into a noble object: it remains the corpse however vigorously it is trained and kept fit."[66] "The very people who burst with proofs of exuberant vitality," Adorno writes in 1951, "could easily be taken for prepared corpses . . ."[67] The context of this fiercely anticorporeal meditation is the age of nazism. "Understandably," Göran Therborn has pointed out, "fascism became a Medusa's head for the Frankfurt School. The result was that the initial attitude of revulsion was *frozen*, instead of developing into a scientific analysis and participation in revolutionary political practice. Sober political analysis seemed morally impossible . . ."[68] The fury Adorno directs at this "Medusa's head" also encompasses the fascist cult of the body; in this sense, the critique of the (male) body is actually a critique of pseudo virility and its potential for sadism. "There is a certain gesture of virility," Adorno writes, "be it one's own or someone else's, that calls for suspicion." He calls this "tough" pose "nothing other than repressed homosexuality presenting itself as the only approved form of heterosexuality."[69] Here is one version of the false virility which appears in *The Authoritarian Personality* as "pseudo-masculinity," the worst form of which is "the Psychopath": "Here go the hoodlums and rowdies, plug-uglies, torturers, and all those who do the 'dirty-work' of a fascist movement," for whom "bodily strength and toughness" are essential criteria of masculinity.[70] The idea of pseudo virility originates, then, within the Frankfurt School's critique of fascism. Its eventual destiny as a form of culture is to be found in the realm of advertising, be it in the guise of "the naked torso of the athletic hero" or the "idolizing of the vital phenomena from the 'blond beast' to the South Sea islanders."[71]

Adorno's treatment of sport is similarly unsparing and ingenious in its range of abuse. The most impressive conceit which appears in *Dialectic of Enlightenment* is the conjoining of sport and the emotionally barren sexuality found in the works of the Marquis de Sade:

The teams of modern sport, whose interaction is so precisely regulated that no member has any doubt about his role, and which provide a reserve for every player, have their exact counterpart in the sexual teams of *Juliette*, which employ every moment usefully, neglect no human orifice, and carry out every function.

The rake without illusions (whom Juliette stands for) transforms himself with the assistance of sex educators, psychoanalysts, and hormone physiologists into the open and practical man who extends his attitude to sport and hygiene to his sexual life.[72]

Here, thanks to the analogical method, sport represents vacuous emotion, an idea which Adorno found in somewhat different form in *The Decline of the West*, where Spengler writes of "consciously practiced idiocy, the relief of intellectual tension through the physical tension of sports." "From this idea," Adorno writes in 1941, "Spengler constructed the thesis that 'art itself becomes a sport.' He knew neither jazz nor quiz programs, but if one were to summarize the most important trends of present-day mass culture, one could hardly find a more pregnant category than that of sports, the hurdling of rhythmic obstacles, the contest, be it between the performers or between the producers and the public."[73] This is an idea Adorno never relinquished. "The aesthetic act," he writes in a denunciation of jazz (1953), "is made into a sport by means of a system of tricks. To master it is also to demonstrate one's practicality. The achievement of the jazz musician and expert adds up to a sequence of successfully surmounted tests."[74] In his *Introduction to the Sociology of Music* (1962), Adorno posits a relationship among music, sport, and the body by employing a compensation theory usually applied to sport:

. . . music seems imaginatively to restore to the body some of the functions which in reality were taken from it by the machines—a kind of ersatz of physical motion, in which the otherwise painfully unbridled motor energies of the young, in particular, are absorbed. In this respect the function of music today is not so very different from the self-evident and yet no less mysterious one of sports. In fact, the type of music listener with expertise on the level of physically measurable performance approximates that of the sports fan. Intensive studies of football habitués and music-addicted listeners might yield surprising analogies.[75]

A more invidious comparison of art and physical dexterity appears in *Dialectic of Enlightenment*, where Horkheimer and Adorno comment acerbically on "the self-justifying and nonsensical skill of riders, acrobats and clowns, in the 'defense and justification of physical as against intellectual art' [Frank Wedekind]."[76] (This condescension toward physical dexterity recalls Hegel's anecdote about "the man who had taught himself to throw lentils through a small opening

without missing. He displayed this skill of his before Alexander, and Alexander presented him with a bushel of lentils as a reward for his frivolous and meaningless art.")[77]
Adorno's longest meditation on sport is in his essay on Thorstein Veblen (1941). Adorno's only complaint about Veblen's portrayal of sport as a savage and even vicious primitivism is that it fails to see sport's modernistic and masochistic elements:

> According to Veblen, the passion for sports is of a regressive nature: "The ground of an addiction to sports is an archaic spiritual constitution." But nothing is more modern than this archaism; athletic events were the models for totalitarian mass rallies. As tolerated excesses, they combine cruelty and aggression with an authoritarian moment, the disciplined observance of the rules—legality, as in the pogroms of Nazi Germany and the people's republics.
>
> Veblen's analyses, of course, should be expanded. For sport includes not merely the drive to do violence to others but also the wish to be attacked oneself and suffer. Only Veblen's rationalist psychology prevents him from seeing the masochistic moment in sports. It is this which makes sports not so much a relic of a previous form of society as perhaps an initial adjustment to its menacing new form . . .[78]

Adorno and Roland Barthes are two of the ablest intellectuals ever to think about sport as a cultural theme. What is more, both are fierce critics of bourgeois civilization. But the basic dispositions they bring to sport, despite important similarities, are in the end very different.

Barthes and Adorno coincide, most importantly, in their disdain of the body as a cultural ideal. This is the basis of Barthes's critique of Poujadism, both its calculated effluvium of virility and its own (essentially fascist) critique of the "corporeal mediocrity" of the intellectuals. "We touch here," Barthes says, "upon the profound idea of any morality of the human body: the idea of race." Similarly, Barthes's scorn for the ideals of "a boy-scout civilization," for courage which is merely "a formal and empty action," for "the old myth of 'character,'"[79] recalls the Veblen of whom Adorno so thoroughly approves.

What separates them is Barthes's ability to distinguish between the sphere of the body as a cultic space and sport as a form of social life which is not devoid of value. The principal accusation Barthes directs against Poujadist anti-intellectualism, after all, is that it must result in "the destruction of sociability."[80] But this is not necessarily the case with sport. Barthes's famous essay on the Tour de France, for example, makes of this bicycle racers' *agon* "a great epic" while avoiding sentimental *Schwärmerei*. But by making the Tour a genuinely social event, the appeals of which are not necessarily homologous with the appeals of fascism, Barthes has done something Adorno never did. "Modern sports, one will perhaps say," Adorno writes in the essay on Veblen, "seek to restore to the body some of the functions of which the machine has deprived it. But they do so only in order to train men all the more inexorably to serve the machine. Hence sports belong to the realm of unfreedom, no matter where they are organized."[81] Barthes does not partake of this nightmare, even as he, too, conjoins sport and unfreedom. "What saves the Tour from the discomforts of freedom," he writes, "is that it is by definition *the world of characterial essences*." Of course Barthes knows that the "psychology of essences" is one of "the traditional impostures," and that the Tour itself is a "generator of ideological alibis." But the Tour also has a transcendent dimension which, *pace* Adorno, cannot be written off as pathology: "This does not keep the Tour from being a fascinating national phenomenon insofar as the epic expresses that fragile moment in History in which man, however clumsy and deceived, nonetheless contemplates through his impure fables a perfect adequation between himself, the community, and the universe."[82] It is not for nothing that Barthes's analysis of the Tour is based upon the idea of its ambiguity, a dimension of sport culture Adorno systematically refused to see. In the last analysis, then, the difference between Barthes's treatment of sport and Adorno's is the difference between criticism and jaundice.

Notes

1. Sport in the Age of Ideology

1. "Aber wir haben den Krieg gewonnen," *Der Spiegel*, May 20, 1974: 113.

2. "Cuba Pulls Baseball Team Out of Nicaragua Series," *New York Times*, November 9, 1977.

3. Quoted in Judith N. Shklar, *After Utopia*: 175.

4. The "ideological" content of American sport is implicitly rather than explicitly political. Themes such as the role of *machismo* in sport, the cult of the authoritarian coach, sport as an escapist distraction, and so forth, have political significance but are not treated as official elements of state ideology.

5. Henri Arvon, *Marxist Esthetics*: 23.

6. L. B. Brown, *Ideology*: 10.

7. Sebastiano Timpanaro, *On Materialism*: 242.

8. Jean-Paul Sartre, *Search for a Method*: 5.

9. Henri Lefebvre, *The Sociology of Marx*: 69–70.

10. Clifford Geertz, "Ideology as a Cultural System": 63, 72.

11. Karl Marx and Frederick Engels, *The German Ideology*: 1.

12. Sigmund Freud, *New Introductory Lectures on Psychoanalysis*: 158, 180, 171.

13. See, for example, Daniel Bell, *The End of Ideology*; Chaim I. Waxman, *The End of Ideology Debate*.

14. Mihajlo Mihajlov, "The Necessity of Ideology," *New York Times*, December 23, 1975.

15. Karl Mannheim, *Ideology and Utopia*: 39, 38.

16. Ernst Nolte, *Three Faces of Fascism*: 51.

17. Benito Mussolini, "The Doctrine of Fascism": 48, 49. As an ideological oracle, Mussolini tended to be inconsistent on principle. "I have a horror of dogma," he said, "and fascist dogma is an impossibility." Mussolini's most distinguished biographer describes Mussolini the ideologist in the following terms: "As Mussolini himself confessed, he set little store by coherence of ideas or opinions, though of course this did not stop the propaganda machine from stressing that he was invariably consistent. He had

learnt the effectiveness of alternating menace and conciliation, of being—in his own words—'reactionary or revolutionary according to circumstances'" (Denis Mack Smith, *Mussolini*: 139, 112).

18. Nolte, *Three Faces of Fascism*: 51.

19. As Paul Lendvai has pointed out, "It is irrelevant whether individuals believe in the dogmas as long as the unity of power and ideology is preserved and the effective power of enforcement by the leadership . . . is maintained" (*The Bureaucracy of Truth*: 18).

20. Hadley Cantril, *Soviet Leaders and Mastery of Man*: 78.

21. Czeslaw Milosz, *The Captive Mind*: 3.

22. Erhard Drenkow and Paul Marschner, *Körperliche Grundausbildung in der sozialistischen Schule*: 80; "Neue, höhere Ziele für Körperkultur und Sport," *Neues Deutschland*, March 15, 1978: 5.

23. *New York Times Book Review*, January 14, 1973.

24. Bernard-Henry Lévy, *Barbarism with a Human Face*: 172.

25. See John M. Hoberman, "Defining the Postwar French Ultra-Right: The View from Within," *Proceedings of the Fifth Annual Meeting of the Western Society for French History* (1978): 322–330.

26. Defining "expressionism" in a single comprehensive formula is impossible. For a detailed analysis of expressionism in the arts, see Walter H. Sokel, *The Writer in Extremis*.

27. Kasimir Edschmid, "Über den dichterischen Expressionismus": 62.

28. Quoted in Silvio Vietta and Hans-Georg Kemper, *Expressionismus*: 11.

29. Georg Kaiser, "Man in the Tunnel": 13–14.

30. José Ortega y Gasset, *The Revolt of the Masses*: 43.

31. See Allen Guttmann, *From Ritual to Record*: 15–55; John M. Hoberman, "Political Ideology and the Record Performance": 7–11.

32. R. W. Flint, *Marinetti: Selected Writings*: 118, 154, 94ff., 78, 150.

33. Bertolt Brecht, "Mehr guten Sport," *Berliner Börsen-Courier*, February 6, 1926.

34. John Willett, *Art and Politics in the Weimar Period*: 103.

35. Antonin Artaud, *The Theater and Its Double*: 133.

36. René Fueloep-Miller, *The Mind and Face of Bolshevism*: 121; Nikolai A. Gorchakov, "Meyerhold's Theatre": 136.

37. Fueloep-Miller, *The Mind and Face of Bolshevism*: 121.

38. Ibid.

39. Winfried Joch, *Politische Leibeserziehung und ihre Theorie im Nationalsozialistischen Deutschland*: 156.

40. L. Moholy-Nagy, "Theatre, Circus, Variety": 117.

41. Edschmid, "Über den dichterischen Expressionismus": 65.

42. Flint (ed.), *Marinetti: Selected Writings*: 91, 95.

43. George L. Mosse, *The Nationalization of the Masses*: 30.

44. Henning Eichberg has further elaborated upon Mosse's argument by showing that during the 1920s and early 1930s both the Left and the

Right in Germany developed public rituals featuring athletics, and that the workers' sport movement (*Arbeitersportbewegung*) appears to have initiated such displays before the Nazis. See "Thing-, Fest- und Weihspiele in Nationalsozialismus, Arbeiterkultur und Olympismus: Zur Geschichte des politischen Verhaltens in der Epoche des Faschismus": 18–19. For an account of mass gymnastic displays and their political significance in the Soviet Union, see Christel Lane, *The Rites of Rulers*: 124, 178, 224–226, 270, 276.

45. See Willett, *Art and Politics in the Weimar Period*: esp. 102–103.
46. Wolfgang Rothe, "When Sports Conquered the Republic: A Forgotten Chapter from the 'Roaring Twenties,'" *Studies in Twentieth Century Literature*, 4/1 (Fall 1980): 6.
47. The Soviet Brecht scholar I. Fradkin, quoted in V. Z. Rogovin, "The Discussions on Problems of Daily Life and Culture in Soviet Russia during the 1920s," *Soviet Sociology*, 14/1 (Summer 1976): 30–31.
48. Susan Sontag, "Fascinating Fascism," *New York Review of Books*, February 6, 1975: 26.
49. Philip Rieff, "Aesthetic Functions in Modern Politics": 498.
50. Sontag, "Fascinating Fascism": 27.
51. Ernst Kris, *Psychoanalytic Explorations in Art*: 230, 231, 236.
52. G. W. F. Hegel, *The Philosophy of History*: 243. It should be noted that Hegel does not use the (later) German word *Sport*, but rather *Wettkämpfe* (competitive contest).
53. Jean-Jacques Rousseau, *The Government of Poland*: 15.
54. Friedrich Schiller, *On the Aesthetic Education of Man*: 79 n.
55. Georges Magnane, *Sociologie du sport*: 81.
56. Yukio Mishima, *Sun and Steel*: 45.
57. Lefebvre, *The Sociology of Marx*: 58.
58. See Mosse, *The Nationalization of the Masses*: 163.
59. Ortega y Gasset, *The Revolt of the Masses*: 185.
60. Quoted in Willi Knecht, *Das Medaillenkollektiv*: 30.
61. Helmut Wagner, *Sport und Arbeitersport*: 164, 26.
62. Horst Ueberhorst, *Frisch, frei, stark und treu*: 153.
63. Henry Morton, *Soviet Sport*: 105ff.
64. Ernst von Salomon, *Fragebogen*: 94.
65. Pierre de Coubertin, *Pédagogie sportive*: 130.
66. Joch, *Politische Leibeserziehung und ihre Theorie im Nationalsozialistischen Deutschland*: 26.
67. Jules Monnerot, *Sociology and Psychology of Communism*: 117.
68. Arthur Koestler, *Darkness at Noon*: 78.
69. Oswald Mosley, *My Life*: 60; see also 365.
70. Maurice Bardèche, *Sparte et les sudistes*: 81.
71. Montgomery Belgion, *Epitaph on Nuremberg*: 91–92.
72. "Libros sobre socialismo, Diversión del equipo de Alemania Oriental," *Excelsior* (Mexico City), June 29, 1974; "Bernd Bransch kaptein for det øst-tyske 'kollektiv,'" *Aftenposten* (Oslo), June 29, 1974.

252   Notes to Pages 15–21

73. "Bei uns ist immer Olympia," *Der Spiegel*, August 14, 1972: 92.
74. Olof Lagercrantz, "The Playing Fields of Peking," *New York Times*, June 18, 1971.
75. Morton, *Soviet Sport*: 26.
76. Quoted in Albert Speer, *Inside the Third Reich*: 144; ibid: 232.
77. Joachim C. Fest, *The Face of the Third Reich*: 111.
78. Nikolay Valentinov, *Encounters with Lenin*: 79.
79. Strobe Talbott (ed.), *Khrushchev Remembers*: 131.
80. Yevgeny Yevtushenko, "A Poet against the Destroyers," *Sports Illustrated*, December 12, 1966: 66.
81. "Blood Sport Groups Unite against Ban," *Times* (London), June 26, 1978.
82. Eric Heffer, "The Case for Abolishing Blood Sports," *Times* (London), June 26, 1978; Thomas More, *Utopia*: 95.
83. "Life, Liberty and the Pursuit of Foxes," *Times* (London), June 14, 1978.
84. "Labour to Reconsider Ban on Blood Sports," *Times* (London), June 29, 1978.
85. E. Tangye Lean, *The Napoleonists*: 322–323.
86. J. A. Hobson, *Imperialism*: 213.
87. "Kleiner Bruch," *Der Spiegel*, November 15, 1971: 76. "In all revolutions," says Ortega y Gasset, "the first thing that the 'people' have done was to jump over the fences of the preserves or to tear them down, and in the name of social justice pursue the hare and the partridge. And this after the [French] revolutionary newspapers, in their editorials, had for years and years been abusing the aristocrats for being so frivolous as to . . . spend their time hunting" (*Meditations on Hunting*: 33).
88. *Sports Illustrated*, June 1, 1981: 20.
89. *Dallas Times Herald*, November 12, 1980.
90. Klaus Ullrich, *Tore, die nicht für Geld fielen*: 32.
91. Wagner, *Sport und Arbeitersport*: 112.
92. See, for example, Lane, *The Rites of Rulers*: 271.
93. Smith, *Mussolini*: 114.
94. Eichberg et al., *Massenspiele*: 152–153.
95. "Future of Bullfights Dubious in Portugal under New Regime," *New York Times*, May 25, 1975.
96. "Three Who Killed Bulls in Portugal Hailed after Court Appearance," *New York Times*, May 10, 1977.
97. Richard Wright, in Richard Crossman (ed.), *The God That Failed*: 128.
98. John F. Kennedy, "The Soft American," *Sports Illustrated*, December 26, 1960: 15.
99. Robert F. Kennedy, "A Bold Proposal for American Sport," *Sports Illustrated*, July 27, 1964: 13.
100. Sargent Shriver, "The Moral Force of Sport," *Sports Illustrated*, June 3, 1963: 30.

101. Spiro T. Agnew, "Not Infected with the Conceit of Infallibility," *Sports Illustrated*, June 21, 1971: 66, 67, 72.

102. Russell Kirk, "Professional Brawn in College," *National Review*, April 9, 1963: 284.

103. D. Keith Mano, "Heavyweight Fraud," *National Review*, June 21, 1974: 705.

104. See, for example, Jack Scott, *The Athletic Revolution*.

105. See, for example, Paul Hoch, *Rip Off the Big Game*. This is a shrill and theoretically naive essay by an author who seems unaware of the history of the Left critique of sport.

2. The Labor-Leisure Dialectic and the Origins of Ideology

1. Benito Mussolini, "The Doctrine of Fascism": 48.

2. Lewis S. Feuer, "The Character and Thought of Karl Marx: The Promethean Complex and Historical Materialism": 24–25. John Valentine has pointed out to me that this passage may express only a denial of economic reductionism, which Engels rejected.

3. See, for example, Francis Hearn, "Toward a Critical Theory of Play," *Telos*, 30 (Winter 1976/77): 145–146.

4. Mikhail Lifshitz, *The Philosophy of Art of Karl Marx*: 13.

5. Maynard Solomon, "General Introduction," in Maynard Solomon (ed.), *Marxism and Art*: 4, 5.

6. Ibid.: 18, 22–23.

7. Karl Marx and Frederick Engels, *The German Ideology*: 17.

8. See Melvin Rader, *Marx's Interpretation of History*: 121–122.

9. Marx and Engels, *The German Ideology*: 16.

10. Frederick Engels, *Dialectics of Nature*: 284, 289.

11. Georgi Plekhanov, "The Materialist Conception of History": 113.

12. Georgi Plekhanov, "Labor, Play, and Art": 141, 141–142, 142, 143.

13. Solomon, "Introduction," in *Marxism and Art*: 123, 123, 23, 123.

14. Henri Lefebvre, *The Sociology of Marx*: 58.

15. Henri Lefebvre, *Everyday Life in the Modern World*: 78.

16. Richard Gombin, *The Origins of Modern Leftism*: 64.

17. Lefebvre, *Everyday Life in the Modern World*: 52–53, 53, 54, 184.

18. Karl Marx, "Economic and Philosophical Manuscripts of 1844": 360–361.

19. Karl Marx, *Writings of the Young Marx on Philosophy and Society*: 281.

20. James Riordan, *Sport in Soviet Society*: 59–60, 4.

21. Joffre Dumazedier, "Réalités du loisir et idéologies," *Esprit* (June 1959): 873.

22. Herbert Marcuse, *Five Lectures*: 15, 47.

23. Hearn, "Toward a Critical Theory of Play": 146.

24. Compare Johan Huizinga's discussion of language in *Homo Ludens*: 4.

25. Hearn, "Toward a Critical Theory of Play": 149, 152, 155.

26. Ibid.: 150.

27. Lawrence M. Hinman, "Marx's Theory of Play, Leisure and Unalienated Praxis," *Philosophy and Social Criticism*, 5/2 (July 1977): 193, 194.

28. Ibid.: 207–208.

29. Ibid.: 193, 213.

30. Quoted in ibid.: 213–214.

31. Ibid.: 214, 216.

32. N. Ignatiev and G. Ossipov, "Le communisme et le problème des loisirs," *Esprit* (June 1959): 1061.

33. Willi Knecht, "DDR-Sport—Gütezeichen für sozialistische Lebensweise," *Deutschland Arkiv*, 7/9 (September 1974): 938.

34. Ignatiev and Ossipov, "Le communisme et le problème des loisirs": 1066.

35. Siegfried Wagner, "Freizeit, Kunst und Lebensfreude," *Einheit*, 27 (1972): 1146.

36. Horst Slomma, "Unterhaltungskultur in unserem Leben," *Einheit*, 27 (1972): 1419.

37. Fred Gras, "On the Development of Sport-Sociological Research in the German Democratic Republic": 119.

38. Gerhard Lukas, *Die Körperkultur in frühen Epochen der Menschenentwicklung*: 8, 19, 13, 14, 19, 21.

39. Kurt Meinel, *Bewegungslehre*: 14, 18, 18.

40. Georgi Plekhanov, "Fundamental Problems of Marxism": 61.

41. Meinel, *Bewegungslehre*: 19.

42. Ernst Cassirer, *The Myth of the State*: 217–218.

43. Friedrich Schiller, *On the Aesthetic Education of Man*: 26, 79, 125.

44. Max Scheler, *Ressentiment*: 161.

45. John Raphael Staude, *Max Scheler*: 40–41.

46. Judith N. Shklar, *After Utopia*: 66.

47. Max Scheler, "Erkenntnis und Arbeit": 193.

48. Peter Ludz, *The Changing Party Elite in East Germany*: 331–332.

49. Scheler, *Ressentiment*: 158–160.

50. Staude, *Max Scheler*: 44.

51. For a brief discussion of Scheler's influence on Ortega, see Oliver W. Holmes, *Human Reality and the Social World*: 47–48.

52. José Ortega y Gasset, "The Sportive Origin of the State": 17, 16, 18.

53. Ibid.: 28, 29, 30, 31, 31, 33, 31.

54. Ibid.: 26–27, 15, 16.

55. Karl J. Weintraub, *Visions of Culture*: 211–212.

56. Huizinga, *Homo Ludens*: 103, 213.

57. Ilse N. Bulhof, "Johan Huizinga: Ethnographer of the Past," *Clio* 4/2 (1975): 220.

58. Huizinga, *Homo Ludens*: 3, 5, foreword (n.p.).

59. Ibid.: 5, 1, 75, 15–16.

60. Ibid.: 16.

61. Ortega y Gasset, "The Sportive Origin of the State": 14.

62. J. H. Huizinga, "My Path to History": 269.

63. Huizinga, *Homo Ludens*: 189.

64. For a very different approach to "the ideological presuppositions" of Huizinga's conception of play, see Jacques Ehrmann, "Homo Ludens Revisited": 31–57. Ehrmann also discusses Roger Caillois' *Les jeux et les hommes* (1958), which both extends and criticizes Huizinga's theory of play. Ehrmann has set himself the task of formulating a basic critique of assumptions shared by Huizinga and Caillois. "Our criticism," he says, "bears precisely on this point, namely on the possibility of grounding an anthropology of play in the dual opposition of play and reality, of play and the sacred, this in turn entailing a division between the serious (the real, the sacred) and the non-serious (play) . . ." (p. 41). What Ehrmann does not address is the estrangement from ideology which characterizes both of these thinkers. Huizinga's ahistorical temperament has been discussed by R. L. Colie, "Johan Huizinga and the Task of Cultural History," *American Historical Review*, 69 (1964): 607–630. When, for example, Caillois founded, with Georges Bataille and Michel Leiris, a College de Sociologie in 1938, they specified that it was "not a political organism"; see Georges Bataille, *Oeuvres complètes*: vol. 1, 538, 539. Caillois' affinity for the ahistorical deserves more attention than it has received.

65. Huizinga, *Homo Ludens*: 1, 3.

66. Ibid.: 6, 7.

67. Robert Anchor, "History and Play," *History and Theory*, 1 (1978): 65.

68. Josef Pieper, *Leisure: The Basis of Culture*: 46, 52, 32.

69. Huizinga, *Homo Ludens*: 17; see also Johan Huizinga, *In the Shadow of Tomorrow*: esp. 131.

70. Pieper, *Leisure: The Basis of Culture*: 59, 31ff., 20.

71. Ibid.: 51, 54.

72. Ibid.: 52, 53.

73. Gabriel Marcel, "Being and Nothingness": 178.

74. Pieper, *Leisure: The Basis of Culture*: 44.

75. Jean-Paul Sartre, *Being and Nothingness*: 741–742, 742, 742, 742, 227, 746, 332.

76. Joseph P. Fell, *Heidegger and Sartre*: 141. Judith N. Shklar compares Sartre and Ortega in the following way: "Moreover, Sartre does not believe in the realization of freedom at all, but only in the absence of rational causes. That we will fail in every attempt to be ourselves is quite certain, and our only real chance to prove our independence is to resort to 'a death freely chosen.' Here there is none of the joy of self-creation that Ortega, for instance, as a representative of an older tradition can still feel. For him it is a matter of dramatic struggle, an artistic enterprise, like composing a novel, a proof that history dominates nature" (*After Utopia*: 125).

77. Quoted in Anchor, "History and Play": 93.
78. Gaston Bachelard, *The Psychoanalysis of Fire*: 16.
79. Ortega y Gasset, "The Sportive Origin of the State": 21, 22, 19.
80. Willi Nitschke, *Kann der Sport Neutral Sein?*: 10.
81. Kostas Axelos comments: "Speaking of labor as producing reified values, Marx denounces the inherently uninteresting and unattractive character of that labor, and he says that the worker does not enjoy his activity as the 'play (*Spiel*) of his bodily and mental powers.' But he says nothing further of the possibility of a future opening into the dimension of play" (*Alienation, Praxis, and Technē in the Thought of Karl Marx*: 258).
82. Quoted in Frederick Engels, *Anti-Dühring*: 351.
83. Perry Anderson, *Arguments within British Marxism*: 167–168.
84. Herbert Marcuse, *The Aesthetic Dimension*: 56–57.
85. Huizinga, *In the Shadow of Tomorrow*: 170.
86. Pieper, *Leisure: the Basis of Culture*: 76.
87. Saul K. Padover (ed.), *Karl Marx on Religion*: 35.
88. David McLellan, *Marx before Marxism*: 190.
89. Quoted in ibid.: 191.
90. Huizinga, *Homo Ludens*: 192, 15.
91. Frederick Engels, *The Origin of the Family, Private Property, and the State*: 107–108.
92. Ortega y Gasset, "The Sportive Origin of the State": 33. Huizinga confines himself to asserting only: "A State is never a utilitarian institution pure and simple." He does, however, quote a passage by Marcel Granet which sounds very much like Ortega: "The spirit of competition, which animated the men's societies or brotherhoods and set them against one another during the winter festivities in tournaments of dance and song, comes at the beginning of the lines of development that led to State forms and institutions" (*Homo Ludens*: 175, 55).
93. Anderson, *Arguments within British Marxism*: 161–162.

3. The Body as an Ideological Variable

1. Thomas Hobbes, *Leviathan*: 151.
2. Juan Beneyto, *Los origenes de la ciencia política en España*: 188–189.
3. Curzio Malaparte, "Mussolini and National Syndicalism": 225.
4. Jean Lacouture, *The Demigods*: 251, 264.
5. Martin Heidegger, *An Introduction to Metaphysics*: 31.
6. John M. Hoberman, "Sport and Political Ideology," *Journal of Sport and Social Issues*, 1/2 (April 1977): 110.
7. Gaetano Mosca, *The Ruling Class*: 53–54.
8. Ali A. Mazrui, "Boxer Muhammad Ali and Soldier Idi Amin as International Political Symbols," *Comparative Studies in Society and History*, 19/2 (April 1977): 197, 190.
9. Lacouture, *The Demigods*: 14.

10. Chris Mullin, "Foreign Truths," *Manchester Guardian Weekly*, June 25, 1978.

11. " . . . and in This Corner, Kid Idi Amin," *Boston Herald American*, November 4, 1978.

12. Robert Skidelsky, *Oswald Mosley*: 165.

13. Quoted in ibid.: 279.

14. Quoted in Colin Cross, *The Fascists in Britain*: 24.

15. Oswald Mosley, *My Life*: 131.

16. Skidelsky, *Oswald Mosley*: 501.

17. Lacouture, *The Demigods*: 86, 217–218.

18. Eugen Weber, *Varieties of Fascism*: 35.

19. Simón Bolívar, "The Angostura Address": 189–190.

20. Eric Bentley, *The Cult of the Superman*: 42.

21. Oswald Spengler, *Der Untergang des Abendlandes*: 1112.

22. Mosley, *My Life*: 7–8.

23. The phrase is Skidelsky's, *Oswald Mosley*: 18.

24. Mosley, *My Life*: 280.

25. Spengler, *Der Untergang des Abendlandes*: 1112.

26. Mosley, *My Life*: 316–317, 242.

27. Oswald Mosley, "Which Inheritance? Goethe or the Vicar": 91.

28. Friedrich Nietzsche, *Twilight of the Idols and The Anti-Christ*: 103.

29. Alastair Hamilton, *The Appeal of Fascism*: 70.

30. Jean Meynaud, *Sport et politique*: 131.

31. John Diggins, *Mussolini and Fascism*: 61, 72.

32. José Ortega y Gasset, *The Revolt of the Masses*: 39.

33. Diggins, *Mussolini and Fascism*: 72.

34. Gilbert D. Allardyce, "The Political Transition of Jacques Doriot": 72.

35. Quoted in Hamilton, *The Appeal of Fascism*: 219.

36. René Rémond, *The Right Wing in France*: 372; J. Plumyène and R. Lasierra, *Les fascismes français 1923–63*: 240.

37. Ibid.: 229.

38. Friedrich Nietzsche, *Thus Spoke Zarathustra*: 61–62.

39. Lacouture, *The Demigods*: 118.

40. Ibid.: 3.

41. Quoted in John Starrels and Anita Mallinckrodt, *Politics in the GDR*: 65.

42. Lacouture, *The Demigods*: 119, 119, 120.

43. Georgi Plekhanov, *Fundamental Problems of Marxism*: 176.

44. Nikolay Valentinov, *Encounters with Lenin*: 77.

45. Nikolay Valentinov, *The Early Years of Lenin*: 30–31; Valentinov, *Encounters with Lenin*: 78.

46. Valentinov, *The Early Years of Lenin*: 47. Christel Lane has pointed out that Lenin's heroic ambience has lacked an element of physicality. "But one set of qualities usually associated with heroism, namely physical

strength, daring and military valour, has never been connected with Lenin, while Stalin, in contrast, was commonly presented as 'the man of steel'" (*The Rites of Rulers*: 212).
47. Valentinov, *Encounters with Lenin*: 26.
48. Lacouture, *The Demigods*: 45–46, 46, 46, 47.
49. G. W. F. Hegel, *The Philosophy of History*: 30, 31.
50. Quoted in Winfried Joch, *Politische Leibeserziehung und ihre Theorie im Nationalsozialistischen Deutschland*: 215.
51. Quoted in Robert C. Tucker, *Stalin as Revolutionary 1879–1929*: 324.
52. Ibid.: 74, 76, 84, 134, 414–415.
53. Quoted in Hermann Glaser, *The Cultural Roots of National Socialism*: 71.
54. Katerina Clark, "Utopian Anthropology as a Context for Stalinist Literature": 185.
55. Wilhelm Reich, *The Mass Psychology of Fascism*: 305.
56. Clark, "Utopian Anthropology": 189.
57. Ibid.: 191, 190.
58. Jorge Abelardo Ramos, "Dangers of Empiricism in Latin American Revolutions": 207, 220–221, 221–222.
59. Malaparte, "Mussolini and National Syndicalism": 225.
60. Donald G. MacRae, "Introduction," in Herbert Spencer, *The Man versus the State*: 25; ibid.: 198–199.
61. Bruce Haley, *The Healthy Body and Victorian Culture*: 4, 70.
62. Otto Gierke, *Natural Law and the Theory of Society 1500–1800*: 51, 52.
63. Hobbes, *Leviathan*: 151.
64. Ernest Barker, "Translator's Introduction," in Gierke, *Natural Law and the Theory of Society*: lvi.
65. Gierke, *Natural Law and the Theory of Society*: 52.
66. Quoted in Melvin Rader, *Marx's Interpretation of History*: 66.
67. G. W. F. Hegel, *The Phenomenology of Mind*: 728–729.
68. Ibid.: 728, 729–730.
69. Pitirim A. Sorokin, "Foreword," in Ferdinand Tönnies, *Community and Society*: ix.
70. Tönnies, *Community and Society*: 33–34, 35, 210.
71. Glaser, *The Cultural Roots of National Socialism*: 79.
72. Arthur Mitzman, *Sociology and Estrangement*: 81, 117, 81 n.
73. Lyttelton (ed.), *Italian Fascisms*: 258, 260.
74. José Antonio Primo de Rivera, *Selected Writings*: 55, 90, 70.
75. Lyttelton (ed.), *Italian Fascisms*: 116, 102.
76. Filippo Marinetti, *Selected Writings*: 125, 96, 42, 152.
77. Oswald Spengler, *The Decline of the West*: 361.
78. Joch, *Politische Leibeserziehung und ihre Theorie*: 216, 214, 221, 225.
79. Quoted in Tarmo Kunnas, *Drieu la Rochelle, Céline, Brasillach et la tentation fasciste*: 189.

80. Pierre Drieu la Rochelle, *Mesure de la France*: 125.
81. Maurice Bardèche, *Les temps modernes*: 96, 208.
82. Joch, *Politische Leibeserziehung und ihre Theorie*: 26.
83. Oswald Mosley, *Fascism in Britain*, quoted in R. Osborn, *The Psychology of Reaction*: 60.
84. Spencer, *The Man versus the State*: 147.
85. Lyttelton (ed.), *Italian Fascisms*: 43.
86. Spencer, *The Man versus the State*: 29.
87. Ibid.: 25, 26.
88. Rader, *Marx's Interpretation of History:* 57, 191, 68, 230.
89. Ibid.: 75.
90. Robert Tucker, *Philosophy and Myth in Karl Marx*: 113.
91. Robert F. Wheeler, "Organized Sport and Organized Labour: The Workers' Sport Movement," *Journal of Contemporary History*, 13 (1978): 195.
92. Leo Lowenthal, *Literature and the Image of Man*: 217.
93. Raymond A. Bauer, *The New Man in Soviet Psychology*: 145.
94. Marinetti, *Selected Writings*: 149.

4. The Political Psychologies of the Sportive and Antisportive Temperaments

1. Quoted in Jean-Paul Sartre, *Saint Genet*: 129.
2. Norman H. Baynes, *The Speeches of Adolf Hitler*: vol. 1, 539.
3. Susan Sontag, "Fascinating Fascism," *New York Review of Books*, February 6, 1975: 26.
4. Hans Buchheim, *Totalitarian Rule*: 34.
5. Wilhelm Reich, *The Mass Psychology of Fascism*: 301–302.
6. Horst Ueberhorst, *Frisch, frei, stark und treu*: 153.
7. W. H. Sheldon, *The Varieties of Temperament*: 49–88.
8. Ibid.: 4.
9. Ibid.: 3, 77.
10. Rebecca West, *The Meaning of Treason*: 198, 200.
11. Harold Lasswell, *Psychopathology and Politics*: 40–41.
12. Quoted in Gilles Perrault, *Les parachutistes*: 148.
13. Thorstein Veblen, *The Theory of the Leisure Class*: 149, 152, 148–149, 169, 171, 173, 178, 174, 174, 174.
14. Quoted in Ernst Nolte, *Three Faces of Fascism*: 516.
15. Benito Mussolini, "The Doctrine of Fascism": 47.
16. Karl Radek, "Contemporary World Literature and the Tasks of Revolutionary Art": 120.
17. César Graña, *Modernity and Its Discontents*: 164, 165.
18. J. A. Hobson, *Imperialism*: 213, 215.
19. Pierre de Coubertin, *Essais de psychologie sportive*: 133.
20. Quoted in Robert Wohl, *The Generation of 1914*: 15.
21. Lewis Mumford, *Technics and Civilization*: 306.
22. Quoted in William R. Tucker, *The Fascist Ego*: 142.

23. Quoted in Karl Löwith, *From Hegel to Nietzsche*: 191.
24. Friedrich Nietzsche, *On the Genealogy of Morals*: 97, 118, 111, 58, 31, 41.
25. Jean-Paul Sartre, *Anti-Semite and Jew*: 119, 119, 120, 121, 122.
26. Robert Skidelsky, *Oswald Mosley*: 320.
27. See, for example, George L. Mosse, *The Nationalization of the Masses*: 8–9.
28. Skidelsky, *Oswald Mosley*: 285; also 269.
29. Ivone Kirkpatrick, *Mussolini*: 170.
30. Quoted in Neal Wood, *Communism and British Intellectuals*: 104.
31. Denis Mack Smith, *Mussolini*: 126.
32. Ibid.: 94, 97, 114; Lyttelton (ed.), *Italian Fascisms*: 40.
33. Smith, *Mussolini*: 113, 284, 106, 137.
34. Nolte, *Three Faces of Fascism*: 213, 211–212.
35. R. W. Flint (ed.), *Marinetti: Selected Writings*: 96, 158.
36. Nolte, *Three Faces of Fascism*: 135, 218, 333.
37. Lyttelton (ed.), *Italian Fascisms*: 23.
38. Sartre, *Anti-Semite and Jew*: 120.
39. Quoted in Skidelsky, *Oswald Mosley*: 268–269.
40. Lyttelton (ed.), *Italian Fascisms*: 126.
41. Hugh Thomas (ed.), *José Antonio Primo de Rivera: Selected Writings*: 36, 151, 215.
42. Quoted in ibid.: 32.
43. Maurice Bardèche, *Sparte et les sudistes*: 132.
44. Flint (ed.), *Marinetti: Selected Writings*: 150.
45. Maurice Merleau-Ponty, *Humanism and Terror*: xxxi.
46. Thomas (ed.), *José Antonio Primo de Rivera: Selected Writings*: 101.
47. Karl Marx and Frederick Engels, *The German Ideology*: 99.
48. Mikhail Lifshitz, *The Philosophy of Art of Karl Marx*: 47.
49. Winfried Joch, *Politische Leibeserziehung und ihre Theorie im Nationalsozialistischen Deutschland*: 104, 163, 173, 219.
50. Ursula Wilke, *Risiko und sozialistische Persönlichkeit*.
51. José Ortega y Gasset, *The Revolt of the Masses*: 39–42.
52. George Mosse, *The Crisis of German Ideology*: vii. Mosse provides a more detailed analysis of male symbolism and the use of sportive motifs in fascist ritual in *The Nationalization of the Masses*.
53. [Basil Henry] Liddell Hart, *The Future of Infantry*: 69, 71.
54. Werner Jaeger, *Paideia*: vol. 2, 231.
55. Liddell Hart, *The Future of Infantry*: 31, 41, 42, 26.
56. Joachim C. Fest, *The Face of the Third Reich*: 223, 207, 231.
57. Heinz Höhne, *The Order of the Death's Head*: 146, 147.
58. Hans Buchheim, "Command and Compliance": 320, 339.
59. Höhne, *The Order of the Death's Head*: 358.
60. Ibid.: 159.
61. Skidelsky, *Oswald Mosley*: 318.

62. Höhne, *The Order of the Death's Head*: 54, 461.
63. Smith, *Mussolini*: 151, 107.
64. Fest, *The Face of the Third Reich*: 112, 119, 131.
65. Ibid.: 151.
66. Höhne, *The Order of the Death's Head*: 164. Earlier in life, according to Heydrich's wife, his only interests had been his naval career and sport (p. 169).
67. Buchheim, "Command and Compliance": 339–340.
68. Mosse, *The Crisis of German Ideology*: 5.
69. Gerhard Stöcker, *Volkserziehung und Turnen*: 43.
70. Quoted in Allen Guttmann, *From Ritual to Record*: 87.
71. Stöcker, *Volkserziehung und Turnen*: 7.
72. Mosse, *The Nationalization of the Masses*: 128.
73. Mosse, *The Crisis of German Ideology*: 26.
74. Robert G. L. Waite, *Vanguard of Nazism*: 18.
75. Mosse, *The Crisis of German Ideology*: 175.
76. Waite, *Vanguard of Nazism*: 208, 209, 210, 27.
77. Höhne, *The Order of the Death's Head*: 159.
78. Waite, *Vanguard of Nazism*: 26, 209.
79. Höhne, *The Order of the Death's Head*: 56.
80. Fest, *The Face of the Third Reich*: 210.
81. Buchheim, "Command and Compliance": 327; Höhne, *The Order of the Death's Head*: 159.
82. Buchheim, "Command and Compliance": 328.
83. Mosse, *The Crisis of German Ideology*: 85.
84. James H. Meisel, *The Fall of the Republic*: 177.
85. Perrault, *Les parachutistes*: 138.
86. Ibid.: 87–88, 103, 88.
87. Ibid.: 114, 134.
88. Robert d'Harcourt, quoted in ibid.: 113.
89. Robert O. Paxton, *Vichy France*: 33.
90. Bruce Mazlish, *The Revolutionary Ascetic*: 145.
91. Nolte, *Three Faces of Fascism*: 209.
92. Perrault, *Les parachutistes*: 125, 132.
93. Ibid.: 149–150.
94. Ibid.: 112, 136.
95. Yukio Mishima, *Sun and Steel*: 11–12, 47–48.
96. Ibid.: 81, 41, 85, 87, 87, 49.
97. Ibid.: 15, 45, 30.
98. Ginette Berthaud et al., *Sport, culture et répression*: 6.
99. Allen Guttmann, "Translator's Introduction," in Bero Rigauer, *Sport and Work*: xii–xiii.
100. Quoted in Paul Laurent et al., *Les communistes et le sport*: 6.
101. Quoted in George Steiner, "The Cleric of Treason," *New Yorker*, December 8, 1980: 184.
102. "Le sport ouvrier international a prouvé sa vitalité," *L'Humanité*, July 16, 1924: 1.

103. Walter Sieger, "Zur Körperkultur in der sozialistischen Gesellschaft," *Deutsche Zeitschrift für Philosophie*, 12/8 (1964). This essay, and one by Friedrich Trögsch which immediately follows it, are the only articles on sport to have appeared in this journal, which was founded in 1953. The official organ of the Socialist Unity party, *Einheit*, founded in 1946, has published only four articles on sport: in 1952, 1972 (two), and 1975.

104. John McMurtry, *The Structure of Marx's World-View*: 33 n.

105. Sebastiano Timpanaro, *On Materialism*: 40–41, 119.

106. See Mosse, *The Nationalization of the Masses*: 9.

107. Lyttelton (ed.), *Italian Fascisms*: 14.

108. "R. Palme Dutt, 79, British Marxist," *New York Times*, December 21, 1974.

109. David Caute, *The Fellow-Travellers*: 57; Wood, *Communism and British Intellectuals*: 221.

110. Robert F. Wheeler, "Organized Sport and Organized Labour," *Journal of Contemporary History*, 13 (1978): 195, 205.

111. Fritz Wildung, *Arbeitersport*: 29.

112. Helmut Wagner, *Sport und Arbeitersport*: 127.

113. Leon Trotsky, *Problems of Everyday Life*: 67, 32, 18.

114. Ralph Miliband, *Marxism and Politics*: 51–52.

115. Nikolay Valentinov, *Encounters with Lenin*: 30.

116. Maynard Solomon (ed.), *Marxism and Art*: 239.

117. Leo Lowenthal, *Literature and the Image of Man*: 217.

118. Quoted in Gerhard Vinnai (ed.), *Sport in der Klassengesellschaft*: 191.

119. Max Horkheimer and Theodor W. Adorno, *Dialectic of Enlightenment*: 235.

120. Philip Rieff, "Aesthetic Functions in Modern Politics," *World Politics*, 5/4 (July 1953): 498.

121. Herbert Marcuse, *Five Lectures*: 72.

122. Merleau-Ponty, *Humanism and Terror*: xxxiii.

123. Henri Lefebvre, *L'Existentialisme*: 81; Leon Trotsky, *Literature and Revolution*: 104.

124. Quoted in Michel-Antoine Burnier, *Choice of Action*: 154; quoted in Caute, *The Fellow-Travellers*: 349, 145.

125. Raymond Aron, *The Opium of the Intellectuals*: 65.

126. Renee Winegarten, *Writers and Revolution*: 295, 300, 301.

127. Wood, *Communism and British Intellectuals*: 111.

128. Simone de Beauvoir, *The Prime of Life*: 154; Jean-Paul Sartre, *Life/Situations*: 95–96.

129. Plumyène and R. Lasierra, *Les fascismes français 1923–63*: 186.

130. Alberto Moravia, *The Conformist*: 181.

131. Quoted in Paul Sérant, *Le romantisme fasciste*: 40.

132. Roland Barthes, *The Eiffel Tower and Other Mythologies*: 132.

133. Oswald Mosley, *My Life*: 128, 130.

134. *La Parisienne* (October 1956): 579.

135. Quoted in E. V. Wolfenstein, *The Revolutionary Personality*: 125.
136. Trotsky, *Literature and Revolution*: 255.
137. Trotsky, *Problems of Everyday Life*: 54.
138. Quoted in *New Left Review*, 64 (November–December 1970): 87.
139. G. A. Cohen, *Karl Marx's Theory of History*: 151.
140. Caute, *The Fellow-Travellers*: 252.
141. Quoted in ibid.: 161.
142. Wilhelm Reich, "What Is Class Consciousness?": 301–302.
143. Reich, *The Mass Psychology of Fascism*: 32–33.
144. Mosse, *The Nationalization of the Masses*: 181–182.
145. Henning Eichberg, "Thing-, Fest- und Weihespiele in Nationalsozialismus, Arbeiterkultur und Olympismus": 109, 86, 150.
146. Reich, *The Mass Psychology of Fascism*: 25.
147. Melvin Rader, *Marx's Interpretation of History*: 97; see also Henri Arvon, *Marxist Esthetics*: 114.
148. See David E. Powell, *Antireligious Propaganda in the Soviet Union*: 5, 15.
149. Arvon, *Marxist Esthetics*: 76.
150. Herbert Marcuse, *The Aesthetic Dimension*: 56–57.
151. Havelock Ellis, *The Psychology of Sex*: 63.
152. Barthes, *The Eiffel Tower and Other Mythologies*: 35–36.
153. Ibid.: 130.

5. From Amateurism to Nihilism

1. Karl Mannheim, *Man and Society in an Age of Reconstruction*: 5, 15, 222, 320.
2. Johan Huizinga, *In the Shadow of Tomorrow*: 15, 16, 147.
3. Freud suggests a relationship between sportive activity and sexual energy in *Three Contributions to a Theory of Sex*: 62 n.
4. Walter Laqueur, *Young Germany*: 232, 48.
5. In fact, Brecht's fascination with sport was largely due to his fascination with America, rather than any particular Marxist idea. Brecht's first encounter with Marxism occurred in 1926. His article "Mehr guten Sport," for example, was published in February of that year.
6. Enrico Corradini, "Article from *Il Regno*": 139.
7. Giovanni Papini and Giuseppe Prezzolini, "Can the Bourgeoisie Revive?": 130–131.
8. See, for example, Judith N. Shklar, *After Utopia*: 91; Curzio Malaparte, "Mussolini and National Syndicalism": 226.
9. Giovanni Papini, "A Nationalist Programme": 102.
10. Winfried Joch, *Politische Leibeserziehung und ihre Theorie im Nationalsozialistischen Deutschland*: 180.
11. Alfred Cobban, *In Search of Humanity*: 218–219, 220.
12. Shklar, *After Utopia*: viii.
13. José Ortega y Gasset, *The Modern Theme*: 82.

14. Karl Jaspers, *Man in the Modern Age*: 70–71.
15. Shklar, *After Utopia*: 37.
16. See Allen Guttmann, "On the Alleged Dehumanization of the Sports Spectator," *Journal of Popular Culture*, 14 (Fall 1980): 275–282.
17. See also Friedrich Schiller, *On the Aesthetic Education of Man*: 79.
18. Roland Auguet, *Cruelty and Civilization*: 190, 196, 194, 197.
19. Quoted in Karl Löwith, *From Hegel to Nietzsche*: 293.
20. Quoted in Bruce Haley, *The Healthy Body and Victorian Culture*: 222.
21. Huizinga, *In the Shadow of Tomorrow*: 37.
22. On the sport culture of Victorian England, see Haley, *The Healthy Body and Victorian Culture*.
23. Robert Hessen, *Der Sport*: 83, 13.
24. The definitive study of Coubertin is John J. MacAloon, *This Great Symbol*. See also Eugen Weber, "Pierre de Coubertin and the Introduction of Organised Sport in France," *Journal of Contemporary History*, 5 (1970): 3–26; Richard D. Mandell, *The First Modern Olympics*: 49–73.
25. Robert A. Nye, *The Origins of Crowd Psychology*: 20, 5; André Senay and Robert Hervet, *Monsieur de Coubertin*: 76. MacAloon points out that Coubertin borrowed the concept of *bonheur* from Frédéric Le Play (*This Great Symbol*: 89).
26. MacAloon, *This Great Symbol*: 89.
27. "By analogy as well as in fact," Bruce Haley has noted, "disease and health became the measure of social well-being in nineteenth-century thought. There was ready at hand the medical theory that physical and mental diseases were more or less natural phases of a general life-pattern. Thus, since it was believed that the pattern of life recapitulated that found in societies, periods of history were seen as states of health and disease and as stages of growth and decay. A culture, like a person, may fall into a state of disease even though the larger pattern is one of growth" (*The Healthy Body and Victorian Culture*: 59).
28. Robert A. Nye, "Degeneration, Hygiene and Sports in Fin-de-siècle France" (presented at the Eighth Annual Conference of the Western Society for French History, University of Oregon, Eugene, October 24, 1980: 12). A revised version has appeared under the title "Degeneration, Neurasthenia and the Culture of Sport in *Belle Epoque* France," *Journal of Contemporary History*, 17 (1982): 51–68.
29. Pierre de Coubertin, *Essais de psychologie sportive*: 77, 162, 244–245. The idea that sport was possessed of curative powers was by no means Coubertin's monopoly: "the cure for neurasthenics was self-evident: it required the strengthening of the physique, by means of exercise. French schools were not even capable of supplying this in their gymnastics classes, because their exercises were too complicated and produced nervous exhaustion: they required pupils to use their heads too much" (Theodore Zeldin, *France 1848–1945*: vol. 2, 842). This was precisely the argument Coubertin

had propounded upon returning from his inspection of the public schools of Victorian England. His importance, as we shall see, lies not in originality but in the detailed development of his psychotherapeutic approach to sport.

30. Coubertin, *Essais de psychologie sportive*: 38.

31. See, for example, Fritz Wildung, *Arbeitersport*: 7.

32. Coubertin, *Essais de psychologie sportive*: 79, 166.

33. Ibid.: 154.

34. Pierre de Coubertin, *Notes sur l'éducation publique*: 199.

35. Senay and Hervet, *Monsieur de Coubertin*: 128.

36. Coubertin, *Notes sur l'éducation publique*: 268.

37. Senay and Hervet, *Monsieur de Coubertin*: 76, 9, 69.

38. Coubertin, *Essais de psychologie sportive*: 27, 32, 55, 105.

39. Paul Adam, *La morale des sports*: 325, 12, 447.

40. Coubertin, *Essais de psychologie sportive*: 171, 75.

41. Adam, *La morale des sports*: 401.

42. Coubertin, *Essais de psychologie sportive*: 38; Heinz Risse, *Soziologie des Sports*: 25.

43. Coubertin, *Essais de psychologie sportive*: 87, 133–134. This is not to say that Nietzsche had no influence in France: see André Gide, *L'Immoraliste* (1902) or Adam, *La morale des sports* (1907).

44. Risse, *Soziologie des Sports*: 48, 76, 78.

45. Georg Kaiser, "Man in the Tunnel": 13–14.

46. Risse, *Soziologie des Sports*: 77; see John M. Hoberman, "Political Ideology and the Record Performance," *Arena Review*, 1/2 (1977): 7–11; Coubertin's attitude toward the record performance was ambivalent.

47. Risse, *Soziologie des Sports*: 4, 5, 84, 4.

48. Wolfgang Rothe, "When Sports Conquered the Republic: A Forgotten Chapter from the 'Roaring Twenties,'" *Studies in Twentieth Century Literature*, 4 (1980): 9.

49. Frank Thiess, "Die Geistigen und der Sport," *Die Neue Rundschau*, 38 (1927): 300–301.

50. Risse, *Soziologie des Sports*: 4–5.

51. Julius Deutsch, *Sport und Politik* (1928); Wildung, *Arbeitersport* (1929); Paul Franken, *Vom Werden einer neuen Kultur* (1930); Helmut Wagner, *Sport und Arbeitersport* (1931). For a discussion of these texts, see chapter 7.

52. Karl Jaspers, *Man in the Modern Age*: 68–71; Karl Mannheim, *Man and Society in an Age of Reconstruction*: 313.

53. Risse, *Soziologie des Sports*: 6–7; it should be noted that Risse does not pursue this theme in terms of a specific case study, except (very briefly) in the case of England (p. 25).

54. Ibid.: 8, 19.

55. Ibid.: 24.

56. Ibid.: 47, 53, 60–61.

57. Ibid.: 51, 19, 25.

58. Arnold J. Toynbee, *A Study of History*: vol. 4, 242–243; Lewis

Mumford, *Technics and Civilization*: 303; Mannheim, *Man and Society in an Age of Reconstruction*: 122, 316–317.

59. Risse, *Soziologie des Sports*: 28, 29, 30, 29, 35, 29.

60. Ibid.: 26, 76, 84, 33, 77.

61. Joch, *Politische Leibeserziehung und ihre Theorie im Nationalsozialistischen Deutschland*: 164, 164, 165, 165, 220.

62. Risse, *Soziologie des Sports*, 12, 13, 12, 13; Friedrich Schiller, *On the Aesthetic Education of Man*: 79.

63. Risse, *Soziologie des Sports*: 13.

64. On professionalism among ancient Greek athletes, see, for example, M. I. Finley and H. W. Pleket, *The Olympic Games*: 70–82. Risse, *Soziologie des Sports*: 14.

65. Ibid.: 39.

66. Huizinga, *In the Shadow of Tomorrow*: 173, 179.

67. Risse, *Soziologie des Sports*: 38; see also Mumford, *Technics and Civilization*: 307.

68. Haley, *The Healthy Body and Victorian Culture*: 257.

69. Christian Graf von Krockow, *Sport: Eine Soziologie und Philosophie des Leistungsprinzips*: 100–101, 136, 139, 162–163.

70. Risse, *Soziologie des Sports*: 40, 37, 37, 41.

71. See, for example, Wildung, *Arbeitersport*: 43, 69, 92, 96.

72. See Robert F. Wheeler, "Organized Sport and Organized Labour: The Workers' Sport Movement," *Journal of Contemporary History*, 13 (1978): 191–210.

73. Risse: *Soziologie des Sports*: 28, 64, 81–82; Risse does not mention Max Scheler's *Ressentiment* (1915).

74. Ibid.: 73, 72, 74, 75, 76, 83.

75. Laqueur, *Young Germany*: 4.

76. Ibid.: 8–9.

77. Ibid.: xxi; Robert Wohl, *The Generation of 1914*: 47.

78. Friedrich Nietzsche, *Thus Spoke Zarathustra*: 34–35.

79. Risse, *Soziologie des Sports*: 46.

80. Jaspers, *Man in the Modern Age*: 25.

81. Ibid.: 68, 68, 70.

82. Ibid.: 69, 70, 71.

83. Ibid.: 142.

84. Ibid.: 174.

85. Mannheim, *Man and Society in an Age of Reconstruction*: 222, 87.

86. Ibid.: 87, 348, 313 n.

87. Ibid.: 352–353, 122, 320, 360.

88. Mumford, *Technics and Civilization*: 303, 307.

89. Robert Musil, *Tagebücher, Aphorismen, Essays und Reden*: 818, 819, 820, 819–820.

90. Quoted in Rothe, "When Sports Conquered the Republic": 26; the original is in Musil, *Tagebücher*: 820.

91. Quoted in Rothe, "When Sports Conquered the Republic": 27, 28.

92. Gottfried Benn, "Der Aufbau der Persönlichkeit," in *Gesammelte Werke*: vol. 3, 666.
93. Gottfried Benn, "Geist und Seele künftiger Geschlecter" (1933), in ibid.: 801; "Dorische Welt" (1934), in ibid.: 839, 841; "Provoziertes Leben" (1943), in ibid.: 899.
94. Gottfried Benn, *Primal Vision: Selected Writings*: 120, 140.
95. Martin Heidegger, *An Introduction to Metaphysics*: 31, 31, 39, 39, 39.
96. T. S. Eliot, review of Herbert Read, *Reason and Romanticism*, and Ramon Fernandez, *Messages*, New Criterion, 4 (October 1926): 752–753.
97. Paul Valéry, "Bilan de l'intelligence" (1935): 1083.
98. T. S. Eliot, *The Idea of a Christian Society*: 12.
99. Valéry, "Bilan de l'intelligence": 1083.
100. Antonin Artaud, *The Theater and Its Double*: 133.
101. Eliot, *The Idea of a Christian Society*: 21–22.
102. Shklar, *After Utopia*: 21.
103. Eliot, *The Idea of a Christian Society*: 62–63.
104. Johan Huizinga, *Homo Ludens*: 17.
105. Johan Huizinga, *America: A Dutch Historian's Vision, from Afar and Near*: 115.
106. Huizinga, *In the Shadow of Tomorrow*: 115.
107. Johan Huizinga, "John of Salisbury" (1933): 176; see also *Homo Ludens*: 181.
108. Herbert Marcuse, review of Johan Huizinga, *Im Schatten von Morgen*, Zeitschrift für Sozialforschung, 5 (1936): 23.
109. See, for example, Huizinga, *In the Shadow of Tomorrow*: 207, 111, 131.
110. Huizinga, *Homo Ludens*: 6, 15, 19, 18, 197–198.
111. Ibid.: 3.
112. Huizinga, *In the Shadow of Tomorrow*: 174.
113. Huizinga, *Homo Ludens*: 197, 198, 200, 199.
114. Mumford, *Technics and Civilization*: 306.
115. Huizinga, *In the Shadow of Tomorrow*: 170.
116. Huizinga, *Homo Ludens*: 205, 205.
117. Huizinga, *In the Shadow of Tomorrow*: 175.
118. Max Scheler, *Ressentiment*: 150.
119. Huizinga, *Homo Ludens*: ix, 192.
120. Scheler, *Ressentiment*: 153.
121. Ibid.: 159, 86.
122. Max Scheler, "Begleitwort," in Alfred Peters, *Psychologie des Sports*: xiii.
123. Max Scheler, *Der Mensch im Weltalter des Ausgleichs*: 16–17.
124. John Raphael Staude, *Max Scheler*: 56, 226.
125. Scheler, *Ressentiment*: 107.
126. Lewis A. Coser, "Introduction," in ibid.: 20.
127. Scheler, *Ressentiment*: 159–160.

128. Scheler, "Begleitwort": xiii.
129. Scheler, *Ressentiment*: 58; Scheler, "Begleitwort": xiii.
130. von Krockow, *Sport*: 92.
131. Peters, *Psychologie des Sports*: 3, 64, 94, 92, 34.
132. Ibid.: 58, 77, 78, 90, 91.
133. See Oliver W. Holmes, *Human Reality and the Social World*: 47.
134. See Holmes's discussion of Ortega's "Neither Vitalism nor Rationalism" (1924) in ibid.: 55–56.
135. José Ortega y Gasset, *The Revolt of the Masses*: 12, 20, 100, 34.
136. Wohl, *The Generation of 1914*: 148, 185.
137. Ortega y Gasset, *The Revolt of the Masses*: 47, 42.
138. Ortega y Gasset, *The Modern Theme*: 72, 73, 71, 82, 83, 147.
139. Ibid.: 83.
140. José Ortega y Gasset, *Meditations on Hunting*: 28, 30, 59, 54, 58, 142, 51, 53, 79, 34.
141. Ibid.: 111.
142. Huizinga, *In the Shadow of Tomorrow*: 212.
143. Ortega y Gasset, *The Modern Theme*: 75.
144. Friedrich Nietzsche, *On the Genealogy of Morals*: 69.
145. Guttmann, "On the Alleged Dehumanization of the Sports Spectator": 275.
146. See Louis Burgener, *L'Education corporelle selon Rousseau et Pestalozzi*: 35–37; Jean-Jacques Rousseau, *The Government of Poland*: 14, 8.
147. George L. Mosse, *The Nationalization of the Masses*: 1.
148. Gustave Le Bon, *The Crowd*: 32, 56, 29, 30, 39, 23.
149. Shklar, *After Utopia*: 89.
150. Mannheim, *Man and Society in an Age of Reconstruction*: 356–357.
151. J. A. Hobson, *Imperialism*: 214.
152. Risse, *Soziologie des Sports*: 37.
153. Thiess, "Die Geistigen und der Sport": 300.
154. Ortega y Gasset, *The Revolt of the Masses*: 12.
155. Mumford, *Technics and Civilization*: 303.
156. Quoted in Joch, *Politische Leibeserziehung und ihre Theorie im Nationalsozialistichen Deutschland*: 169; Helmut Wagner, *Sport und Arbeitersport*: 31, 35.
157. See Brecht, "Mehr guten Sport," *Berliner Börsen-Courier*, February 6, 1926.
158. Christopher Lasch, *The Culture of Narcissism*: 104–105.

6. Nazi Sport Theory

1. Hajo Bernett (ed.), *Nationalsozialistische Leibeserziehung*: 18; see Richard D. Mandell, *The Nazi Olympics*; Arnd Krüger, *Die Olympische Spiele 1936 und die Weltmeinung*.
2. Albert Speer, *Inside the Third Reich*: 83.

3. Adolf Hitler, *Mein Kampf*: 5.

4. Gernot Friese, *Anspruch und Wirklichkeit des Sports im Nationalsozialismus*: 9, 11, 12, 37, 38, 82.

5. Hans-Jochen Gamm, quoted in ibid.: 2; *Mein Kampf*, quoted in ibid.: 8.

6. See Bernett (ed.), *Nationalsozialistische Leibeserziehung*: 132, 165, 211.

7. Manfred Wolfson, "Constraint and Choice in the SS Leadership," *Western Political Quarterly*, 18 (1965): 557, 566.

8. Winfried Joch, *Politische Leibeserziehung und ihre Theorie im Nationalsozialistischen Deutschland*: 215, 216.

9. Alfred Baeumler, quoted in Friese, *Anspruch und Wirklichkeit*: 22.

10. Joch, *Politische Leibeserziehung*: 216.

11. Gerhard Stöcker, *Volkserziehung und Turnen*: 42.

12. Hajo Bernett, *Untersuchungen zur Zeitgeschichte des Sports*: 31.

13. Hajo Bernett, "Das Jahn-Bild in der nationalsozialistischen Weltanschauung," *Stadion*, 4 (1978): 235, 233.

14. Joch, *Politische Leibeserziehung*: 182–183.

15. Friese, *Anspruch und Wirklichkeit*: 11.

16. George L. Mosse, *The Nationalization of the Masses*: 28.

17. Hermann Glaser, *The Cultural Roots of National Socialism*: 44, 47, 47–48.

18. David Irwin (ed.), *Winckelmann: Writings on Art*: 62.

19. Bernett (ed.), *Nationalsozialistische Leibeserziehung*: 28, 30.

20. Glaser, *The Cultural Roots of National Socialism*: 221; see also Bernett (ed.), *Nationalsozialistische Leibeserziehung*: 38.

21. Bernett (ed.), *Nationalsozialistische Leibeserziehung*: 39, 44, 45.

22. Quoted in Joch, *Politische Leibeserziehung*: 171.

23. Bernett (ed.), *Nationalsozialistische Leibeserziehung*: 32, 39, 44, 111, 159.

24. Friedrich Nietzsche, *On the Genealogy of Morals*: 38; José Ortega y Gasset, *The Revolt of the Masses*: 118.

25. Bernett (ed.), *Nationalsozialistische Leibeserziehung*: 203 (see also 26), 157, 113.

26. Friese, *Anspruch und Wirklichkeit*: 48.

27. Bernett (ed.), *Nationalsozialistische Leibeserziehung*: 169.

28. Stöcker, *Volkserziehung und Turnen*: 29.

29. Joch, *Politische Leibeserziehung*: 179, 216–217.

30. Bernett (ed.), *Nationalsozialistische Leibeserziehung*: 195.

31. Joch, *Politische Leibeserziehung*: 170.

32. Bernett (ed.), *Nationalsozialistische Leibeserziehung*: 60.

33. Ibid.: 22; Joch, *Politische Leibeserziehung*: 161.

34. Bernett (ed.), *Nationalsozialistische Leibeserziehung*: 37, 42.

35. Joch, *Politische Leibeserziehung*: 113.

36. Bernett (ed.), *Nationalsozialistische Leibeserziehung*: 61, 210, 219, 222; see also Friese, *Anspruch und Wirklichkeit*: 28.

37. Joch, *Politische Leibeserziehung*: 220.

38. Bernett (ed.), *Nationalsozialistische Leibeserziehung:* 97.
39. Joch, *Politische Leibeserziehung:* 185, 165.
40. Ibid.: 178, 164, 183, 169.
41. Ibid.: 216, 225.
42. Bernett (ed.), *Nationalsozialistische Leibeserziehung:* 26, 87; see, for example, 195.
43. Joch, *Politische Leibeserziehung:* 91–92; for another account of Baeumler's differences with Hitler, see Friese, *Anspruch und Wirklichkeit:* 34–39.
44. Joch, *Politische Leibeserziehung:* 158, 163, 160.
45. Bernett (ed.), *Nationalsozialistische Leibeserziehung:* 45.
46. See Joch, *Politische Leibeserziehung:* 162, 163, 165, 173, 175, 219.
47. Bernett (ed.), *Nationalsozialistische Leibeserziehung:* 86.
48. Ibid.: 132, 165, 211.
49. Quoted in Joch, *Politische Leibeserziehung:* 45.

7. The Origins of Socialist Sport

1. V. Z. Rogovin, "The Discussions on Problems of Daily Life and Culture in Soviet Russia during the 1920s," *Soviet Sociology* (1976): 23.
2. James Riordan, *Sport in Soviet Society:* 82–83.
3. Quoted in Henry W. Morton, *Soviet Sport:* 37.
4. Riordan, *Sport in Soviet Society:* 95–96.
5. Paul Magriel, a world-class backgammon player, quoted in *New Yorker*, December 5, 1977: 41. See also Alexander Cockburn, *Idle Passion:* "The Russians ban blindfold chess, as potentially damaging to the player" (p. 221).
6. Andrzej Wohl, "Fifty Years of Physical Culture in the U.S.S.R.": 182.
7. Riordan, *Sport in Soviet Society:* 101–102.
8. Wohl, "Fifty Years of Physical Culture in the U.S.S.R.": 182.
9. Henri Arvon, *Marxist Esthetics:* 57, 58.
10. Wohl, "Fifty Years of Physical Culture in the U.S.S.R.": 181–183.
11. Riordan, *Sport in Soviet Society:* 96, 98 n.
12. Fyodor Dostoyevsky, *The Possessed:* 111.
13. Leon Trotsky, *Literature and Revolution:* 254–255, 256, 256, 231.
14. Riordan, *Sport in Soviet Society:* 98.
15. Bruce Mazlish, *The Revolutionary Ascetic:* 103.
16. Dostoyevsky, *The Possessed:* 355.
17. Nikolay Valentinov, *Encounters with Lenin:* 79–81.
18. René Fuelœp-Miller, *The Mind and Face of Boshevism:* 24–25.
19. Yuri Olesha, *Envy and Other Works:* 19–20, 15, 103, 108, 108, 49, 84.
20. Fuelœp-Miller, *The Mind and Face of Bolshevism:* 133.
21. Riordan, *Sport in Soviet Society:* 102.
22. Fuelœp-Miller, *The Mind and Face of Bolshevism:* 149.
23. Vsevolod Meyerhold, "Biomechanics": 197, 200.

24. Carola Stern, *Ulbricht:* 9.

25. Rolf Dietz, "Sports Acrobats in the GDR," *GDR Review,* 4 (1959): 7.

26. Hans Magnus Enzensberger, "On the Irresistibility of the Petty Bourgeoisie," *Telos,* 30 (Winter 1976/77): 165.

27. On the workers' culture movement, see Wilfried van der Will and Rob Burns (eds.), *Arbeiterkulturbewegung in der Weimarer Republik;* and Gerhard A. Ritter, "Workers' Culture in Imperial Germany," *Journal of Contemporary History,* 13 (1978): 165–189. On the European workers' sport movements, see Robert F. Wheeler, "Organized Sport and Organized Labour," *Journal of Contemporary History,* 13 (1978): 191–210; David A. Steinberg, "The Workers' Sport Internationals 1920–28," *Journal of Contemporary History,* 13 (1978): 233–251. On the German movement, see Horst Ueberhorst, *Frisch, frei, stark und treu;* Heinz Timmermann, *Geschichte und Struktur der Arbeitersportbewegung 1893–1933; Theater in der Weimarer Republik;* H.-J. Teichler, "Arbeitersport als soziales und politisches Phänomen im wilhelminischen Klassenstaat": 443–484; Henning Eichberg et al., *Massenspiele;* on the French movement, see Alain Ehrenberg, "Note sur le sport rouge (1910–1936)," *Recherches,* 43 (April 1980): 75–81; on the Swedish movement, see Rolf Pålbrant, *Arbetarrörelsen och idrotten 1919–1939;* on the Norwegian movement, see Rolf Hofme, "Idrett og politikk," *Kontrast* (1972): 26–40.

28. Wheeler, "Organized Sport and Organized Labor": 196.

29. Helmut Wagner, *Sport und Arbeitersport:* 26, 79, 98.

30. Fritz Wildung, *Arbeitersport:* 73, 32.

31. Wagner, *Sport und Arbeitersport:* 147.

32. Wildung, *Arbeitersport:* 67, 67; Wagner, *Sport und Arbeitersport:* 130.

33. Wagner, *Sport und Arbeitersport:* 157.

34. Wildung, *Arbeitersport:* 5, 68, 75, 62, 143.

35. Ibid.: 39, 40, 79.

36. Wagner, *Sport und Arbeitersport:* 12.

37. See Sheila Fitzpatrick (ed.), *Cultural Revolution in Russia, 1928–1931.*

38. Wildung, *Arbeitersport:* 4, 38, 64, 66.

39. Wagner, *Sport und Arbeitersport,* 17, 13, 15, 15.

40. Leon Trotsky, "Vodka, the Church, and the Cinema": 34–35, 32.

41. Wilhelm Reich, "What Is Class Consciousness?": 301–302.

42. Julius Deutsch, *Sport und Politik:* 15.

43. Paul Franken, *Vom Werden einer neuen Kultur:* 7.

44. Ibid.: 29.

45. Leon Trotsky, "The Struggle for Cultured Speech" (1923): 54.

46. Franken, *Vom Werden einer neuen Kultur:* 39, 40, 42, 58.

47. Wildung, *Arbeitersport:* 43, 4, 4.

48. Wagner, *Sport und Arbeitersport:* 147.

49. Franken, *Vom Werden einer neuen Kultur:* 7.

50. Deutsch, *Sport und Politik:* 16, 18.

51. Franken, *Vom Werden einer neuen Kultur*: 5, 60.
52. Wildung, *Arbeitersport*: 35.
53. Franken, *Vom Werden einer neuen Kultur*: 8.
54. Ibid.: 26, 56–57.
55. Ibid.: 30, 31–32.
56. Deutsch, *Sport und Politik*: 20, 21, 22, 22–23.
57. Sigmund Freud, *Three Contributions to a Theory of Sex*: 62 n.
58. Wildung, *Arbeitersport*: 41.
59. Wagner, *Sport und Arbeitersport*: 150, 149, 150.
60. Ibid.: 90.
61. Wilhelm Reich, *The Mass Psychology of Fascism* (1933): 141.
62. Wildung, *Arbeitersport*: 36.
63. Quoted in Ueberhorst, *Frisch, frei, stark und treu*: 46.
64. Susan Sontag, "Fascinating Fascism," *New York Review of Books*, February 6, 1975: 26.
65. Deutsch, *Sport und Politik*: 41.
66. Quoted in Ueberhorst, *Frisch, frei, stark und treu*: 175.
67. *Kleine Enzyklopädie: Körperkultur und Sport*: 592–594.
68. Franken, *Vom Werden einer neuen Kultur*: 52, 57.
69. Wildung, *Arbeitersport*: 72.
70. Wheeler, "Organized Sport and Organized Labour": 195.
71. Nikolay Valentinov, *Encounters with Lenin*: 81.
72. See Pålbrant, *Arbetarrörelsen och idrotten 1919–1939*: 72–76; see also *Theater in der Weimarer Republik*: 609.
73. "Forsinker idretten ungdommens åndelige utvikling?" *Friheten* (Oslo), December 4, 1946: 6.
74. Eventually this rationalism would contribute to the catastrophe of 1933. As Heinz Timmermann has pointed out, "It was precisely the belief in the power of reason which made the workers' sportsmen helpless when confronted with the irrational dynamic of the Nazis: success on the part of the fascists seemed unthinkable, because it was in conflict with reason" (*Geschichte und Struktur der Arbeitersportbewegung*: 118; see also p. 132).
75. Ibid.: 28; Jürgen Fischer and Peter-Michael Meiners, *Proletarische Körperkultur + Gesellschaft*: 46, 50.
76. Timmermann, *Geschichte und Struktur der Arbeitersportbewegung*: 35; Fischer and Meiners, *Proletarische Körperkultur*: 39.
77. Timmermann, *Geschichte und Struktur der Arbeitersportbewegung*: 19; Fischer and Meiners, *Proletarische Körperkultur*: 46, 48.
78. Fischer and Meiners, *Proletarische Körperkultur*: 48. Fischer and Meiners also claim that the rapprochement achieved by 1919 was occasioned by the SPD's interest in integrating the workers' sport movement into the capitalist system of the Weimar Republic (p. 64).
79. Timmermann, *Geschichte und Struktur der Arbeitersportbewegung*: 19, 66, 69.
80. Ibid.: 19.
81. Fischer and Meiners, *Proletarische Körperkultur*: 46, 58.

82. Timmermann, *Geschichte und Struktur der Arbeitersportbewegung*: 45.

83. Fischer and Meiners, *Proletarische Körperkultur*: 44–45, 58.

84. Timmermann, *Geschichte und Struktur der Arbeitersportbewegung*: 26.

8. Sport in the Soviet Union

1. John N. Washburn, "Sport as a Soviet Tool," *Foreign Affairs* (April 1956): 490.

2. Avery Brundage, "I Must Admit—Russian Athletes Are Great!" *Saturday Evening Post*, April 30, 1955.

3. Jerry Cooke, "Sports in the U.S.S.R.," *Sports Illustrated*, December 2, 1957.

4. Brundage, "I Must Admit—Russian Athletes Are Great!"

5. Don Canham, "Russia Will Win the 1956 Olympics," *Sports Illustrated*, October 25, 1954.

6. James Riordan, *Sport in Soviet Society*: 56.

7. Henry W. Morton, *Soviet Sport*: 112, 174f.

8. "Kein Charakter," *Der Spiegel* (1979: 40): 207.

9. Peter C. Ludz, *The Changing Party Elite in East Germany*: 325.

10. Riordan, *Sport in Soviet Society*: 127.

11. Katerina Clark, "Utopian Anthropology as a Context for Stalinist Literature": 183.

12. Raymond A. Bauer, *The New Man in Soviet Psychology*: 22. As Bauer notes, however, the Soviet ideological premise "that man, or at least Soviet man, is infinitely capable of controlling the universe" may well conceal "the desire of the practical man of Soviet politics to reassure himself that the world is not beyond his powers of control" (p. 192).

13. Ibid.: 5, 93, 102, 133, 168.

14. Clark, "Utopian Anthropology as a Context for Stalinist Literature": 185, 186.

15. Willi Knecht, *Das Medaillenkollektiv*: 145–146.

16. Riordan, *Sport in Soviet Society*: 124.

17. Sheila Fitzpatrick, "Cultural Revolution as Class War": 35.

18. David Caute, *The Fellow-Travellers*: 54.

19. Perry Anderson, *Arguments within English Marxism*: 171–172.

20. James Bowen, *Soviet Education*: 193.

21. "Kein Charakter": 209.

22. "Trinker, Raucher und Raufbold," *Der Spiegel*, February 19, 1958: 44.

23. "Soviet Drops Hockey Star for Drinking and Egotism," *New York Times*, December 27, 1978.

24. Yevgeny Yevtushenko, "A Poet against the Destroyers," *Sports Illustrated*, December 12, 1966: 106.

25. Andrzej Wohl, "Competitive Sport and Its Social Functions," *International Review of Sport Sociology*, 5 (1970): 122.
26. "An Individual On and Off the Field," *Sport in the USSR*, 7 (1979): 3.
27. Frits Alstrøm, "Russisk ishockeys ideologi," *Politiken* (Copenhagen), April 16, 1973.
28. See, for example, *The New Soviet Society* (New York: New Leader, 1962): 208–209.
29. *Atlas World Press Review* (June 1981): 15.
30. James E. Oberg, *Red Star in Orbit*: 151.
31. E. Arab-Ogly, "Giant or Dwarf? Modern Myths about the Antagonism between Man and Machines," *Reprints from the Soviet Press*, March 21, 1969: 28.
32. Wohl, "Competitive Sport and Its Social Functions": 119–120.
33. Andrzej Wohl, *Die gesellschaftlich-historischen Grundlagen des bürgerlichen Sports*: 114.
34. This is why the East German cosmonaut Sigmund Jähn was hailed in *Neues Deutschland* (September 26, 1978) in the context of a celebration of the sporting achievements of the GDR.
35. The Soviet Academician S. L. Sobolev, quoted in V. I. Koriukin and Iu. P. Lobastov, "Living Beings, Artificial Creations, and Cybernetics," *Soviet Studies in Philosophy*, 3/4 (Spring 1965): 33.
36. Riordan, *Sport in Soviet Society*: 55–56.
37. A. Popovsky, quoted in Gustav Wetter, *Dialectical Materialism*: 478.
38. David Joravsky, "The Construction of the Stalinist Psyche": 125.
39. Wetter, *Dialectical Materialism*: 478; A. von Kultschytsky, quoted in ibid.: 476, 479.
40. On the identification of the cosmonaut and the athlete in the Soviet Union, see F. D. Gorbov and F. P. Kosmolinskiy, "From Aviation Psychology to Space Psychology," *Soviet Review*, 10 (1969): 3–13; E. Ozolin, "Science Helps Sport," *Soviet Military Review*, 5 (1981): 63–64; and "Overcoming Weightlessness," *Soviet Military Review*, 6 (1981): 62–64.
41. Katerina Clark, "Little Heroes and Big Deeds: Literature Responds to the First Five-Year Plan": 192–193.
42. Riordan, *Sport in Soviet Society*: 199.
43. "Soviet Unit Speaks: Contract Bridge Nyet," *Los Angeles Times*, January 27, 1973: 18.
44. Riordan, *Sport in Soviet Society*: 201.
45. "Pumping Body-Building," *Sports Illustrated*, November 14, 1977.
46. Riordan, *Sport in Soviet Society*: 201.
47. Y. Khromov, "Karate," *Sport in the USSR* (1979: 3): 38.
48. Riordan, *Sport in Soviet Society*: 201.
49. "Soviet Unit Speaks: Contract Bridge Nyet."
50. Alex Inkeles, *Social Change in Soviet Russia*: 82.
51. On the Soviet critique of "bourgeois" sport, see Morton, *Soviet Sport*: 106ff.

52. Arab-Ogly, "Giant or Dwarf? Modern Myths about the Antagonism between Man and Machines": 31.

53. Wohl, *Die gesellschaftlich-historischen Grundlagen des bürgerlichen Sports*: 136.

9. The Sport Culture of East Germany

1. Sebastiano Timpanaro, *On Materialism*: 82.

2. Ibid.: 62; on East German sport medicine, see Peter Kühnst, *Der mißbrauchte Sport*: 65–68.

3. For example, in 1981 the GDR, a nation of seventeen million, ranked first in the world in track and field (*Track and Field News*, December 1981: 17). See also Doug Gilbert, *The Miracle Machine*.

4. "Bogicevic Remains the Cosmic Rebel," *New York Times*, March 7, 1979.

5. "Bei uns ist immer Olympia," *Der Spiegel*, August 14, 1972: 89.

6. "Ins Abseits," *Der Spiegel*, December 12, 1977: 170.

7. See Jonathan Steele, *Inside East Germany*: 218–220.

8. See Willi Knecht, *Das Medaillenkollektiv*: 51–54; Carola Stern, *Ulbricht*: 9; Kühnst, *Der mißbrauchte Sport*: 43–49.

9. Knecht, *Das Medaillenkollektiv*: 59.

10. "Eurocommunism Reaches East Germany," *Atlas World Press Review* (March 1978): 19. I have quoted from this translation.

11. "'Korruption, wohin man blickt': Das Manifest der ersten organisierten Opposition in der DDR," *Der Spiegel* (1978: 2): 30. For a documentation of this controversy, see *DDR. Das Manifesto der Opposition*, in which the passage on sport appears on p. 37.

12. Kühnst, *Der mißbrauchte Sport*: 49–50.

13. Knecht, *Das Medaillenkollektiv*: 52–53.

14. Quoted in Steele, *Inside East Germany*: 226.

15. See, for example, Künst, *Der mißbrauchte Sport*: 35ff.

16. See, for example, Helmut Klein, *Bildung in der DDR*: 44.

17. Fred Müller, "Von den wissenschaftlichen Körpererziehung in der Sowjetunion lernen!" *Einheit*, 7 (1952): 679–688.

18. Gerhard Engelhardt, *Die Leibeserziehung an den Schulen in der Sowjetischen Besatzungszone*: 14.

19. Klein, *Bildung in der DDR*: 24, 42, 26.

20. *The New Soviet Society* (New York: New Leader, 1962): 208–209.

21. Klein, *Bildung in der DDR*: 43, 51.

22. James Bowen, *Soviet Education*: 39, 137–138.

23. Karl Marx, *On Religion*: 64; Raymond A. Bauer, *The New Man in Soviet Psychology*: 80.

24. Loyd D. Easton and Kurt H. Guddat (eds.), *Writings of the Young Marx on Philosophy and Society*: 424–425.

25. Engelhardt, *Die Leibeserziehung an den Schulen*: 19.

26. Walter Laqueur, *Young Germany*: 223.

27. Engelhardt, *Die Leibeserziehung an den Schulen*: 13–14, 19, 33, 69–70.

28. In Hans-Dieter Krebs, "Sport als Lehrfach," *Deutschland Arkiv*, 6/9 (September 1973): 990.

29. "Bei uns ist immer Olympia," *Der Spiegel*, July 31, 1972: 70.

30. "Rührt euch, weitermachen," *Der Spiegel*, October 27, 1975: 203.

31. See, for example, *Zur Geschichte der Marxistisch-Leninistischen Philosophie in der DDR*: 309–310, 326; and Rudi Hellmann, "Körperkultur und Sport in unserer Gesellschaft," *Einheit* (1975): 520–528. In *Leisure: The Basis of Culture* (1947), Josef Pieper comments sarcastically on the appearance of "humanism" in East Germany (p. 47).

32. Willi Nitschke, *Kann der Sport Neutral Sein?*: 9.

33. Fred Gras, "On the Development of Sport-Sociological Research in the German Democratic Republic": 119.

34. Quoted in Knecht, *Das Medaillenkollektiv*: 7.

35. Siegfried Wagner, "Freizeit, Kunst und Lebensfreude," *Einheit* (1972): 1146. For a discussion of the labor-leisure dialectic in the GDR, see chapter 2.

36. Helmut Hanke, *Freizeit in der DDR*: 28, 165–167, 182.

37. Ibid.: 182, 110.

38. Engelhardt, *Die Leibeserziehung an den Schulen*: 73.

39. Horst Slomma, "Unterhaltungskultur in unserem Leben," *Einheit* (1972): 1419.

40. Willi Nitschke and Lothar Kleine, "Lebensphilosophie und Körpererziehung": 589, 591, 592, 592; Nitschke, *Kann der Sport Neutral Sein?*: 10. For a brief discussion of this argument, see Dieter Voigt, *Soziologie in der DDR*: 29.

41. Voigt, *Soziologie in der DDR*: 30.

42. Gerhard Lukas, *Die Körperkultur in frühen Epochen der Menschheitsentwicklung*: 13ff.

43. G. Lukas, "Bemerkungen zu dem Artikel von W. Eichel: 'Die Entwicklung der Körperübungen in der Urgemeinschaft'": 61.

44. Kühnst, *Der mißbrauchte Sport*: 41.

45. See, for example, Georg Klaus, "Zur Soziologie der 'Mensch-Maschine-Symbiose,'" *Deutsche Zeitschrift für Philosophie*, 10 (1962): 885–902; Peter C. Ludz, *The Changing Party Elite in East Germany*: 367, 354.

46. For a brief account of Klaus's "long-term Utopian vision," see Steele, *Inside East Germany*: 125.

47. Georg Klaus, "Erkenntnis-Modell-Spiel und Mensch," *Marxistische Blätter*, 3/5 (September/October 1965): 2, 3.

48. See, for example, Voigt, *Soziologie in der DDR*: 40.

49. Nitschke and Kleine, "Lebensphilosophie und Körpererziehung": 589.

50. W. Sieger, quoted in Voigt, *Soziologie in der DDR*: 40.

51. Quoted in Knecht, *Das Medaillenkollektiv*: 148.

52. See, for example, Voigt, *Soziologie in der DDR*: 37.

53. Ludz, *The Changing Party Elite in East Germany*: 3.

54. See, for example, Steele, *Inside East Germany*: 77.

55. Barbara Hille, "Zum Stellenwert des Sports bei Jugendlichen in der Bundesrepublik und in der DDR," *Deutschland Arkiv*, 9/6 (June 1976): 601.

56. Quoted in Jean-Marie Brohm, *Critiques du sport*: 37.

57. Brian Chapman, "East of the Wall," *Runner's World* (March 1978): 61.

58. "Bei uns ist immer Olympia," *Der Spiegel*, August 14, 1972: 89.

59. See Kühnst, *Der mißbrauchte Sport*: 65–68.

60. Brian Chapman, "East Germany's Scientific Cycling Program," *Bike World* (April 1977): 17.

61. Walter Sieger, "Zur Körperkultur in der sozialistischen Gesellschaft," *Deutsche Zeitschrift für Philosophie*, 12 (1964): 931.

62. "Bei uns ist immer Olympia," *Der Spiegel*, August 14, 1972: 90; Paul Katz, "East Germany's Olympic Secrets," *Atlas World Press Review* (April 1977): 52.

63. "Hormon-strid om øst-tyske svømmersker," *Aftenposten* (Oslo), August 24, 1974: 17.

64. Knecht, *Das Medaillenkollektiv*: 139–140.

65. "DDR: Schluck Pillen oder kehr Fabriken aus," *Der Spiegel* (1979: 12): 206, 204, 205, 206, 204.

66. "Bei uns ist immer Olympia," *Der Spiegel*, August 14, 1972: 84.

67. Ludz, *The Changing Party Elite in East Germany*: 353, 359.

68. Günther Wonneberger, *Deutsche Arbeitersportler gegen Faschisten und Militaristen 1929–1933*: 15; *Zur Geschichte der Marxistisch-Leninistischen Philosophie in der DDR*: 616.

69. Kurt Meinel, *Bewegungslehre*: 42, 43, 43.

70. Engelhardt, *Die Leibeserziehung an den Schulen*: 15.

71. See, for example, Sieger, "Zur Körperkultur in der sozialistischen Gesellschaft": 934.

72. Quoted in Steele, *Inside East Germany*: 210.

73. Siegfried Wollgast, *Tradition und Philosophie*: 10, 7, 9, 12, 13, 94, 95.

74. John Starrels and Anita Mallinckrodt, *Politics in the GDR*: 35, 34.

75. Richard D. Mandell, *The Nazi Olympics*: 11.

76. Quoted in Arnd Krüger, *Sport und Politik*: 18.

77. Wonneberger, *Deutsche Arbeitersportler*: 57.

78. Günter Wonneberger, "Mehr als ein 'Turnvater,'" *Neues Deutschland*, August 11, 1978: 5.

79. "Interest in Prussia Reviving," *New York Times*, December 18, 1978.

80. "East Germany Puts King Back on His Pedestal," *New York Times*, December 14, 1980.

81. Willi Schröder, "Das Jahnbild in der deutschen Turnbewegung": 397.

82. Wolfgang Eichel et al., *Die Körperkultur in Deutschland von 1789 bis 1917*: vol. 2, 59, 60.

83. Some exceptions are a series of articles titled "Auf den Spuren der Roten Sportler" (In the Tracks of the Red Sportsmen) which appeared in the youth magazine *Junge Generation* (nos. 5, 6, 9) during 1973, and four articles in *Neues Deutschland* on Werner Seelenbinder which appeared in the issues of July 28/29, August 2, October 24, and October 29, 1979.

84. Kühnst, *Der mißbrauchte Sport*: 35–36.

85. "Ein Arbeitersportler und unbeugsamer Kommunist," *Neues Deutschland*, August 2, 1979: 4.

86. Quoted in Henry W. Morton, *Soviet Sport*: 71; see also David A. Steinberg, "The Workers' Sport Internationals 1920–28," *Journal of Contemporary History*, 13 (1978): 233–251.

87. See, for example, Hans Simon et al., *Die Körperkultur in Deutschland von 1917 bis 1945*: vol. 3, 94ff.; H. Schuster, *Arbeiterturner im Kampf um die Jugend*.

88. Wonneberger, *Deutsche Arbeitersportler*: 28, 68; see Fritz Wildung, *Arbeitersport*: 32; Helmut Wagner, *Sport und Arbeitersport* (1931): 130, 158.

89. Wildung, *Arbeitersport*: 129; Wagner, *Sport und Arbeitersport*: 75.

90. Hanns Eisler, "Our Revolutionary Music" (1932): 59.

91. Hanns Eisler, "The Builders of a New Musical Culture" (1931): 54.

92. Hanns Eisler, "Progress in the Workers' Music Movement" (1931): 34.

93. Czeslaw Milosz, *The Captive Mind*: 223.

94. "Boxsport—einmal ganz anders gezeigt," *Neues Deutschland*, November 1, 1949: 3. On June 11, 1950, *Neues Deutschland* printed a criticism of professional bicycle riding. For a more recent critique of professional sport, see Klaus Ullrich, *Tore, die nicht für Gelt fielen*.

95. Kühnst, *Der mißbrauchte Sport*: 57.

96. Klaus Ullrich, "Wurde Angelo Jacopucci ein Opfer der Manager?" *Neues Deutschland*, August 4, 1978: 8.

97. Klaus Ullrich, *Kreuzritter im Stadion*: 50.

10. Purism and the Flight from the Superman

1. This is not to suggest that the Chinese psychologists have shown no interest in psychotechnology. One study describes Chinese scientists moving from experimental psychology "into a very modern, highly sophisticated interdisciplinary area involving mathematics and communications engineering as well as psychology. This type of work can be said to belong to the general rubric of what the Soviets call 'man and technology' and what the West labels 'human engineering'"; such research can be applied, for example, to the selection and evaluation of aviators (Robert Chin and Ai-li Chin, *Psychological Research in Communist China*: 117, 208).

2. Bill Brugger, *China: Radicalism to Revisionism 1962–1979*: 14.

3. Frederic Wakeman, Jr., has suggested that the attraction Maoist

China had for the American New Left of the 1960s was in part the result of its technophobia. "It is difficult to make sweeping generalizations about so eclectic a movement, but one dominant impulse behind it has certainly been a deep concern with the dehumanization of the individual in technologically advanced societies, and a consequent tendency to look to Maoist China for evidence of the reconcilability of individual and mass" (*History and Will*: 68).

4. Wakeman, *History and Will*: 325–326.

5. This is the judgment of Stuart R. Schram in his introduction to Mao Ze-dong, *Une étude de l'éducation physique*: 32, 41; see Roy A. Clumpner and Brian B. Pendleton, "The People's Republic of China": 107.

6. Mao Ze-dong, *Une étude de l'éducation physique*: 43, 44, 44, 49, 49.

7. Wakeman, *History and Will*: 212; Mao Ze-dong, *Une étude de l'éducation physique*: 36, 41.

8. Ibid.: 49.

9. Wakeman, *History and Will*: 65.

10. Ibid.: 157.

11. Ibid.: 165.

12. Mao Ze-dong, *Une étude de l'éducation physique*: 25.

13. Wakeman, *History and Will*: 39.

14. Ibid.: 201, 202, 202.

15. Ibid.: 306.

16. Riordan (ed.), *Sport under Communism*: 110, 111, 120.

17. "By the Numbers Red China Gets into Shape," *Sports Illustrated*, June 12, 1961.

18. "Drei Meter vorhalten," *Der Spiegel*, November 23, 1981: 202.

19. Dick Miles, "One for All, But Not All for One," *Sports Illustrated*, April 18, 1977: 79.

20. "Plan für Moskau," *Der Spiegel*, January 22, 1979: 159.

21. "Historische Strömung," *Der Spiegel*, September 16, 1974: 122.

22. "China's Fourth Straight at Hong Kong Women's Basketball Championships": *Survey of People's Republic of China Press*, 6219–6223 (November 15–19, 1976): 221.

23. Quoted in Jonathan Kolatch, *Sports, Politics and Ideology in China*: 95.

24. Wakeman, *History and Will*: 163, 99.

25. Quoted in Jonathan Spence, *The Gate of Heavenly Peace*: 66.

26. Quoted in Wakeman, *History and Will*: 134; see also Spence, *The Gate of Heavenly Peace*: 70.

27. Quoted in Wakeman, *History and Will*: 236, 236, 237.

28. Ibid.: 32.

29. This rule does not apply to fascist societies to the same degree, since fascism tends to promote a vitalism which grants special authority to the (champion's) body. At the same time, however, it should be noted that Nazi ideology long opposed the cult of the champion athlete as being too individualistic.

30. Wakeman, *History and Will*: 237.

31. See, for example, Brugger, *China: Radicalism to Revisionism* *1962–1979*: 14–16.

32. Wakeman, *History and Will*: 23; a recent report has it that "knowl-edgeable China" now admits that Mao was carried down the Yangtse by a strong current ("Medaillen statt Mao," *Der Spiegel*, December 27, 1982: 102).

33. East German sport ideology (see chapter 9) argues that sportive and labor performances are actually equivalent in the eyes of the state authorities.

34. Wakeman, *History and Will*: 326.

35. Brugger, *China: Radicalism to Revisionism 1962–1979*: 95, 145.

36. Spence, *The Gate of Heavenly Peace*: 381.

37. Christopher S. Wren, "Peking's New Line Calls for New Heroes," *New York Times*, January 16, 1983.

38. "Socialist Sport Must Benefit the Largest Number of People," *Xin tiyu* (1976: 7): 17.

39. "Teng Again Says Chinese May Move against Vietnam," *New York Times*, February 1, 1979. In 1981 Deng was named "bridge personality of the year by the International Bridge Press Association" (*New York Times*, November 6, 1981).

40. Riordan (ed.), *Sport under Communism*: 129, 119.

41. "Medaillen statt Mao": 102.

42. Simon Leys [Pierre Ryckmans], *Chinese Shadows*: 42.

43. "China Is Extending Purge to Ministries of Arts and Sports," *New York Times*, December 7, 1976.

44. Leys, *Chinese Shadows*: 122.

45. "Uphold the Revolution in the Domain of the Superstructure by Doing a Good Job in Socialist Sport," *Xin tiyu* (1975: 1); "Socialist Sport Must Benefit the Largest Number of People," ibid.: 16; "Uphold the Revo-lution": 5; "Break the Legalistic Point of View of the Capitalist Class, in Which Skills Are Private Property," *Xin tiyu* (1975: 5): 12; "In Favor of Woman Umpires," ibid.: 16; "Uphold the Revolution": 6; "Study to Under-stand Theory, to Further the Revolution Successfully," *Xin tiyu* (1975: 6): 9; "Socialist Sport Must Benefit the Largest Number of People": 17.

46. "Plan für Moskau": 159; see also *Xin tiyu* (1978: 11): 2.

47. "Training Methods in Middle and Long Distance Running Develop Continuously through Praxis," *Xin tiyu* (1978: 11): 5–6; "Profis nach Pe-king," *Der Spiegel*, April 2, 1979: 196.

48. "Plan für Moskau": 159.

49. See "Freunde aus Fernwest," *Der Spiegel*, January 15, 1973: 98; *Newsweek*, January 7, 1980: 33.

50. "Plan für Moskau": 160.

51. "Uphold the Revolution": 5.

52. "Breakthrough into the 'Death-Zone'—The Truth Emerges from Praxis," *Xin tiyu* (1978: 11): 4.

53. Fox Butterfield, "Love and Sex in China," *New York Times Maga-zine*, January 13, 1980: 17.

54. "Uphold the Revolution": 5.

55. "How a Male Instructor Should Give Sports Lessons to Female Students," *Xin tiyu* (1981: 2): 26.

56. "You Wish Your Body to Be Healthy and Beautiful? Some Notes on Sports Aesthetics," *Xin tiyu* (1981: 2): 30.

57. An analogous expression appeared in the April 13, 1978, issue of the East German party newspaper *Neues Deutschland* (p. 8), where a sport enthusiast refers to himself as a "handball nut" (*Handballverrückten*).

58. "Brilliant Visual Experience of Overwhelming Beauty: A Review of the Color Documentary 'Beautifully Executed Movement,'" *Xin tiyu* (1978: 11): 29.

59. Thorstein Veblen, *The Theory of the Leisure Class*: 170.

60. Leys, *Chinese Shadows*: 16.

61. Riordan (ed.), *Sport under Communism*: 127; "Medaillen statt Mao": 102; on the night of November 16, 1981, tens of thousands of Chinese, defying a ban on unauthorized gatherings in Peking's Tian An Men Square, held "boisterous celebrations that prompted the police to rush in reinforcements and seal off some adjacent streets"—all of this to celebrate the first world title of the Chinese women's volleyball team (Christopher S. Wren, "Peking Celebrates Volleyball Sweep," *New York Times*, November 18, 1981).

11. Toward the Abolition of "Sport"

1. Gerhard Vinnai, *Fußballsport als Ideologie*: 9.

2. Fritz Wildung, *Arbeitersport*: 3.

3. Arthur Koestler describes the appearance of the women in his party cell in Berlin as follows: "They were all dowdily dressed, and their faces had a neglected appearance, as if they disdained the effort to be pretty as a bourgeois convention . . . " (in Richard Crossman, [ed.], *The God That Failed*: 25).

4. Wilhelm Reich, "What Is Class Consciousness?": 305–306.

5. See Robert F. Wheeler, "Organized Sport and Organized Labour," *Journal of Contemporary History*, 13 (1978): 198–199. A brief description of workers' sport in France is Alain Ehrenberg, "Note sur le sport rouge (1910–1936)," *Recherches*, 43 (1980): 75–81.

6. Wildung, *Arbeitersport*: 4, 67ff, 57; Helmut Wagner, *Sport und Arbeitersport* (1931): 180; Wildung, *Arbeitersport*: 10, 69, 4, 149, 33, 82; Wagner, *Sport und Arbeitersport*: 107, 111; Wildung, *Arbeitersport*: 4; Wagner, *Sport und Arbeitersport*: 155; Paul Franken, *Vom Werden einer neuen Kultur*: 52.

7. See, for example, Christine Kulke, "Emanzipation oder gleiches Recht auf 'Trimm Dich'? Diskussionsbeitrag zum Problem des Frauensports in der BRD": 98; Ilse Modelmoog, "Philosophische Anthropologie und Sportwissenschaft": 108; Sven Güldenpfennig, *Gewerkschaftliche Sportpolitik*: 14, 15, 48. Joachim Neu claims that a sport radical named Dieter Bott, cofounder of an "Anti-Olympic Committee," is to be credited with having made

the West German New Left aware of the pre-1933 workers' sport movement. See "Studentschaft zwischen 'Olympismus' und 'Anti-Olympia'": 199.
    8. Jürgen Fischer and Peter-Michael Meiners, *Proletarische Körperkultur + Gesellschaft*: 71, 73, 66.
    9. Ibid.: 58, 43, 44, 45, 46.
    10. Vinnai (ed.), *Sport in der Klassengesellschaft*: 11.
    11. Ginette Berthaud et al., *Sport, culture et répression*: 5.
    12. Daniel Cohn-Bendit and Gabriel Cohn-Bendit, *Obsolete Communism*: 67.
    13. Daniel Cohn-Bendit, *Le grand bazar*: 50.
    14. Fischer and Meiners, *Proletarische Körperkultur + Gesellschaft*: 66.
    15. Alfred Grosser, *Germany in Our Time*: 391.
    16. Reimut Reiche, *Sexuality and Class Struggle*: 146-147.
    17. Ibid.: 149.
    18. Göran Therborn, "The Frankfurt School," *New Left Review*, 63 (September-October 1970): 95.
    19. Paul Connerton, *The Tragedy of Enlightenment*: 3.
    20. Reiche, *Sexuality and Class Struggle*: 147.
    21. Richard Gombin, *The Origins of Modern Leftism*: 40, 75-76.
    22. For an excellent account of Lefebvre's role in French intellectual life, see Mark Poster, *Existential Marxism in Postwar France*: 238-260.
    23. Henri Lefebvre, *Everyday Life in the Modern World*: 144.
    24. Herbert Marcuse, *The Aesthetic Dimension*: 16.
    25. For a discussion of the Situationists, see Gombin, *The Origins of Modern Leftism*: 61ff. Lefebvre mentions the Situationists in his *Introduction à la modernité*: 336.
    26. This phrase, coined by Walter Benjamin, is applied to the Frankfurt School (primarily Theodor Adorno and Max Horkheimer) by Michael Landmann in his "Foreword," in Zoltán Tar, *The Frankfurt School*: xiv-xv; Lefebvre, *Everyday Life in the Modern World*: 36.
    27. Poster, *Existential Marxism in Postwar France*: 248 n.
    28. Paul Laurent, Robert Barran, and Jean-Jacques Faure, *Les communistes et le sport*: 8, 34, 32, 32, 9.
    29. Berthaud et al., *Sport, culture et répression*: 7. See also Jean-Marie Brohm, *Critiques du sport*: 18ff., 60, 135, 136, 142, 143, 144, 219, 8, 43, 66.
    30. Jean-Marie Brohm, "Vers l'analyse institutionelle du sport de compétition," *L'Homme et la Société* (1973: 29/30): 182. For a schematic presentation of the opposing positions of East German sport ideology and its leftist critics, see Arnd Krüger, *Sport und Politik*: 166-167.
    31. Vinnai (ed.), *Sport in der Klassengesellschaft*: 7.
    32. Jac-Olof Böhme et al., *Sport im Spätkapitalismus*: 26-30.
    33. Cohn-Bendit and Cohn-Bendit, *Obsolete Communism*: 67.
    34. Michael Schneider, *Neurosis and Civilization*: x.
    35. Sherry Turkle, *Psychoanalytic Politics*: 6, 8.
    36. Berthaud et al., *Sport, culture et répression*: 99, 98, 126.

37. Böhme et al., *Sport im Spätkapitalismus*: 33–41.

38. Vinnai, *Fußballsport als Ideologie*: 89, 24.

39. Vinnai (ed.), *Sport in der Klassengesellschaft*: 20.

40. Berthaud et al., *Sport, culture et répression*: 20.

41. Christian Graf von Krockow, *Sport*: 62; see, for example, Hans Lenk, "Sport, Achievement, and the New Left Criticism," *Man and World*, 5 (1972): 179–192; idem, *Leistungssport*: 19–42; idem, *Social Philosophy of Athletics*: 81–118.

42. Herbert Marcuse, *Eros and Civilization*: xi.

43. Brohm, "Vers l'analyse institutionelle du sport de compétition": 180.

44. Quoted in Berthaud et al., *Sport, culture et répression*: 7, 12.

45. Vinnai, *Fußballsport als Ideologie*: 23, 25, 25.

46. Berthaud et al., *Sport, culture et répression*: 20.

47. Vinnai, *Fußballsport als Ideologie*: 48, 18; Henning Eichberg, *Der Weg des Sports in die industrielle Zivilisation*: 17; see F. G. Jünger, *Die Spiele*.

48. Poster, *Existential Marxism in Postwar France*: 255; Ronald Bruzina, "Translator's Introduction," in Kostas Axelos, *Alienation, Praxis, and Technē in the Thought of Karl Marx*: xxvii.

49. Henri Lefebvre, *Critique de la vie quotidienne* (Paris: l'Arche Editeur, 1958): 40–42, 45.

50. Lefebvre, *Everyday Life in the Modern World*: 190–191.

51. Gombin, *The Origins of Modern Leftism*: 74, 70.

52. Raoul Vaneigem, *Traité de savoir-vivre à l'usage des jeunes générations*: 268.

53. See, for example, Vinnai (ed.), *Sport in der Klassengesellschaft*: 50; Berthaud et al., *Sport, culture et répression*: 54; Brohm, *Critiques du sport*: 37, 136, 138, 143; Ulrike Prokop, *Soziologie der Olympischen Spiele*; Berthaud et al., *Sport, culture et répression*: 121, 153; Vinnai (ed.), *Sport in der Klassengesellschaft*: 66; Reiche, *Sexuality and Class Struggle*: 62, 71; Berthaud et al., *Sport, culture et répression*: 13, 54; Vinnai (ed.), *Sport in der Klassengesellschaft*: 8, 11, 44, 179.

54. Vinnai (ed.), *Sport in der Klassengesellschaft*: 154.

55. Eichberg, *Der Weg des Sports in die industrielle Zivilisation*; Wilhelm Hopf, *Kritik der Sportsoziologie*. For a critical discussion in English, see Allen Guttmann, *From Ritual to Record*: 64–69.

56. Hopf, *Kritik der Sportsoziologie*: 78.

57. Eichberg, *Der Weg des Sports in die industrielle Zivilisation*: 87.

58. Ibid.

59. Hopf, *Kritik der Sportsoziologie*: 64; Eichberg, *Der Weg des Sports in die industrielle Zivilisation*: 20; Vinnai (*Fußballsport als Ideologie*: 69), quoted in ibid.: 56.

60. Ibid.: 124, 125, 126.

61. Marcuse, *Eros and Civilization*: 41.

62. Adorno, quoted in Tar, *The Frankfurt School*: 155–156.

63. Ibid.: 42–43, 100–101, 170, 170.

64. Quoted in ibid.: 19.

65. Theodor W. Adorno, *Prisms*: 80.

66. Max Horkheimer and Theodor W. Adorno, *Dialectic of Enlightenment*: 234, 234.

67. Theodor Adorno, *Minima Moralia*: 59.

68. Therborn, "The Frankfurt School": 94–95.

69. Adorno, *Minima Moralia*: 45, 46.

70. T. W. Adorno et al., *The Authoritarian Personality*: 428, 763.

71. Horkheimer and Adorno, *Dialectic of Enlightenment*: 140, 233.

72. Ibid.: 88, 109.

73. Adorno, *Prisms*: 56.

74. Ibid.: 132.

75. Theodor W. Adorno, *Introduction to the Sociology of Music*: 49–50.

76. Horkheimer and Adorno, *Dialectic of Enlightenment*: 143.

77. G. W. F. Hegel, "On Art": 73.

78. Adorno, *Prisms*: 80, 81.

79. Roland Barthes, *The Eiffel Tower and Other Mythologies*: 132, 35.

80. Ibid.: 134.

81. Adorno, *Prisms*: 81.

82. Barthes, *The Eiffel Tower*: 87, 87, 88.

Bibliography

I. Books

Adam, Paul. *La morale des sports*. Paris: Librairie mondiale, 1907.

Adorno, Theodor W. *Prisms*. London: Neville Spearman, 1967 (1953).

———. *Minima Moralia: Reflections from Damaged Life*. London: New Left Books, 1974 (1951).

———. *Introduction to the Sociology of Music*. New York: Seabury Press, 1976 (1962).

——— et al. *The Authoritarian Personality*. New York: Norton Library, 1969 (1950).

Anderson, Perry. *Arguments within British Marxism*. London: New Left Books, 1980.

Aron, Raymond. *The Opium of the Intellectuals*. New York: Norton, 1962.

Artaud, Antonin. *The Theater and Its Double*. New York: Grove Press, 1958 (1938).

Arvon, Henri. *Marxist Esthetics*. Ithaca: Cornell University Press, 1973 (1970).

Auguet, Roland. *Cruelty and Civilization: The Roman Games*. London: George Allen and Unwin, 1972.

Axelos, Kostas. *Alienation, Praxis, and Technē in the Thought of Karl Marx*. Austin: University of Texas Press, 1976 (1969).

Bachelard, Gaston. *The Psychoanalysis of Fire*. Boston: Beacon Press, 1968.

Bardèche, Maurice. *Les temps modernes*. Paris: Les Sept Couleurs, 1956.

———. *Sparte et les sudistes*. Paris: Les Sept Couleurs, 1969.

Barthes, Roland. *The Eiffel Tower and Other Mythologies*. New York: Hill and Wang, 1979.

———. *Mythologies*. New York: Hill and Wang, 1982 (1957).

Bataille, Georges. *Oeuvres complètes*. Paris: Gallimard, 1970.

Bauer, Raymond A. *The New Man in Soviet Psychology*. Cambridge, Mass.: Harvard University Press, 1952.

Baynes, Norman H. *The Speeches of Adolf Hitler*, Vol. 1. London: Oxford University Press, 1942.

Beauvoir, Simone de. *The Prime of Life*. New York: Laneer Books, 1966.

Belgion, Montgomery. *Epitaph on Nuremberg*. London: Falcon Press, 1946.

Bell, Daniel. *The End of Ideology*. New York: Free Press, 1965 (1960).
Beneyto, Juan. *Los origenes de la ciencia política en España*. Madrid: Instituto de Estudios Políticos, 1949.
Benn, Gottfried. *Primal Vision: Selected Writings*. London: Bodley Head, 1961.
———. *Gesammelte Werke*, Vol. 3. Wiesbaden: Limes Verlag, 1968.
Bentley, Eric. *The Cult of the Superman*. Philadelphia and New York: J. P. Lippincott, 1947.
Bernett, Hajo. *Untersuchungen zur Zeitgeschichte des Sports*. Schorndorf bei Stuttgart: Verlag Karl Hofmann, 1973.
——— (ed.). *Nationalsozialistische Leibeserziehung*. Schorndorf bei Stuttgart: Verlag Karl Hofmann, 1966.
Berthaud, Ginette et al. *Sport, culture et répression*. Paris: François Maspero, 1972.
Böhme, Jac-Olof et al. *Sport im Spätkapitalismus*. Frankfurt/M.: Limpert, 1971.
Bowen, James. *Soviet Education: Anton Makarenko and the Years of Experiment*. Madison: University of Wisconsin, 1965.
Brohm, Jean-Marie. *Critiques du sport*. Paris: Christian Bourgois, 1976.
Brown, L. B. *Ideology*. Harmondsworth: Penguin Books, 1973.
Brugger, Bill. *China: Radicalism to Revisionism 1962–1979*. London: Croom Helm, 1981.
Buchheim, Hans. *Totalitarian Rule: Its Nature and Characteristics*. Middletown, Conn.: Wesleyan University Press, 1968.
Burgener, Louis. *L'Education corporelle selon Rousseau et Pestalozzi*. Paris: Librairie Philosophique J. Vrin, 1973.
Burnier, Michel-Antoine. *Choice of Action: The French Existentialists in Politics*. New York: Random House, 1968.
Caillois, Roger. *Les jeux et les hommes*. Paris: Gallimard, 1958.
Cantril, Hadley. *Soviet Leaders and Mastery of Man*. New Brunswick: Rutgers University Press, 1960.
Cassirer, Ernst. *The Myth of the State*. Garden City, N.Y.: Doubleday Anchor Books, 1955 (1946).
Caute, David. *The Fellow-Travellers: A Postscript to the Enlightenment*. New York: Macmillan, 1973.
Chin, Robert and Ai-li Chin. *Psychological Research in Communist China*. Cambridge, Mass.: MIT Press, 1969.
Cobban, Alfred. *In Search of Humanity*. London: Jonathan Cape, 1960.
Cockburn, Alexander. *Idle Passion: Chess and the Dance of Death*. New York: Village Voice/Simon and Schuster, 1974.
Cohen, G. A. *Karl Marx's Theory of History: A Defence*. Princeton: Princeton University Press, 1980.
Cohn-Bendit, Daniel. *Le grand bazar*. Paris, Pierre Belfond, 1975.
——— and Gabriel Cohn-Bendit. *Obsolete Communism: The Left-Wing Alternative*. New York: McGraw-Hill, 1968.
Connerton, Paul. *The Tragedy of Enlightenment: An Essay on the Frankfurt School*. Cambridge: Cambridge University Press, 1980.

Coubertin, Pierre de. *Notes sur l'éducation publique*. Paris: Hachette, 1901.
————. *Essais de psychologie sportive*. Lausanne and Paris: Librairie Payot, 1913.
————. *Pédagogie sportive*. Lausanne: Bureau International de Pédagogie Sportive, 1922.
Cross, Colin. *The Fascists in Britain*. London: Barrie and Rockliff, 1961.
Crossman, Richard (ed.). *The God That Failed*. New York: Bantam Books, 1959 (1950).
DDR. *Das Manifest der Opposition: Eine Dokumentation*. Munich: Wilhelm Goldmann Verlag, 1978.
Deutsch, Julius. *Sport und Politik*. Berlin: Verlag J. H. W. Dietz Nachfolger, 1928.
Diggins, John. *Mussolini and Fascism: The View from America*. Princeton: Princeton University Press, 1972.
Dostoyevsky, Fyodor. *The Possessed*. New York: New American Library, 1962.
Drenkow, Erhard and Paul Marschner. *Körperliche Grundausbildung in der sozialistischen Schule*. Berlin: Volkseigener Verlag, 1975.
Drieu la Rochelle, Pierre. *Mesure de la France*. Paris: Editions Bernard Grasset, 1964.
Ehrmann, Jacques (ed.). *Game, Play, Literature*. Boston: Beacon Press, 1971.
Eichberg, Henning. *Der Weg des Sports in die industrielle Zivilization*. Baden-Baden: Nomos, 1973.
———— et al. *Massenspiele: NS-Thingspiel, Arbieterweihespiel und olympisches Zeremoniell*. Stuttgart-Bad Cannstatt: Frommann-holzboog, 1977.
Eichel, Wolfgang et al. *Die Körperkultur in Deutschland von 1789 bis 1917*, Vol. 2. Berlin: Sportverlag, 1973.
Eisler, Hanns. *A Rebel in Music*. New York: International Publishers, 1978.
Eliot, T. S. *The Idea of a Christian Society*. New York: Harcourt, Brace: 1940.
Ellis, Havelock. *The Pyschology of Sex*. New York: Mentor Books, 1964 (1932).
Engelhardt, Gerhard. *Die Leibeserziehung an den Schulen in der Sowjetischen Besatzungszone*. Bonn and Berlin: Bundesministerium für Gesamtdeutsche Fragen, 1965.
Engels, Frederick. *Dialectics of Nature*. New York: International Publishers, 1963 (1st Eng. ed. 1925).
————. *The Origin of the Family, Private Property, and the State*. New York: International Publishers, 1970 (1884).
————. *Anti-Dühring*. New York: International Publishers, 1972 (1st Eng. ed. 1935).
Fell, Joseph P. *Heidegger and Sartre*. New York: Columbia University Press, 1979.
Fest, Joachim C. *The Face of the Third Reich: Portraits of the Nazi Leadership*. New York: Ace Books, 1963.

Finley, M. I. and H. W. Pleket. *The Olympic Games: The First Thousand Years*. London: Chatto and Windus, 1976.

Fischer, Jürgen and Peter-Michael Meiners, *Proletarische Körperkultur + Gesellschaft: Zur Geschichte des Arbeitersports*. Giessen: Edition 2000, 1973.

Fitzpatrick, Sheila (ed.). *Cultural Revolution in Russia, 1928–1931*. Bloomington: Indiana University Press, 1978.

Flint, R. W. (ed.). *Marinetti: Selected Writings*. New York: Farrar, Straus and Giroux, 1972.

Franken, Paul. *Vom Werden einer neuen Kultur*. Berlin: E. Laubsche Verlagsbuchhandlung, 1930.

Freud, Sigmund. *Three Contributions to a Theory of Sex*. New York: Dutton, 1962 (1905).

———. *New Introductory Lectures on Psychoanalysis*. New York: Norton, 1965 (1933).

Friese, Gernot. *Anspruch und Wirklichkeit des Sports im Nationalsozialismus*. Ahrensburg bei Hamburg: Verlag Ingrid Czwalina, 1974.

Fueloep-Miller, René. *The Mind and Face of Bolshevism*. New York: Harper Torchbooks, 1965 (1926).

Gide, André. *The Immoralist*. New York: Vintage Books, n.d. (1902).

Gierke, Otto. *Natural Law and the Theory of Society 1500–1800*. Boston: Beacon Press, 1957.

Gilbert, Doug. *The Miracle Machine*. New York: Coward, McCann and Geoghegan, 1980.

Glaser, Hermann. *The Cultural Roots of National Socialism*. Austin: University of Texas Press, 1978.

Gombin, Richard. *The Origins of Modern Leftism*. Baltimore: Penguin Books, 1975 (1971).

Graña, César. *Modernity and Its Discontents*. New York: Harper Torchbooks, 1967.

Grosser, Alfred. *Germany in Our Time: A Political History of the Postwar Years*. Harmondsworth: Pelican Books, 1974.

Güldenpfennig, Sven. *Gewerkschaftliche Sportpolitik*. Cologne: Pahl-Rugenstein, 1978.

Guttmann, Allen. *From Ritual to Record: The Nature of Modern Sports*. New York: Columbia University Press, 1978.

Haley, Bruce. *The Healthy Body and Victorian Culture*. Cambridge, Mass.: Harvard University Press, 1978.

Hamilton, Alastair. *The Appeal of Fascism*. New York: Macmillan, 1971.

Hanke, Helmut. *Freizeit in der DDR*. Berlin: Dietz Verlag, 1979.

Hegel, G. W. F. *The Philosophy of History*. New York: Dover, 1956 (1830–1831).

———. *The Phenomenology of Mind*. New York: Harper Torchbooks, 1967 (1807).

———. *On Art, Religion, Philosophy*. New York: Harper Torchbooks, 1970 (1835–1838).

Heidegger, Martin. *An Introduction to Metaphysics*. New York: Anchor Books, 1961.

Hessen, Robert. *Der Sport*. Frankfurt am Main: Literarische Anstalt Rütten und Loenning, 1908.

Hitler, Adolf. *Mein Kampf*. Boston: Houghton Mifflin, 1943 (1925).

Hobbes, Thomas. *Leviathan*. Baltimore: Penguin Books, 1976 (1651).

Hobson, J. A. *Imperialism: A Study*. Ann Arbor: University of Michigan Press, 1972 (1902).

Hoch, Paul. *Rip Off the Big Game*. Garden City, N.Y.: Anchor Books, 1973.

Höhne, Heinz. *The Order of the Death's Head*. London: Secker and Warburg, 1969.

Holmes, Oliver W. *Human Reality and the Social World: Ortega's Philosophy of History*. Amherst: University of Massachusetts Press, 1975.

Hopf, Wilhelm. *Kritik der Sportsoziologie*. Lollar/Lahn: Aschenbach, 1979.

Horkheimer, Max and Theodor W. Adorno. *Dialectic of Enlightenment*. New York: Seabury Press, 1969 (1944).

Huizinga, Johan. *In the Shadow of Tomorrow*. New York: Norton, 1936.

———. *Homo Ludens: A Study of the Play-Element in Culture*. Boston: Beacon Press, 1955 (1938).

———. *America: A Dutch Historian's Vision, from Afar and Near*. New York: Harper Torchbooks, 1972.

Inkeles, Alex. *Social Change in Soviet Russia*. Cambridge, Mass.: Harvard University Press, 1968.

Irwin, David (ed.). *Winckelmann: Writings on Art*. London: Phaidon, 1972.

Jaeger, Werner. *Paideia: The Ideals of Greek Culture*, Vol. 2. New York: Oxford University Press, 1943.

Jaspers, Karl. *Man in the Modern Age*. Garden City, N.Y.: Doubleday Anchor, 1957 (1931).

Joch, Winfried. *Politische Leibeserziehung und ihre Theorie im Nationalsozialistischen Deutschland*. Frankfurt/M.: Peter Lang, 1976.

Jünger, Friedrich Georg. *Die Spiele: Ein Schlüssel zu ihrer Bedeutung*. Frankfurt/M.: Vittorio Klostermann, 1953.

Kirkpatrick, Ivone. *Mussolini: A Study in Power*. New York: Avon Books, 1968.

Klein, Helmut. *Bildung in der DDR*. Reinbek bei Hamburg: Rowohlt, 1974.

Kleine Enzyklopädie: Körperkultur und Sport. Leipzig: Verlag Enzyklopädie, 1960.

Knecht, Willi. *Das Medaillenkollektiv*. Berlin: Verlag Gebr. Holzapfel, 1978.

Koestler, Arthur. *Darkness at Noon*. New York: Bantam Books, 1979.

Kolatch, Jonathan. *Sports, Politics and Ideology in China*. New York: Jonathan David Publishers, 1972.

Kretschmer, Ernst. *Die Persönlichkeit der Athletiker*. Leipzig: Georg Thieme Verlag, 1936.

Kris, Ernst. *Pscyhoanalytic Explorations in Art*. New York: Schocken Books, 1964 (1952).

Krockow, Christian Graf von. *Sport: Eine Soziologie und Philosophie des Leistungsprinzips.* Hamburg: Hoffmann und Campe, 1974.

Krüger, Arnd. *Die Olympischen Spiele 1936 und die Weltmeinung.* Berlin-Munich-Frankfurt/M.: Verlag Bartels und Wernitz KG, 1972.

――. *Sport und Politik: Von Turnvater Jahn zum Staatsamateur.* Hannover: Fackelträger-Verlag, 1975.

Kühnst, Peter. *Der Mißbrauchte Sport: Die politische Instrumentalisierung des Sports in der SBZ und DDR 1945–1957.* Cologne: Verlag Wissenschaft und Politik, 1982.

Kunnas, Tarmo. *Drieu la Rochelle, Céline, Brasillach et la tentation fasciste.* Paris: Les Sept Couleurs, 1972.

Lacouture, Jean. *The Demigods: Charismatic Leadership in the Third World.* New York: Knopf, 1970.

Lane, Christel. *The Rites of Rulers: Ritual in Industrial Society—The Soviet Case.* Cambridge: Cambridge University Press, 1981.

Laqueur, Walter Z. *Young Germany: A History of the German Youth Movement.* New York: Basic Books, 1962.

Lasch, Christopher. *The Culture of Narcissism.* New York: Norton, 1978.

Lasswell, Harold. *Psychopathology and Politics.* New York: Viking Press, 1960.

Laurent, Paul, Robert Barran, and Jean-Jacques Faure. *Les communistes et le sport: A l'heure de Munich.* Paris: Editions Sociales, 1972.

Lean, E. Tangye. *The Napoleonists: A Study in Political Disaffection 1760/ 1960.* London: Oxford University Press, 1970.

Le Bon, Gustave. *The Crowd.* New York: Viking Press, 1960 (1895).

Lefebvre, Henri. *L'Existentialisme.* Paris: Editions du Sagittaire, 1946.

――. *Introduction à la modernité.* Paris: Editions de Minuit, 1962.

――. *Vers le cybernanthrope.* Paris: Editions Denoël, 1967–1971.

――. *The Sociology of Marx.* New York: Vintage Books, 1969 (1966).

――. *Everyday Life in the Modern World.* New York: Harper Torchbooks, 1971 (1968).

Lendvai, Paul. *The Bureaucracy of Truth: How Communist Governments Manage the News.* Boulder: Westview Press, 1981.

Lenk, Hanks. *Leistungssport: Ideologie oder Mythos?* Stuttgart: Verlag W. Kohlhammer, 1972.

――. *Social Philosophy of Athletics.* Champaign, Ill.: Stipes, 1979.

Lévy, Bernard-Henry. *Barbarism with a Human Face.* New York: Colophon Books, 1980.

Leys, Simon [Pierre Ryckmans]. *Chinese Shadows.* New York: Penguin Books, 1978.

Liddell Hart, [Basil Henry]. *The Future of Infantry.* Harrisburg, Pa.: Military Service Publishing, 1936.

Lifshitz, Mikhail. *The Philosophy of Art of Karl Marx.* London: Pluto Press, 1973.

Lowenthal, Leo. *Literature and the Image of Man.* Boston: Beacon Press, 1955.

Löwith, Karl. *From Hegel to Nietzsche.* Garden City, N.Y.: Doubleday Anchor Books, 1967.

Ludz, Peter C. *The Changing Party Elite in East Germany.* Cambridge, Mass.: MIT Press, 1972.

Lukas, Gerhard. *Die Körperkultur in frühen Epochen der Menschheitsentwicklung.* Berlin: Sportverlag, 1969.

Lyttelton, Adrian (ed.). *Italian Fascisms: From Pareto to Gentile.* New York: Harper Torchbooks, 1975.

MacAloon, John J. *This Great Symbol: Pierre de Coubertin and the Origins of the Modern Olympic Games.* Chicago: University of Chicago Press, 1981.

McLellan, David. *Marx before Marxism.* New York: Harper Torchbooks, 1971.

McMurtry, John. *The Structure of Marx's World-View.* Princeton: Princeton University Press, 1978.

Magnane, Georges. *Sociologie du sport.* Paris: Gallimard, 1964.

Mandell, Richard D. *The Nazi Olympics.* New York: Macmillan, 1971.

———. *The First Modern Olympics.* Berkeley: University of California Press, 1976.

Mannheim, Karl. *Ideology and Utopia.* New York: Harvest Books, n.d. (1929).

———. *Man and Society in an Age of Reconstruction.* New York: Harvest Books, n.d. (1935).

Mao Ze-dong. *Une étude de l'éducation physique.* Paris and The Hague: Mouton, 1962 (1917).

Marcuse, Herbert, *Eros and Civilization.* New York: Vintage Books, 1955.

———. *Five Lectures.* Boston: Beacon Press, 1970.

———. *The Aesthetic Dimension.* Boston: Beacon Press, 1978.

Marinetti, Filippo. *Selected Writings.* New York: Farrar, Straus and Giroux, 1972.

Marx, Karl. *Writings of the Young Marx on Philosophy and Society.* Ed. Loyd D. Easton and Kurt H. Guddat. Garden City, N.Y.: Anchor Books, 1967.

———. *On Religion.* Ed. Saul K. Padover. New York: McGraw-Hill, 1974.

——— and Frederick Engels. *The German Ideology.* New York: International Publishers, 1968 (1846).

Mazlish, Bruce. *The Revolutionary Ascetic.* New York: Basic Books, 1976.

Meinel, Kurt. *Bewegungslehre.* Berlin: Volkseigener Verlag, 1977.

Meisel, James H. *The Fall of the Republic: Military Revolt in France.* Ann Arbor: University of Michigan Press, 1962.

Merleau-Ponty, Maurice. *Humanism and Terror.* Boston: Beacon Press, 1969.

Meynaud, Jean. *Sport et politique.* Paris: Payot, 1966.

Miliband, Ralph. *Marxism and Politics.* New York: Oxford University Press, 1977.

Milosz, Czeslaw. *The Captive Mind.* New York: Vintage Books, 1951.

Mishima, Yukio. *Sun and Steel.* New York: Grove Press, 1970.

Mitzman, Arthur. *Sociology and Estrangement.* New York: Knopf, 1973.
Monnerot, Jules. *Sociology and Psychology of Communism.* Boston: Beacon Press, 1960 (1949).
Moravia, Alberto. *The Conformist.* New York: Ace Books, 1970 (1951).
More, Thomas. *Utopia.* New York: Penguin Books, 1978.
Morton, Henry W. *Soviet Sport: Mirror of Soviet Society.* New York: Collier Books, 1963.
Mosca, Gaetano. *The Ruling Class.* New York: McGraw-Hill, 1939.
Mosley, Oswald. *Fascism in Britain.* Quoted in R. Osborn. *The Psychology of Reaction.* London: Victor Gollancz, 1938.
———. *My Life.* New Rochelle, N.Y.: Arlington House, 1972 (1968).
Mosse, George L. *The Nationalization of the Masses.* New York: New American Library, 1975.
———. *The Crisis of German Ideology: Intellectual Origins of the Third Reich.* New York: Schocken Books, 1981.
Mumford, Lewis. *Technics and Civilization.* New York: Harbinger Books, 1963 (1933).
Musil, Robert. *Tagebücher, Aphorismen, Essays und Reden.* Hamburg: Rowohlt, 1955.
Nietzsche, Friedrich. *Twilight of the Idols and The Anti-Christ.* Baltimore: Penguin Books, 1968 (1889).
———. *On the Genealogy of Morals.* New York: Vintage Books, 1969 (1887).
———. *Thus Spoke Zarathustra.* Baltimore: Penguin Books, 1969 (1883–1892).
Nitschke, Willi. *Kann der Sport Neutral Sein?* Berlin: Sportverlag, 1961.
Nolte, Ernst. *Three Faces of Fascism.* New York: Mentor Books, 1969.
Nye, Robert A. *The Origins of Crowd Psychology: Gustave Le Bon and the Crisis of Mass Democracy in the Third Republic.* Beverly Hills: SAGE, 1975.
Oberg, James E. *Red Star in Orbit.* New York: Random House, 1981.
Olesha, Yuri. *Envy and Other Works.* Garden City, N.Y.: Doubleday Anchor, 1967.
Ortega y Gasset, José. *The Revolt of the Masses.* New York: W. W. Norton, 1957 (1930).
———. *The Modern Theme.* New York: Harper Torchbooks, 1961 (1931).
———. *Meditations on Hunting.* New York: Scribner, 1972 (1943).
Osborn, R. *The Psychology of Reaction.* London: Victor Gollancz, 1938.
Pålbrant, Rolf. *Arbetarrörelsen och idrotten 1919–1939.* Uppsala: Acta Universitatis Upsaliensis, 1977.
Paxton, Robert O. *Vichy France: Old Guard and New Order.* New York: Knopf, 1972.
Perrault, Gilles. *Les parachutistes.* Paris: Editions du Seuil, 1961.
Pieper, Josef. *Leisure: The Basis of Culture.* New York: New American Library, 1947.
Plekhanov, Georgi. *Fundamental Problems of Marxism.* New York: International Publishers, 1969.

Plumyène, J. and R. Lasierra. *Les fascismes français 1923–63*. Paris: Editions du Seuil, 1963.

Poster, Mark. *Existential Marxism in Postwar France*. Princeton: Princeton University Press, 1977.

Powell, David E. *Antireligious Propaganda in the Soviet Union*. Cambridge, Mass.: MIT Press, 1975.

Primo de Rivera, José Antonio. *Selected Writings*. Ed. Hugh Thomas. New York: Harper Torchbooks, 1975.

Prokop, Ulrike. *Soziologie der Olympischen Spiele*. Munich: Carl Hanser Verlag, 1971.

Rader, Melvin. *Marx's Interpretation of History*. New York: Oxford University Press, 1979.

Reich, Wilhelm. *The Mass Psychology of Fascism*. New York: Noonday, 1970 (1933).

Reiche, Reimut. *Sexuality and Class Struggle*. New York: Praeger, 1971.

Rémond, René. *The Right Wing in France: From 1815 to de Gaulle*. Philadelphia: University of Pennsylvania Press, 1966.

Rigauer, Bero, *Sport and Work*. New York: Columbia University Press, 1981.

———. *Sportsoziologie*. Reinbek bei Hamburg: Rowohlt, 1982.

Riordan, James. *Sport in Soviet Society*. Cambridge: Cambridge University Press, 1977.

——— (ed.). *Sport under Communism: The U.S.S.R., Czechoslovakia, the G.D.R., China, Cuba*. London: C. Hurt, 1978.

Risse, Heinz. *Soziologie des Sports*. Berlin: Verlag von August Reher, 1921.

Rousseau, Jean-Jacques. *The Government of Poland*. New York: Library of Liberal Arts, 1972 (1772).

Salomon, Ernst von. *Fragebogen*. Garden City, N.Y.: Doubleday, 1955.

Sartre, Jean-Paul. *Anti-Semite and Jew*. New York: Schocken Books, 1965.

———. *Search for a Method*. New York: Vintage Books, 1968.

———. *Saint Genet: Actor and Martyr*. New York: New American Library, 1971.

———. *Being and Nothingness*. New York: Pocket Books, 1975.

———. *Life/Situations*. New York: Pantheon Books, 1977.

Scheler, Max. *Der Mensch im Weltalter des Ausgleichs*. Berlin: Deutsche Hochschule für Politik, 1928.

———. *Ressentiment*. New York: Schocken Books, 1972 (1915).

Schiller, Friedrich. *On the Aesthetic Education of Man*. New York: Frederick Ungar, 1977 (1795).

Schneider, Michael. *Neurosis and Civilization: A Marxist/Freudian Synthesis*. New York: Seabury Press, 1975.

Schulke, Hans-Jürgen (ed.). *Sport, Wissenschaft und Politik in der BRD*. Cologne: Pahl-Rugenstein, 1975.

——— (ed.). *Die Zukunft der olympischen Spiele*. Cologne: Pahl-Rugenstein, 1976.

Schuster, H. *Arbeiterturner im Kampf um die Jugend*. Berlin: Sportverlag, 1962.

Scott, Jack. *The Athletic Revolution*. New York: Free Press, 1970.

Senay, André and Robert Hervet. *Monsieur de Coubertin*. Paris: Points et Contrepoints, 1960.

Sérant, Paul. *Le romantisme fasciste*. Paris: Fasquelle Editeurs, 1959.

Sheldon, W. H. *The Varieties of Temperament*. New York: Harper and Brothers, 1942.

Shklar, Judith N. *After Utopia: The Decline of Political Faith*. Princeton: Princeton University Press, 1969 (1957).

Simon, Hans et al. *Die Körperkultur in Deutschland von 1917 bis 1945*, Vol. 3. Berlin: Sportverlag, 1964.

Skidelsky, Robert. *Oswald Mosley*. New York: Holt, Rinehart and Winston, 1975.

Smith, Denis Mack. *Mussolini*. New York: Knopf, 1982.

Sokel, Walter H. *The Writer in Extremis: Expressionism in Twentieth-Century German Literature*. Stanford: Stanford University Press, 1959.

Solomon, Maynard (ed.). *Marxism and Art*. New York: Vintage Books, 1974.

Speer, Albert. *Inside the Third Reich*. New York: Avon Books, 1971.

Spence, Jonathan. *The Gate of Heavenly Peace*. New York: Penguin Books, 1982.

Spencer, Herbert. *The Man versus the State*. Baltimore: Penguin Books, 1969 (1881).

Spengler, Oswald. *The Decline of the West*. New York: Knopf, 1928 (1918).

———. *Der Untergang des Abendlandes*. Munich: C. H. Beck, 1969.

Starrels, John and Anita Mallinckrodt. *Politics in the GDR*. Cambridge, Mass.: MIT Press, 1975.

Staude, John Raphael. *Max Scheler: An Intellectual Portrait*. New York: Free Press, 1967.

Steele, Jonathan. *Inside East Germany*. New York: Urizen Books, 1977.

Stern, Carola. *Ulbricht: A Political Biography*. New York: Praeger, 1965.

Stöcker, Gerhard. *Volkserziehung und Turnen: Untersuchung der Grundlagen des Turnens von Fr. L. Jahn*. Schorndorf bei Stuttgart: Verlag Karl Hofmann, 1971.

Talbott, Strobe (ed.). *Khrushchev Remembers*. New York: Bantam Books, 1971.

Tar, Zoltán. *The Frankfurt School*. New York: John Wiley and Sons, 1977.

Theater in der Weimarer Republik. Cologne: Kunstamt Kreuzberg und Institut für Theaterwissenschaft der Universität Köln, 1977.

Timmermann, Heinz. *Geschichte und Struktur der Arbeitersportbewegung 1893–1933*. Ahrensburg bei Hamburg: Verlag Ingrid Czwalina, 1973.

Timpanaro, Sebastiano. *On Materialism*. London: NLB, 1975 (1970).

Tönnies, Ferdinand. *Community and Society*. East Lansing: Michigan State University Press, 1964.

Toynbee, Arnold J. *A Study of History*, Vol. 4. London: Oxford University Press, 1939.

Trotsky, Leon. *Literature and Revolution*. Ann Arbor: University of Michigan Press, 1966.

———. *Problems of Everyday Life*. New York: Monad Press, 1973.

Tucker, Robert C. *Philosophy and Myth in Karl Marx*. Cambridge: Cambridge University Press, 1972.

———. *Stalin as Revolutionary 1879–1929*. New York: Norton Library, 1974.

Tucker, William R. *The Fascist Ego: A Political Biography of Robert Brasillach*. Berkeley: University of California Press, 1975.

Turkle, Sherry. *Psychoanalytic Politics: Freud's French Revolution*. New York: Basic Books, 1978.

Ueberhorst, Horst. *Frisch, frei, stark und treu: Die Arbeitersportbewegung in Deutschland 1893–1933*. Düsseldorf: Droste Verlag, 1973.

Ullrich, Klaus. *Tore, die nicht für Geld fielen: Fakten und Zusammenhänge zum Thema Sport und Profit*. East Berlin: Sportverlag, 1975.

———. *Kreuzritter im Stadion: Bemerkungen zum Antikommunismus im Sport*. East Berlin: Sportverlag, 1978.

Valentinov, Nikolay. *Encounters with Lenin*. London: Oxford University Press, 1968.

———. *The Early Years of Lenin*. Ann Arbor: University of Michigan Press, 1969.

van der Will, Wilfried and Rob Burns. *Arbeiterkulturbewegung in der Weimarer Republik*. Berlin, Vienna: Ullstein, 1982.

Vaneigem, Raoul. *Traité de savoir-vivre à l'usage des jeunes générations*. Paris: Gallimard, 1967.

Veblen, Thorstein. *The Theory of the Leisure Class*. New York: New American Library, 1960 (1899).

Vietta, Silvio and Hans-Georg Kemper. *Expressionismus*. Munich: Wilhelm Fink Verlag, 1975.

Vinnai, Gerhard. *Fußballsport als Ideologie*. Frankfurt am Main: Europäische Verlagsanstalt, 1970.

——— (ed.). *Sport in der Klassengesellschaft*. Frankfurt/M.: Fischer Taschenbuch Verlag, 1972.

Voigt, Dieter. *Soziologie in der DDR*. Cologne: Verlag Wissenschaft und Politik, 1975.

Wagner, Helmut. *Sport und Arbeitersport*. Cologne: Pahl-Rugenstein, 1973 (1931).

Waite, Robert G. L. *Vanguard of Nazism: The Free Corps Movement in Postwar Germany 1918–1923*. Cambridge, Mass.: Harvard University Press, 1952.

Wakeman, Frederic, Jr. *History and Will: Philosophical Perspectives of Mao Tse-Tung's Thought*. Berkeley: University of California Press, 1973.

Waxman, Chaim I. *The End of Ideology Debate*. New York: Clarion Books, 1969 (1968).

Weber, Eugen. *Varieties of Fascism*. New York: Van Nostrand Reinhold, 1964.

Weintraub, Karl J. *Visions of Culture*. Chicago: University of Chicago Press, 1966.

West, Rebecca. *The Meaning of Treason*. New York: Viking Press, 1947.

Wetter, Gustav. *Dialectical Materialism*. New York: Praeger, 1963.

Wildung, Fritz. *Arbeitersport*. Berlin: Bücherkreis G.M.B.H., 1929.
Wilke, Ursula. *Risiko und sozialistische Persönlichkeit*. Berlin: VEB Deut-
scher Verlag der Wissenschaften, 1977.
Willett, John. *Art and Politics in the Weimar Period*. New York: Pantheon,
1978.
Winegarten, Renee. *Writers and Revolution*. New York: New Viewpoints,
1974.
Wohl, Andrzej. *Die gesellschaftlich-historischen Grundlagen des bürger-
lichen Sports*. Cologne: Pahl-Rugenstein, 1973.
Wohl, Robert. *The Generation of 1914*. Cambridge, Mass.: Harvard Univer-
sity Press, 1979.
Wolfenstein, E. V. *The Revolutionary Personality*. Princeton: Princeton
University Press, 1971.
Wollgast, Siegfried. *Tradition und Philosophie*. Berlin: VEB Deutscher Ver-
lag der Wissenschaften, 1975.
Wonneberger, Günther. *Deutsche Arbeitersportler gegen Faschisten und
Militaristen 1929–1933*. Berlin: Sportverlag, 1959.
Wood, Neal. *Communism and British Intellectuals*. New York: Columbia
University Press, 1959.
Zeldin, Theodore. *France 1848–1945*, Vol. 2. New York: Oxford University
Press, 1977.
Zur Geschichte der Marxistisch-Leninistischen Philosophie in der DDR.
Berlin: Dietz Verlag, 1979.

2. Articles

"Aber wir haben den Krieg gewonnen." *Der Spiegel*, May 20, 1974.
Agnew, Spiro T. "Not Infected with the Conceit of Infallibility." *Sports Illus-
trated*, June 21, 1971.
Allardyce, Gilbert D. "The Political Transition of Jacques Doriot." In Walter
Laqueur and George L. Mosse (eds.), *International Fascism 1920–1945*.
New York: Harper Torchbooks, 1966.
Alstrøm, Frits. "Russisk ishockeys ideologi." *Politiken* (Copenhagen), April
16, 1973.
Anchor, Robert. "History and Play: Johan Huizinga and His Critics." *His-
tory and Theory*, 1 (1978).
". . . and in This Corner, Kid Idi Amin." *Boston Herald American*, Novem-
ber 4, 1978.
"An Individual On and Off the Field." *Sport in the USSR*, 7 (1979).
Arab-Ogly, E. "Giant or Dwarf? Modern Myths about the Antagonism be-
tween Man and Machines." *Reprints from the Soviet Press*, March 21,
1969.
"Bei uns ist immer Olympia." *Der Spiegel*, July 31, August 14, 1972.
"Bernd Bransch kaptein for det øst-tyske 'kollektiv.'" *Aftenposten* (Oslo),
June 29, 1974.
Bernett, Hajo. "Das Jahn-Bild in der nationalsozialistischen Weltanschau-
ung." *Stadion*, 4 (1978).

Bibliography 297

"Blood Sport Groups Unite against Ban." *Times* (London), June 26, 1978.
"Bogicevic Remains the Cosmic Rebel." *New York Times*, March 7, 1979.
Bolívar, Simón. "The Angostura Address" (February 15, 1819). In John J. Johnson, *Simon Bolívar and Spanish American Independence: 1783–1830*. New York: Van Nostrand Reinhold, 1968.
"Boxsport—einmal ganz anders gezeigt." *Neues Deutschland*, November 1, 1949.
Brecht, Bertolt. "Mehr guten Sport." *Berliner Börsen-Courier*, February 6, 1926. In *Schriften zum Teater I 1918–1933*. Frankfurt am Main: Suhrkamp, 1963.
Brohm, Jean-Marie. "Vers l'analyse institutionnelle du sport de compétition." *L'Homme et la Société* (1973).
Brundage, Avery. "I Must Admit—Russian Athletes Are Great!" *Saturday Evening Post*, April 30, 1955.
Buchheim, Hans. "Command and Compliance." In Helmut Krausnick et al. (eds.), *Anatomy of the SS State*. New York: Walker, 1968.
Bulhof, Ilse N. "Johan Huizinga; Ethnographer of the Past: An Analysis of Johan Huizinga's Approach to History." *Clio*, 4/2 (1975).
Butterfield, Fox. "Love and Sex in China." *New York Times Magazine*, January 13, 1980.
"By the Numbers Red China Gets into Shape." *Sports Illustrated*, June 12, 1961.
Canham, Don. "Russia Will Win the 1956 Olympics." *Sports Illustrated*, October 25, 1954.
Chapman, Brian. "East Germany's Scientific Cycling Program." *Bike World* (April 1977).
———. "East of the Wall." *Runner's World* (March 1978).
"China Is Extending Purge to Ministries of Arts and Sports." *New York Times*, December 7, 1976.
"China's Fourth Straight at Hong Kong Women's Basketball Championships." *Survey of People's Republic of China Press*, 6219–6223 (November 15–19, 1976).
Clark, Katerina. "Utopian Anthropology as a Context for Stalinist Literature." In Robert C. Tucker (ed.), *Stalinism: Essays in Historical Interpretation*. New York: Norton, 1977.
———. "Little Heroes and Big Deeds: Literature Responds to the First Five-Year Plan." In Sheila Fitzpatrick (ed.), *Cultural Revolution in Russia, 1928–1931*. Bloomington: Indiana University Press, 1978.
Clumpner, Roy A. and Brian B. Pendleton. "The People's Republic of China." In James Riordan (ed.), *Sport under Communism: The U.S.S.R., Czechoslovakia, the G.D.R., China, Cuba*. London: C. Hurt, 1978.
Colie, R. L. "Johan Huizinga and the Task of Cultural History." *American Historical Review*, 69 (1964).
Cooke, Jerry. "Sports in the U.S.S.R." *Sports Illustrated*, December 2, 1957.
"Cuba Pulls Baseball Team Out of Nicaragua Series." *New York Times*, November 9, 1977.
"DDR: Schluck Pillen oder kehr Fabriken aus." *Der Spiegel*, 12 (1979).

Dietz, Rolf. "Sports Acrobats in the GDR." *GDR Review*, 4 (1959).

"Drei Meter vorhalten." *Der Spiegel*, November 23, 1981.

Dumazedier, Joffre. "Réalities du loisir et idéologies." *Esprit* (June 1959).

"East Germany Puts King Back on His Pedestal." *New York Times*, December 14, 1980.

Edschmid, Kasimir. "Über den dichterischen Expressionismus." In Otto F. Best (ed.), *Theorie des Expressionismus*. Stuttgart: Reclam, 1976.

Ehrenberg, Alain. "Note sur le sport rouge (1910–1936)." *Recherches*, 43 (April 1980).

Ehrmann, Jacques. "Homo Ludens Revisited." In Jacques Ehrmann (ed.), *Game, Play, Literature*. Boston: Beacon Press, 1971.

"Ein Arbeitersportler und unbeugsamer Kommunist." *Neues Deutschland*, August 2, 1979.

Eliot, T. S. Review of Herbert Read, *Reason and Romanticism*, and Ramon Fernandez, *Messages*. *New Criterion*, 4 (October 1926).

Enzensberger, Hans Magnus. "On the Irresistibility of the Petty Bourgeoisie." *Telos* 30 (Winter 1976/77).

"Eurocommunism Reaches East Germany." *Atlas World Press Review* (March 1978).

Feuer, Lewis S. "The Character and Thought of Karl Marx: The Promethean Complex and Historical Materialism." In *Marx and the Intellectuals*. Garden City, N.Y.: Anchor Books, 1969.

Fitzpatrick, Sheila. "Cultural Revolution as Class War." In Sheila Fitzpatrick (ed.), *Cultural Revolution in Russia, 1928–1931*. Bloomington: Indiana University Press, 1978.

"Forsinker idretten ungdommens åndelige utvikling?" *Friheten* (Oslo), December 4, 1946.

"Freunde aus Fernwest." *Der Spiegel*, January 15, 1973.

"Future of Bullfights Dubious in Portugal under New Regime." *New York Times*, May 25, 1975.

Geertz, Clifford. "Ideology as a Cultural System." In David Apter (ed.), *Ideology and Discontent*. Glencoe: Free Press, 1964.

Gorbov, F. D. and F. P. Kosmolinskiy. "From Aviation Psychology to Space Psychology." *Soviet Review*, 10 (1969).

Gorchakov, Nikolai A. "Meyerhold's Theatre." In E. T. Kirby (ed.), *Total Theatre: A Critical Anthology*. New York: E. P. Dutton, 1969.

Gras, Fred. "On the Development of Sport-Sociological Research in the German Democratic Republic." In *Sociological Research in the German Democratic Republic*. Berlin: VEB Deutscher Verlag der Wissenschaften, 1970.

Guttmann, Allen. "On the Alleged Dehumanization of the Sports Spectator." *Journal of Popular Culture*, 14 (Fall 1980).

Hearn, Francis. "Toward A Critical Theory of Play." *Telos*, 30 (Winter 1976/77).

Heffer, Eric. "The Case for Abolishing Blood Sports." *Times* (London), June 26, 1978.

Hellmann, Rudi. "Körperkultur und Sport in unserer Gesellschaft." *Einheit* (1975).
Hille, Barbara. "Zum Stellenwert des Sports bei Jugendlichen in der Bundesrepublik und in der DDR." *Deutschland Arkiv*, 9/6 (June 1976).
Hinman, Lawrence M. "Marx's Theory of Play, Leisure and Unalienated Praxis." *Philosophy and Social Criticism*, 5 (July 1977).
"Historische Strömung." *Der Spiegel*, September 16, 1974.
Hoberman, John M. "Political Ideology and the Record Performance." *Arena Review*, 1/2 (February 1977).
———. "Sport and Political Ideology." *Journal of Sport and Social Issues*, 1 (April 1977).
———. "Defining the Postwar French Ultra-Right: The View from Within." *Proceedings of the Fifth Annual Meeting of the Western Society for French History* (1978).
"Hormon-strid om øst-tyske svømmersker." *Aftenposten* (Oslo), August 24, 1974.
Hu Hsiao-ming. "You Wish Your Body to Be Healthy and Beautiful? Some Notes on Sports Aesthetics." *Xin tiyu* (1981: 2).
Huizinga, J. H. "My Path to History." In *Dutch Civilisation in the Seventeenth Century and Other Essays*. New York: Frederick Ungar, 1968.
———. "John of Salisbury: A Pre-Gothic Mind" (1933). In *Men and Ideas*. New York: Harper Torchbooks, 1970.
Ignatiev, N. and G. Ossipov. "Le communisme et le problème des loisirs." *Esprit* (June 1959).
"Ins Abseits." *Der Spiegel*, December 12, 1977.
"Interest in Prussia Reviving." *New York Times*, December 18, 1978.
Joravsky, David. "The Construction of the Stalinist Psyche." In Sheila Fitzpatrick (ed.), *Cultural Revolution in Russia, 1928–1931*. Bloomington: Indiana University Press, 1978.
Kaiser, Georg. "Man in the Tunnel." In Walter H. Sokel, *Anthology of German Expressionist Drama*. Garden City, N.Y.: Anchor Books, 1963.
Katz, Paul. "East Germany's Olympic Secrets." *Atlas World Press Review* (April 1977).
"Kein Charakter." *Der Spiegel* (1979: 40).
Kennedy, John F. "The Soft American." *Sports Illustrated*, December 26, 1960.
Kennedy, Robert F. "A Bold Proposal for American Sport." *Sports Illustrated*, July 27, 1964.
Khromov, Y. "Karate." *Sport in the USSR* (1979: 3).
Kirk, Russell. "Professional Brawn in College." *National Review*, April 9, 1963.
Klaus, Georg. "Zur Soziologie der 'Mensch-Maschine-Symbiose.'" *Deutsche Zeitschrift für Philosophie*, 10 (1962).
———. "Erkenntnis-Modell-Spiel und Mensch." *Marxistische Blätter*, 3 (September/October 1965).
"Kleiner Bruch." *Der Spiegel*, November 15, 1971.

Knecht, Willi. "DDR-Sport—Gütezeichen für sozialistische Lebensweise." *Deutschland Arkiv*, 7/9 (September 1974).

Koriukin, V. I. and Iu. P. Lobastov. "Living Beings, Artificial Creations, and Cybernetics." *Soviet Studies in Philosophy*, 3 (1965).

"'Korruption, wohin man blickt': Das Manifest der ersten organisierten Opposition in der DDR." *Der Spiegel*, 2 (1978).

Krebs, Hans-Dieter. "Sport als Lehrfach." *Deutschland Arkiv*, 6/9 (September 1973).

Kulke, Christine. "Emanzipation oder gleiches Recht auf 'Trimm Dich'? Diskussionsbeitrag zum Problem des Frauensports in der BRD." In Gerhard Vinnai (ed.), *Sport in der Klassengesellschaft* Frankfurt am Main: Fischer Taschenbuch Verlag GmbH, 1972.

"Labour to Reconsider Ban on Blood Sports." *Times* (London), June 29, 1978.

Lagercrantz, Olof. "The Playing Fields of Peking." *New York Times*, June 18, 1971.

Lenk, Hans. "Sport, Achievement, and the New Left Criticism." *Man and World*, 5 (1972).

"Libros sobre socialismo, Diversión del equipo de Alemania Oriental." *Excelsior* (Mexico City), June 29, 1974.

"Life, Liberty and the Pursuit of Foxes." *Times* (London), June 14, 1978.

Lukas, G. "Bemerkungen zu dem Artikel von W. Eichel: 'Die Entwicklung der Körperübungen in der Urgemeinschaft.'" *Theorie und Praxis der Körperkultur* (1953: 6).

Malaparte, Curzio. "Mussolini and National Syndicalism." In Adrian Lyttelton (ed.), *Italian Fascisms: From Pareto to Gentile*. New York: Harper Torchbooks, 1975.

Mano, D. Keith. "Heavyweight Fraud." *National Review*, June 21, 1974.

Marcel, Gabriel. "Being and Nothingness." In *Homo Viator*. New York: Harper Torchbooks, 1962.

Marcuse, Herbert. Review of Johan Huizinga, *Im Schatten von Morgen*. *Zeitschrift für Sozialforschung*, 5 (1936).

Marx, Karl. "Economic and Philosophical Manuscripts of 1844." In *Early Writings*. New York: Vintage Books, 1975.

Mazrui, Ali A. "Boxer Muhammad Ali and Soldier Idi Amin as International Political Symbols: The Bioeconomics of Sport and War." *Comparative Studies in Society and History*, 19/2 (April 1977).

"Medaillen statt Mao." *Der Spiegel*, December 27, 1982.

Meyerhold, Vsevolod. "Biomechanics." In Edward Braun, *Meyerhold on Theatre*. London: Methuen, 1969.

Mihajlov, Mihajlo. "The Necessity of Ideology." *New York Times*, December 23, 1975.

Miles, Dick. "One for All, But Not All for One." *Sports Illustrated*, April 18, 1977.

Modelmoog, Ilse. "Philosophische Anthropologie und Sportwissenschaft: Ein Beitrag zur Soziologie des Sports." In Hans-Jürgen Schulke (ed.), *Sport, Wissenschaft und Politik in der BRD*. Cologne: Pahl-Rugenstein, 1975.

Moholy-Nagy, L. "Theatre, Circus, Variety." In E. T. Kirby, *Total Theatre: A Critical Anthology*. New York: E. P. Dutton, 1969.

Mosley, Oswald. "Which Inheritance? Goethe or the Vicar." In *Mosley: Policy and Debate*. London: Euphorion Press, 1954.

Müller, Fred. "Von den wissenschaftlichen Körpererziehung in der Sowjetunion lernen!" *Einheit*, 7 (1952).

Mullin, Chris. "Foreign Truths." *Manchester Guardian Weekly*, June 25, 1978.

Mussolini, Benito. "The Doctrine of Fascism." In Adrian Lyttelton (ed.), *Italian Fascisms: From Pareto to Gentile*. New York: Harper Torchbooks, 1975.

"Neue, höhere Ziele für Körperkultur und Sport." *Neues Deutschland*, March 15, 1978.

Nitschke, Willi and Lothar Kleine. "Lebensphilosophie und Körpererziehung." *Theorie und Praxis der Körperkultur* (1960).

Nye, Robert A. "Degeneration, Neurasthenia and the Culture of Sport in *Belle Epoque* France." *Journal of Contemporary History*, 17 (1982).

Ortega y Gasset, José. "The Sportive Origin of the State." In *History as a System*. New York: Norton, 1961 (1924).

"Overcoming Weightlessness." *Soviet Military Review*, 6 (1981).

Ozolin, E. "Science Helps Sports." *Soviet Military Review*, 5 (1981).

"Plan für Moskau." *Der Spiegel*, January 22, 1979.

"Den politiske idretten." *Kontrast* (Oslo), 4 (1972).

"Profis nach Peking." *Der Spiegel*, April 2, 1979.

"Pumping Body-Building." *Sports Illustrated*, November 14, 1977.

"R. Palme Dutt, 79, British Marxist." *New York Times*, December 21, 1974.

Radek, Karl. "Contemporary World Literature and the Tasks of Revolutionary Art." In A. Zhdanov et al., *Problems of Soviet Literature*. New York: International Publishers, n.d.

Ramos, Jorge Abelardo. "Dangers of Empiricism in Latin American Revolutions." In Luis E. Aguilar (ed.), *Marxism in Latin America*. Philadelphia: Temple University Press, 1978.

Reich, Wilhelm. "What Is Class Consciousness?" In *Sex-Pol: Essays 1929–1934*. New York: Vintage Books, 1972.

Rieff, Philip. "Aesthetic Functions in Modern Politics." *World Politics*, 5/4 (July 1953).

Ritter, Gerhard A. "Workers' Culture in Imperial Germany: Problems and Points of Departure for Research." *Journal of Contemporary History*, 13 (1978).

Rogovin, V. Z. "The Discussions on Problems of Daily Life and Culture in Soviet Russia during the 1920s." *Soviet Sociology*, 14/1 (1976).

Rothe, Wolfgang. "When Sports Conquered the Republic: A Forgotten Chapter from the 'Roaring Twenties.'" *Studies in Twentieth Century Literature*, 4/1 (1980).

"Rührt euch, weitermachen." *Der Spiegel*, October 27, 1975.

Scheler, Max. "Begleitwort." In Alfred Peters, *Psychologie des Sports*. Leipzig: Neue Geist Verlag, 1927.

———. "Erkenntnis und Arbeit." In *Die Wissensformen und die Gesellschaft*. Bern: Francke Verlag, 1960.

Schröder, Willi. "Das Jahnbild in der deutschen Turnbewegung." *Theorie und Praxis der Körperkultur* (1959).

Shriver, Sargent. "The Moral Force of Sport." *Sports Illustrated*, June 3, 1963.

Sieger, Walter. "Zur Körperkultur in der sozialistischen Gesellschaft." *Deutsche Zeitschrift für Philosophie*, 12/8 (1964).

Slomma, Horst. "Unterhaltungskultur in unserem Leben." *Einheit*, 27 (1972).

Sontag, Susan. "Fascinating Fascism." *New York Review of Books*, February 6, 1975.

"Soviet Drops Hockey Star for Drinking and Egotism." *New York Times*, December 27, 1978.

"Soviet Unit Speaks: Contract Bridge Nyet." *Los Angeles Times*, January 27, 1973.

"Le sport ouvrier international a prouvé sa vitalité." *L'Humanité*, July 16, 1924.

Steinberg, David A. "The Workers' Sport Internationals 1920–28." *Journal of Contemporary History*, 13 (1978).

Steiner, George. "The Cleric of Treason." *New Yorker*, December 8, 1980.

Teichler, H.-J. "Arbeitersport als soziales und politisches Phänomen im wilhelminischen Klassenstaat." In Horst Ueberhorst (ed.), *Geschichte der Leibesübungen*, 3/1. Berlin, Munich, Frankfurt a.M.: Verlag Bartels und Wernitz KG, 1980.

"Teng Again Says Chinese May Move against Vietnam." *New York Times*, February 1, 1979.

Therborn, Göran. "The Frankfurt School." *New Left Review*, 63 (1970).

"Three Who Killed Bulls in Portugal Hailed after Court Appearance." *New York Times*, May 10, 1977.

"Trinker, Raucher und Raufbold." *Der Spiegel*, February 19, 1958.

Ullrich, Klaus. "Wurde Angelo Jacopucci ein Opfer der Manager?" *Neues Deutschland*, August 4, 1978.

Valéry, Paul. "Bilan de l'intelligence" (1935). In *Oeuvres*, Vol. 1. Paris: Pléiade, 1957.

Wagner, Siegfried. "Freizeit, Kunst und Lebensfreude." *Einheit*, 27 (1972).

Washburn, John N. "Sport as a Soviet Tool." *Foreign Affairs* (April 1956).

Weber, Eugen. "Pierre de Coubertin and the Introduction of Organised Sport in France." *Journal of Contemporary History*, 5 (1970).

Wheeler, Robert F. "Organized Sport and Organized Labour: The Workers' Sports Movement." *Journal of Contemporary History*, 13 (1978).

Wohl, Andrzej. "Fifty Years of Physical Culture in the U.S.S.R.: Reflections and Conclusions." *International Review of Sport Sociology* (Warsaw), 3 (1968).

———. "Competitive Sport and Its Social Functions." *International Review of Sport Sociology*, 5 (1970).

Wolfson, Manfred. "Constraint and Choice in the SS Leadership." *Western Political Quarterly*, 18 (1965).

Wonneberger, Günter. "Mehr als ein 'Turnvater': Friedrich Ludwig Jahn." *Neues Deutschland*, August 11, 1978.

Wren, Christopher S. "Peking Celebrates Volleyball Sweep." *New York Times*, November 18, 1981.

———. "Peking's New Line Calls for New Heroes." *New York Times*, January 16, 1983.

Yevtushenko, Yevgeny. "A Poet against the Destroyers." *Sports Illustrated*, December 12, 1966.

Index

Meiners, Peter-Michael, 189
Mendès-France, P., 115, 234
Merleau-Ponty, Maurice, 96, 114
Meyerhold, Vsevolod, 10, 176–177
Mihajlov, Mihajlo, 4–5
Miliband, Ralph, 111
Mill, James, 31, 33; *Elements of Political Economy* (1844), 31, 33
Milosz, Czeslaw, 6, 218
Minh, Ho Chi, 64, 69
Mishima, Yukio, 11, 13, 106–109; *Sun and Steel* (1970), 106
Mittenzwei, Dr. Ingrid, 215–216
Mitzman, Arthur, 76
Modernity, 7, 11, 148, 168
Moholy-Nagy, L., 10
Monnerot, Jules, 15; *Sociology and Psychology of Communism* (1949), 15
Montherlant, Henry de, 95, 105, 123
Morand, Paul, 123
Moravia, Alberto, 115
More, Sir Thomas, 17; *Utopia* (1516), 17
Morgan, Lewis H., 25; *Tribal Society* (1877), 25
Mosca, Gaetano, 54
Mosley, Oswald, 15, 56, 57, 60, 61, 62, 79, 82, 91, 94, 99, 115
Mosse, George, 11, 97, 101, 103, 118, 160, 163; *The Crisis of German Ideology* (1981), 97
Mumford, Lewis, 89, 138, 145–146, 153, 161
Music, 217, 246
Musil, Robert, 123, 146
Mussolini, Benito, 5, 19, 23, 53, 56, 61, 71, 80, 88, 91, 92, 93, 94, 96, 99, 125, 154, 162
Muths, Guths, 189, 206

Narcissism, 20, 53, 56, 57, 58, 70, 80, 82, 84, 85, 89, 92, 120, 195, 198, 228, 234, 244
Nasser, Gamal Abdel, 57, 63, 64
Nationalism: in America, 21; in

Germany, 1, 11, 101, 215; Marx on, 81
Nealson, Buddy, 19
Neo-Hellenism, 21, 127
Neo-Marxists. *See* chapter 11
Neuendorff, Edmund von, 163, 215
Neufeld, Renate, 212
New Economic Policy (NEP), 171
New Sobriety, 11
Nicaragua, 1, 18
Nietzsche, Friedrich, 38, 49, 59, 60–61, 63, 67, 74, 79, 89, 90, 91, 112, 126, 129, 135, 139, 141, 142, 147, 155, 160, 161, 165; *On the Genealogy of Morals* (1887), 38, 90, 161; *Thus Spoke Zarathustra* (1883–1892), 63, 67, 112, 126; *Twilight of the Idols* (1889), 60–61
Nietzscheanism, 43, 61, 130, 137, 153
Nitschke, Willi, 208, 209
Nkrumah, Kwame, 53, 64
Nolte, Ernst, 5, 92–94
Nuremberg Trials, 15
Nye, Robert, 131
Nyerere, Julius, 56

Olesha, Yuri, 174–175; *Envy* (1927), 174–175
Olympics: ancient, 167, 229; modern, 15, 21, 101, 109, 118, 129, 130, 131, 162, 165, 191, 209, 210, 213, 216, 227, 233, 238, 241
Organic state concept, 73
Origin of the state: P. Anderson on, 51–52; E. Cassirer on, 37; F. Engels on, 51; J. Huizinga on, 44; J. Ortega y Gasset on, 41–42
Ortega y Gasset, José, 8, 13, 16, 17, 23, 25, 28, 37, 41, 43, 44, 45, 49, 51, 61, 97, 116, 123, 124, 126, 156, 157–159, 161, 165, 167, 208, 209; *Meditations on Hunting* (1943), 17, 158–159; *The Modern Theme* (1931), 158; *The Revolt of the Masses* (1930), 61, 97, 157–